Sentence Processing

What are the psychological processes involved in comprehending sentences? How do we process the structure of sentences and how do we understand their meaning? Do children, bilinguals and people with language impairments process sentences in the same way as healthy monolingual adults? These are just some of the many questions that sentence-processing researchers have tried to answer by conducting ever more sophisticated experiments, making this one of the most productive and exciting areas in experimental language research in recent years.

This book is the first to provide a comprehensive, state-of-the-art overview of this critical field. It contains 10 chapters written by world-leading experts, which discuss influential theories of sentence processing and important experimental evidence, with a focus on recent developments in the area. The chapters analyse research that has explored how people process the structure and meaning of sentences, and how sentences are understood within their context. They also discuss studies that have investigated healthy monolingual adults as well as children, bilinguals and people with language impairments.

This comprehensive and authoritative work will appeal to students and researchers in the field of sentence processing, and also to anyone with an interest in psychology and linguistics.

Roger P. G. van Gompel is a Senior Lecturer in the School of Psychology at the University of Dundee. His research interests concern the psychological processes underlying language production and comprehension, with a special interest in sentence processing. He has published research articles on discourse and sentence processing and has written several reviews of the literature on sentence comprehension.

Current Issues in the Psychology of Language
Series Editor: Trevor A. Harley

Current Issues in the Psychology of Language is a series of edited books that will reflect the state-of-the-art in areas of current and emerging interest in the psychological study of language.

Each volume is tightly focused on a particular topic and consists of seven to ten chapters contributed by international experts. The editors of individual volumes are leading figures in their areas and provide an introductory overview.

Example topics include: language development, bilingualism and second language acquisition, word recognition, word meaning, text processing, the neuroscience of language, and language production, as well as the inter-relations between these topics.

Visual Word Recognition Volume 1
Edited by James S. Adelman

Visual Word Recognition Volume 2
Edited by James S. Adelman

Sentence Processing
Edited by Roger P. G. van Gompel

Sentence Processing

Edited by
Roger P. G. van Gompel

Taylor & Francis Group
LONDON AND NEW YORK

First published 2013
by Psychology Press
27 Church Road, Hove, East Sussex BN3 2FA

Simultaneously published in the USA and Canada
by Psychology Press
711 Third Avenue, New York NY 10017

Psychology Press is an imprint of the Taylor & Francis Group, an informa business

© 2013 Psychology Press

The right of the editor to be identified as the author of the editorial material, and of the authors for their individual chapters, has been asserted in accordance with sections 77 and 78 of the Copyright, Designs and Patents Act 1988.

All rights reserved. No part of this book may be reprinted or reproduced or utilised in any form or by any electronic, mechanical, or other means, now known or hereafter invented, including photocopying and recording, or in any information storage or retrieval system, without permission in writing from the publishers.

Trademark notice: Product or corporate names may be trademarks or registered trademarks, and are used only for identification and explanation without intent to infringe.

British Library Cataloguing in Publication Data
A catalogue record for this book is available from the British Library

Library of Congress Cataloging in Publication Data
Sentence processing/Edited by Roger P. G. Van Gompel.
  pages cm
  Includes bibliographical references and index.
  1. English language—Sentences. 2. English language—Semantics.
  3. English language—Psychological aspects. 4. Psycholinguistics.
  I. Van Gompel, Roger P. G. editor of compilation.
  PE1441.S39 2013
  415—dc23   2012049194

ISBN: 978-1-84872-063-3 (hbk)
ISBN: 978-1-84872-131-9 (pbk)
ISBN: 978-203-77283-6 (ebk)

Typeset in Times New Roman
by Florence Production Ltd, Stoodleigh, Devon, UK

Printed and bound by CPI Group (UK) Ltd, Croydon, CR0 4YY

Contents

List of illustrations	vii
List of contributors	ix
Preface	xi

1 **Sentence processing: An introduction**   1
ROGER P. G. VAN GOMPEL

2 **Syntax in sentence processing**   21
LYN FRAZIER

3 **Constraint-based models of sentence processing**   51
KEN MCRAE AND KAZUNAGA MATSUKI

4 **Memory and surprisal in human sentence comprehension**   78
ROGER LEVY

5 **Putting syntax in context**   115
MICHAEL J. SPIVEY, SARAH E. ANDERSON, AND THOMAS A. FARMER

6 **Syntactic constraints on referential processing**   136
PATRICK STURT

7 **Semantic interpretation of sentences**   160
STEVEN FRISSON AND MATTHEW J. TRAXLER

8 **Children's sentence processing**   189
JESSE SNEDEKER

9 **Sentence processing in bilinguals**   221
LEAH ROBERTS

**10 Syntactically based sentence comprehension in aging and
individuals with neurological disease** 247
DAVID CAPLAN

Index 269

Illustrations

Figures

1.1a	Attachment of *the solution* as the direct object of *forgot*	4
1.1b	Attachment of *the solution* as part of the complement clause of *forgot*	4
3.1	Schematic of McRae et al.'s (1998) competition–integration model	63
3.2	Predicting ambiguity effects (reduction effect: the difference between ambiguous reduced and unambiguous relative clauses) with the competition–integration model	65
3.3	The architecture of a simple recurrent network (SRN)	68
3.4	Example visual scene from Knoeferle et al. (2005)	70
4.1	Deep inside a multiply center-embedded sentence in the stack-depth model of Yngve (1960)	81
4.2	The two incremental analyses for sentence (15) pre-disambiguation	93
4.3	Broad-coverage transitivity-distinguishing PCFG assessed on (17)	96
4.4	Surprisal as optimal perceptual discrimination	98
4.5	Syntactically constrained contexts with preceding dependents	101
5.1	When instructed to "Put the spoon on the napkin in the bowl," participants often mis-parse the syntactic attachment of the initial prepositional phrase when there is only one visible referent for "spoon" (panel A), but not when there are two such referents (panel B)	127
8.1	Example of a display for the verb bias and prosody experiments. Printed words are for illustration only. The target sentence was: *Tickle the pig with the fan*	200

Tables

4.1	A small PCFG for the sentences in section on *surprisal and garden-path disambiguation*	92
4.2	Surprisals at ambiguity resolution in (16) and (16a), and at ambiguity onset and resolution in (17), using small PCFG	95

Contributors

Sarah E. Anderson, Department of Psychology, University of Cincinnati, USA

David Caplan, Neuropsychology Laboratory, Massachusetts General Hospital, USA

Thomas A. Farmer, Department of Psychology, The University of Iowa, USA

Lyn Frazier, Department of Linguistics, University of Massachusetts, USA

Steven Frisson, School of Psychology, University of Birmingham, UK

Roger Levy, Department of Linguistics, University of California at San Diego, USA

Kazunaga Matsuki, Department of Psychology, University of Western Ontario, Canada

Ken McRae, Department of Psychology and Neuroscience Program, University of Western Ontario, Canada

Leah Roberts, Centre for Language Learning Research, Department of Education, University of York, UK

Jesse Snedeker, Department of Psychology, Harvard University, USA

Michael J. Spivey, School of Social Sciences, Humanities, and Arts, University of California at Merced, USA

Patrick Sturt, The School of Philosophy Psychology and Language Sciences, University of Edinburgh, UK

Matthew J. Traxler, Psychology Department, University of California at Davis, USA

Roger P. G. van Gompel, School of Psychology, University of Dundee, UK

Preface

This volume in the *Current Issues in the Psychology of Language* series contains chapters that provide a critical review of the state-of-the-art in sentence-processing research. Together, they aim to give a comprehensive overview of work in this prominent area of psycholinguistic research. This volume would not have been possible without Trevor Harley, the series editor, who suggested me for the editor, and who, as the Dean of the School of Psychology where I work, has ensured that I can do my research in a very supportive and pleasurable environment. Obviously, it would also have been impossible without the authors, who wrote the chapters with no other incentive than the honour of having their work appear in this volume. Many of the authors also reviewed chapters. I would also like to thank the other chapter reviewers, Kathy Conklin, Christoph Scheepers and Juhani Järvikivi, as well as Adrian Staub and the other (anonymous) reviewers of an earlier version of the complete volume. Finally, I am very grateful to the team from Psychology Press for their support and patience, in particular Becci Edmondson, Michael Fenton, Sharla Plant, Laura Ellis, Jack Howells and Aimee Miles.

1 Sentence processing
An introduction

Roger P. G. van Gompel

Introduction

The sentence forms a special unit in language. Many writing systems have evolved to mark its beginning and end (e.g., with a capital and full stop), reflecting the fact that the sentence functions as a semantic and syntactic unit. Semantically, it can be considered the smallest group of words that expresses a complete thought or idea. Syntactically, it is often considered the largest independent unit of language structure: grammatical rules apply within the sentence, but generally not outside it.

Not surprisingly then, the sentence has been the focus of much language research. In theoretical linguistics, this research led to the rise of transformational-generative grammars from the 1950s onwards (e.g., Chomsky, 1957, 1965), formal grammars which consist of syntactic rules that aim to describe all well-formed/grammatical sentences and rule out all sentences which are ungrammatical. In psycholinguistics, early experimental work tested whether language comprehenders applied these rules, in particular, whether sentences that required more transformational rules were harder to process. However, in the early seventies, it was realised that the transformational rules formulated by theoretical linguists did not account for processing difficulty during sentence processing (e.g., Fodor, Bever, & Garrett, 1974). Furthermore, because these rules could not be applied until the end of the sentence, they were incompatible with experimental evidence for incrementality, that is, for the most part, language comprehenders interpret sentences word-by-word rather than delaying their interpretation until the end (Just & Carpenter, 1980; Marslen-Wilson, 1973, 1975).

Experimental methods

The finding that sentence processing is highly incremental led to the realisation that research needs to employ on-line methods, that is, methods that measure processing *while* language users process the sentence rather than off-line methods, which measure experimental participants' responses at the end of the sentence. An example of an off-line method is grammaticality judgement, in which participants have to indicate as quickly as possible whether a sentence is grammatical; slower decision times and a higher proportion of 'no' responses suggest that participants found the sentence hard to process.

The most frequently used on-line methods have been self-paced reading and eye-tracking during reading. With all methods, participants (generally 20–40 university students) read several sentences from each condition, that is, several sentences that have the same experimental manipulation (generally 6–10 per condition). For example, in all the example sentences below, the (a) and (b) versions are two different conditions from a single item. The sentences are presented following a Latin-square design, so that each participant sees all conditions and all items in an experiment, but only one condition of each item. In the self-paced reading method, participants press a button to make each word or phrase visible while the previous word or phrase disappears. Button press times are taken as a measure of processing difficulty. In eye tracking, participants' eye fixations are recorded while they read sentences. Eye fixation times and positions are recorded and various eye fixation measures are calculated for regions of interest in the sentence by summing fixations in different ways. An important advantage of this method is that it allows the investigation of sentence processing in a naturalistic way, without an additional task such as button pressing. Another advantage is that the different eye-tracking measures may tap into processes that occur at different points in time. For example, the first-pass measure (the sum of fixations from first entering the region until first leaving it, provided that a subsequent region has not been fixated) reflects relatively early processing, whereas the total time measure (sum of all fixations) also includes fixations that occur during re-reading.

A slightly later development has been the recording of event-related brain potentials (ERPs) during sentence processing. ERPs are changes in electrical activity in the brain, which are recorded with electrodes on participants' scalps. ERP research has shown that ungrammatical sentences (e.g., *The cat will eating*) elicit a positive electrical response around 600 ms after the onset of the ungrammatical word relative to grammatical sentences (e.g., Hagoort, Brown, & Groothusen, 1993; Osterhout & Nicol, 1999). This has been dubbed the P600 effect. A similar P600 also occurs when a structurally ambiguous sentence is disambiguated towards the less preferred analysis (e.g., Osterhout & Holcomb, 1992, 1993; Van Berkum, Brown, & Hagoort, 1999). In some studies, the P600 is preceded by a negative brain response in left-anterior brain regions (e.g., Friederici, Hahne, & Mecklinger, 1996). Thus, these ERP signals can be taken as evidence for difficulty during the processing of structurally ambiguous sentences. Interestingly, the nature of the brain response to syntactic processing difficulty is different from that to semantic processing difficulty, which elicits a negative brain wave at around 400 ms following a semantic anomaly (e.g., Kutas & Hillyard, 1980, 1984).

Important advances in our understanding of sentence processing have also been made using the visual-world method (e.g., Altmann & Kamide,

1999; Cooper, 1974; Tanenhaus, Spivey-Knowlton, Eberhard, & Sedivy, 1995). In this method, participants listen to a sentence while their eye-movements to pictures of words in the sentence are monitored. As will become clear later in this chapter, which picture participants fixate can give researchers a fine-grained temporal record of which structure participants adopt while they process a structurally ambiguous sentence. Thus, in contrast to the other methods mentioned above, the visual-world method measures interpretation preferences rather than processing difficulty.

The garden-path theory

Modern work on sentence processing started with the development of theories that explain how sentence structure is built up word-by-word by incrementally incorporating each word into the previously built syntactic structure (e.g., Frazier & Fodor, 1978; Kimball, 1973). In cases where the structure is unambiguous, it is assumed that determining the sentence structure is generally straightforward, because the processor does not need to choose between different grammatical possibilities. Instead, the main focus of these theories has been on explaining how structurally ambiguous sentences are processed: they stipulate parsing strategies that explain why, in cases of structural ambiguity, certain syntactic structures are preferred over others.

By far the most influential theory has been the garden-path theory by Frazier (1979, 1987; Frazier & Rayner, 1982). Frazier proposed two language-universal processing strategies, minimal attachment and late closure. As explained by Frazier (this volume), these processing strategies were motivated by general cognitive constraints, in particular, the need for the processor to reduce memory demands. According to the minimal attachment principle, language comprehenders prefer the structure that is syntactically least complex in terms of number of tree structure nodes. For example, the phrase *the solution* in (1a) and (1b) is temporarily ambiguous, because it can be interpreted as the direct object of *forgot*, as in (1a), or as the subject of a subsequent complement clause, as in (1b).[1]

(1a) The student forgot *the solution* immediately.
      (direct object structure)

(1b) The student forgot *the solution* **was** in the book.
      (complement clause structure)

Minimal attachment stipulates that language comprehenders initially adopt the direct object analysis (Figure 1.1a), because it involves fewer tree structure nodes than the complement clause analysis (Figure 1.1b). Difficulty ensues in (1b) when the processor encounters *was*, notices that the initial analysis is impossible, and has to reanalyse (see e.g., Frazier & Rayner, 1982 for evidence and Frazier, this volume, for an overview of theories of reanalysis).

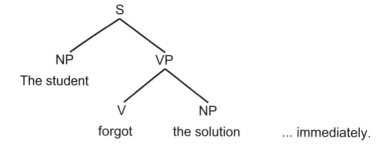

Figure 1.1a Attachment of *the solution* as the direct object of *forgot*.

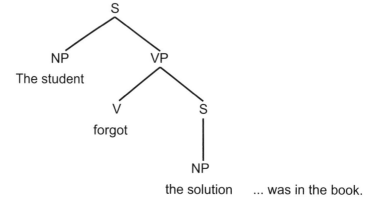

Figure 1.1b Attachment of *the solution* as part of the complement clause of *forgot*.
Abbreviations: S = clause, NP = noun phrase, VP = verb phrase, V = verb.

In cases where both analyses of an ambiguous structure have the same number of nodes, the principle of late closure comes into play, which states that an ambiguous phrase preferentially attaches to the phrase that is currently being processed, in other words, to the most recent phrase. For example, the adverbial phrases *yesterday* in (2a) and *tomorrow* in (2b) are structurally ambiguous, because they can be part of either the first or second clause. However, the tense of the verb and the adverb rule out attachment to the first clause in (2a) and to the second clause in (2b).

(2a) Tom will brush the dog he washed ***yesterday***.
      (attachment to clause 2)

(2b) Tom will brush the dog he washed ***tomorrow***.
      (attachment to clause 1)

According to late closure, language comprehenders should initially adopt attachment to the more recent clause in both (2a) and (2b), but because this is ruled out by tense in (2b), reanalysis has to take place, resulting in processing difficulty. Consistent with this, Altmann, Van Nice, Garnham, and Henstra (1998) found that (2b) took longer to read than (2a) (though importantly, the preference was also affected by context).

Many experiments conducted in the 1980s suggested that minimal attachment and late closure, later supplemented by a third principle, the active filler strategy (Frazier, this volume; Frazier & Flores d'Arcais, 1989) accounted for the processing of a range of structural ambiguities (e.g., Ferreira & Clifton, 1986; Ferreira & Henderson, 1990; Frazier & Clifton, 1989; Frazier & Rayner, 1982; Rayner, Carlson, & Frazier, 1983).

The use of non-syntactic information

Although initial research provided evidence for the garden-path theory, later research has questioned its assumptions. One critical finding (Cuetos & Mitchell, 1988) was that, in Spanish, translations of (3) showed a preference for attachment of the relative clause (*who shot himself/herself*) to the first noun phrase (*the daughter*), even though late closure predicts a preference for the second, more recent, noun phrase (*the colonel*).

(3a)   The daughter of the colonel *who shot himself* was on the balcony.
       (attachment to noun phrase 2)

(3b)   The daughter of the colonel *who shot herself* was on the balcony.
       (attachment to noun phrase 1)

This contrasted with results from English, which showed a preference for the second noun phrase (e.g., Carreiras & Clifton, 1993, 1999). The findings from Spanish resulted in modifications to the garden-path theory (Frazier & Clifton, 1996) and various other proposals for explaining cross-linguistic relative clause processing differences (e.g., Gibson, Pearlmutter, Canseco-Gonzalez, & Hickok, 1996; Mitchell, Cuetos, Corley, & Brysbaert, 1995). Since then, an important question has been to what extent sentence-processing strategies are language universal. Frazier (this volume) reviews current research on this topic.

Most research, however, has investigated another fundamental assumption of the garden-path theory, which is that the sentence processor is modular. That is, when determining the syntactic structure of the sentence, the processor initially only uses syntactic category information (e.g., whether a word is a verb or noun) and structural strategies (minimal attachment and late closure). Other potentially useful sources of information are only used during a subsequent stage of processing. As summarised by McRae and Matsuki (this volume), this has generated much research on the use of such information. The research has mainly focused on three types of information: context, semantics, and structural frequency.

Crain and Steedman (1985) and Altmann and Steedman (1988) proposed the referential theory to explain how context affects sentence processing. They argued that the prepositional phrase modifier *with the new lock* in (4b) selects one safe from a set of other safes, so it suggests the presence of more than one safe. However, no other safes are mentioned (because there is no context), so language comprehenders instead prefer attachment of the prepositional phrase to the verb phrase, as in (4a), where *the safe* remains unmodified.

(4a) The burglar blew open the safe *with the dynamite*.
(verb phrase attachment)

(4b) The burglar blew open the safe *with the new lock*.
(noun phrase attachment)

In contrast, when the preceding context mentions two locks, noun phrase attachment should be preferred, because it is unclear which safe is referred to unless it is modified. Consistent with these predictions, a self-paced reading study by Altmann and Steedman (1988) showed that noun phrase attachment took less time to read than verb phrase attachment following contexts that mentioned two safes (whereas verb phrase attachment was preferred if one safe was mentioned). This provided evidence against the garden-path theory, because minimal attachment predicts a preference for verb phrase attachment, and this preference should not be affected by context during early processing.

Spivey, Anderson, and Farmer (this volume) review other studies on context effects. The general finding is that context can have very rapid effects on structural ambiguity resolution, but whether it can neutralise the difficulty with the less preferred structure depends for a large part on how strong the preference is in the absence of context (Britt, 1994; MacDonald, Pearlmutter, & Seidenberg, 1994). Evidence that even non-linguistic contexts have a rapid effect comes from visual-world studies (e.g., Chambers, Tanenhaus, & Magnuson, 2004; Knoeferle, Crocker, Scheepers, & Pickering, 2005; Tanenhaus et al., 1995). Tanenhaus et al. (1995) asked participants to follow auditory instructions such as (5).

(5a) Put the apple *on the towel* **in the box**.
(temporarily ambiguous noun phrase attachment)

(5b) Put the apple **that's** on the towel in the box.
(unambiguous noun phrase attachment)

They were presented with either a one-referent scene containing a single apple on a towel, or a two-referent scene containing two apples, one of which was on a towel. Both scenes also contained an empty towel without an apple, and a box. When viewing the one-referent scene, people looked more often at the empty towel when hearing (5a) than (5b). Hence, they appeared to initially misinterpret *on the towel* in the temporarily ambiguous sentence (5a) as modifying the verb *put* and took it as the destination for the apple, rather than as the modifier of *the apple*, which is the correct interpretation. But most importantly, in the two-referent scene, no such difference was observed, suggesting that participants immediately interpreted *on the towel* as a modifier of *the apple*. Hence, Tanenhaus et al. argued that visual referential context immediately affected syntactic ambiguity resolution.

Other research has investigated whether semantic information affected syntactic ambiguity resolution (see Spivey et al., this volume). Most of this research has focused on the reduced relative clause ambiguity in (6a).

(6a)   The defendant *examined* **by the lawyer** was unreliable.
       (reduced relative clause)

(6b)   The defendant **that** was examined by the lawyer was unreliable.
       (unambiguous relative clause)

When the first noun phrase (e.g., *the defendant*) is a plausible agent of the subsequent verb (*examined*), the verb is preferentially interpreted as part of the main clause (e.g., *the defendant examined something*) rather than as part of a reduced relative clause, which is the correct interpretation in (6a). Hence, the disambiguating region *by the lawyer* in (6a) takes longer to read than the same region in a sentence with an unambiguous relative clause (6b). The question of interest is whether this is still the case if the first noun phrase (e.g., *the evidence*) is not a plausible agent of the verb (e.g., ⁇ *the evidence examined something*) and only the reduced relative clause analysis is plausible. Eye-tracking results from Trueswell, Tanenhaus, and Garnsey (1994) showed that in such cases, a reduced relative clause takes no longer to read than an unambiguous relative clause, suggesting that semantic information has a strong and rapid effect on syntactic ambiguity resolution, *contra* the garden-path theory. However, in an experiment that tested more materials, Clifton et al. (2003) found that semantic information did not completely eliminate the difficulty with reduced relatives.

One final source of information that has received much attention is structural frequency, in particular whether structural preferences associated with verbs affect syntactic ambiguity resolution. Trueswell, Tanenhaus, and Kello (1993) investigated ambiguities such as (1). They contrasted verbs such as *forgot*, which occurs more frequently with a direct object than a complement clause, with verbs such as *hoped*, which occurs more frequently with a complement clause. Their eye-tracking reading results showed that, with direct-object biased verbs, temporarily ambiguous complement clauses as in (1b) took longer to read at the disambiguating region (*was in the*) than unambiguous complement clauses with the word *that* after *forgot*, consistent with the predictions of minimal attachment. However, no difference between the temporarily ambiguous and unambiguous sentences was observed when the verb was biased towards the complement clause analysis. Other studies have also found evidence for rapid effects of frequency information (e.g., Snedeker & Trueswell, 2004;

Staub, 2007; Trueswell, 1996), though it does not always completely neutralise difficulty with the structurally preferred analysis (Pickering, Traxler, & Crocker, 2000).

Constraint-based theories

Much discussion about the use of context, semantics and frequency has centred on the question of how rapidly this information affects structural processing (e.g., Clifton & Ferreira, 1989). If the use of non-structural information is delayed relative to that of structural parsing principles, then this would be consistent with a modular account such as the garden-path theory. One possibility is that with some methods, such as self-paced reading, the initial structural stage of processing may not be detectable. However, even the most sensitive methods, eye-tracking during reading and the visual-world method, often fail to show evidence for a delay of non-structural information. This led to the rise of constraint-based theories, which are reviewed in more detail in McRae and Matsuki (this volume). Initially, these theories consisted of no more than the assumption that the sentence processor is interactive, that is, all potentially relevant sources of information (constraints) are used immediately during sentence processing. However, several constraint-based theories have now been computationally implemented and are therefore much more explicit (e.g., McRae, Spivey-Knowlton, & Tanenhaus, 1998; Tabor & Tanenhaus, 1999). Generally, these theories assume that all syntactic analyses of an ambiguous sentence are activated in parallel. The analysis that receives most support from the various constraints becomes most activated and is selected. Selection is fast when one analysis is more strongly activated than its alternatives, but when two or more analyses receive similar activation, this results in strong competition before one analysis is selected, slowing down processing.

Whether competition is indeed the cause of processing difficulty is questionable: Van Gompel, Pickering, Pearson, and Liversedge (2005; Van Gompel, Pickering, & Traxler, 2001) found that syntactically ambiguous sentences such as (7a), in which both relative clause attachment analyses are equally preferred and semantically plausible, took *less* time to process than sentences such as (7b) and (7c), in which only one of the analyses is plausible.

(7a) I read that the bodyguard of the governor *retiring after the troubles* is very rich.
(globally ambiguous)

(7b) I read that the governor of the province *retiring after the troubles* is very rich.
(attachment to noun phrase 1)

(7c) I read that the province of the governor *retiring after the troubles* is very rich.
(attachment to noun phrase 2)

This is the opposite from what is predicted by competition. Instead, the results suggest that readers adopt either one or the other structure, and if this structure is implausible, then reanalysis results in processing difficulty (see Green & Mitchell, 2006 for a different explanation).

However, it seems clear that constraint-based theories can account for more experimental findings in the literature than the garden-path theory. In contrast, the garden-path theory is more parsimonious: whereas the garden-path theory assumes only three parsing principles (at least for initial processing), in principle there are an unlimited number of constraints in constraint-based theories, and the relative importance/weight of each constraint has to be independently determined, for example by analysing production data. This makes constraint-based theories very powerful, but also less predictive. Thus, it is very difficult to compare the garden-path theory and constraint-based theories: the relative strength of the theories depends on whether one favours coverage or parsimony.

Structural complexity

While most sentence-processing research has focused on structural ambiguity, a different strand of research has tried to explain how the structural complexity of (generally) unambiguous sentences affects comprehension difficulty. As discussed by Levy (this volume), there are currently three influential theories that aim to account for structural complexity. These theories can be illustrated by a prominent finding in the literature, evidence that object relative clauses (8b) take longer to process than subject relative clauses (8a) (e.g., Gordon, Hendrick, & Johnson, 2001; King & Just, 1991; Traxler, Morris, & Seely, 2002).

(8a) The reporter who attacked the senator admitted the error.
     (subject relative)

(8b) The reporter who the senator attacked admitted the error.
     (object relative)

Gibson (1998, 2000) proposed the dependency locality theory (DLT) to account for processing difficulty in these and various other structures. This theory assumes that two factors contribute to processing complexity. The first is storage cost, which occurs when a syntactic dependency between two words is predicted and spans intervening discourse referents. For example, in (8b) the embedded subject *who* predicts a dependency with a later verb (*attacked*), and this dependency prediction has to be maintained in memory during the processing of the discourse referent *the senator*. The second factor is integration cost, which arises when a syntactic dependency is established. This is also assumed to be larger the more intervening discourse referents the dependency spans. For example, integration cost occurs at *attacked* in (8b) because the dependency with *who* is established and this dependency spans the discourse referent *the senator*. Thus, both storage and memory cost are higher in (8b) than (8a) due to the fact that *the senator* intervenes between *who* and *attacked* in (8b) but not in (8a).

More recently, two alternative theories have been proposed. The similarity-based interference account (Lewis & Vasishth, 2005; Lewis, Vasishth, & Van Dyke, 2006) claims that processing difficulty occurs when two linguistic items are simultaneously retrieved and cause interference in working memory. Interference at the verb *attacked* is strong in (8b) because *who* and *the senator* have to be integrated simultaneously, whereas in (8a) only *who* has to be integrated when the verb is being processed. This account claims that retrieval interference is largest when other items in the sentence are very similar. For example, the predicate *was standing in the hallway* in (9) is part of the complement clause headed by *forgot*. Similarity-based interference predicts more interference during attachment of the predicate in (9b) than (9a) because in (9b) there is another verb that can take a complement clause (*knew*), whereas there is not in (9a). Furthermore, in (9b) there is another subject (*the exam*) that interferes with *the student*, whereas in (9a) *the exam* is not a subject. Consistent with this, Van Dyke and Lewis (2003) found that *was standing* took longer to read in (9b) than (9a).

(9a) The executive assistant forgot that the student who was waiting for the exam was standing in the hallway.
(no interfering structure)

(9b) The executive assistant forgot that the student who knew that the exam was important was standing in the hallway.
(interfering structure)

A second alternative account is surprisal theory (Hale, 2001; Levy, 2008). It claims that the parser predicts structural analyses that are possible at the next word and allocates attentional resources to them on the basis of their probability. Processing difficulty is due to the amount of re-ranking of allocational resources that is needed when the next word is processed: the less predictable it is, the more re-ranking is needed, and the longer it takes to process the word. As explained in detail by Levy (this volume), surprisal theory accounts for many ambiguity as well as complexity effects. For example, because object relatives are less frequent than subject relatives, the predictability of the noun phrase *the senator* in (8b) should be lower than that of the verb *attacked* in (8a), making object relatives harder to process. Current evidence does not strongly favour either the DLT, similarity-based interference or surprisal, suggesting that storage and integration cost, interference, and surprisal may all contribute to processing difficulty (see Levy, this volume).

Beyond syntactic ambiguity resolution and structural complexity

In recent years, research on sentence processing has also started to examine aspects other than syntactic ambiguity resolution and structural complexity.

As discussed by Sturt (this volume), one topic that has received interest is the extent to which syntactic constraints affect the processing of pronouns (*he*, *him*, *she*, *her*, often called anaphora in this research area) and reflexives (*himself*, *herself*). In theoretical linguistics, syntactic constraints have been proposed to explain why *him* in (10a) can refer to *Jonathan* but not to *the surgeon*, whereas *himself* in (10b) can only refer to *the surgeon*.

(10a) Jonathan remembered that the surgeon had pricked him.
(pronoun)

(10b) Jonathan remembered that the surgeon had pricked himself.
(reflexive)

The critical question in sentence-processing research has been when such syntactic constraints affect on-line processing and whether other, non-syntactic influences also play a role. It is clear that although structural constraints have a strong effect during on-line processing, language comprehenders sometimes do ignore them (e.g., Badecker & Straub, 2002; Kennison, 2003; Sturt, 2003) and consider interpretations that are inconsistent with them (e.g., consider *himself* as referring to *Jonathan*). One possibility, suggested by the results from Sturt (2003), is that language comprehenders initially only consider references that are consistent with syntactic constraints, but later also consider other possibilities.

Another topic that is receiving more and more interest is the question of how language comprehenders semantically interpret sentences. Until recently, almost all sentence-processing research focused on how the human parser determines structural relations, but, obviously, sentence processing is more than that: language comprehenders also need to derive a semantic interpretation of the sentence. To do this, they generally need to build a syntactic structure (though in some cases, this may be bypassed, see Ferreira, 2003; Townsend & Bever, 2001). However, as pointed out by Frisson and Traxler (this volume), this is often not sufficient. For example, to understand that *The teenager began the novel* means 'the teenager began reading the novel', it is not sufficient to analyse *the novel* as the direct object of *began*: the comprehender has to add semantic content. There is now considerable research showing that this operation is costly, and one explanation is that this cost occurs because a novel is not an event, but has to be reconceptualised as an event in order to interpret *began the novel* (e.g., McElree, Frisson, & Pickering, 2006).

Frisson and Traxler (this volume) discuss various other aspects of semantic interpretation. One central question in this research has been the time-course of semantic interpretation. As discussed by Frazier (this volume), there is considerable evidence that syntactic processing is very rapid and highly automatic. The general finding is that many semantic processes are also very rapid. For example, Boland, Tanenhaus, Garnsey, and Carlson (1995) showed that the recipient semantic role in (11) is assigned even before the whole syntactic structure is processed: participants indicated that distributing science exams to a car salesman (rather than uneasy pupils) is implausible at *science exams*, before they had reached *to*, which syntactically licenses the recipient (see also Kamide, Altmann, & Haywood, 2003).

(11)   Which car salesman/uneasy pupils did Harriet distribute the science exams to in class?

Sentence processing in other populations

Most research has investigated how healthy, adult native speakers of a language (usually university students) process sentences. However, as the research field has developed, an increasing number of researchers have started examining other populations such as young children, older people, bilinguals and aphasic patients (patients with a language disorder resulting from brain damage). The main question that drives this research is whether these language users process sentences differently from healthy, adult native speakers.

For a long time, it was difficult to investigate on-line sentence processing in young children, because the best available methods (self-paced reading and eye-tracking during reading) required children to be able to read. The ERP method does allow investigation of spoken sentences and has been used in a few studies (Snedeker, this volume), but is often not practical with young children, because it requires the presentation of many experimental materials and, to get data without too much noise, participants need to avoid muscle movements. As reviewed by Snedeker (this volume), the introduction of the visual-world method, which allows the on-line investigation of spoken language, therefore resulted in important advances in our understanding of children's sentence processing. Visual-world research suggests that at the age of five, children rapidly use structural frequency information (Snedeker & Trueswell, 2004) and prosody (Snedeker & Trueswell, 2003) during syntactic ambiguity resolution, but, interestingly, they rely much less on referential context than adults do and are much worse at revising initial interpretations than adults are (Trueswell, Sekerina, Hill, & Logrip, 1999). Another important finding is that three-year-olds find it easier to process a sentence when it is preceded by a sentence with the same structure (structural priming) even if none of the content words in the sentences is the same (Thothathiri & Snedeker, 2008). This suggests that even very young children use abstract syntactic representations (rather than merely word-based representations, as suggested by Tomasello, 1992).

Sentence-processing research investigating bilinguals has generally focused on proficient late learners, who learnt a second language during or after puberty. Like first-language users, these bilinguals usually show evidence of rapid processing difficulty when a temporarily ambiguous sentence is disambiguated towards the non-preferred structure, indicating that they process sentence structure incrementally (Roberts, this volume). They also rapidly use non-syntactic information such as structural preferences of verbs in the second language (Dussias & Cramer Scaltz, 2008; Frenck-Mestre & Pynte, 1997) and animacy (whether a noun phrase refers to a living or non-living thing, Jackson & Roberts, 2010). However, specific aspects of sentence processing appear to be delayed. For example, Roberts and Felser (2011) found that late learners experienced more difficulty at *the song/beer* in (12b) than (12a), indicating that they quickly realised that the direct object analysis *the band played the beer* is implausible.

(12a) While the band played *the song* **pleased** all the customers.
(plausible direct object)

(12b) While the band played *the beer* **pleased** all the customers.
(implausible direct object)

However, learners did not immediately use this information to rule out this analysis, so at the syntactic disambiguation (*pleased*), they experienced the same difficulty in (12a) and (12b). This contrasts with the results from native speakers (see also Dussias & Piñar, 2010). Furthermore, Jackson (2008) found that in German, low-proficient learners delayed syntactic analysis until the end of the sentence if the thematic verb (the verb containing lexical information rather than an auxiliary or copula) was at the end, unlike native speakers and high-proficient learners, who processed these sentences incrementally.

Clahsen and Felser (2006) have argued that late second language learners are generally good at using non-syntactic information, but do not construct a full syntactic analysis of the sentence. They refer to this as the shallow structure hypothesis, which assumes that native speakers use structural strategies (e.g., minimal attachment and recency), whereas late language learners cannot do this, because they do not construct a complete syntactic analysis. Instead, learners rely more on lexical and semantic information for sentence interpretation. There is indeed some evidence that learners' structural analysis of sentences is shallower (Marinis, Roberts, Felser, & Clahsen, 2005; Felser & Roberts, 2007), but whether they instead rely more on non-syntactic information needs further investigation. As Roberts (this volume) points out, whether the shallow structure hypothesis provides an accurate account of second language processing also depends to a large extent on how one defines syntax. Felser, Cunnings, Batterham, and Clahsen (2012) tested sentences such as (13), where *the magazine/shampoo* cannot be the direct object of *read*.

(13) Everyone liked the magazine/shampoo that the hairdresser who read extensively and with such enormous enthusiasm bought before going to the salon.

Indeed, neither native speakers nor second language learners adopted this ungrammatical analysis, as indicated by the finding that neither group experienced more difficulty at or shortly following *read* when this analysis was implausible (*shampoo*) than plausible (*magazine*). Given that the impossibility of the direct object analysis is generally assumed to be due to hard-core syntactic constraints (e.g., Chomsky, 1973), the results suggest that second language learners do construct a detailed syntactic analysis, *contra* the shallow structure hypothesis. However, some researchers have argued that rather than due to syntactic constraints, this is due to memory limitations (Kluender, 2004), in which case the results do not rule out the shallow structure hypothesis.

Research investigating sentence processing in older people (generally over 65) and aphasic patients has mainly focused on structurally complex sentences (e.g., (8)). Most research suggests that older participants slow down more when they process complex structures than young adults (e.g., Kemper & Liu, 2007; Caplan, DeDe, Waters, Michaud, & Tripodis, 2011), though some studies have found no evidence that processing difficulty is affected by aging (Waters & Caplan, 2001, 2005). Caplan (this volume) suggests that this difference in findings may be due to different processing strategies: when older participants read a complex sentence, they may either slow down more relative to younger participants, or they may read the sentence equally quickly, but process it less fully or accurately.

There is a much longer tradition of research on aphasic patients, but as Caplan (this volume) points out, early research mostly measured end-of-sentence responses. Over the years, research on aphasics has started to focus more on on-line sentence comprehension. This research indicates that on-line sentence comprehension is often more intact than suggested by end-of-sentence methods (e.g., Dickey & Thompson, 2005; Thompson & Choy, 2009; Tyler, 1985). It raises the possibility that at least some of the difficulty that aphasics face during sentence comprehension is due to processes following initial structure building (Linebarger, 1995; Thompson & Choy, 2009). This would be consistent with evidence that sentence-processing effects in aphasics are often task dependent (e.g., Caplan, DeDe, & Michaud, 2006).

As argued by Caplan (this volume), evidence for the idea that specific syntactic operations are impaired in aphasic patients (e.g., Grodzinsky, 2000) is currently weak. Rather, most studies suggest that syntactic processing is impaired across the board. One possibility is that the syntactic comprehension deficits in patients is due to a lower general working memory capacity compared to healthy controls (e.g., Just & Carpenter, 1992; Miyake, Carpenter, & Just, 1994). However, Caplan and Waters (1999; Caplan, this volume) have argued against this, because syntactic processing of patients with a low general working memory capacity such as Alzheimer patients tends to be similar to that of healthy control participants (e.g., Almor, MacDonald, Kempler, Andersen, & Tyler, 2001) and aphasic patients' sentence comprehension is unaffected by an additional working memory task they have to perform during sentence processing (Caplan & Waters, 1996). These results are more consistent with the idea that rather than using general working memory resources, syntactic processing employs a working memory component that is specifically dedicated to it

(Caplan & Waters, 1999; Waters & Caplan, 1996), and it is this dedicated working memory component that is impaired in aphasic patients.

Conclusions

The last 40 years or so have seen major advances in our understanding of how language users process sentences. It is clear that syntactic processing is highly incremental and that various non-syntactic sources of information generally have rapid effects on syntactic ambiguity resolution. Even many aspects of semantic interpretation are very quick. Although the main focus has been on syntactic ambiguity resolution, research on (usually unambiguous) syntactically complex structures suggests that factors such as storage in working memory, integration cost, similarity-based interference and surprisal affect processing. Finally, there is an increasing body of research that has investigated to what extent sentence processing in children, older people, bilinguals and aphasic patients differs from that of healthy, adult native speakers. The current volume presents a series of chapters that provide more in-depth reviews of the different (but strongly interconnected) research areas within sentence processing. Written by senior authors in the respective research fields, together they give an overview of the state-of-the-art in sentence-processing research.

Note

1 Throughout this chapter, italics in the example sentences indicate the structurally ambiguous region, and bold type marks the word(s) that provide syntactically or semantically disambiguating information.

References

Almor, A., MacDonald, M. C., Kempler, D., Andersen, D. S., & Tyler, L. K. (2001). Comprehension of long distance number agreement in probable Alzheimer's disease. *Language and Cognitive Processes, 16*, 35–63.

Altmann, G., & Steedman, M. (1988). Interaction with context during human sentence processing. *Cognition, 30*, 191–238.

Altmann, G. T. M., & Kamide, Y. (1999). Incremental interpretation at verbs: Restricting the domain of subsequent reference. *Cognition, 73*, 247–264.

Altmann, G. T.M., van Nice, K. Y., Garnham, A., & Henstra, J. A. (1998). Late closure in context. *Journal of Memory and Language, 38*, 459–484.

Badecker, W., & Straub, K. (2002). The processing role of structural constraints on the interpretation of pronouns and anaphora. *Journal of Experimental Psychology: Learning, Memory, and Cognition, 28*, 748–769.

Boland, J. E., Tanenhaus, M. K., Garnsey, S. M., & Carlson, G. N. (1995). Verb argument structure in parsing and interpretation: Evidence from *wh*-questions. *Journal of Memory and Language, 34*, 774–806.

Britt, M. A. (1994). The interaction of referential ambiguity and argument structure in the parsing of prepositional phrases. *Journal of Memory and Language, 33*, 251–283.

Caplan, D., & Waters. G. S. (1996). Syntactic processing in sentence comprehension under dual-task conditions in aphasic patients. *Language and Cognitive Processes*, *11*, 525–551.

Caplan, D., & Waters, G. S. (1999). Verbal working memory and sentence comprehension. *Behavioral and Brain Sciences*, *22*, 77–126.

Caplan, D., DeDe, G., & Michaud, J. (2006). Task-independent and task-specific syntactic deficits in aphasic comprehension. *Aphasiology*, *20*, 893–920.

Caplan, D., DeDe, G., Waters, G. S., Michaud, J., & Tripodis, Y. (2011). Effects of age, speed of processing and working memory on comprehension of sentences with relative clauses. *Psychology and Aging*, *26*, 439–450.

Carreiras, M., & Clifton, C. (1993). Relative clause interpretation preferences in Spanish and English. *Language and Speech*, *36*, 353–372.

Carreiras, M., & Clifton, C. (1999). Another word on parsing relative clauses: Eye-tracking evidence from Spanish and English. *Memory & Cognition*, *27*, 826–833.

Chambers, C. G., Tanenhaus, M. K., & Magnuson, J. S. (2004). Actions and affordances in syntactic ambiguity resolution. *Journal of Experimental Psychology: Learning Memory and Cognition*, *30*, 687–696.

Chomsky, N. (1957). *Syntactic structures*. The Hague: Mouton.

Chomsky, N. (1965). *Aspects of the theory of syntax*. Cambridge, MA: MIT Press.

Chomsky, N. (1973). Conditions on transformations. In S. R. Anderson and P. Kiparsky (Eds.), *A Festschrift for Morris Halle* (pp. 232–286). New York, NY: Holt, Rinehart, & Winston.

Clahsen, H., & Felser, C. (2006). Grammatical processing in language learners. *Applied Psycholinguistics*, *27*, 3–42.

Clifton, C., & Ferreira, F. (1989). Ambiguity in context. *Language and Cognitive Processes*, *4*, 77–104.

Clifton, C., Traxler, M. J., Mohamed, M. T., Williams, R. S., Morris, R. K., & Rayner, K. (2003). The use of thematic role information in parsing: Syntactic processing autonomy revisited. *Journal of Memory and Language*, *49*, 317–334.

Cooper, R. M. (1974). The control of eye fixation by the meaning of spoken language: A new methodology for the real-time investigation of speech perception, memory, and language processing. *Cognitive Psychology*, *6*, 84–107.

Crain, S., & Steedman, M. (1985). On not being led up the garden path: The use of context by the psychological syntax processor. In D. R. Dowty, L. Karttunen, & A. M. Zwicky (Eds.), *Natural language parsing: Psychological, computational and theoretical perspectives* (pp. 320–358). Cambridge: Cambridge University Press.

Cuetos, F., & Mitchell, D. C. (1988). Cross-linguistic differences in parsing: Restrictions on the use of the Late Closure strategy in Spanish. *Cognition*, *30*, 73–105.

Dickey, M., & Thompson, C. (2005) Real-time comprehension of *wh-* movement in aphasia: Evidence from eyetracking while listening. *Brain and Language*, *100*, 2.

Dussias, P. E., & Cramer Scaltz, T. R. (2008). Spanish–English L2 speakers' use of subcategorization bias information in the resolution of temporary ambiguity during second language reading. *Acta Psychologica*, *128*, 501–513.

Dussias, P. E., & Piñar, P. (2010). Effects of reading span and plausibility in the reanalysis of *wh*-gaps by Chinese-English L2 speakers. *Second Language Research*, *26*, 443–472.

Felser, C., & Roberts, L. (2007). Processing *wh*-dependencies in a second language: A cross-modal priming study. *Second Language Research*, *23*, 9–36.

Felser, C., Cunnings, I., Batterham, C. & Clahsen, H. (2012). The Timing of Island Effects in Nonnative Sentence Processing. *Studies in Second Language Acquisition, 34*, 67–98.

Ferreira, F. (2003). The misinterpretation of noncanonical sentences. *Cognitive Psychology, 47*, 164–203.

Ferreira, F., & Clifton, C. (1986). The independence of syntactic processing. *Journal of Memory and Language, 25*, 348–368.

Ferreira, F., & Henderson, J. M. (1990). Use of verb information in syntactic parsing: Evidence from eye-movements and word-by-word self-paced reading. *Journal of Experimental Psychology: Learning, Memory, and Cognition, 16*, 555–568.

Fodor, J., Bever, T., & Garrett, M. (1974). *The psychology of language.* New York: McGraw-Hill.

Frazier, L. (1979). *On comprehending sentences: Syntactic parsing strategies.* Ph.D. Dissertation. Indiana University Linguistics Club. University of Connecticut.

Frazier, L. (1987). Sentence processing: A tutorial review. In M. Coltheart (Ed.), *Attention and performance XII: The psychology of reading* (pp. 559–586). Hillsdale, NJ: Lawrence Erlbaum Associates.

Frazier, L., & Clifton, C. Jr. (1989). Successive cyclicity in the grammar and the parser. *Language and Cognitive Processes, 4*, 93–126.

Frazier, L., & Clifton, C. Jr. (1996). *Construal.* Cambridge, MA: MIT Press.

Frazier, L., & Flores D'Arcais, G. B. (1989). Filler driven parsing: A study of gap filling in Dutch. *Journal of Memory and Language, 28*, 331–344.

Frazier, L., & Fodor, J. D. (1978). The sausage machine: A new two-stage parsing model. *Cognition, 6*, 291–325.

Frazier, L., & Rayner, K. (1982). Making and correcting errors during sentence comprehension: Eye-movements in the analysis of structurally ambiguous sentences. *Cognitive Psychology, 14*, 178–210.

Frenck-Mestre, C., & Pynte, J. (1997). Syntactic ambiguity resolution while reading in second and native languages. *Quarterly Journal of Experimental Psychology, 50A*, 119–148.

Friederici, A. D., Hahne, A., & Mecklinger, A. (1996). Temporal structure of syntactic parsing: Early and late event-related brain potential effects. *Journal of Experimental Psychology: Learning Memory and Cognition, 22*, 1219–1248.

Gibson, E. (1998). Linguistic complexity: Locality of syntactic dependencies. *Cognition, 68*, 1–76.

Gibson, E. (2000). The dependency locality theory: A distance-based theory of linguistic complexity. In A. Marantz, Y. Miyashita, and W. O'Neil (Eds.), *Image, Language, Brain* (pp. 95–126). Cambridge, MA: MIT Press.

Gibson, E., Pearlmutter, N., Canseco-Gonzalez, E., & Hickok, G. (1996). Recency preference in the human sentence processing mechanism. *Cognition, 59*, 23–59.

Gordon, P. C., Hendrick, R., & Johnson, M. (2001). Memory interference during language processing. *Journal of Experimental Psychology: Learning Memory and Cognition, 27*, 1411–1423.

Green, M., & Mitchell, D. (2006). Absence of real evidence against competition during syntactic ambiguity resolution. *Journal of Memory and Language, 55*, 1–17.

Grodzinsky, Y. (2000). The neurology of syntax: Language use without Broca's area. *Behavioral and Brain Sciences, 23*, 47–117.

Hagoort, P., Brown, C., & Groothusen, J. (1993). The syntactic positive shift (SPS) as an ERP measure of syntactic processing. *Language and Cognitive Processes, 8*, 439–483.

Hale, J. (2001). A probabilistic Earley parser as a psycholinguistic model. In *Proceedings of NAACL* (Vol. 2, pp. 159–166).

Jackson, C. N. (2008). Proficiency level and the interaction of lexical and morphosyntactic information during L2 sentence processing. *Language Learning, 58*, 875–909.

Jackson, C., & Roberts, L. (2010). Animacy affects the processing of subject-object ambiguities in L2 processing: Evidence from self-paced reading with German L2 learners of Dutch. *Applied Psycholinguistics, 31*, 671–691.

Just, M. A., & Carpenter, P. A. (1980). A theory of reading: From eye fixations to comprehension. *Psychological Review, 87*, 329–354.

Just, M. A., & Carpenter, P. A. (1992). A capacity theory of comprehension: Individual differences in working memory. *Psychological Review, 99*, 122–149.

Kamide, Y., Altmann, G. T. M., & Haywood, S. L. (2003). The time-course of prediction in incremental sentence processing: Evidence from anticipatory eye-movements. *Journal of Memory and Language, 49*, 133–156.

Kemper, S. & Liu, C-J. (2007). Eye-movements of young and older adults during reading. *Psychology and Aging, 22*, 84–93.

Kennison, S. M. (2003). Comprehending the pronouns her, him, and his: Implications for theories of referential processing. *Journal of Memory and Language, 49*, 335–352.

Kimball, J. (1973). Seven principles of surface structure parsing in natural language. *Cognition, 2*, 15–47.

King, J., & Just, M. A. (1991). Individual differences in syntactic processing: The role of working memory. *Journal of Memory and Language, 30*, 580–602.

Kluender, R. (2004). Are subject islands subject to a processing account? In V. Chand, A. Kelleher, A. J. Rodríguez & B. Schmeiser (Eds.), *Proceedings of the 23rd WCCFL*. Somerville, MA: Cascadilla Press.

Knoeferle, P., Crocker, M. W., Scheepers, C., & Pickering, M. J. (2005). The influence of the immediate visual context on incremental thematic role-assignment: Evidence from eye-movements in depicted events. *Cognition, 95*, 95–127.

Kutas, M., & Hillyard, S. A. (1980). Reading senseless sentences: Brain potentials reflect semantic incongruity. *Science, 207*, 203–205.

Kutas, M., & Hillyard, S. A. (1984). Brain potentials during reading reflect word expectancy and semantic association. *Nature, 307*, 161–163.

Levy, R. (2008). Expectation-based syntactic comprehension. *Cognition, 106*, 1126–1177.

Lewis, R. L., & Vasishth, S. (2005). An activation-based model of sentence processing as skilled memory retrieval. *Cognitive Science, 29*, 1–45.

Lewis, R. L., Vasishth, S., & Van Dyke, J. A. (2006). Computational principles of working memory in sentence comprehension. *Trends in Cognitive Science, 10*, 447–454.

Linebarger, M. C. (1995). Agrammatism as evidence about grammar. *Brain and Language, 50*, 52–91.

MacDonald, M. C., Pearlmutter, N. J., & Seidenberg, M. S. (1994). The lexical nature of syntactic ambiguity resolution. *Psychological Review, 101*, 676–703.

Marinis, T., Roberts, L., Felser, C., & Clahsen, H. (2005). Gaps in second language processing. *Studies in Second Language Acquisition, 27*, 53–78.

Marslen-Wilson, W. (1973). Linguistic structure and speech shadowing at very short latencies. *Nature, 244*, 522–523.

Marslen-Wilson, W. (1975). Sentence perception as an interactive parallel process. *Science, 189*, 226–228.

McElree, B., Frisson, S., & Pickering, M. J. (2006). Deferred interpretations: Why starting Dickens is taxing but reading Dickens isn't. *Cognitive Science*, *30*, 181–192.

McRae, K., Spivey-Knowlton, M. J., & Tanenhaus, M. K. (1998). Modeling the influence of thematic fit (and other constraints) in on-line sentence comprehension. *Journal of Memory and Language*, *38*, 283–312.

Mitchell, D. C., Cuetos, F., Corley, M. M.B., & Brysbaert, M. (1995). Exposure-based models of human parsing: Evidence for the use of coarse-grained (nonlexical) statistical records. *Journal of Psycholinguistic Research*, *24*, 469–488.

Miyake, A., Carpenter, P., & Just, M. (1994). A capacity approach to syntactic comprehension disorders: Making normal adults perform like aphasic patients. *Cognitive Neuropsychology*, *11*, 671–717.

Osterhout, L. & Holcomb, P. J. (1992). Event-related brain potentials elicited by syntactic anomaly. *Journal of Memory and Language*, *31*, 785–806.

Osterhout, L., & Holcomb, P. J. (1993). Event-related potentials and syntactic anomaly: Evidence of anomaly detection during the perception of continuous speech. *Language and Cognitive Processes*, *8*, 413–437.

Osterhout, L., & Nicol, J. (1999). On the distinctiveness, independence, and time-course of the brain responses to syntactic and semantic anomalies. *Language and Cognitive Processes*, *14*, 283–317.

Pickering, M. J., Traxler, M. J., & Crocker, M. W. (2000). Ambiguity resolution in sentence processing: Evidence against frequency-based accounts. *Journal of Memory and Language*, *43*, 447–475.

Rayner, K., Carlson, M., & Frazier, L. (1983). The interaction of syntax and semantics during sentence processing: Eye-movements in the analysis of semantically biased sentences. *Journal of Verbal Learning and Verbal Behavior*, *22*, 358–374.

Roberts, L., & Felser, C. (2011). Plausibility and recovery from garden-paths in second language sentence processing. *Applied Psycholinguistics*, *32*, 299–331.

Snedeker, J., & Trueswell, J. (2003). Using prosody to avoid ambiguity: Effects of speaker awareness and referential context. *Journal of Memory and Language*, *48*, 103–130.

Snedeker, J., & Trueswell, J. C. (2004). The developing constraints on parsing decisions: The role of lexical-biases and referential scenes in child and adult sentence processing. *Cognitive Psychology*, *49*, 238–299.

Staub, A. (2007). The parser doesn't ignore intransitivity, after all. *Journal of Experimental Psychology: Learning, Memory, and Cognition*, *33*, 550–569.

Sturt, P. (2003). The time-course of the application of binding constraints in reference resolution. *Journal of Memory and Language*, *48*, 542–562.

Tabor, W., & Tanenhaus, M. K. (1999). Dynamical models of sentence processing. *Cognitive Science*, *23*, 491–515.

Tanenhaus, M. K., Spivey Knowlton, M. J., Eberhard, K. M., & Sedivy, J. C. (1995). Integration of visual and linguistic information in spoken language comprehension. *Science*, *268*, 1632–1634.

Thompson, C. K., & Choy, J. (2009). Pronominal resolution and gap filling in agrammatic aphasia: Evidence from eye-movements. *Journal of Psycholinguistic Research*, *38*, 255–283.

Thothathiri, M., & Snedeker, J. (2008). Syntactic priming during language comprehension in three- and four-year-old children. *Journal of Memory and Language*, *58*, 188–213.

Tomasello, M. (1992). *First verbs: A case study in early grammatical development.* Cambridge: Cambridge University Press.

Townsend, D. J., & Bever, T. G. (2001) *Sentence comprehension: The integration of habits and rules.* Cambridge, MA: MIT Press.

Traxler, M. J., Morris, R. K., & Seely, R. E. (2002). Processing subject and object relative clauses: Evidence from eye-movements. *Journal of Memory and Language, 47,* 69–90.

Trueswell, J. C. (1996). The role of lexical frequency in syntactic ambiguity resolution. *Journal of Memory and Language, 35,* 566–585.

Trueswell, J. C., Sekerina, I., Hill, N. M., & Logrip, M. L. (1999). The kindergarten-path effect: Studying on-line sentence processing in young children. *Cognition, 73,* 89–134.

Trueswell, J. C., Tanenhaus, M. K., & Garnsey, S. M. (1994). Semantic influences on parsing: Use of thematic role information in syntactic ambiguity resolution. *Journal of Memory and Language, 33,* 285–318.

Trueswell, J. C., Tanenhaus, M. K., & Kello, C. (1993). Verb-specific constraints in sentence processing: Separating effects of lexical preference from garden-paths. *Journal of Experimental Psychology: Learning, Memory, and Cognition, 19,* 528–553.

Tyler, L. (1985). Real-time comprehension processes in agrammatism: A case study. *Brain and Language, 26,* 259–275.

Van Berkum, J., Brown, C., & Hagoort, P. (1999). Early referential context effects in sentence processing: Evidence from event-related potentials. *Journal of Memory and Language, 41,* 147–182.

Van Dyke, J. A. & Lewis, R. L. (2003). Distinguishing effects of structure and decay on attachment and repair: A retrieval interference theory of recovery from misanalysed ambiguities. *Journal of Memory and Language, 49,* 285–316.

Van Gompel, R. P. G., Pickering, M. J., & Traxler, M. J. (2001). Reanalysis in sentence processing: Evidence against current constraint-based and two-stage models. *Journal of Memory and Language, 45,* 225–258.

Van Gompel, R. P. G., Pickering, M. J., Pearson, J., & Liversedge, S. P. (2005). Evidence against competition during syntactic ambiguity resolution. *Journal of Memory and Language, 52,* 284–307.

Waters, G. S., & Caplan, D. (1996). The capacity theory of sentence comprehension: Critique of Just and Carpenter (1992). *Psychological Review, 103,* 761–772.

Waters, G. S. & Caplan, D. (2001). Age, working memory and on-line syntactic processing in sentence comprehension. *Psychology and Aging, 16,* 128–144.

Waters, G. S. & Caplan, D. (2005). The relationship between age, processing speed, working memory capacity, and language comprehension. *Memory, 13,* 403–413.

2 Syntax in sentence processing

Lyn Frazier

Introduction

Today it may be taken for granted by some that listeners and readers compute a syntactic structure when they comprehend a sentence or discourse. Nevertheless, it seems appropriate to review the evidence for the existence of syntax, and some of the arguments and evidence that it is computed automatically, rather than strategically, during ordinary language comprehension. If syntax is computed without awareness in a reflexive manner, this fits with a view of the human language ability where the (acquisition and) processing of syntax is assumed to be biologically given to some important extent (though presumably automatic systems need not be biologically fixed in any direct way). If on the other hand processing syntax is a consciously controlled cognitive process, this would undermine the view that humans have a species-specific communication system. Consequently, some very basic arguments for the existence of automatic syntactic processing will be addressed before taking up the principles proposed to govern the construction of syntactic structures, and reviewing various theories of syntactic processing (though sidestepping for the most part those theories taken up in later chapters).

In constructing a theory of language comprehension, the goal is to construct a theory that can explain language processing regardless of whether the input language is English, Swahili or Mongolian. English, and processing English sentences, has been investigated intensively. It is well-known that English is a Verb Object (VO) language, that it generally does not permit phonologically null subjects (*Called me*), it has impoverished Case except in the pronoun system (*I like him*, not **Me like he*) and it contains overt determiners (hence, *The girl laughed*, not **Girl laughed*). Further, English tends to mark the information (given/new) status of phrases prosodically rather than by moving the phrase to a particular syntactic position. On the other hand, when it comes to question formation, English moves the interrogative phrase (*who, what*) rather than leaving it in place ("in situ"). Whether any of these properties matter in the sense of explaining the properties of syntactic processing that have been documented will remain unknown until languages without these properties have been investigated in detail. Thus, after discussing properties of syntactic processing motivated primarily by work in English and a handful of European languages, we will take up the issue of what is known about processing Object Verb (OV) languages, languages with null subjects, languages with a rich set of Case markers, languages that mark information structure through movement ("scrambling") and, finally, languages where the interrogative phrase remains *in situ* in questions. Languages like Japanese and Turkish differ from English with respect to all of the mentioned properties as they are head-final, permit null subjects, contain rich Case, lack overt determiners, are able to scramble given or contrasted phrases and form questions with *in situ* interrogative phrases. Languages like Finnish show a mixture of properties, e.g., VO basic word order, but permitting scrambling, showing that although particular properties often co-occur, they need not.

The existence of syntax

Standard linguistic argumentation, characterizing the intuitively well-formed sentences of languages in an insightful manner, distinguishing them from similar but ill-formed structures, suffices to demonstrate the existence of sentence structure ("syntax"). Sentences are not just strings of words. Rather, words are organized into larger units according to the grammatical principles of a language. If the language is English, then the head of a phrase (e.g., the verb in a verb phrase, the noun in a noun phrase, and so on) precedes its object(s) as in *Ian examined the problem*; *examination of the problem*. The properties of English, such as head initiality, do not hold for all languages. The grammar of a language must specify what combinations and orders of words and phrases are well formed. Although the actual restrictions are mind-boggling in their subtlety when one looks at the data carefully, the basic restrictions can be captured using a highly limited syntactic vocabulary (verb, noun, . . .) and a small number of structural relations defined over tree structures (dominate, "c-command," . . . ; cf. Adger, 2003, and Radford, 1997).

Native speakers of a language are able to produce an indefinite number of novel sentences in their language, along with predictable meanings for them. Without syntax, it is entirely unclear how this could be possible. However, some researchers seem to remain skeptical of this argument. After all, the actual sentences people encounter may be short, semi-familiar and possibly boring. Perhaps syntax isn't needed in order to understand familiar sentences (Townsend & Bever, 2001), or perhaps it serves merely as a backup when other means don't suffice or it is computed on an as-needed basis depending on task demands or the goal of a conversation (Ferreira, 2003; Ferreira & Patson, 2007).

The problem with this approach is that it presupposes that a listener can suspend syntactic analysis. This is not at all clear. For example, Event Related Potential (ERP) evidence from a task in which subjects attended to auditory non-speech stimuli in the left ear and passively listened to speech in the right ear, revealed an effect of ungrammaticality of the unattended speech stimuli already at 150 ms post-onset (Pulvermüller, Shtyrov, Hasting & Carlyon, 2008). Further, the ERP effect was unaffected by the attentional load of the distracting task (a demanding auditory discrimination task involving the non-speech stimuli or a passive task, watching a video, which was also present in the high attentional load condition).

In some models of processing, syntax may play a role, but it does not play a distinguished role, defining a separate level of representation, as in constraint satisfaction models (MacDonald, Pearlmutter, & Seidenberg, 1994; Tanenhaus, Spivey-Knowlton, Eberhard, & Sedivy, 1995). The existence of "automatic" (non-directed, non-resource demanding) syntactic analysis may be problematic for such models. For example, native speakers of English report computing the silly analysis of (1), where a boy is in a box. If syntactic analysis is automatic, the general syntactic preference for low or local attachment of *in a box* as a modifier of *a boy* as illustrated by the brackets in (1a) can explain why this analysis is computed rather than the correct analysis shown in (1b). But if syntax is used only as a backup for complex or highly novel input or always used along with semantics, it becomes mysterious why a silly interpretation would be computed when a perfectly sensible conventional interpretation is possible (where the gift to a boy is what is in the box).

(1) A gift to a boy in a box . . .

    a. [A gift to [a boy in a box]]
    b. [[A gift to a boy] in a box]

(Example due to Steve Abney)

Syntactic priming in production (Bock, 1986; Pickering & Branigan, 1999) and comprehension (Arai, Van Gompel, & Scheepers, 2007; Sturt, Keller, & Dubey, 2010) further suggest that a syntactic representation is constructed automatically during language processing. Processing of a structure is faster in comprehension if a similar structure has been processed recently, and, in production, the probability of choosing a particular structure is increased by the recent production or comprehension of the same structure. There is no indication that participants in these priming studies are aware of the structures they are producing or comprehending: the priming effects are not dependent on conscious awareness of the structure, suggesting that basic implicit learning or processing mechanisms are involved, not controlled strategies. Even amnesics show priming (Ferreira, Bock, Wilson, & Cohen, 2008). Flores d'Arcais (1987) did a series of studies investigating the processing and detection of different types of violations, including "spelling" (non-word) errors, semantic anomalies and syntactic violations involving incorrect or missing prepositions (2).

(2) a. The old lady spifted the white chair.
       ("spelling" error)

b. The old lady sat the white chair.
(syntactic violation)

c. The old lady drank the white chair.
(semantic anomaly)

Detection rates were lowest (28 percent) for syntactic violations and substantially higher for semantic (67 percent) and "spelling" errors (78 percent). The interesting finding, however, is that when eye-movements were measured during reading, there was a penalty even for syntactic errors, in terms of more fixations and longer fixations, independent of whether the violation was detected. This result too suggests that syntactic analysis automatically occurs, but does not necessarily get noticed consciously when a sensible interpretation can be assigned to the sentence.

One might think that at least in the case of comprehending idioms, prototypical examples of familiar conventionalized language, syntax would not play a role. But syntax is computed even during idiom recognition (e.g., Tabossi, Wolf, & Koterle, 2009). Indeed, in general, frequency or familiarity cannot substitute for syntax. Bader and Häussler (submitted) collected speeded acceptability judgment data and corpus data on German verbs that take either an accusative object or both an accusative and dative object. They showed that grammaticality cannot be reduced to frequency: although a particular verb occurring with a particular object or set of objects with high frequency in a corpus entails being grammatical, and being ungrammatical entails low frequency in the corpus, occurring with low frequency in the corpus does not entail ungrammaticality.

The construction of syntax

Syntactic analysis proceeds as soon as a syntactic category label (noun, verb, determiner, . . .) for an input word becomes available from the comprehender's stored knowledge about words. Syntactic analysis proceeds systematically, by incorporating each new word into a connected phrase marker, favoring grammatical analyses over ungrammatical ones. Although sometimes the input itself will be ungrammatical or fragmented, under conditions when a globally well-formed analysis *is* available, typically it is identified by the language processor (e.g., Frazier & Rayner, 1982). It is possible though that ungrammatical sentence analyses, analyses without successful revision, do occasionally arise and persist. For example, Tabor, Galantucci, and Richardson (2004) (see also Konieczny, 2005) argued that comprehenders will analyze the sentence in (3) as two locally well-formed phrases, as in the beginning of a conjoined verb phrase (*The player tossed a ball, threw a frisbee, and left the park*), but fail to successfully reanalyze the structure to a reduced relative clause structure (as in *Who threw the frisbee? The player tossed the ball threw the frisbee*) where *The player tossed the ball* is analyzed as "the player who was tossed the ball."

(3) The player tossed the ball threw a frisbee.

Evidence from various sources indicates that, generally, grammatical analyses of a sentence are computed. Increases in fixation durations are found immediately on a verb, *fell* in (4), when a post-verbal phrase cannot be interpreted as the object of the verb in reading.

(4) a. While Mary was mending the sock *fell* off her lap.
    b. While Mary was mending the sock it fell off her lap.

In ERP studies, a characteristic pattern (late positivity or "P600") is observed in the ERP record immediately at a syntactically deviant word, italicized in the examples below. Osterhout and Holcomb (1992) investigated garden-path sentences like (5) and observed a P600; Hagoort, Brown, and Groothusen (1993) investigated examples like (6) and also found a late positivity.

(5) The broker persuaded *to* sell the stock . . .

(6) The child *throw* the toys . . .

Evidence of long processing times or other indicators of a syntactic violation such as the P600 could only occur immediately at the point of the deviant word if syntax is computed immediately. If a connected syntactic representation were not built, then no violation should occur in examples like (2b) above, because each of the syntactic chunks, taken by itself, is well-formed: The old lady, sat, the white chair. It is only in virtue of syntactically analyzing these as a connected syntactic structure that a violation emerges.

These properties of syntactic analysis were captured by, among other models, the garden-path model of sentence comprehension. In this model, once syntactic category information for a new item becomes available, syntactic inferences trigger attachment of the item into the syntactic representation of the portion of the sentence received so far. The model was developed in the context of the assumption that the syntactic processing sub-system is "modular" in the sense that grammatical inferences are stated in terms of a highly limited and specialized vocabulary governing the permissible sets of phrases and the way they can combine, e.g., a verb phrase consists of a verb and its object(s). Inferences following from syntactic conditions thus give rise to rapid automatic structuring of linguistic input (Forster, 1979; Fodor, 1983), with semantic and pragmatic evidence influencing the interpretation of a phrase (and perhaps reanalysis of a hastily computed syntactic structure).

The garden-path model emphasized the need to get an analysis quickly as the motivation for the preferences the processor exhibits. The difficulty of maintaining unanalyzed material in memory, together with the limits imposed by the size of immediate memory, were seen as the pressure behind the need to adopt the first syntactic analysis available. This resulted in minimal attachment, namely, attachment into the current syntactic representation postulating only as many new phrases as required by the grammar. In (7) *and her sister* could be incorporated into the object phrase *Mary*, creating a conjoined noun phrase, as in (7a), rather than postulating a new clause and making *her sister* the subject of that clause, as in (7b). Late closure attachments resulted in attachment, e.g., of *yesterday* in (8), to the most recently received material, assumed to be most readily available in memory. This would result in *yesterday* being interpreted as modifying the lower clause *Bill died*, as in (8a), rather than the higher clause *John announced*, as in (8b).

(7) a. Jesse kissed Mary and her sister . . . yesterday.
(minimal attachment)

b. Jesse kissed Mary and her sister . . . laughed.
(non-minimal attachment)

(8) John announced that Bill died yesterday.

a. Bill died yesterday.
(late closure interpretation)

b. John announced something yesterday.
(early closure interpretation)

Dependencies between the basic position of a phrase (the "gap") and the position where the phrase appears in the sentence (e.g., typically the beginning of the sentence for interrogative phrases like *what* in (9)) were processed by the active filler strategy. The active filler strategy requires each moved phrase to be assigned to the first grammatically permissible gap position available. In (9), this is the potential gap after *whisper*, even though *whisper* is a preferred intransitive verb and need not take an object at all. Nevertheless, readers do not overlook early gap sites, and thus a continuation consistent with the active filler strategy analysis (9a) is read more quickly than one inconsistent with it (9b): see Frazier and Clifton, 1989; Pickering and Traxler, 2003. (See Frazier, 1987, for an overview of evidence; Omaki, Lau, Davidson White, Dakan, & Phillips, submitted, for evidence about the timing of gap-filling decisions; and Warren & Gibson, 2002, for evidence about the effect of intervening phrases.)

(9) a. What did the old man whisper to his fiancee about the movie?
(active filler predicts less difficulty)

b. What did the old man whisper to his fiancee about?
(active filler predicts difficulty)

In the garden-path theory, a fast automatic inference machine produced the first structural analysis of a linguistic input in a word by word fashion.

The initially constructed analysis was revised if later information, subsequent syntactic information or semantic/pragmatic information resulting from interpretation of the structured input, provided evidence that the initial analysis was in need of revision. So the garden-path account needed an accompanying theory of reanalysis.

Theories of reanalysis

Some theories of sentence processing were motivated primarily by the attempt to distinguish easy reanalysis from difficult or impossible reanalysis. Pritchett's (1988) theory of sentence processing, for example, was based on the Theta-attachment principle requiring every argument to have one and only one thematic role, favoring the maximal theta grid of a verb, as in (10a) where *took* can be analyzed as taking two objects. But reanalysis was claimed to be easy providing that a phrase stayed within the theta-domain of the same verb, as in (10b).

(10) Ian took her money.
      (Predicted interpretation: Ian took her the money.)

   a. Ian took [her] [money].
      (What Ian took her was money.)

   b. Ian took [her money].
      (What Ian took was her money.)

Clifton, Kennison and Albrecht (1997) investigated the processing of Case ambiguous (*her*) and Case unambiguous *(him)* pronouns, and found evidence for a more complicated picture. They suggested that an underspecified syntactic representation, one neutral between the determiner phrase (DP) and the possessor analysis, is built initially. The ease of finding an antecedent for the pronoun eventually determines its specific syntactic analysis.

Ferreira and Henderson (1998) also focus on thematic roles in accounting for difficulty in reanalysis. Difficult reanalysis results when thematic roles interact, as in (11a) where *the dog* will initially be attached in the first clause and must therefore be reanalyzed by being eliminated from the theta grid of *scratched* and taken to be an argument of *yawned* instead. Reanalysis is also predicted to be difficult when one thematic domain is embedded inside another. Thus, reanalysis is more difficult when the ambiguous phrase is lengthened with material that introduces a theta assigner, the verb *hates* in (11b), that intervenes between the head of the ambiguous phrase (*dog*) and the disambiguating word *yawned*. When the ambiguous phrase is lengthened by material that does not intervene between the head of the ambiguous phrase and the disambiguating word, for example by the prenominal modifiers *big and hairy* in (11c), no comparable difficulty is observed. Specifically, in speeded grammaticality judgments, there is no drop in the percentage of sentences judged grammatical when the lengthening material does not intervene between the head of the ambiguous phrase and the disambiguating word.

(11) a. When the boy scratched the dog yawned.

b. When the boy scratched the dog that Sally hates yawned loudly.

c. When the boy scratched the big and hairy dog yawned loudly.

Ferreira, Christianson and Hollingworth (2000) examined reanalysis in sentences like (12). They argued that reanalysis is partly successful in the sense that the post-verbal phrase *the baby that was small and cute* was correctly reanalyzed as the subject of the following clause *spit up on the bed*. But, nevertheless, the original thematic role assignment lingered, with the baby taken as the theme of the verb *dressed*, as shown in the answers of participants to questions about who did what to whom. In a series of fascinating studies Christianson, Hollingworth, Halliwell, and Ferreira (2001) further showed that the original thematic role assignment lingers even in sentences like (12) containing reflexive verbs that have very different interpretations depending on whether they are analyzed as having an overt post-verbal object (the baby) or a reflexive "intransitive" interpretation (where Anna dressed herself).

(12) While Anna dressed the baby that was small and cute spit up on the bed.

Participants correctly analyzed *baby* as the subject of the main clause but still responded that *Anna dressed the baby* when asked who Anna dressed. This intriguing result was the original basis for what the authors eventually labeled the "Good enough" approach to processing: the claim that the processor assigns only as much structure and interpretation as is required for the task at hand (Ferreira & Patson, 2007). An alternative approach to these data might be to assume that at the end of the clause (... *small and cute*) the syntactic and thematic analysis of the clause is made available for integration into a discourse representation, which is not automatically updated when syntactic reanalysis of the post-verbal phrase takes place. This might explain why both interpretations persist.

Perhaps the best-known theory of reanalysis is the diagnosis model. Fodor and Inoue (1994, 1998, 2000) argued for two stages of revision: diagnosis and repair. They suggested that no kind of repair is intrinsically costly; the cost depends on the difficulty of diagnosing the problem. To diagnose an error easily and reliably a "positive" symptom is needed. For example, it is easy to misparse the German interrogative phrase *Welche Vertreterin* in (13a) as binding the subject gap, since the *wh*-phrase's Case-marking is ambiguous in differentiating between Nominative and Accusative.

(13) a. *Welche Vertreterin der Gewerkschaft hat [subject gap] der Minister kritisiert?

Which delegate of the trade union (NOM or ACC) has [subject gap] the minister (NOM) criticized?

"Which delegate of the trade union has criticized the minister?" (expected analysis)

Correct analysis:

b. Welche Vertreterin der Gewerkschaft hat der Minister [object gap] kritisiert?

Which delegate of the trade union has the minister [object gap] criticized?

"Which delegate of the trade union have the ministers criticized?"

However, when the reader encounters the unambiguously Nominative phrase *der Minister*, it is obvious that *the minister* must be the subject of the sentence, and consequently the *Vertreterin* must be the object. Case-disambiguation is an obvious symptom, and reanalysis is easy. On the other hand, with Number disambiguation, as in (14), the number of the interrogative phrase conflicts with the verb's (*haben*) unambiguously plural number, violating Subject–Verb number agreement. But in the diagnosis model, this only disconfirms the first analysis with the subject gap; it does not guide the parser to the correct analysis with an object gap, perhaps explaining why Case is a better disambiguator (see Meng & Bader, 2002 for data; Fodor & Inoue, 2000 for why number is a "negative" symptom).

(14) Welche Vertreterin der Gewerkschaft haben [subject gap] die Minister kritisiert?

Which delegate (Singular, NOM or ACC) have-plural [subject gap] the ministers (Plural, NOM or ACC) criticized?

"Which delegate of the trade union has criticized the minister?"

The other central constraint in the diagnosis model is the need for a chain of grammatical dependencies between the error signal and the node in need of repair.

Event Related Potential (ERP) studies provide qualitative evidence about different electroencephalography (EEG) components, their onset and amplitude. Friederici (1998) proposed that ERPs reflect the two stages of revision, diagnosis and repair, in separate parameters. The onset latency of a positivity associated with a revision may reflect diagnosis of the error, and the duration of the positivity may reflect the actual structural alterations performed (though see too Dillon, Nevens, Austin, & Phillips, 2011).

In a ground-breaking paper on implicit prosody and its impact on repairs, Bader (1998) showed that silent reading of German sentences involves more expensive revisions when both the prosody and the syntax of the original analysis need to be repaired as compared to when only the syntax must be repaired (see Bader & Meng 1999 for a different argument that foreshadows the point). The study thus experimentally shows that prosody is assigned during silent reading (see also Fodor, 2002) but also implies that reanalysis costs are not determined by syntax alone. Others have argued that the cost of syntactic reanalysis can indeed be influenced by non-syntactic factors such as the semantic and pragmatic plausibility of the first analysis and of the target analysis (Frazier & Clifton, 1998; Pickering & Traxler, 1998). Theories of repair processes and repair difficulty tend to be partial theories that are for the most part mutually compatible in the sense that the cost of revisions may depend on both the amount and type of evidence available to diagnose the error, and on the thematic or semantic consequences of making the revision.

Parallel construction of syntax

In some models of sentence processing, multiple syntactic analyses of an input are constructed at the same time. For example, in Crain and Steedman's (1985) highly influential referential theory, multiple syntactic analyses of each new word are constructed, and then the semantically and pragmatically best analysis is chosen and pursued. In particular, Crain and Steedman proposed the principle of Parsimony, which favors whatever analysis has the fewest presupposition violations, though the model also favors analyses that are plausible in terms of world-knowledge ("Plausibility") and analyses that permit phrases to refer to entities already present in the discourse model ("Referential success").

(15) The horse raced past the barn fell.
      (Compare: The horse ridden past the barn fell.)

In Crain and Steedman's analysis, restrictive relative clauses presuppose the existence of a context set of entities of the type of the head nominal (*horses* in (15)). Since this presupposition will not be satisfied in a null context, comprehenders will choose the main clause analysis of *raced past the barn* in (15) to avoid a presupposition violation. In a context with several horses, one of them ridden past the barn, the presupposition will be satisfied so the processor will not avoid the correct reduced relative clause analysis.

In recent years, theories of repair have been backgrounded. In part this is because repair plays a less central role in models where multiple syntactic structures are computed. Further, visual-world studies have impressed on investigators that in the presence of rich visual contexts structural errors may be avoided in the first place. This is commonly accounted for in a parallel constraint satisfaction model where all analyses of an input compete, and the one with the most activation wins (quickly if all evidence favors that analysis, and slowly if evidence is equally consistent with two or more analyses, see MacDonald et al., 1994, Tanenhaus et al., 1995, and McRae and Matsuki, this volume, for discussion).

On most assumptions (though see Green & Mitchell, 2006), the competition predicted by constraint satisfaction models should be especially great in fully ambiguous sentences in neutral contexts where evidence does not clearly favor one analysis over alternatives. Thus fully ambiguous sentences are predicted to take longer to process than their temporarily ambiguous counterparts. But this prediction has been disconfirmed (Clifton & Staub, 2008; Traxler, Pickering, & Clifton, 1998; Van Gompel, Pickering, Pearson, & Liversedge, 2005).

One model that can account for effects of context and the ease of processing fully ambiguous syntactic structures is the unrestricted race model (Van Gompel, Pickering & Traxler, 2000, 2001). In response to evidence showing effects of non-syntactic (contextual and discourse) information before the disambiguation point in a sentence and the existence of evidence arguing against competition, Van Gompel and colleagues propose the unrestricted race model in which all sources of information may influence the selection of a single analysis, which is then the only analysis pursued unless or until it becomes untenable.

Distinct kinds of dependencies processed differently

It is not uncommon for researchers to assume that the dependency between a pronoun and its antecedent in discourse is processed differently from a movement dependency such as that found in questions (where a "filler" (*who*) has been moved from its normal position, e.g., after the verb if it is acting as object, as in *Who did Justin call ___?*). The movement dependency is processed predictively: the processor searches for the first position from which the filler might have been moved (see discussion of the active filler strategy above). By contrast, in the usual case where a pronoun follows its antecedent, the processor has no knowledge of the existence of the upcoming pronoun and therefore could not process it predictively. When the pronoun arrives, the processor finds an antecedent either in the same sentence as the pronoun, or possibly an antecedent in the discourse representation.[1]

Phillips, Wagers, and Lau (2011) examined a wider class of dependencies, focusing on the contrast between distinct classes of grammatical dependencies. They note that some are processed accurately, despite their complexity. These include "filler-gap" relations governed by the active filler strategy (even though such dependencies obey complex grammatical conditions "island constraints"; Crain & Fodor, 1985; Stowe, 1986; Traxler & Pickering, 1996a). They also include cases where a pronoun precedes its "antecedent" (Kazanina, Lau, Lieberman, Yoshida, & Phillips, 2007), and thus may be processed predictively. In addition, standard reflexives such as *himself* (Nicol & Swinney, 1989; Sturt, this volume) seem to be processed accurately. What is striking is that such dependencies seem to be processed accurately despite the complex conditions governing the well-formedness of the dependencies.

By contrast, other types of dependencies are error prone. For example, agreement between the grammatical number of the verb and its subject is not enforced accurately in sentences like *The key to the cabinets are here* (Wagers, Lau, & Phillips, 2009; Staub, 2010a, among many others). Similar processing errors have been documented in the area of grammatical Case. Case is a grammatical feature licensed for particular arguments or positions: Nominative Case (*I*, *he*) is typically grammatical only in subject position (**I like he*); Accusative Case is typically only grammatical in object position *(*Him arrived)*. But in a language with a rich set of Cases, in some structures, ungrammatical sentences seem to be acceptable due to the presence of an intervening phrase bearing the particular Case that is needed (see Bader, Meng, & Bayer, 2000). Thus Case like number is not processed without error. Processing "negative polarity" items such as *any* or *ever*, that must be licensed by negative or negative-like elements, is also at times characterized as being error prone (Drenhaus, Saddy, & Frisch, 2005; but also Xiang, Dillon, & Phillips, 2009). Phillips and colleagues (2011) suggest that all of these dependencies are accessing the same mental representation, a syntactic representation, but distinct access mechanisms may be involved. Bottom-up information may determine which access mechanism is used, permitting structure to guide memory search under some conditions but not others. In this view, analysis guided by hard grammatical constraints will be error free in the sense that only structurally well-formed dependencies will be created. When memory retrieval is not guided by structure or is guided by "soft" constraints, phrases in incorrect positions may be retrieved, resulting in errors.

Fully specified syntax

Any model of syntactic processing must characterize the representations that are constructed during syntactic analysis. These representations may be fully specified or they may be underspecified with respect to some particular property or some particular class of constructions, or simply allow underspecification under particular communicative circumstances.

In models like the garden-path model, a fully specified syntactic phrase marker is constructed for an input sentence. When a word or phrase is attached into the syntactic representation, e.g., a tree structure, the attachment indicates the mother of the new syntactic phrase and the sister of that phrase. The position of the phrase in the tree structure is thus fully determined. If a structural relation must be changed at some later point in the parsing process, then the tree structure must be changed, not simply elaborated.

By contrast, in description theory, a tree structure is described using the predicate "dominance," not "immediate dominance" (see Marcus, Hindle, & Fleck, 1983 for discussion). In description theory, underspecification of structural (immediate-domination) relations is permitted since adding a syntactic node in between two already connected nodes amounts to adding a new statement to the description of the tree, but not a change of already present (domination) statements. Consequently, in this theory, lowering of a syntactic phrase, by adding a new phrase that dominates it, should be cost free: lowering involves an elaboration of (the description of) the tree, not a revision of existing relations. Sturt, Pickering, and Crocker (1999) investigated the processing of sentences like those in (16). In (16a) *the famous doctor* is first analyzed as the simple direct object of *see* and later must be analyzed instead as the subject of the verb *drink*.

(16) a. The Australian woman saw the famous doctor had been drinking quite a lot.

b. Before the woman visited the famous doctor had been drinking quite a lot.

As a consequence, *the famous doctor* ends up as the subject of a sentential object of *see*—a position where it is still dominated by the verb *see*. In (16b), *the famous doctor* must also be reanalyzed, from being the object of one verb (*visit*) to being the subject of another verb (*drink*). However, after this phrase is reanalyzed in (16b), it is no longer dominated by the original verb (*visit*). Sturt and colleagues showed that reanalysis of a simple direct object as subject of a sentential complement, as in (16a), took less time than reanalyzing the direct object of a subordinate clause as subject of the main clause, as in (16b). This could be viewed as evidence supporting the description theory prediction that lowering is less costly than other revisions of the syntactic tree. (See also Gorrell, 1995.)

Frazier and Clifton (1996) proposed a revision of the garden-path model to include a very specific type of underspecification. In simplified form, the theory predicted that in the absence of evidence about their correct attachment, adjuncts could "associate" with a thematic domain. Their sisterhood and immediate domination relations within that domain could be determined by prosodic, semantic or pragmatic factors. However, this did not imply the complete absence of a syntactic relation between the phrase marker and the adjunct. If the adjunct needed to be reanalyzed outside of its initial thematic domain, reanalysis effects were predicted to occur.

As noted above, Ferreira and Patson (2007) proposed that underspecification could be driven by task demands. Comprehenders on this view only need to construct analyses that are "good enough" for the demands of the current task. In the case of syntax, the model is at odds with the notion of fast automatic syntactic analysis, which is thought not to be under strategic control. In the case of semantics, presumably Ferreira and Patson's primary concern, strategic control of the amount of processing and the allocation of attention seems less problematic (e.g., Sanford & Sturt, 2002), though one still needs an explicit characterization of which aspects of interpretation can be omitted and which cannot.

Cross-language differences

As mentioned in the introduction, in linguistic theory, some of the major typological differences among languages include differences in head direction such as whether the verb precedes or follows its object(s), the availability or non-availability of phonologically null subjects, the availability or non-availability of "scrambling," a particular type of movement to mark focus and other information structure properties, and the use of overt *wh*-movement versus *in situ* interrogative phrases to form questions. The impact of each of these parameters on sentence processing will be taken up in turn, after discussing the most intensely investigated cross-language issue, namely, attachment of relative clauses immediately preceded by a complex head noun phrase.

Cross-language differences

The central aim of a theory of sentence processing, at least in models like the garden-path theory, is to construct a theory of the human language processing system where one could literally take out the grammar of one language, plug in the grammar of another language, and, if the theory is correct, predict and explain the processing of that language. If this sort of strongly universal theory is not correct, then of course one wants to identify the principles from which it follows that particular grammatical parameters have an impact on the way sentence analysis takes place, and others do not.

In their seminal article on processing ambiguous relative clause attachment in the Spanish counterpart to (17), Cuetos and Mitchell (1988) found a majority of early closure (high attachment of the relative clause to *daughter*) interpretations in Spanish.

(17) The journalist interviewed the daughter of the colonel who was on the balcony.

Since late closure of phrases to the lowest/most recent attachment site (*colonel* in (17)) had been observed in many structures in English, they proposed that Spanish was an early closure language and English was a late closure language. Their proposed tuning model specified that attachment is exposure based, i.e., speakers of a language adopt whatever analysis is most likely to turn out to be correct given their experience with the language (see too Mitchell, Cuetos, Corley & Brysbaert, 1995). Cuetos and Mitchell's work launched extensive cross-language investigation into the factors influencing attachment preferences in this particular structure. One approach to these data is to note that attachment preferences in this structure are very mild, near 50 percent, especially in sentences with definite determiners (**the daughter of the colonel**) and a non-theta assigning preposition (**of**) (Gilboy, Sopena, Clifton, & Frazier, 1995). Perhaps the lack of a strong preference is related to the clause-peripheral adjunct status of the relative clause and the fact that, by definition, the relative clause is a clausal adjunct. In any case, although preferences across languages may tend to be a bit above 50 percent high attachment or a bit below, to my knowledge the biases rarely involve strong, say 80 percent, biases for some particular attachment in the particular types of structures that show cross-language variation. This suggests that we may be looking at a structure where the absence of a strong syntactic bias allows non-syntactic factors to carry the day. Indeed, Fodor (2002) has argued that prosodic differences between languages determine whether the preference in a language is for high or low attachment of a relative clause with a complex head, as in (17).

We turn now to possible effects of grammatical parameters on how a sentence is processed, beginning with whether a head of phrase precedes or follows its object(s).

Head direction

Some languages, like English, are head-initial and the verb precedes its object(s). By contrast, in a head-final language like Turkish, Korean or Japanese, the head of a phrase follows its object(s). Several researchers have proposed head-driven processing in one form or another. The head of a phrase (the verb in a verb phrase, the adjective in an adjective phrase, and so on) is the obligatory member of a phrase and it determines the syntactic type of the entire phrase. Given the importance of the head of a phrase in linguistic theory, it might seem natural to assume that phrases are projected or constructed if and when the head of the phrase is encountered. The proposal that a phrase is built from its head (Abney, 1989) runs into empirical problems, however. It predicts a phrase is not built until its head has been encountered in the input string. In head-final languages, this predicts that assigning any phrase a structure external to that phrase would be delayed until the end of the verb phrase, which is typically at the end of a clause. Empirical results do not support the prediction in German verb final clauses (Bader & Lasser, 1994), Korean (Kim, 1999), Japanese (Miyamoto, 2002) or to my knowledge in any other head final language (see Yamashita, Hirose, & Packard, 2010).[2] Instead, what one finds is that structure is built as soon as there is evidence for it.

Are head-final languages difficult to process? Apparently there is a processing-relevant generalization about head-final languages. Ueno and Polinsky (2009) argue that head-final languages tend to have more intransitive predicates than head-initial languages do. They suggest that this facilitates processing by reducing the number of pre-verb arguments. Presumably pre-head arguments are costly to process since their interpretation is dependent on the (upcoming) head. However, on-going semantic interpretation is not well understood at present, and thus the presumed cost of processing pre-head constituents remains somewhat speculative.

It's an interesting question why natural languages permit both VO and OV word order especially if OV languages are difficult to comprehend. Indeed, Langus and Nespor (2010) suggest that VO order may be basic in the human computational system, but that the cognitive, non-linguistic, communication systems favor OV order, as in gestural systems.

Null subject parameter

Another cross-language difference that one might expect to have large consequences for the syntactic analysis of sentences is whether a language permits a phonologically null pronominal (pro) subject, or not. In many head-final languages (e.g., Japanese, Korean, Turkish), phonologically null subjects are permitted. Some head-initial languages such as Spanish and Italian also permit null subjects. In "null-subject" languages, a phonologically null subject is generally available for third-person subjects as well as first- and second-person subjects and for most or all tenses. One might have expected that the syntactic possibility of a null subject would have a huge impact on the analysis of all sentences in these languages. In SOV languages, a sentence-initial phrase could be analyzed as either an overt subject or the object of a transitive clause with a null subject, for example.

However, in Turkish at least, the availability of a null subject analysis does not seem to entail that the first argument is analyzed as an object.

(18) a. Dün adam kadını gördü.
Yesterday man woman (ACC) see (Past 3rd Person Singular).
"The man saw the woman yesterday."

b. Dün adam ben gördüm.
Yesterday man I see (Past 1st Person Singular).
"I saw (a) man yesterday."

In sentences like (18a) and (18b) where the first argument could be object or subject, independent of animacy of the first argument (only animates are illustrated), ERP research has found a broadly distributed positivity in sentences when the first argument was disambiguated by verb number to be an object as in (18b) (Demiral, Schlesewsky, & Bornkessel-Schlesewsky, 2008). This suggests that the null subject analysis is not the default in null subject languages, but rather comprehenders take the initial overt phrase to be the subject.

In contrast to Turkish, Italian sentences can be ambiguous in differentiating between an analysis involving a pre-verbal null subject ("pro V object"), as in (19a), and an analysis involving a verb-initial sentence with a post-verbal subject "V subject," as in (19b). According to De Vincenzi (1991) the null subject analysis is preferred in Italian, even in contexts without an antecedent for the null subject. Consequently, Italian participants preferred (19a) to (19b) in their interpretation of ambiguous sentences with optionally transitive verbs.

(19) a. *pro* ha chiamato Gianni.
"Someone has called Gianni."
(Transitive clause with a null pronominal subject)

b. *e* ha chiamato Gianni.
   "Gianni has called."
   (Intransitive clause with a post-verbal subject linked to "e" in pre-verbal position)

The preference for the null subject analysis was attributed to a simplicity principle, see discussion of the "minimal chain principle" in De Vincenzi (1991). (See Bornkessel & Schlesewsky, 2006b, and Bornkessel-Schlesewsky & Schlesewsky, 2009, for evidence suggesting that transitive clauses may be generally favored across languages.) Why Turkish and Italian would differ in their analysis of an initial DP is unclear (though perhaps it is important that the alternative analysis to postulating a null subject involves postulating a post-verbal subject in the Italian studies but not in the Turkish study).

In a corpus study of subject-dropping in English, Spanish, Japanese and Turkish, Ueno and Polinsky (2009) found that null subjects are more prevalent in clauses with two arguments than in clauses with one argument. This fits with their hypothesis that processing is facilitated by minimizing the number of overt arguments in a sentence (assuming that the greatest reduction in complexity due to reducing the number of overt arguments will occur in the most complex sentences, i.e., those with more overt arguments). However, the bias to drop subjects more often in transitive than in intransitive clauses was unrelated to head direction: pro-drop occurred more often in two argument than in one argument clauses independent of whether the language was VO or OV. (See too Bornkessel-Schlesewsky & Schlesewsky, 2009.)

Languages with or without rich case

It has often been claimed that syntax plays a different or lesser role in languages with a rich set of Case markers, e.g., that superficial cues to the relation between arguments and verbs are weighted according to their "cue validity" and "cue availability" and thus Case cues are stronger in a language with rich case than a language with impoverished case (MacWhinney, Bates & Kliegl, 1984). It is certainly true that different types of Case systems exist across languages. An interesting array of languages has now been investigated using ERP methods (Bornkessel & Schlesewsky, 2006b, Bornkessel-Schlesewsky & Schlesewsky, 2009). There is also evidence that "structural" cases like the Nominative and Accusative may be processed differently from lexically determined cases like the Dative (Bader, Meng & Bayer, 2000). However, what is not clear is that Case plays any smaller role in a language like English when Case is available than it does in a language with a rich set of Cases. Indeed, results from an eye-movement study of Traxler and Pickering (1996b) suggest an immediate effect of Case in disambiguating structure in English when Case is informative.

Syntactic encoding of information structure (topic, focus, contrastive focus) and information status (discourse-given, hearer-given, new)

Languages differ in how information structure (topic, focus) and information status (given versus new) are marked. In some languages like English, prosody typically is exploited: new phrases may not be deaccented, and contrastive focus is conveyed prosodically (*JOHN left*). In other languages, syntax is exploited instead. For example, often there is a fixed position where contrastively focused phrases appear, e.g., in pre-verbal position in Hungarian. It's an open question whether the two types of languages exhibit distinct processing profiles.

In languages with scrambling (syntactic movement) of given phrases, it is clear that contextual information about information structure can eliminate or nearly eliminate the cost of the greater syntactic complexity resulting from moving a phrase (e.g., in reading time, Kaiser & Trueswell, 2004). Kaiser and Trueswell (2004) also conducted a visual-world study in Finnish in which participants listened to descriptions of pictures and then answered questions about them while their eye-movements were measured. In Finnish, already mentioned objects may scramble to the beginning of a sentence (with a previously unmentioned subject appearing in post-verbal position). Given a picture of an already mentioned nurse and an unmentioned nurse, participants rapidly looked at the already mentioned nurse in a sentence beginning with (the Finnish equivalent of) *nurse*, suggesting that information structure and positional information were rapidly exploited by Finnish listeners.

Bornkessel and Schlesewsky (2006a) used ERPs to study scrambling in German, where the object can precede the subject under particular discourse conditions. They investigated the processing of scrambled sentences in contexts where contrastive focus (20) or corrective focus (21) motivated the scrambled (object-before-subject) word order. Contrastive focus involved an explicit comparison to alternative foci in context. Corrective focus, illustrated in (21), involved actual correction of an expectation set up in context. (The bolded material in the contexts was not bolded in the experiment, and naturally the context and target sentence were both presented in German to native speakers of German.)

(20) a. Of the twenty students who had begun studying chemistry in the first semester, only Toralf and Dietmar remained after four years. Unfortunately, only one of them passed the final exam. **Who did the professors fail?**

b. Ich habe gehört, dass den Dietmar-Acc ein besonders gemeiner Prüfer hat durchfallen lassen.

"I heard that (the) Dietmar a particularly nasty examiner has failed let."

(I heard that it was Dietmar who was failed by a particularly nasty examiner.)

(21) a. Of the twenty students who had begun studying chemistry in the first semester, only Toralf and Dietmar remained after four years. Unfortunately, only one of them passed the final exam. **I suspect that it was Toralf.**

b. Ich habe gehört, dass den Dietmar-Acc ein besonders gemeiner Prüfer hat durchfallen lassen.

"I heard that (the) Dietmar a particularly nasty examiner has failed let."

(I heard that it was Dietmar who was failed by a particularly nasty examiner.)

The results differed from those of Kaiser and Trueswell's study in that contrast globally licensed scrambling, resulting in high acceptability of the scrambled order, but it did not reduce the local cost of computing the scrambled structure, as indicated by significant positivity in the ERP record. However, corrective focus did eliminate the local cost of scrambled word order when the scrambled object corrected information just presented. (See Bader & Meng (1999) for further evidence of a local scrambling cost in German sentences presented in isolation in a speeded acceptability judgment task.)

Interrogative phrases move to an interrogative operator or remain in situ

There has been considerable research on processing questions in languages where the interrogative phrase like *who* or *what* must move to the interrogative operator at the beginning of the sentence, as in German, Spanish and English, for example, as illustrated in (22a). In English, an "*in situ*" question is also possible, as in (22b), but primarily only as an Echo question, where the speaker has not heard a preceding statement accurately.

(22) a. What has John bought __?
(*what* has moved from object position)

b. John has bought what?
(*what* remains *in situ*)

There has been less research on the processing of questions in languages where the questioned constituent always remains *in situ*, as in (22b). Mandarin, and many other languages, have only *in situ wh*-words. Using the speed accuracy tradeoff paradigm, in which a decision is made repeatedly at regular intervals, Xiang, Dillon, Wagers, Liu, and Guo (2010) found that the processing of *in situ* questions in Mandarin Chinese shows many of the same properties as processing of English-type questions where the interrogative phrase moves to the front of the sentence. For example, the *in situ* Mandarin questions are processed more slowly than their non-*wh* controls (possibly this is also a property of questions involving movement, such as fronting *what* in *What have you done?*).

In English the length of a dependency between an interrogative and its gap (indicated by the underlining in (22a)) is expected to increase the difficulty of processing a question (Warren & Gibson, 2002; see Staub, 2010b, for evidence of complexity both early, as soon as a dependency-type can be inferred, and at the position of the gap). One question is whether a question that does not involve overt movement of the interrogative phrase would also exhibit greater difficulty with longer dependencies, e.g., on the assumption that the scope of the question corresponds to the scope of an interrogative operator at some covert level of structure. Xiang and colleagues (2010) and Xiang, Wagers, and Dillon (submitted) found that longer dependencies did lead to a drop in accuracy, but did not influence the rate of computing the dependency. (In the speed accuracy tradeoff paradigm, language processing often shows effects on accuracy but not speed). In any case, the fact that the distance between interrogative phrase and the presumed position of the null operator at the beginning of a clause influenced complexity, as revealed by accuracy, is suggestive. If two positions must be related to create a grammatical dependency, it may not matter very much which of the two positions is marked by the presence of the critical phrase (the interrogative phrase). Whether what is important for processing questions is the entire dependency or primarily the interrogative phrase itself is something that must be determined. Looking only at languages with movement of the interrogative phrase it would be far less obvious what properties of interrogatives matter with respect to processing complexity. Even identifying the important issues in parsing depends on recognizing the range of possible variation across languages. (For the production and comprehension of Japanese questions see Hirotani, 2004 and Hirose & Kitagawa, 2010.)

Cross-language research on language processing is exciting and very much an on-going concern. At present such investigation is in its infancy, even the questions are unclear, not to mention the possible and plausible answers. The rich diversity in the properties of natural languages might amount to superficial differences with little impact on how sentences are processed. The small amount of currently available evidence on question formation, discussed immediately above, supports this speculation. However, deep semantically relevant properties like the lack of overt determiners, or the semantic type of basic categories like nouns, may reveal a quite different picture, with pervasive ramifications throughout the entire comprehension system. To figure out which of these answers is more representative, we must investigate well-chosen case studies in detail.

Prosody is another area where there are enormous cross-language differences. In what follows, due to space limitations, there is no attempt to deal systematically with languages other than English. But discussion of the English facts surrounding how people compute prosody and use it to constrain their syntactic analysis should suffice to give an idea of just how complicated the problem is.

Prosody

What is the input to the syntactic processing sub-system? The most natural assumption in the case of speech is presumably that the input is a phonologically and prosodically structured lexically labeled representation of the input. Christophe, Peperkamp, Pallier, Block, and Mehler (2004), for example, showed that prosody influences the segmentation of the input for purposes of lexical analysis. If it's true that the syntactic sub-system takes a prosodically structured object as its input, then it would be expected that prosodic structure would influence syntactic analysis. Prosody clearly can bias or disambiguate constituent structure ambiguities (Carlson, 2002; Cutler, Dahan, & van Donselaar, 1997; Nespor & Vogel, 1986; Price, Ostendorf, Shattuck-Huffnagel, & Fong, 1991, see Wagner & Watson, 2010, for a review). A prosodic phrase groups words together. In English, a prosodic phrase boundary is typically indicated by the presence of a boundary tone, lengthening of the pre-boundary constituent and perhaps a pause. The clearest influence of prosody on syntactic processing occurs in cases where the grammar requires a prosodic boundary at a certain syntactic location, or prohibits a prosodic boundary at a particular syntactic location. In such cases, prosody should disambiguate the input if only one syntactic structure is permissible given the particular prosody of the input. Nespor and Vogel (1986) present evidence from Italian supporting the claim.

If it is assumed that the end of an initial subordinate clause requires a prosodic boundary in English, then the evidence from Kjelgaard and Speer (1999) shows that an obligatory prosodic boundary fully disambiguates what would otherwise be an ambiguous syntactic structure in English. In their study, listeners judged the phonosyntactic well-formedness of early closure (23a) and late closure (23b) sentences in a timed judgment task. With neutral prosody, "late closure" sentences, where a late closure syntactic analysis is correct, were responded to more quickly and accurately than "early closure" sentences. But when an early closure sentence like (23a) was spoken with a prosodic boundary at the end of the initial subordinate clause, the general tendency to misanalyze the post-verbal phrase (*the house*) as the object of the verb was entirely eliminated in the judgment data. Further, there was no response time penalty for early closure sentences that were prosodically disambiguated (though the penalty persisted for sentences spoken with a neutral prosody).

(23) a. When Roger leaves the house is dark.
 b. When Roger leaves the house it's dark.

Schafer, Speer, Warren, and White (2000) present further evidence that listeners can use prosodic boundaries to avoid late closure syntactic errors using non-laboratory speech, despite considerable variability in the detailed prosody of the input. They recorded speakers in a structured elicitation task (24), where participants played a scripted game involving a Slider, who gave directions, and a Driver, who carried them out. Only certain limited moves were permitted. The participants' speech was recorded. They spontaneously placed the largest prosodic boundary in a sentence after the initial subordinate clause in sentences like those in (24c) (after *square*) and (24d) (after *moves*). In a subsequent comprehension study, listeners exploited this regularity, placing the largest prosodic boundary at the end of the subordinate clause, thereby allowing the prosody to disambiguate the syntax.

(24) a. DRIVER: I want to change the position of the square with the triangle.

b. SLIDER: Which triangle do you want to change the position of the square?

c. DRIVER: The red one. When that moves the square it should land in a good spot.

d. SLIDER: Good choice. When that moves the square will encounter a cookie.

(See Steinhauer, Alter, & Friederici, 1999; Steinhauer & Friederici, 2001, for evidence that prosodic boundaries also syntactically disambiguate German sentences.)

Anderson and Carlson (2010) also find that speakers produce prosodies that disambiguate early/late closure sentences (e.g., (23)), but they do not produce prosodies that disambiguate object/subject structures (e.g., (16a)): specifically, with object/subject structures, speakers produced distinct prosodies for the object structure versus the subject structure, but listeners did not use those prosodies to disambiguate the syntax in a listening task. This result highlights the need to understand the syntax–prosody mapping rules of a language in order to characterize the effects of prosodic differences on listeners' syntactic processing. Presumably prosodic differences required by the grammar are the differences that will show stable robust effects in comprehension.

Another case where the prosody might influence syntactic analysis is when more than one prosodic structure for a sentence is permitted by the grammar. In such cases, the speaker's choice of one prosody from among a larger set of possible prosodies should have pragmatic consequences. Carlson, Clifton and Frazier (2001) investigated examples like (25), where the italicized phrase may attach low into the embedded clause where it modifies *telephoned* or high into the matrix clause where it modifies *learned.*

(25) Susie learned that Bill telephoned *after John visited.*

If (25) is spoken with an intermediate-sized prosodic boundary before the italicized ambiguous phrase, this will bias the analysis toward high attachment of the italicized phrase to *learned* if there is no earlier prosodic boundary, or if that boundary is smaller than any prosodic boundary after *telephoned.*

However, precisely the same prosodic boundary before the italicized phrase will bias toward low attachment of the phrase if the earlier boundary is larger than the boundary before the italicized phrase. Thus a larger prosodic boundary followed by a smaller prosodic boundary will be taken as evidence for low attachment of the constituent following the smaller boundary, whereas a smaller boundary followed by a larger boundary will be taken as evidence for high attachment of the constituent following the larger boundary, where the new phrase is not part of the preceding phrase. Clifton, Carlson, and Frazier (2002) present evidence from a range of syntactic structures showing that the interpretation of prosodic boundary information is non-local and relative, i.e., it involves a global prosodic representation containing information about prosodic boundaries earlier in the sentence. Clifton, Frazier, and Carlson (2006) argue for a pragmatic account of prosodic boundary effects based on evidence showing that when phonological properties of the input (the length of phrases) would justify the presence and size of a prosodic boundary, the boundary has a lesser impact on syntactic analysis than when only the syntax would justify the presence of the boundary.

In recent work, Snedeker and Casserly (2010) compare an Absolute boundary size hypothesis with a Relative Boundary Size hypothesis (discussed above). They find evidence for effects of relative boundary size (when absolute boundary size is held constant) in comprehension, but in production they find that absolute boundary size is more important, with only a modest effect from relative boundary size.

Watson and Gibson (2004) argue for a model where the presence of a prosodic boundary is determined by the length of constituents. The existence of a prosodic boundary at a particular location could be viewed as a consequence of planning upcoming material, or a consequence of the processing demands of having just produced a long or complex constituent. Thus prosodic boundaries tend to flank long constituents, which will involve more planning and more processing time. Their model is extremely simple and yet has considerable empirical coverage.

Conclusions

The evidence that humans rapidly compute a syntactic structure for a linguistic input is overwhelming. Further, the vast majority of evidence suggests syntax is computed incrementally in a systematic manner, not as a random set of surface cues or on some "as needed" basis. The syntactic sub-system works with a specialized vocabulary of syntactic constraints, giving rise to rapid analysis. Syntactic analysis is information driven rather than strictly knowledge driven (top-down), input driven (bottom-up) or head driven. Structure is postulated as soon as evidence for it becomes available. For the most part, the structures computed appear to be fully specified, and they do not violate the prosodic constraints of the language.

A large body of interesting work on sentence processing now exists. Cross-language research is beginning to address fundamental questions about the relation between non-superficial grammatical properties and their impact on the (neural) representation and processing of syntax. Existing studies clearly pave the way for an exciting program of research exploring a larger range of languages and taking up explicit hypotheses about the parsing consequences of specific grammatical parameters.

If the remarkable ability of humans to understand novel sentences, even implausible ones about the future or the past, is to be understood and explained, understanding the role of syntax is crucial, along with the way it interfaces with lexical processing, prosody, and semantic and pragmatic interpretation. Linguistic and non-linguistic context is also essential to language comprehension. But whatever our ultimate theory of language comprehension turns out to be, it must accommodate both the fact that language is often used in predictable ways to convey predictable messages largely recoverable from context and prior world-knowledge and the fact that our language ability at its core is a system capable of generating novel structures with compositionally determined meanings. Without syntax, this would be impossible.

Acknowledgments

This work was supported by HD-18708 to the University of Massachusetts, and by the Center for Advanced Studies in Oslo. I am particularly grateful to Chuck Clifton, Brian Dillon, Roger van Gompel and an anonymous reviewer for detailed comments on this manuscript.

Notes

1. Frazier and Clifton (2002) argue that discourse linked phrases like *which girl* are immediately related to a discourse referent in a representation that is distinct from the syntactic representation. For discussion of the properties distinguishing syntactic and discourse representations, see Frazier and Clifton (2005).
2. Note that principles like Theta-attachment (Pritchett, 1988) or other thematically driven processing systems encounter essentially the same problem if the initial syntactic analysis cannot be performed until the theta-assigner is encountered.

References

Abney, S. P. (1989). A computational model of human parsing. *Journal of Psycholinguistic Research*, *18*, 129–144.

Adger, D. (2003). *Core syntax: A minimalist approach*. Oxford University Press.

Anderson, C., & Carlson, K. (2010). Syntactic structure guides prosody in temporarily ambiguous sentences. *Language and Speech*, *53*, 472–93.

Arai, M., Van Gompel, R. P. G., & Scheepers, C. (2007). Priming ditransitive structures in comprehension. *Cognitive Psychology*, *54*, 218–250.

Bader, M. (1998). Prosodic influences on reading syntactically ambiguous sentences. In J. D. Fodor & F. Fereirra (Eds.), *Reanalysis in sentence processing* (pp. 1–46). Dordrecht: Kluwer.

Bader, M., & Häussler, J. (Submitted). The primacy of grammaticality.
Bader, M., & Laser, I. (1994). German verb-final clauses and sentence processing: Evidence for immediate attachment. In C. Clifton, L. Frazier & K. Rayner (Eds.), *Perspectives on sentence processing*. Hilldale, NJ: Lawrence Erlbaum Associates.
Bader, M., & Meng, M. (1999). Subject-object ambiguities in German embedded clauses: An across-the-board comparison. *Journal of Psycholinguistic Research, 28* (2), 121–143.
Bader, M., Meng, M., & Bayer, J. (2000). Case and reanalysis. *Journal of Psycholinguistic Research, 29*, 37–52.
Bock, J. K. (1986). Syntactic persistence in language production. *Cognitive Psychology, 18*, 355–387.
Bornkessel, I., & Schlesewsky, M. (2006a). The role of contrast in the local licensing of scrambling in German: Evidence from on-line comprehension. *Journal of Germanic Linguistics, 18* (1), 1–43.
Bornkessel, I., & Schlesewsky, M. (2006b). The Extended Argument Dependency Model: A neurocognitive approach to sentence comprehension across languages. *Psychological Review, 113*, 787–821.
Bornkessel-Schlesewsky, I., & Schlesewsky, M. (2009). The role of prominence information in real time comprehension of transitive constructions: A cross-linguistic approach. *Language and Linguistics Compass, 3* (1), 19–58.
Carlson, K. (2002). *Parallelism and prosody in the processing of ellipsis sentences*. Outstanding Dissertations in Linguistics. New York: Routledge.
Carlson, K., Clifton, C. Jr., & Frazier, L. (2001). Prosodic boundaries in adjunct attachment. *Journal of Memory & Language, 45*, 58–81.
Christianson, K., Hollingworth, A., Halliwell, J. F., & Ferreira, F. (2001). Thematic roles assigned along the garden path linger. *Cognitive Psychology, 42*, 368–407.
Christophe, A. Peperkamp, S., Pallier, C., Block, E., & Mehler, J. (2004). Phonological phrase boundaries constrain lexical access, I. Adult data. *Journal of Memory and Language, 51*, 523–547.
Clifton, C. Jr., Carlson, K., & Frazier, L. (2002). Informative prosodic boundaries. *Language and Speech, 45*, 87–114.
Clifton, C. Jr., Frazier, L., & Carlson, K. (2006). Tracking the What and Why of speakers' choices: Prosodic boundaries and the length of constituents. *Psychonomic Bulletin & Review, 13*, 854–861.
Clifton, C. Jr., Kennison, S., & Albrecht, J. (1997). Reading the words Her, His, Him: Implications for parsing principles based on frequency and structure. *Journal of Memory and Language, 36*, 276–292.
Clifton, C. Jr., & Staub, A. (2008). Parallelism and competition in syntactic ambiguity resolution. *Language and Linguistics Compass, 2*, 234–250.
Crain, S., & Fodor, J. D. (1985). How can grammars help parsers? In D. R. Dowty, L. Karttunen, & A. M. Zwicky (Eds.), *Natural language parsing: Psychological, computational and theoretical perspectives* (pp. 94–128). Cambridge: Cambridge University Press.
Crain, S., & Steedman, M. (1985). On not being led up the garden path: The use of context by the psychological syntax processor. In D. R. Dowty, L. Karttunen, & A. M. Zwicky (Eds.), *Natural language parsing: Psychological, computational and theoretical perspectives* (pp. 320–358). Cambridge: Cambridge University Press.
Cuetos, F., & Mitchell, D. (1988). Cross linguistic differences in parsing: Restrictions on the use of the late closure strategy in Spanish. *Cognition, 3*, 73–105.

Cutler, A., Dahan, D., & van Donselaar, W. (1997). Prosody in the comprehension of spoken language: A literature review. *Language and Speech*, *40* (2), 141–201.

Demiral, S. B., Schlesewsky, M., & Bornkessel-Schlesewsky, I. (2008). On the universality of language comprehension strategies: Evidence from Turkish. *Cognition*, *106*, 484–500.

De Vincenzi, M. (1991). *Syntactic parsing strategies in Italian*. Dordrecht: Kluwer Academic Publishers.

Dillon, B., Nevins, A., Austin, A., & Phillips, C. (2011). Syntactic and semantic predictors of tense in Hindi: An ERP investigation. *Language and Cognitive Processes*, *26* (8).

Drenhaus, H., Saddy, D., & Frisch, S. (2005). Intrusion effects in the processing of negative polarity items. In S. Kepser & M. Reis (Eds.), *Proceedings of the international conference on Linguistic Evidence* (pp. 41–46). Tubingen.

Ferreira, F. (2003). The misinterpretation of non-canonical sentences. *Cognitive Psychology*, *47*, 164–203.

Ferreira, F., Christianson, K., & Hollingworth, A. (2000). Misinterpretations of garden path sentences: Implications for models of sentence processing and reanalysis. *Journal of Psycholinguistic Research*, *30* (1), 3–20.

Ferreira, F., & Henderson, J. (1998). Syntactic reanalysis, thematic processing and sentence comprehension. In J. D. Fodor & F. Ferreira (Eds.), *Reanalysis in sentence processing*. Dordrecht: Kluwer Academic Publishers.

Ferreira, F., & Patson, N. (2007). The 'Good Enough' approach to language comprehension. *Language and Linguistic Compass*, *1*, 71–83.

Ferreira, V., Bock, K., Wilson, M. P., & Cohen, N. J. (2008). Memory for syntax despite amnesia. *Psychological Sciences*, *19* (9), 940–946.

Flores d'Arcais, G. (1987). Syntactic processing during reading for comprehension. In M. Coltheart (Ed.), *Attention and Performance XII: The psychology of reading*. Hillsdale, NJ: Lawrence Erlbaum Associates.

Fodor, J. A. (1983). *Modularity of mind*. Cambridge, MA: MIT Press.

Fodor, J. D. (2002). Prosodic disambiguation in silent reading. In M. Hirotani (Ed.), *Proceedings of the North East Linguistic Society, 32* (pp. 113–132). Amherst: GLSA.

Fodor, J. D & Inoue, A. (1994). The diagnosis and cure of garden paths. *Journal of Psycholinguistic Research*, *23(5)*.

Fodor, J. D., & Inoue, A. (1998). Attach anyway. In J. D. Fodor & F. Ferreira (Eds.), *Reanalysis in sentence processing*. Dordrecht: Kluwer Academic Publishers.

Fodor, J. D., & Inoue, A. (2000). Syntactic features in reanalysis: Positive and negative symptoms. *Journal of Psycholinguistic Research*, *29* (1), 25–36.

Forster, K. (1979). Levels of processing and the structure of the language processor. In W. E. Cooper & E. C. T. Walker (Eds.), *Sentence processing: Psycholinguistic studies presented to Merrill Garrett*. Hillsdale, NJ: Lawrence Erlbaum Associates.

Frazier, L. (1987). Sentence processing: A tutorial review. In M. Coltheart (Ed.), *Attention and performance XII* (pp. 601–618). Hillsdale, NJ: Erlbaum.

Frazier, L., & Clifton, C. Jr. (1989) Comprehending sentences with long-distance dependencies. In M. Tanenhaus & G. Carlson (Eds.), *Linguistic structure in language processing*. Kluwer Series in Theoretical Psycholinguistics. Dordrecht, The Netherlands.

Frazier, L., & Clifton, C. Jr. (1996). *Construal*. Cambridge, MA: MIT Press.

Frazier, L., & Clifton, C. Jr. (1998). Sentence reanalysis, and visibility. In J. D. Fodor & F. Ferrerira (Eds.), *Reanalysis in sentence processing*. Dordrecht: Kluwer Academic Publishers.

Frazier, L., & Rayner, K. (1982). Making and correcting errors during sentence comprehension: Eye-movements in the analysis of structurally ambiguous sentences. *Cognitive Psychology, 14*, 178–210.

Friederici, A. (1998). Diagnosis and reanalysis: Two processing aspects the brain may differentiate. In J. D. Fodor & F. Ferreira (Eds.), *Reanalysis in sentence processing*. Dordrecht: Kluwer Academic Publishers.

Gilboy, E., Sopena, J., Clifton, C. Jr., & Frazier, L. (1995). Argument structure and association preferences. *Cognition, 54*, 131–167.

Gorrell, P. (1995). *Syntax and parsing*. Cambridge: Cambridge University Press.

Green, M. J., & Mitchell, D. C. (2006). Absence of real evidence against competition during syntactic ambiguity resolution. *Journal of Memory and Language, 55*, 1–17.

Hagoort, P., Brown, C., & Groothusen, J. (1993). The syntactic positive shift (SPS as an ERP measure of syntactic processing). *Language and Cognitive Processes, 8* (4), 439–483.

Hirose, Y., & Kitagawa, Y. (2010). Production-perception asymmetry in *Wh*-scope marking. In H. Yamashita, Y. Hirose & J. L. Packard (Eds.), *Processing and producing head-final structures*. Studies in Theoretical Psycholinguistics, *38*. Dordrecht, Heidelberg, London and New York: Springer.

Hirotani, M. (2004). *Prosody & LF interpretation: Processing Japanese wh-questions*. Ph.D. dissertation. University of Massachusetts.

Kaiser, E., & Trueswell, J. C. (2004). The role of discourse context in the processing of a flexible word-order language. *Cognition, 94*, 113–147.

Kazanina, N., Lau, E. F., Lieberman, M. Yoshida, M., & Phillips, C. (2007). The effect of syntactic constraints on the processing of backwards anaphora. *Journal of Memory and Language, 56*, 384–409.

Kim, Y. (1999). The effects of case marking information on Korean sentence processing. *Language and Cognitive Processes, 14*, 687–714.

Kjelgaard, M., & Speer, S. (1999). Prosodic facilitation and Interference in the resolution of temporary syntactic closure ambiguity. *Journal of Memory and Language, 40*, 153–194.

Konieczny, L. (2005). The psychological reality of local coherences in sentence processing. *27th Annual Conference on Cognitive Science*, August 2005, Stresa, Italy.

Langus, A., & Nespor, M. (2010). Cognitive systems struggling for word order. *Cognitive Psychology, 60* (4), 291–318.

MacDonald, M. C., Pearlmutter, N. J., & Seidenberg, M. S. (1994). The lexical nature of syntactic ambiguity resolution. *Psychological Review, 101*, 676–703.

MacWhinney, B., Bates, E., & Kliegl, R. (1984). Cue validity and sentence interpretation in English, German, and Italian. *Journal of Verbal Learning and Verbal Behavior, 23*, 127–150.

Marcus, M., Hindle, D., & Fleck, M. (1983). D-theory: Talking about talking about trees. In *Proceedings of the 21st annual meeting of the Association for Computational Linguistics* (pp. 129–136), Cambridge, MA.

Meng, J., & Bader, M. (2002). Mode of disambiguation and garden path strength: An investigation of subject-object ambiguities in German. *Language and Speech, 43*, 43–74.

Mitchell, D. C., Cuetos, F., Corley, M. M. B., & Brysbaert, M. (1995). Exposure-based models of human parsing: Evidence for the use of coarse-grained (nonlexical) statistical records. *Journal of Psycholinguistic Research, 24*, 469–488.

Miyamoto, E. (2002). Case markers as clause boundary inducers in Japanese. *Journal of Psycholinguistic Research, 31*, 307–347.

Nespor, M., & Vogel, I. (1986). Prosodic structure above the word. In A. Cutler & R. Ladd (Eds.) *Prosody: Models and measurements* (pp. 123–140). Berlin: Springer-Verlag.

Nicol, J., & Swinney, D. (1989). The role of structure in co-reference assignment during sentence comprehension. *Journal of Psycholinguistic Research, 18*, 5–19.

Omaki, A., Lau, E., Davidson White, I., Dakan, M., & Phillips, C. (Submitted). Hyperactive gap filling: Pre-verbal object gap creation in English filler-gap dependency processing.

Osterhout, L, & Holcomb, P. J. (1992). Event-related brain potentials elicted by syntactic anomaly. *Journal of Memory and Language, 31* (6), 785–806.

Pickering, M. J., & Branigan, H. (1999). Syntactic priming in language production. *Trends in Cognitive Sciences, 3*, 136–141.

Pickering, M. J., & Traxler, M. J. (1998). Plausibility and recovery from garden paths: An eye-tracking study. *Journal of Experimental Psychology: Learning, Memory, and Cognition, 24*, 940–961.

Pickering, M. J., & Traxler, M. J. (2003). Evidence against the use of subcategorisation frequency in the processing of unbounded dependencies. *Language & Cognitive Processes, 18*, 469–503.

Phillips, C., Wagers, M., & Lau, E. (2011). Grammatical illusions and selective fallibility in real-time language comprehension. In J. Runner (Ed.), *Experiments at the Interfaces, Syntax & Semantics*, Vol. 37. Bingley, UK: Emerald Publications.

Price, P. J., Ostendorf, M., Shattuck-Huffnagel, S., & Fong, C. (1991). The use of prosody in syntactic disambiguation. *Journal of the Acoustical Society of America, 90*, 2956–2970.

Pritchett, B. (1988). Garden path phenomena and the grammatical basis of language processing. *Language, 64*.

Pulvermüller, F., Shtyrov, Y., Hasting, A. S., & Carlyon, R. P. (2008). Syntax as reflex: Neurophysiological evidence for early automaticity of grammatical processing. *Brain and Language, 104*, 244–253.

Radford, A. (1997). *Syntax: A minimalist introduction*. Cambridge: Cambridge University Press.

Sanford, A., & Sturt, P. (2002). Depth of processing in language comprehension: Not noticing the evidence. *Trends in Cognitive Science, 6* (9), 382–386.

Schafer, A. J., Speer, S., Warren, P., & White, S. D. (2000). Intonational disambiguation in sentence production and comprehension. *Journal of Psycholinguist Research, 29*, 169–182.

Snedeker, J., & Casserly, E. (2010). Is it all relative? Effects of prosodic boundaries on the comprehension and production of attachment ambiguities. *Language and Cognitive Processes, 25* (7–9), 1234–1264.

Staub, A. (2010a). On the interpretation of the number attraction effects: Response time evidence. *Journal of Memory and Language, 60* (2), 308–327.

Staub, A. (2010b). Eye-movements and processing difficulty in object relative clauses. *Cognition, 116* (1), 71–86.

Steinhauer, K., Alter, K., & Friederici, A. D. (1999). Brain potentials indicate immediate use of prosodic cues in natural speech processing. *Nature Neuroscience, 2*, 191–196.

Steinhauer, K., & Friederici, A. (2001). Prosodic boundaries, comma rules, and brain responses: The Closure Positive Shift in ERPs as a universal marker for prosodic phrasing in listeners and readers. *Journal of Psycholinguistic Research, 30*, 267–295.

Stowe, L. A. (1986). Parsing *Wh*-constructions: Evidence for on-line gap location. *Language and Cognitive Processes*, *3*, 227–245.
Sturt, P., Keller, F., & Dubey, A. (2010). Syntactic priming in comprehension: Parallelism effects with and without coordination. *Journal of Memory and Language*, *62* (4), 333–351.
Sturt, P., Pickering, M. J., & Crocker, M. W. (1999). Structural change and reanalysis difficulty in language comprehension. *Journal of Memory and Language*, *40*, 136–150.
Tabor, W., Galantucci, B., & Richardson, D. (2004). Effects of merely local syntactic coherence on sentence processing, *Journal of Memory and Language*, *50* (4), 355–370.
Tabossi, P., Wolf, K., & Koterle, S. (2009). Idiom syntax: Idiosyncratic or principled? *Journal of Memory and Language*, *61*, 77–96.
Tanenhaus, M. K., Spivey-Knowlton, M. J., Eberhard, K. M., & Sedivy, J. C. (1995). Integration of visual and linguistic information in spoken language comprehension. *Science*, *268*, 1632–1634.
Townsend, D. J., & Bever, T. G. (2001). *Sentence comprehension: The integration of habits and rules*. Cambridge, MA: MIT Press.
Traxler, M. J., & Pickering, M. J. (1996a). Plausibility and the processing of unbounded dependencies: An eye tracking study. *Journal of Memory and Language*, *35*, 454–475.
Traxler, M. J., & M. J. Pickering. (1996b). Case-marking in the parsing of complement sentences: Evidence from eye-movements. *Quarterly Journal of Experimental Psychology*, *49A* (4), 991–1004.
Traxler, M. J., Pickering, M. J., & Clifton, C. Jr. (1998). Adjunct attachment is not a form of lexical ambiguity resolution. *Journal of Memory & Language*, *39*, 558–592.
Ueno, M., & Polinsky, M. (2009). Does headedness affect processing? A new look at the VO–OV contrast. *Linguistics*, *45*, 675–710.
Van Gompel, R. P. G., Pickering, M. J., Pearson, J., & Liversedge, S. P. (2005). Evidence against competition during syntactic ambiguity resolution. *Journal of Memory and Language*, *52*, 284–307.
Van Gompel, R. P. G., Pickering, M. J., & Traxler, M. J. (2000). Unrestricted race: A new model of syntactic ambiguity resolution. In A. Kennedy, R. Radach, D. Heller, & J. Pynte (Eds.), *Reading as a perceptual process*, 621–648. Oxford: Elsevier.
Van Gompel, R. P. G., Pickering, M. J., & Traxler, M. J. (2001). Reanalysis in sentence processing: Evidence against current constraintbased and two-stage models. *Journal of Memory & Language*, *45*, 225–258.
Wagers, M. W., Lau, E. F., & Phillips, C. (2009). Agreement attraction in comprehension: Representations and processes. *Journal of Memory and Language*, *61* (2), 206–237.
Wagner, M., & Watson, D. (2010). Experimental and theoretical advances in prosody: A review. *Language and Cognitive Processes*, *25* (7), 905–945.
Warren, T., & Gibson, E. (2002). The influence of referential processing on sentence complexity. *Cognition*, *85*, 79–112.
Watson, D., & Gibson, E. (2004). The relationship between intonational phrasing and syntactic structure in language production. *Language and Cognitive Processes*, *19*, 713–755.
Xiang, M., Dillon, B., & Phillips, C. (2009). Illusory licensing effects across dependency types: ERP evidence. *Brain and Language*, *108*, 40–55.
Xiang, M., Dillon, B., Wagers, M., Liu, F., & Guo, T. (2010). Processing *wh*-movement dependencies in a language without *wh*-movement. Poster presented at the *23rd Annual CUNY Conference on Human Sentence Processing*, March 18–20, 2010. New York University.

Xiang, M., Wagers, M., & Dillon, B. (submitted to Journal of East Asian Linguistics). Processing covert dependencies: An SAT study on Mandarin *wh*-in-situ questions.

Yamashita, H., Hirose, Y., & Packard, J. (Eds.), (2010). *Processing and producing head-final structure*. Studies in Theoretical Psycholinguistics. Dordrecht, Heidelberg, London and New York: Springer.

3 Constraint-based models of sentence processing

Ken McRae and Kazunaga Matsuki

Introduction

A number of sentence comprehension models have been developed over the past 30 years or so. Many of these have been aimed at the central issue of explaining how people resolve temporary syntactic (and/or semantic) ambiguities. Because language is processed incrementally as spoken or written input is encountered over time, temporary ambiguities are rampant in natural language. A comprehender's ability to interpret sentences containing such ambiguities is an important subject of investigation, and provides insights into the comprehension system. The goal of this chapter is to review developments in constraint-based modeling. We begin by presenting some background, and then discuss advances in sentence-processing research that are due to researchers' attempts to specify the constraint-based approach. Consider the following four sentences.

(1)   The horse raced past the barn fell.

(2)   The landmine buried in the sand exploded.

(3)   The actor forgot his lines were supposed to be spoken with a Scottish accent.

(4)   The woman wished her husband was a better person.

The first two are examples of the main clause/reduced relative clause ambiguity that has been used as a tool in many studies. These sentences need to be understood as containing the less frequent and more syntactically complex reduced relative in which the initial noun phrase (*The horse* or *The landmine*) is the patient of the initial verb (i.e., they are being *raced* or *buried*), which is part of the reduced relative. Both (1) and (2) are temporarily ambiguous at the initial verb because many verbs have the same past tense and past participle inflection (as used in a main clause and in a reduced relative, respectively), and because English speakers can drop the relative pronoun and auxiliary (e.g., *that was*) prior to the initial verb.

Sentence (1) causes a great deal of difficulty because all of the initial cues point toward the incorrect main clause interpretation. Consider the moment when someone has read or heard up to *raced*. People's real-world knowledge about horses includes the fact that they often race, and thus *horse* is a great agent of *raced*. Although *raced* is ambiguous between a past tense and passive participle reading, it is usually used as a past tense verb. Therefore, comprehenders are likely to interpret the initial portion of (1) as if it will continue as a main clause, although it does not. In addition, the main clause reading carries smoothly through the prepositional phrase (PP, *past the barn*) because *raced* can be used intransitively (without a direct object, DO), and a horse racing past a barn is a plausible event. Furthermore, there is no context that contains multiple horses that might pragmatically be distinguished using a reduced relative (i.e., picking out the one that was raced past the barn). Therefore, even after *barn* is read or heard, it is very difficult to reject the main clause reading and to correctly interpret the temporarily ambiguous reduced relative. The main verb *fell* syntactically disambiguates (1) as having contained a reduced relative, but the sentence remains difficult to comprehend even at this point due to the strong constraints that all work together to cue the incorrect interpretation.

On the other hand, sentence (2) is quite easy to understand because the constraints point to a reduced relative interpretation. Because landmines do not bury things, *landmine* is a terrible agent for *buried*. Also, landmines are typically buried, and thus are a great fit as a patient. Furthermore, although *buried* is ambiguous, it is used more frequently as a passive participle than as a past tense verb. Thus, all of these cues support the reduced relative reading, even at the initial verb.

The latter two sentences are examples of the direct object/sentential complement ambiguity, another commonly used ambiguity in sentence comprehension research. In general, a sentential complement follows a verb less frequently than does a direct object. Sentences (3) and (4) are temporarily ambiguous because *that* following the verb can be dropped in English. Sentence (3) is quite difficult to understand for a few reasons. Given our knowledge of actors and what they do, we know that an actor can forget things. The potential direct object, *his lines*, is a great example of something that an actor might forget, and thus strongly supports the direct object interpretation. In addition, *forgot* is used much more often with a direct object than a sentential complement. Therefore, when a comprehender encounters *were supposed to*, which syntactically signals a sentential complement reading, difficulties arise because all of the other information prior to that point cues an interpretation in which the actor forgot his lines, rather than forgot something about his lines. In contrast, (4) is much easier than (3) because *wished* rarely takes a direct object, and is followed by a sentential complement with a high probability. Furthermore, because it makes perfect sense for a woman to wish something about *her husband*, and it makes little sense for *her husband* to be the direct object of *wished*, all of this information cues a sentential complement.

A major goal of sentence comprehension models is to explain why some temporary syntactic ambiguities cause more difficulty than do others. For a number of years, the garden-path model dominated (Frazier, 1987; Frazier & Rayner, 1982; see Chapter 2 in this volume). In this model, when each word is read or heard, a modular first stage of processing uses only the syntactic structure to that point, the major syntactic category of that word (i.e., noun, verb, etc.), and general syntactic rules to compute a single analysis. Outputting a single analysis designates it as a serial model. After the first stage is completed, the second stage (thematic processor) uses all available information (and so is not modular) to check the plausibility of the single first-stage analysis, and then to reanalyze if necessary. Van Gompel et al.'s race model (Van Gompel, Pickering, Pearson, & Liversedge, 2005; Van Gompel, Pickering, & Traxler, 2001) is also serial in that a single analysis wins a race and thus is passed on for further processing. When each word is read or heard, its major category is combined with all information regarding the previous words and discourse to produce a single candidate syntactic structure. If this analysis turns out to be incorrect, reanalysis is necessary. Finally, constraint-based models are not modular in that all available information and knowledge is used to weigh potential interpretations over time. They are also parallel in that multiple possible interpretations are entertained, and these interpretations often compete.

This chapter is organized as follows. First, we describe the general properties of constraint-based models. Next, we discuss constraints that have been hypothesized and tested, and how they have been measured. In the final section, we present various implemented constraint-based models to illustrate how constraints can be weighted and combined.

Properties of constraint-based models

The first principle underlying constraint-based models is that multiple sources of information (or "constraints") are used for comprehending sentences and resolving ambiguities. These constraints can include general syntactic biases, probabilistic lexically specific syntactic information, word meaning, selectional restrictions of verbs, knowledge of common events, contextual pragmatic biases, intonation and prosody of speech, and other types of information gleaned from intra-sentential and extra-sentential context, including both linguistic and visual contexts. This property is not unique to constraint-based models because all theories assume that all relevant information and knowledge is used eventually to interpret language.

In constraint-based models, it is assumed that there is little or no delay in information availability. This distinguishes them from the garden-path and race model. Computing some types of information might conceivably take longer than others, however. For example, computing information that requires conceptually combining the meanings of multiple words might take longer than information tied to a single word, such as verb subcategorization preferences.

The third property is that there is no delay in information usage once it becomes available. That is, once a constraint is computed or accessed, it is used immediately for comprehension. Therefore, there is no time during processing when only the major syntactic category of the current word is available.

Fourth, multiple potential alternative interpretations are activated probabilistically in parallel. An alternative way to state this is that, at any given moment, comprehenders activate (or construct) multiple relevant interpretations of the given sentential input, and these are weighted probabilistically. This contrasts with the serial models discussed above.

Finally, many constraint-based models include anticipation or expectation of structure and content. Elman's (1990) simple recurrent network, and models based on that architecture, are the clearest examples of this.

Development of constraint-based models

During the late 1980s and early 1990s, researchers began using constraint-based models to account for experimental data and to motivate psycholinguistic experiments, in large part by contrasting them with the garden-path model. At that time, constraint-based models essentially consisted of the statement that all types of contextual information that are relevant to interpretation are used rapidly. This is, of course, a vague theoretical stance. As Tanenhaus and Trueswell (1995) stated, constraint-based models were highly underspecified in a number of ways. This was nicely summed up by MacDonald (1994), who stated, "There is little evidence available about the range of probabilistic constraints that affect ambiguity resolution, the relative strength of these constraints, or how they interact with one another" (p. 160). As a consequence of this underspecification, constraint-based models were criticized for being unfalsifiable (Frazier, 1995). If a theory corresponds to stating that all types of information matter, that information types are differentially manipulated in any specific experiment, and that constraints can be weighted differently, then the theory is unduly malleable, and such criticism is justifiable. On the positive side, valid criticism often results in progress, and it did in this case. To address underspecification, and to move the field forward, a major challenge was to make constraint-based models more specific in multiple ways. Below are four major issues that needed to be addressed, and on which progress has been made.

1. What constraints are relevant to particular contexts, ambiguities, and sentences? For understanding and interpreting experimental results, what constraints were manipulated in a particular experiment, and what other constraints matter, regardless of whether or not they were purposely manipulated?
2. What are the values or strengths of the relevant constraints? Answering this question demands careful, valid measurement. Part of the issue concerns how best to quantify constraints, including over what elements they are best conditionalized (grain size).

3. What are the relative weights on the constraints in particular contexts/ sentences? That is, how does a researcher specify how strongly each constraint influences potential interpretations? Do weights differ by the linguistic environment stipulated by a specific context and construction? How do they differ over time as a sentence is processed incrementally?
4. How are constraints combined? What mechanism can be used to combine the influence of multiple constraints? Should this mechanism combine constraints in a linear or a non-linear fashion?

The constraints

A major aspect of elucidating constraint-based theory involves identifying important constraints. Over approximately the past 25 years, progress has been made in that a substantial number of constraints have been identified and tested. The Appendix lists many of them. These constraints cover a large range of information types and vary along numerous dimensions. For example, some are syntactic (subcategorization preferences), whereas others are semantic or pragmatic (referential pragmatics). Some are tied to single words (transitivity) whereas others are conditionalized over combinations of words (syntactic probabilities given *verbed by*; event-specific thematic fit). Finally, some are based on the physical linguistic signal (prosody of speech) whereas others are not linguistic at all (aspects of the visual environment accompanying an utterance).

At a general level, there are global syntactic biases, such as the subject–verb–object (SVO) bias in English (Bever, 1970). Such global biases, which take into account only the major syntactic category of each word, can be viewed as corresponding to, for example, the principle of minimal attachment (i.e., build the syntactically simplest possible structure consistent with the sentence fragment up to that point; Rayner, Carlson, & Frazier, 1983). In constraint-based models, however, such biases are probabilistic, rather than binary principles.

A number of constraints are tied to single words, partly due to well-developed theories of lexical representations, and partly due to the relative ease of identifying them. A central aspect of constraint-based models has been the constraint-based lexicalist account (MacDonald, Pearlmutter, & Seidenberg, 1994; Trueswell, 1996). In this approach, syntactic ambiguity resolution is similar to, and depends crucially on, lexical ambiguity resolution (i.e., resolving ambiguities inherent to single words). This view has spurred a great deal of investigation into lexically specific syntactic biases (Carlson & Tanenhaus, 1988; MacDonald et al., 1994; Trueswell, Tanenhaus, & Kello, 1993). One is a verb's bias toward being used in its past tense versus passive participle form. For example, Trueswell (1996) showed that the relative frequency with which an ambiguous verb is used as a past tense verb versus a past participle influences resolution of the main clause/reduced relative ambiguity (e.g., *searched* has low passive participle bias whereas *selected* has high passive participle bias).

Another well-studied issue concerns people's knowledge of the probability that a specific verb is followed by alternative structures. Many verbs can be used in multiple structures, and verbs vary in terms of the relative frequencies with which they appear in different structures. For example, verbs such as *insist* are never used transitively (with a direct object) and are often followed by a sentential complement (*She insisted she was right.*), whereas verbs such as *confirm* are strongly biased toward being followed by a direct object (*She confirmed her reservation.*). Some studies of verb subcategorization preferences have illustrated their rapid influence on resolving the direct object/sentential complement ambiguity (Garnsey, Pearlmutter, Meyers, & Lotocky, 1997; Trueswell et al., 1993), whereas other have found null or delayed effects (Ferreira & Henderson, 1990; Kennison, 2001). Another subcategorization bias involves verb transitivity, i.e., whether or not a verb takes a direct object. Several studies have shown that these verb biases are used rapidly to resolve ambiguity during reading (Garnsey et al., 1997; MacDonald, 1994; Tanenhaus, Boland, Garnsey, & Carlson, 1989; Trueswell et al., 1993; Staub, 2007; but cf. Mitchell, 1987).

In some cases, the manner in which a constraint is viewed has been refined in systematic ways. For example, verbs such as *admit* have multiple senses. Roland and Jurafsky (2002) noted that subcategorization biases can differ by verb sense. In the case of *admit*, the "let in" sense is strongly direct object biased, whereas the "acknowledge" mental process sense is biased toward being followed by a sentential complement. Hare, McRae, and Elman (2003) found that such sense-contingent syntactic biases rapidly influence direct object/ sentential complement ambiguity resolution. In addition, Hare, McRae, and Elman (2004) showed that conditionalizing subcategorization biases over verb sense reconciled previously conflicting results (rapid effects in Trueswell et al., 1993, and Garnsey et al., 1997, versus null effects in Ferreira & Henderson, 1990, and Kennison, 2001).

Structural constraints also have been conditionalized over combinations of words. For example, Spivey-Knowlton and Sedivy (1995) measured the probability that a *with*-prepositional phrase (PP) includes a noun that modifies either a verb (*The fireman smashed down a door with an axe.*) or a noun (*The teacher despised the student with the bad attitude.*). Using the Brown corpus (Kuçera & Francis, 1967), they measured overall attachment bias of a verb followed by a *with*-PP, the biases of both action and psych verbs followed by a *with*-PP, and the same biases when the direct object noun phrase (NP) contained either a definite (*the*) or indefinite (*a*) determiner. They found that *with*-PPs have a moderate overall bias toward verb phrase-attachment (VP-attachment), which is largely due to the overwhelming bias toward VP-attachment when the direct object is a definite NP. When the direct object is an indefinite NP, there is actually a moderate statistical bias toward NP-attachment. Moreover, the bulk of that pattern is due to action verbs (which are frequent) rather than verbs of perception (which are comparatively rare). In Spivey-Knowlton and Sedivy's corpus analysis, action verbs showed a bias toward VP-attachment even when the direct object was an indefinite NP, and verbs of perception showed a bias toward NP-attachment even when the direct object was a definite NP. They presented self-paced reading results demonstrating people's sensitivity to these contingencies.

Constraints involving thematic roles of verbs have played a major role in multiple ways. The thematic roles that a verb assigns to its arguments, such as agent, patient, and instrument, are assumed in many theories to be stored in a verb's argument structure (Levin & Rappaport, 1986; Tanenhaus & Carlson, 1989). Research focusing on thematic roles has dealt with thematic fit, the fit between noun concepts and the potential thematic roles assigned by the verbs. As was the case with verb biases, the scope of this constraint has been refined in systematic ways. Many studies have investigated verb-general thematic fit (i.e., not tied to any specific verb) in the form of binary selectional restrictions, such as the fact that agents of actions tend to be animate (Caplan, Hildebrandt, & Waters, 1994; Clifton et al., 2003; Ferreira & Clifton, 1986; Trueswell, Tanenhaus, & Garnsey, 1994). Some researchers have viewed thematic roles as verb-specific or event-specific concepts that are continuous rather than binary in nature (McRae, Ferretti, & Amyote, 1997). That is, thematic role assignment is based on people's general knowledge about the roles that specific entities and objects play in specific types of events denoted by the verbs. McRae, Spivey-Knowlton, and Tanenhaus (1998) demonstrated that the relative likelihood of a sentence-initial noun being the agent or patient of the event denoted by a verb (as in *The cop arrested* . . . versus *The crook arrested* . . .) immediately influences resolution of the main clause/reduced relative ambiguity.

Constraints that cross sentence boundaries also have been shown to influence ambiguity resolution (see Chapter 5 in this volume). Most language is understood within a broader context, both linguistic (other sentences; a conversation) and physical (the sights, sounds, and smells of a real-life context). The incremental interactive theory of sentence comprehension developed by Crain and Steedman (1985) and Altmann and Steedman (1988) focused on contextual factors, most notably, referential pragmatics. These researchers stressed that the context in which an ambiguity was embedded could strongly influence preferences. What is particularly crucial are the ways in which potential syntactic structures best match the pragmatic constraints of the discourse model. For example, one discourse function of a relative clause is to select among alternatives. If there were two actresses, and one was the favorite of the director, and the other of the producer, it would make pragmatic sense to begin a sentence with *The actress favored by the director*, and such a reduced relative is more easily interpreted (see Spivey & Tanenhaus, 1998).

Finally, although a great deal of research testing constraint-based models has been conducted with written language, some studies have used spoken language. A number of studies have shown rapid influences of visual context on ambiguity resolution (Chambers, Tanenhaus, & Magnuson, 2004; Tanenhaus, Spivey-Knowlton, Eberhard, & Sedivy, 1995), including developmental studies (Trueswell & Gleitman, 2004), using the visual-world paradigm in which participants' eye movements to the visual scene or objects are monitored while sentences are heard. Using this paradigm, the influence of pictures that match one or another interpretation of an utterance has been illustrated, often in terms of predicting or anticipating the structure and semantic content of sentences. These can include the number of referents, location of referents, or implied events in a scene. Other research using spoken language has demonstrated that various aspects of prosody and intonation of speech are important constraints for resolving syntactic ambiguities (Beach, 1991; Speer, Kjelgaard, & Dobroth, 1996).

In summary, the field of sentence processing has moved over the years from vague statements of the type that all constraints matter, to investigations in which many constraints have been identified and shown to rapidly influence syntactic ambiguity resolution.

Measuring constraints

In constraint-based models, the vast majority of constraints are viewed as probabilistic. Therefore, carefully measuring the relevant probabilities is critical to understanding their influence. Predicting the speed and strength with which a specific constraint affects comprehension requires valid measures of not only the constraint of primary interest, but also the other constraints at work in experimental items. This is important both for generating hypotheses and for understanding precisely why specific results were obtained. In general, rather than speculating about the influence that various constraints might have, or using intuition to explain why certain results were obtained, quantifying all relevant factors produces a deeper understanding of the empirical phenomena.

It is interesting to note the parallel between a major influence of connectionist modeling in general, and that of constraint-based models of sentence comprehension (which are often connectionist models themselves, or incorporate many of the same principles). For connectionist models, one consequence of the emphasis on learning environmental distributional statistics was a focus on the importance of quantifying relevant aspects of the environment (Daugherty & Seidenberg, 1992). The development of constraint-based models was likewise tied to quantifying linguistic and extra-linguistic constraints. Critical to this endeavor was the development of many types of norming methods designed to tap people's linguistic and world knowledge. Furthermore, advances in computational linguistics have played a vital role in constraint-based modeling, and in language research in general.

A major method for measuring constraint strength is to use human judgments or productions. In many off-line production norming tasks, participants are given sentence fragments such as *The defendant examined* and are asked to complete them. Researchers then count the frequencies of the syntactic structures that participants have produced. This type of norming provides quantitative estimates for experimental items. Given that much of the debate surrounding constraint-based versus garden-path models hinges on precisely when a constraint influences comprehension, off-line norms provide estimates of people's knowledge and its influences when they have time to consider the options. Results also can be considered to be an estimate of the degree to which people predict various structures given some context/fragment. Finally, it is possible to gauge the influence of the words in a sentence incrementally by using gated completion norms in which completions for successively longer fragments are collected (McRae et al., 1998).

There are a number of issues regarding completion norms, however. Sentence completion is a production task, so it necessarily combines comprehension of the given fragment with production of the completion. Depending on one's view of the extent to which comprehension and production rely on independent processes or representations, this may be an issue. Because shorter, less complex structures are easier and faster to produce, completion tasks may overestimate the frequency of shorter, less complex structures. Another issue is that sentence fragments sometimes combine multiple constraints. For example, participants might be given a context sentence or sentences, an initial NP, and a verb. Because it is unclear which constraint or set of interacting constraints are influencing participants' completions, such completion tasks do not necessarily provide information about the influence of specific constraints.

Potential production biases can be alleviated via rating tasks. For example, participants might be given fragments of sentences and be asked to rate the degree to which they are grammatical or plausible. One potential issue is that it can be difficult to disentangle structural influences from the influences of people's knowledge about real-world events. Each of the two judgments may be influenced by variables from the other domain. For example, two sentences describing the same event may be given different plausibility ratings because syntax leaks into the judgment.

For these reasons, particularly when measuring people's semantic or event knowledge, researchers have tapped this knowledge outside of particular sentences. For example, thematic fit ratings have been used in numerous studies (McRae et al., 1998; Pado, Crocker, & Keller, 2009). People are asked to rate, for example, how common it is for a spoon to be used for stirring. One can also ask participants to list things that people use to stir.

In corpus analyses, researchers calculate probabilities of interest by either examining parsed corpora (e.g., Penn Treebank), or randomly sampled sets from unparsed corpora (Jurafsky, 1996). The assumption is that corpora reflect subsets of inputs that comprehenders experience as language learners, and from which they acquire their knowledge regarding the distributional properties of words or phrases within certain syntactic contexts. Corpus analyses have played a crucial role in quantifying constraints for experiments and modeling.

Estimating constraint weights from corpora is not without its challenges, as discussed by Roland, Dick, and Elman (2007). There is a quality versus quantity issue, because parsed corpora tend to be smaller in size, and the choice of automatically, semi-automatically, or manually parsing corpora, or random sampling, is associated with a tradeoff between accuracy and costs. This is a potential issue when a researcher's goal is to obtain estimates that are conditionalized over multiple items. For example, less familiar verbs occur rarely in corpora, and if the goal is to estimate their occurrence in various structures in specific environments, estimates will be based on sparse data. Finally, corpora vary in genre and thus their content; compare Wall Street Journal corpora to those based on internet postings. Corpora also differ in register (from relatively free spoken conversation to heavily edited written newspapers or books). Researchers such as Gahl, Jurafsky, and Roland (2004) have shown that such differences can lead to systematic cross-corpus variability.

In summary, a great deal of progress has been made on estimating the strengths of numerous constraints, and this progress has had a major positive influence on sentence processing research. Norming methodologies have played a crucial role, and the possible types of norms are limited only by one's imagination. Advances in corpus techniques have enabled greatly improved experimental predictions and modeling. Every method has associated complications, but researchers continue to develop an appreciation for precisely what is being measured and how estimates can be influenced by specific factors.

Weighting and combining constraints

Even when the relevant constraints have been identified and their strengths estimated, there remain the critical issues of how they are weighted relative to one another, and how they are combined or integrated. A great deal of debate has centered on precisely how and when various constraints influence ambiguity resolution. The simplest view is that if a researcher manipulates one constraint (e.g., thematic fit) in a way that biases readers toward the less frequent, syntactically more complex interpretation of an ambiguous sentence (e.g., the reduced relative interpretation of a sentence containing a main clause/reduced relative ambiguity), then ambiguity effects that would otherwise occur without such a manipulation should be eliminated. This view makes perfect sense at first glance, and numerous studies have used this logic. However, there are two issues.

First, the theoretical stance that all relevant constraints matter entails that predicting self-paced reading times or eye-movement latencies requires taking into account the influences of all constraints and their strengths. If, for example, a researcher manipulates a single constraint, but all other constraints strongly oppose it, it is unlikely that the manipulated constraint will have a major influence on comprehension, and almost certainly will not eliminate comprehension difficulty. Such a result could be interpreted as supporting the garden-path model, and often has been (Ferreira & Clifton, 1986; Rayner, Carlson, & Frazier, 1983). However, such a result could also be interpreted as supporting the constraint-based theory because the majority of constraints favor a specific analysis.

The second issue is that even if the manipulation of a non-syntactic constraint eliminates the ambiguity-driven difficulty in self-paced reading or early eye-tracking measures such as first fixation duration or first-pass reading times, proponents of garden-path or race models can argue that the second stage of processing (or reanalysis) kicks in with a small, but real, time delay. This logic has been used as well (Clifton & Ferreira, 1989; Frazier, 1995). Thus, the field was left in the position that there was no signature data pattern that clearly discriminated constraint-based from other models (McRae et al., 1998).

One potential solution is to use computational modeling. Computational modeling forces researchers to make explicit decisions regarding parameters and mechanisms. Implementation requires decisions regarding the constraints to incorporate, their strengths, how they are weighted, and how they are combined. Simulations can help to adjudicate among theories because the output can be compared to human performance, and that output does not always match researchers' intuitions. In general, simulations increase a theory's falsifiability. Of course, computational modeling is not a panacea because there are typically some free parameters that influence a model's performance, but the exercise of implementing a model is highly beneficial in terms of clarifying what choices have to be made, how parameters can be set, and how parameter values influence the model's behavior.

Implemented constraint-based models

In this section, we present implemented constraint-based models. A number of researchers have conducted simulations to generate and test predictions for on-line reading-time experiments. As discussed in detail by Hintzman (1991), there are a number of advantages of implemented models. These include overcoming hindsight bias ("Of course my model would account for that result."), the latitude in explanation that is available when using verbally described models, and the extreme difficulty of using intuition to predict the performance or output of a fully interacting non-linear system that changes over time.

We begin with the competition–integration model because it was the first implementation of a constraint-based model and it has been used most frequently in the literature. We then describe Tabor's dynamical systems model (Tabor, Juliano, & Tanenhaus, 1997). Finally, we present the coordinated interplay account network that has been used to simulate visual-world eye-tracking data (Mayberry, Crocker, & Knoeferle, 2009).

The competition–integration model

Spivey and colleagues (McRae et al., 1998; Spivey & Tanenhaus, 1998; Spivey-Knowlton, 1994; Spivey-Knowlton, 1996) developed a model that simulates on-line reading latency data. The competition–integration model has been implemented in a number of studies (Binder, Duffy, & Rayner, 2001; Elman, Hare, & McRae, 2004; Ferretti & McRae, 1999; Green & Mitchell, 2006; Hanna, Spivey-Knowlton, & Tanenhaus, 1996; McRae et al., 1998; Spivey &

Tanenhaus (1998); Tanenhaus, Spivey-Knowlton, & Hanna, 2000). It has been used to study the main clause/reduced relative ambiguity, direct object/sentential complement ambiguity, agentive/locative prepositional phrase ambiguity, and relative clause attachment. A number of structural, lexically syntactic, thematic, and referential constraints have been included. Thus, it has been applied reasonably widely to account for self-paced reading and eye-tracking data.

Although some details differ, there are mostly commonalities across the various implementations. The competition–integration model consists of input constraint nodes, output interpretation nodes, and weights connecting them. McRae et al.'s (1998) implementation is shown in Figure 3.1. The two hexagons in the center represent the interpretations of interest, main clause and reduced relative. With one exception (Ferretti & McRae, 1999), the competition–integration model has simulated competition between two interpretations. The activation values of interpretation nodes vary between 0 and 1 to capture the probability of, or the model's confidence in, competing interpretations, which changes over time as constraints interact and new input arrives. The model does not generate syntactic alternatives on its own. Instead, it simulates resolving a syntactic ambiguity once it is encountered. It accomplishes this by evaluating the relevant constraints, and using them to support various alternatives. Therefore, the competition–integration model was designed to simulate ambiguity effects when matched ambiguous and unambiguous sentences are compared (Tanenhaus et al., 2000).

The rectangles surrounding the hexagons in Figure 3.1 are input nodes corresponding to relevant constraints. The circles within each type of input represent the constraint values specific to one interpretation. How those values are estimated varies across constraints, and values are not necessarily in the same scale, but are treated as similar to probabilities during computations. That is, they are transformed to range from 0 to 1 and add up to 1 for each type of input. As shown in Figure 3.1, not all input nodes exert an influence from the beginning of a sentence or region; only the relevant constraints are included in computations, and inputs are added as they become applicable. In McRae et al. (1998), thematic fit of the initial NP, the main clause bias, the *by* bias, and the verb tense/voice constraint are operative at the verb+by region. Thematic fit of the agent NP comes into play at the agent NP region and the main verb bias becomes operative at the main verb region.

Constraints are integrated using a normalized recurrence algorithm developed by Spivey-Knowlton (1996). Each cycle of competition consists of three steps:

1. Each value within each input node is divided by the sum of those values to normalize activation within each constraint.
2. The activation of each interpretation node is the sum of supporting input activations scaled by the connecting weights.
3. The input nodes receive feedback from the interpretation nodes proportional to the activation of that input in Step 2.

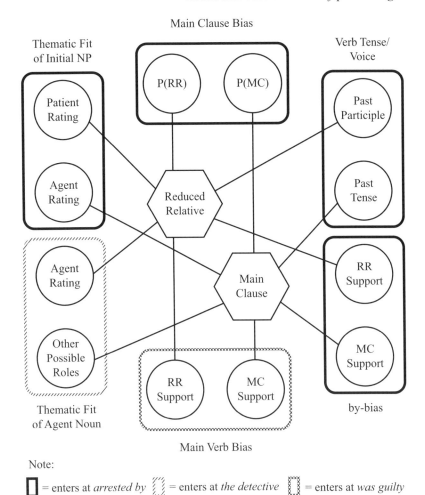

Figure 3.1 Schematic of McRae et al.'s (1998) competition–integration model.

Source: Reprinted from *Journal of Memory and Language, 38 (3)*, K. McRae, M. J. Spivey-Knowlton, & M. K. Tanenhaus, Modeling the influence of thematic fit (and other constraints) in on-line sentence comprehension, 283–312, © 1998, with permission from Elsevier.

These three steps comprise one cycle of competition and are repeated until the activation level of one of the output nodes reaches a criterion value. The criterion changes dynamically as a function of number of cycles and a constant called Δcrit, which makes the threshold more lenient as the number of competition cycles increases, and ensures that competition terminates. This dynamic criterion is needed because fixation durations are partially determined by a preset timing program so that a reader spends only so long on a fixation before making a saccade (Rayner & Pollatsek, 1989; Vaughan, 1983). This logic holds for self-paced reading in that readers attempt to resolve competition at each segment for only so long before pressing the key for more information. Because it is not clear what value of Δcrit is the most appropriate, researchers either choose a fixed Δcrit after exploring the parameter space with multiple data sets (Spivey & Tanenhaus, 1998), or choose a range of values and average across simulations (McRae et al., 1998). These models use a Δcrit for which competition is not halted too quickly, to allow for differences among conditions to be observed. After simulating the interpretation of each sentence, the mean number of cycles is compared to the ambiguity effect found in behavioral data (e.g., the mean difference in reading time in each region between the ambiguous and unambiguous conditions). All published models have used a linear transformation to compare human ambiguity effects and the model's cycles of competition.

The model receives information incrementally. Thus, its changing interpretation can be measured on a moment-by-moment basis. When simulating ambiguity effects across multiple regions, the model takes various constraints assumed to be available at each region as its inputs, and iterates until the criterion is reached before moving on to the next region. The model then adds new constraints and associated weights, while retaining all activations from the previous region as the initial state. The constraints for the word or region currently being read are given one-half of the overall weight. Weights are normalized for each region. At the initial region, if the constraints support the interpretations relatively equally, substantial competition results. At subsequent regions, competition increases with the degree to which new constraints oppose the carried-over interpretation and constraint values.

McRae et al. (1998) simulated data from a self-paced reading study using the main clause/reduced relative ambiguity (Figure 3.2). The human data indicated that a number of constraints influenced interpretation: the main clause bias, the verb tense/voice constraint, and the *by* bias. In particular, readers were sensitive to the goodness of fit of the initial noun as a potential agent or patient of the specific verb (thematic fit). For example, *The cop arrested* . . . favored a main clause reading whereas *The crook arrested* . . . favored the reduced relative. McRae et al. used both off-line data from role/filler typicality ratings (thematic fit) and corpus analyses (for the other constraints) to estimate the degree to which each constraint supported each interpretation. They also used off-line gated sentence completion data to determine the weights. They tested a large set of weight configurations and averaged over a subset of models that yielded the smallest root mean square error values to the off-line completion proportions. With these inputs and parameters, the model provided a close quantitative fit to the reading time data. Additionally, they delayed the availability of thematic fit and lexically specific syntactic information, so that only the configural constraint (main clause bias) operated initially. The delayed version deviated significantly from the empirical data, supporting the view that all constraints immediately influence ambiguity resolution.

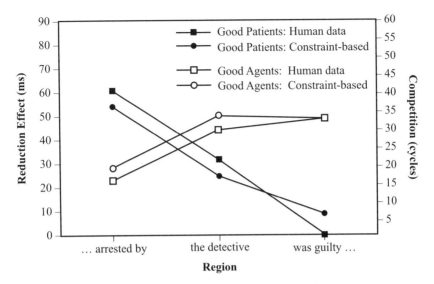

Figure 3.2 Predicting ambiguity effects (reduction effect: the difference between ambiguous reduced and unambiguous relative clauses) with the competition–integration model.

Source: Reprinted from *Journal of Memory and Language*, 38 (3), K. McRae, M. J. Spivey-Knowlton, & M. K. Tanenhaus, Modeling the influence of thematic fit (and other constraints) in on-line sentence comprehension, 283–312, © 1998, with permission from Elsevier.

The competition–integration model has been used to investigate other constraints and ambiguities. Spivey and Tanenhaus (1998) simulated data from several studies showing the influence of extra-sentential referential context on the main clause/reduced relative ambiguity (Murray & Liversedge, 1994; Spivey-Knowlton, Trueswell, & Tanenhaus, 1993). They determined constraint values using off-line norms and corpora analyses. For practical reasons, Spivey and Tanenhaus used equal weights for each constraint rather than estimating them from off-line norming data. Their model simulated both eye-tracking and self-paced reading data. The competition–integration model also has been used to simulate the direct object/sentential complement ambiguity (Elman et al., 2004; Ferretti & McRae, 1999), and the agentive/locative *by*-phrase ambiguity (Hanna et al., 1996; Tanenhaus et al., 2000). Furthermore, Tanenhaus et al. (2000) present an illuminating set of simulations in which they successfully simulated data from a range of experiments that had been interpreted as evidence for both constraint-based and garden-path models.

There have been challenges to the competition–integration model. It has been claimed that the model predicts (prolonged) processing difficulty under the circumstance in which constraints are balanced between alternative interpretations because competition cannot be easily resolved under such circumstances (Traxler, Pickering, & Clifton, 1998; Van Gompel et al., 2001; Van Gompel et al., 2005). In contrast, in sentences with adjunct or relative clause modifiers, reading times were shorter when structural ambiguity was present than when it was absent. For example, Van Gompel et al. (2005) used materials like the following.

(5)   I read that the governor of the province retiring after the troubles is very rich.

(6)   I read that the province of the governor retiring after the troubles is very rich.

(7)   I read that the bodyguard of the governor retiring after the troubles is very rich.

Sentences (5) and (6) are initially temporally ambiguous until *retiring* is encountered, but the ambiguity can be resolved using thematic fit in favor of high-attachment in (5) or low-attachment in (6). In both cases, *the governor* is, but *the province* is not, a semantically plausible subject of *retiring*. Sentence (7) is globally ambiguous because the relative clause can modify either *the bodyguard* or *the governor*. Because there is no strong bias toward one of the interpretations before or after *retiring*, Van Gompel et al. (2005) argued that competition models predict greatest competition in (7). However, participants spent less time reading the potentially disambiguating word (*retiring*) in (7) than in (5) or (6), referred to as an ambiguity advantage.

Green and Mitchell (2006) argued that Traxler et al.'s (1998) and Van Gompel et al.'s (2005) assumptions are based on a misinterpretation of the model. Green and Mitchell investigated how McRae et al.'s (1998) model behaves given various inputs. One issue concerned whether the model displays maximal competition given a new input that is balanced between two interpretations. The second issue concerned whether the model can display an ambiguity advantage.

The competition–integration model exhibits maximal competition when the bias of new inputs opposes the model's values inherited from the previous region, whereas there is less competition when new inputs are balanced. Balanced new inputs produce a high degree of competition when both the inputs and inherited activations are perfectly balanced. Green and Mitchell showed that this seldom occurs because the model amplifies early biases in a region, so that tiny biases in early phases of competition become large values by the time the model moves to the next phase of competition. They concluded that "Balanced legacies are very rare indeed" (p. 10). Second, the model displays an ambiguity advantage much like that reported by Traxler et al. and Van Gompel et al. in some circumstances. For instance, when there is an inherited bias from previous regions toward some interpretation, which Green and Mitchell argued is extremely likely, a balanced ambiguity leads to faster processing. For Van Gompel et al.'s studies, it could be argued that the activations in the competition model, as currently implemented, would be balanced because the ambiguity begins at *retiring*. However, this may be an implementational rather than a theoretical issue. In a complete model of this type, one would assume that evidence for numerous interpretations builds throughout a sentence. Therefore, from the initial word onward, various interpretations would be favored, producing an unbalanced state when entering any subsequent region. This has not been simulated definitively, however.

In summary, the implemented competition–integration model has contributed to sentence-processing research because it forced researchers to make specific decisions regarding the four key issues defined above. Simulations enabled explicit testing of ideas regarding the relevant constraints, their strengths, how they are weighted, and how they combine. It also made it possible to simulate experiments that had been interpreted as support for two types of verbally described models, thus moving the field forward. However, there are clear limitations with current implementations. The model does not construct potential interpretations, rather, it simulates competition among assumed possible constructions. Given that simulations have included only a small number of alternatives, there are open issues regarding scalability. Furthermore, it does not compute the actual meaning of utterances, whereas computing meaning is presumably the major reason why people process language. Finally, potentially free parameters exist, such as the precise mapping of cycles of competition to human reading times.

The visitation set gravitation model

Several researchers have implemented connectionist models to capture the computational dynamics of sentence comprehension using simple recurrent networks (SRN; Elman, 1990; see Figure 3.3). An SRN consists of three feed-forward layers (input, hidden, and output) as well as a context layer that stores a copy of activations of the hidden layer at the previous time step, and feeds its activation to the hidden layer during the current time step. The network can be trained on English-like sequences of words, each represented by a random vector and presented one at a time, and teaching it to predict the next word at each step. One of the interesting aspects of the model is that the activation of its hidden layer represents the "mental space" or "parse state" of the model. Analyses of hidden layer activation reveal that the patterns evoked in response to each word correspond to category membership of the words (e.g., verbs versus nouns, transitive versus intransitive verbs, animate versus inanimate nouns; Elman 1991). When the hidden layer's activation is viewed as a vector or a point in a metric space, the model forms, over the course of training, a set of clusters (the centers of which are called *attractors*) within the space where contextually (i.e., syntactically, thematically, or semantically) similar patterns are placed near one another. For a given sequence of input (a sentence), the network displays continuous movement (or a trajectory) through the multi-dimensional space of mental states (Elman, 1993). Thus, sentence comprehension can be characterized as the behavior of a dynamical system (Elman, 1995).

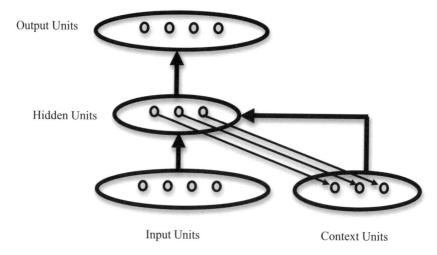

Figure 3.3 The architecture of a simple recurrent network (SRN). The input units are typically fully interconnected with the hidden units, which are then fully interconnected with the output units. The input and output units are the same. Weights from input and context units to hidden units, and from hidden units to output units are trained using the back propagation learning algorithm. The hidden unit activations are copied back to the context units.

Building on the SRN and the dynamical system metaphor, Tabor and colleagues (Tabor, Juliano, & Tanenhaus, 1997; Tabor & Tanenhaus, 2001) developed the visitation set gravitation (VSG) model to explore syntactic ambiguity resolution. In the VSG, the hidden layer representations of a trained SRN are analyzed to map representational states onto structural interpretations and to generate reading-time predictions. Gravitation time, which is the time required for a given hidden-layer state to move toward or "gravitate" into an attractor, corresponds to reading time for a word. When a sentence is ambiguous, multiple attractors pull with different gravitational strengths that are determined by their distance from the starting point. The model predicts processing disruption as a function of the relative proximity of the starting point of a trajectory to the attractors, and the relative strengths of the attractors' gravitational pull, both of which are determined by the model's experience during training. Tabor and Tanenhaus (2001) used the model to simulate the influence of thematic fit in the main clause/reduced relative ambiguity. Tabor et al. (1997) simulated the general pattern of contingent frequency effects in the determiner/complementizer ambiguity of *that*. The relative frequency with which *that* is used as a determiner (*The lawyer insisted that cheap hotel would be safe*) versus as a complementizer (*The lawyer insisted that cheap hotels would be safe*) is contingent on whether it appears before (35 percent versus 11 percent) or after the main verb of the sentence (93 percent versus 6 percent), and reading times to *that–adjective–noun* reflect this.

One important aspect of this modeling is that, unlike the competition–integration model whose inputs and weights are estimated using norms and corpora analyses, the model acquires the relevant statistics and constraints from the input corpus. This is a crucial step toward a more complete constraint-based model of language comprehension, although the SRN part of the VSG model has to date been trained on relatively simplified sets of input sentences.

The coordinated interplay account network (CIANet)

Mayberry, Crocker, and Knoeferle (2009) developed a model of situated language comprehension named CIANet, which also is based on an SRN. Unlike the models discussed so far, which focus exclusively on linguistically available constraints, an explicit aim of CIANet is to simulate the role of visual context during sentence comprehension. Before describing this model in some detail, we first review studies by Knoeferle and her colleagues (Knoeferle & Crocker, 2006; Knoeferle et al., 2005) to illustrate the type of phenomena the model was designed to simulate.

Knoeferle et al. (2005) monitored participants' eye-movements to a depicted scene while listening to sentences describing the event. For example, given a scene depicting a pirate, a princess carrying a bucket and a sponge, a fencer carrying a paint pallet and brush, and a few other common objects (not depicted in Figure 3.4), they listened to one of the following sentences:

(8) SVO sentence: Die Prinzessin wäscht offensichtlich den Pirat.
(The princess$_{AMBIGUOUS}$ washes apparently the pirate$_{ACC}$.)

(9) OVS sentence: Die Prinzessin malt offensichtlich der Fechter.
(The princess$_{AMBIGUOUS}$ paints apparently [is apparently painted by] the fencer$_{NOM}$.)

In German, the nominative and accusative case are different for masculine noun phrases such as *Pirat* (*der* and *den* respectively), but are identical for feminine noun phrases such as *Prinzessin* (*die* in both cases). Because German allows scrambling of nouns, without any context, sentences (8) and (9) are temporarily ambiguous in terms of the thematic role of the initial noun phrase (*Die Prinzessin*) until the case-marked determiner of the second noun phrase is encountered (*den* vs. *der*). However, sentence (8) can be disambiguated much earlier at the verb because the combined information in the scene and in the sentence up to the verb constrains the possible role of the mentioned referent (i.e., the princess is more likely the agent of washing because she is carrying the bucket and sponge in the picture). Eye-movement patterns indicated that participants made use of this constraint to resolve the ambiguity. More specifically, immediately after the verb was heard, participants looked more to the soon-to-be-mentioned thematic role fillers of the event denoted by the verb than to other objects in the scene (in sentence (8), *the pirate* fulfills the patient

Figure 3.4 Example visual scene from Knoeferle et al. (2005).

Source: Reprinted from *Cognition*, *95(1)*, P. Knoeferle, M. W. Crocker, C. Scheepers, & M. J. Pickering, The influence of the immediate visual context on incremental thematic role assignment: evidence from eye-movements in depicted events, 95–127, © 2004, with permission from Elsevier.

role of the washing event, whereas in sentence (9), *the fencer* is the agent of painting).

Knoeferle and Crocker (2006) used the same methodology to investigate how prior knowledge about events in general comes into play. Of particular interest is the relative importance of immediate visual context and general thematic role knowledge of verbs. Participants were shown a scene with, for example, a wizard with a monocle, and a detective with some food and a pipe, facing toward a pilot, while they listened to one of the sentences below:

(10)   Den Piloten bespitzelt gleich der Detektiv.
    (The pilot$_{ACC}$ spies-on soon the detective$_{NOM}$.)

(11)   Den Piloten bespitzelt gleich der Zauberer.
    (The pilot$_{ACC}$ spies-on soon the wizard$_{NOM}$.)

Whereas general world-knowledge would predict the detective to be the more likely agent of *spying*, the visual scene depicts *the wizard* to be more likely. At the verb, the wizard was fixated more than the other objects, suggesting that participants relied more on the immediate visual context than general knowledge. Only when the linguistic input revealed otherwise at the second noun phrase in (10) did people fixate the contextually conflicting but thematically more likely object (i.e., *detective*).

Based on these results, Knoeferle and Crocker (2006) proposed the coordinated interplay account (CIA) of situated language comprehension. Its central tenet is that incremental and anticipatory processing of linguistic input guides people's attention to a simultaneously present visual context. Furthermore, this guided attention toward mentioned and/or yet-to-be mentioned visual referents influences how the relevant visual context is used during sentence comprehension. The account also assumes that the visual contextual information takes priority over more general event knowledge when they conflict.

CIANet is the computational instantiation of the CIA. Mayberry et al. (2009) used CIANet to simulate the key findings of Knoeferle et al. (2005), Knoeferle and Crocker (2006), and several other visual-world experiments. In addition to including an SRN, CIANet consists of an input layer representing the visual input of a depicted scene coded in terms of event constituents (e.g., agent, action, and patient). During simulations, two events from the same scene are presented (e.g., *painting* and *washing* event from Figure 3.4), only one of which is described by the linguistic input. CIANet contains a layer of sigma-pi units (units that have multiplicative rather than additive connections) that gate attention to event constituents, enabling attention shifting. That is, the more the model attends to one event, the less it attends to the other, producing a competitive aspect to processing. The model's performance is analyzed quantitatively by comparing its outputs to the pattern of the behavioral data from the visual-world paradigm, or by generating a neurobehavioral equivalent from the pattern of hidden layer activation (see Crocker, Knoeferle, & Mayberry, 2010, for mapping of the model's hidden layer patterns to ERP data). Simulating Knoeferle et al.'s (2005) results, CIANet displayed predictive ambiguity resolution at the same point in time in the sentence (i.e., immediately after the verb). The model also simulated the human data from Knoeferle and Crocker's (2006) research, where participants relied on both constraints from the depicted event as well as their knowledge about common events, but relied more on the former when the two sources conflicted. Also note that as in the VSG, CIANet learned the constraints and their relevance from the input over the course of training. A final contribution of CIANet is that it simulates processing in a language other than English, and thus incorporates different constraints and investigates issues such as the on-line influence of case-marking.

Conclusions

Constraint-based models have been used to demonstrate how constraints are integrated over time both within and across the regions of an unfolding sentence. They have been used to simulate data originating from a number of syntactic ambiguities, methods, and languages. Constraint-based models have evolved from a general statement that all types of constraints matter, to multiple implemented models with carefully measured constraints, which has reduced theoretical degrees of freedom, and made them falsifiable. These explicit implementations were an important advance because of the difficulty in distinguishing among similar verbally described theories.

Acknowledgments

This work was supported by National Institutes of Health grant HD053136 and Natural Sciences and Engineering Council Grant OGP0155704 to Ken McRae.

References

Altmann, G., & Steedman, M. (1988). Interaction with context during human sentence processing. *Cognition, 30,* 191–238.

Beach, C. (1991). The influence of prosodic patterns at points of syntactic structure ambiguity: Evidence for cue trading relations. *Journal of Memory & Language, 30,* 627–643.

Bever, T. G. (1970). The cognitive basis for linguistic structure. In J. R. Hayes (Ed.), *Cognitive development of language* (pp. 279–362). New York: Wiley.

Binder, K. S., Duffy, S. A., & Rayner, K. (2001). The effects of thematic fit and discourse context on syntactic ambiguity resolution. *Journal of Memory and Language, 44,* 297–324.

Caplan, D., Hildebrandt, N., & Waters, G. S. (1994). Interaction of verb selectional restrictions, noun animacy, and syntactic form in sentence processing. *Language and Cognitive Processes, 9,* 549–585.

Carlson, G. N., & Tanenhaus, M. K. (1988). Thematic roles and language comprehension. In W. Wilkins (Ed.), *Thematic relations* (pp. 263–288). New York: Academic Press.

Chambers, C. G., Tanenhaus, M. K., & Magnuson, J. S. (2004). Actions and affordances in syntactic ambiguity resolution. *Journal of Experimental Psychology: Learning, Memory, and Cognition, 30,* 687–696.

Clifton, C. Jr., & Ferreira, F. (1989). Ambiguity in context. *Language and Cognitive Processes, 4,* 77–104.

Clifton, C. Jr., Traxler, M. J., Mohamed, M. T., Williams, R. S., Morris, R. K., & Rayner, K. (2003). The use of thematic role information in parsing: Syntactic processing autonomy revisited. *Journal of Memory and Language, 49,* 317–334.

Crain, S., & Steedman, M. (1985). On not being led up the garden path: The use of context by the psychological parser. In D. Dowty, L. Karttunen, & A. Zwicky (Eds.), *Natural language processing: Psychological, computational and theoretical perspectives* (pp. 320–358). Cambridge: Cambridge University Press.

Crocker, M. W., Knoeferle, P., & Mayberry, M. R. (2010). Situated sentence processing: The coordinated interplay account and a neurobehavioral model. *Brain & Language, 112,* 189–201.

Daugherty, K., & Seidenberg, M.S. (1992). Rules or connections? The past tense revisited. In *Proceedings of the 14th annual meeting of the Cognitive Science Society.* Hillsdale, NJ: Erlbaum.

Elman, J. L. (1990). Finding structure in time. *Cognitive Science, 14,* 179–211.

Elman, J. L. (1991). Representation and structure in connectionist model. In G. Altman (Ed.), *Cognitive models of speech processing: Psycholinguistic and computational perspectives.* (pp. 345–382). Cambridge, MA: MIT Press.

Elman, J. L. (1993). Learning and development in neural networks: The importance of starting small. *Cognition, 48,* 71–99.

Elman, J. L. (1995). Language as a dynamical system. In R. Port & T. van Gelder (Eds.), *Mind as motion* (pp. 195–223). Cambridge, MA: MIT Press.

Elman, J. L., Hare, M., & McRae, K. (2004). Cues, constraints, and competition in sentence processing. In M. Tomasello & D. Slobin (Eds.), *Beyond nature–nurture: Essays in honor of Elizabeth Bates* (pp. 111–138). Mahwah, NJ: Lawrence Erlbaum Associates.

Ferreira, F., & Clifton, C. Jr. (1986). The independence of syntactic processing. *Journal of Memory and Language*, 25, 348–368.

Ferreira, F., & Henderson, J. M. (1990). Use of verb information in syntactic parsing: Evidence from eye-movements and word-by-word self-paced reading. *Journal of Experimental Psychology: Learning, Memory, and Cognition*, 16, 555–568.

Ferretti, T. R., & McRae, K. (1999). Modeling the role of plausibility and verb-bias in the direct object/sentence complement ambiguity. In *Proceedings of the twenty-first annual conference of the Cognitive Science Society* (pp. 161–166). Hillsdale NJ: Erlbaum.

Frazier, L. (1987). Sentence processing: A tutorial review. In M. Coltheart (Ed.), *Attention and performance XII: The psychology of reading* (pp. 559–586). Hillsdale, NJ: Erlbaum.

Frazier, L. (1995). Constraint satisfaction as a theory of sentence processing. *Journal of Psycholinguistic Research*, 24, 437–468.

Frazier, L. & Clifton, Jr., C. (2005) The syntax-discourse divide: Processing ellipsis. *Syntax*, 8(2), 121–174.

Frazier, L., & Rayner, K. (1982). Making and correcting errors during sentence comprehension: Eye-movements in the analysis of structurally ambiguous sentences. *Cognitive Psychology*, 143, 178–210.

Gahl, S., Jurafsky, D., & Roland, D. (2004). Verb subcategorization frequencies, American English corpus data, methodological studies, and cross-corpus comparisons. *Behavior Research Methods, Instruments, & Computers*, 36, 432–443.

Garnsey, S. M., Pearlmutter, N., Meyers, E., & Lotocky, M. A. (1997). The contribution of verb-bias and plausibility to the comprehension of temporarily ambiguous sentences. *Journal of Memory and Language*, 37, 58–93.

Green, M. J., & Mitchell, D. C. (2006). Absence of real evidence against competition during syntactic ambiguity resolution. *Journal of Memory and Language*, 55, 1–17.

Hanna, J. E., Spivey-Knowlton, M. J., & Tanenhaus, M. K. (1996). Integrating discourse and local constraints in resolving lexical thematic ambiguities. In G. Cottrell (Ed.), *Proceedings of the eighteenth annual conference of the Cognitive Science Society* (pp. 266–271). Hillsdale, NJ: Erlbaum.

Hare, M., McRae, K., & Elman, J. L. (2003). Sense and structure: Meaning as a determinant of verb subcategorization preferences. *Journal of Memory and Language*, 48, 281–303.

Hare, M., McRae, K., & Elman, J. L. (2004). Admitting that admitting verb sense into corpus analyses makes sense. *Language and Cognitive Processes*, 19, 181–224.

Hintzman, D. L. (1991). Why are formal models useful in psychology? In W. E. Hockley and S. Lewandowsky, (Eds.), *Relating theory and data: Essays on human memory in honor of Bennet B. Murdock* (pp. 39–56). Hillsdale, NJ: Erlbaum.

Jurafsky, D. (1996). A probabilistic model of lexical and syntactic access and disambiguation. *Cognitive Science*, 20, 137–194.

Kennison, S. M. (2001). Limitations on the use of verb information during sentence comprehension. *Psychonomic Bulletin & Review*, 8, 132–138.

Knoeferle, P., & Crocker, M. W. (2006). The coordinated interplay of scene, utterance, and world knowledge: Evidence from eye-tracking. *Cognitive Science, 30*, 481–529.

Knoeferle, P., Crocker, M. W., Scheepers, C., & Pickering, M. J. (2005). The influence of the immediate visual context on incremental thematic role-assignment: Evidence from eye-movements in depicted events. *Cognition, 95*, 95–127.

Kuçera, H., & Francis, W. N. (1967). *A computational analysis of present-day American English*. Providence, RI: Brown University Press.

Levin, B., & Rappaport, M. (1986). The formation of adjectival passives. *Linguistic Inquiry, 17*, 623–661.

MacDonald, M. C. (1994). Probabilistic constraints and syntactic ambiguity resolution. *Language and Cognitive Processes, 9*, 157–201.

MacDonald, M. C., Pearlmutter, N. J., & Seidenberg, M. S. (1994). The lexical nature of syntactic ambiguity resolution. *Psychological Review, 101*, 483–506.

McRae, K., Ferretti, T. R., & Amyote, L. (1997). Thematic roles as verb-specific concepts. *Language and Cognitive Processes, 12*, 137–176.

McRae, K., Spivey-Knowlton, M. J., & Tanenhaus, M. K. (1998). Modeling the influence of thematic fit (and other constraints) in on-line sentence comprehension. *Journal of Memory and Language, 38*, 283–312.

Mayberry, M. R., Crocker, M. W., & Knoeferle, P. (2009). Learning to attend: A connectionist model of situated language comprehension. *Cognitive Science, 33*, 449–496.

Mitchell, D. C. (1987). Lexical guidance in human parsing: Locus and processing characteristics. In M. Coltheart (Ed.), *Attention and performance XII: The psychology of reading* (pp. 601–618). Hillsdale, NJ: Erlbaum.

Murray, W., & Liversedge, S. (1994). Referential context and syntactic processing. In C. Clifton, L. Frazier, & K. Rayner (Eds.), *Perspectives on sentence processing* (pp. 359–388). Hillsdale, NJ: Erlbaum.

Pado, U., Crocker, M. W., & Keller, F. (2009). A probabilistic model of semantic plausibility in sentence processing. *Cognitive Science, 39*, 794–838.

Rayner, K., Carlson, M., & Frazier, L. (1983). The interaction of syntax and semantics during sentence processing. *Journal of Verbal Learning and Verbal Behavior, 22*, 358–374.

Rayner, K., & Pollatsek, A. (1989). *The psychology of reading*. Englewood Cliffs, NJ: Prentice Hall.

Roland, D., Dick, F., & Elman, J. L. (2007). Frequency of basic English grammatical structures: A corpus analysis. *Journal of Memory and Language, 57*, 348–379.

Roland, D., & Jurafsky, D. (2002). Verb sense and verb subcategorization probabilities. In S. Stevenson & P. Merlo (Eds.), *The lexical basis of sentence processing: Formal, computational, and experimental issues* (pp. 325–346). Philadelphia, PA: John Benjamins Publishing.

Speer, S. R., Kjelgaard, M. M., & Dobroth, K. M. (1996). The influence of prosodic structure on the resolution of temporary syntactic closure ambiguities. *Journal of Psycholinguistic Research, 25*, 249–271.

Spivey, M. J., & Tanenhaus, M. K. (1998). Syntactic ambiguity resolution in discourse: Modeling the effects of referential context and lexical frequency. *Journal of Experimental Psychology: Learning, Memory and Cognition, 24*, 1521–1543.

Spivey-Knowlton, M. (1994). Quantitative predictions from a constraint-based theory of syntactic ambiguity resolution. In M. C. Mozer, D. S. Touretzky, & P. Smolensky (Eds.), *Proceedings of the 1993 connectionist models summer school* (pp. 130–137). Hillsdale, NJ: Lawrence Erlbaum.

Spivey-Knowlton, M. (1996). Integration of linguistic and visual information: Human data and model simulations. Unpublished doctoral dissertation, University of Rochester.

Spivey-Knowlton, M., & Sedivy, J. (1995). Resolving attachment ambiguities with multiple constraints. *Cognition*, *55*, 227–267.

Spivey-Knowlton, M., Trueswell, J. C., & Tanenhaus, M. K. (1993). Context effects in syntactic ambiguity resolution: Discourse and semantic influences in parsing reduced relative clauses. *Canadian Journal of Experimental Psychology*, *37*, 276–309.

Staub, A. (2007). The parser doesn't ignore intransitivity, after all. *Journal of Experimental Psychology: Learning, Memory, and Cognition*, *33*, 550–569.

Tabor, W., Juliano, C., & Tanenhaus, M. K. (1997). Parsing in a dynamical system: An attractor-based account of the interaction of lexical and structural constraints in sentence processing. *Language and Cognitive Processes*, *12*, 211–271.

Tabor, W., & Tanenhaus, M. K. (2001). Dynamical systems for sentence processing. In M. H. Christiansen & N. Chater (Eds.), *Connectionist psycholinguistics* (pp. 177–211). Westport, CT: Ablex Publishing.

Tanenhaus, M. K., Boland, J. E., Garnsey, S. M., & Carlson, G. N. (1989). Lexical structure in parsing long-distance dependencies. *Journal of Psycholinguistic Research: Special Issue on Sentence Processing*, *18*, 37–50.

Tanenhaus, M. K., & Carlson, G. N. (1989). Lexical structure and language comprehension. In W. Marslen-Wilson (Ed.), *Lexical representation and process* (pp. 529–561). Cambridge, MA: MIT Press.

Tanenhaus, M. K., Spivey-Knowlton, M. J., Eberhard, K. M., & Sedivy, J. E. (1995). Integration of visual and linguistic information in spoken language comprehension. *Science*, *268*, 1632–1634.

Tanenhaus, M. K., Spivey-Knowlton, M. J., & Hanna, J. E. (2000). Modeling thematic and discourse context effects on syntactic ambiguity resolution within a multiple constraints framework: Implications for the architecture of the language processing system. In M. Pickering, C. Clifton, & M. Crocker (Eds.), *Architecture and mechanisms of the language processing system* (pp. 90–118). Cambridge: Cambridge University Press.

Tanenhaus, M. K., & Trueswell, J. C. (1995). Sentence comprehension. In P. Eimas & J. Miller (Eds.), *Handbook in perception and cognition, Volume 11: Speech, language, and communication* (pp. 217–262). San Diego, CA: Academic Press.

Traxler, M. J., Pickering, M. J., & Clifton, C. Jr. (1998). Adjunct attachment is not a form of lexical ambiguity resolution. *Journal of Memory and Language*, *39*, 558–592.

Trueswell, J. C. (1996). The role of lexical frequency in syntactic ambiguity resolution. *Journal of Memory and Language*, *35*, 566–585.

Trueswell, J. C., & Gleitman, L.R. (2004). Children's eye-movements during listening: Evidence for a constraint-based theory of parsing and word learning. In J. M. Henderson & F. Ferreira (Eds.), *Interface of language, vision, and action: Eye-movements and the visual world* (pp. 319–346). New York: Psychology Press.

Trueswell, J. C., Tanenhaus, M. K., & Garnsey, S. (1994). Semantic influences on parsing: Use of thematic role information in syntactic ambiguity resolution. *Journal of Memory and Language*, *33*, 285–318.

Trueswell, J. C., Tanenhaus, M. K., & Kello, K. (1993). Verb-specific constraints in sentence processing: Separating effects of lexical preference from garden-paths. *Journal of Experimental Psychology: Learning, Memory, and Cognition*, *19*, 528–553.

Van Gompel, R. P. G., Pickering, M. J., Pearson, J., & Liversedge, S. P. (2005). Evidence against competition during syntactic ambiguity resolution. *Journal of Memory and Language, 52,* 284–307.

Van Gompel, R. P. G., Pickering, M. J., & Traxler, M. J. (2001). Reanalysis in sentence processing: Evidence against current constraint-based and two-stage models. *Journal of Memory and Language, 45,* 225–258.

Vaughan, J. (1983). Control of fixation duration in visual search and memory search: Another look. *Journal of Experimental Psychology: Human Perception & Performance, 8,* 709–723.

Appendix: Some of the constraints that have been identified and tested

- probabilistic global syntactic biases
    - subject–verb–object (SVO) construction
    - passive constructions

- lexically specific syntactic biases

    - verb subcategorization frames/argument structure

        ○ direct object/sentence complement
        ○ sense-specific verb subcategorization biases
        ○ transitivity biases
        ○ dative alternations
        ○ verb tense probabilities (past tense versus past participle)

    - prepositions (*by, with, on, in*)
    - *that* preferences

- combinatorial preferences

    - verb + preposition (verbed + *by*)
    - psych verb + *with*
    - action verb + *with*
    - verb + *that*

- thematic biases

    - thematic grids: probabilities of thematic roles of a verb
    - verb-general selectional restrictions (e.g., ±animacy as subject or direct object)
    - verb-specific selectional restrictions (e.g., *eat*: ±edible)
    - verb-specific thematic fit (e.g., *cop* versus *crook* as agent or patient of *arrested*)
    - sense-specific thematic fit (e.g., *brakes* versus *spelling* as patient of *mechanic checked* versus *editor checked*)

- physical aspects of speech
  - intonation, prosody, contrastive stress, duration of, e.g., final syllable of a verb

- extra-sentential linguistic context
  - reference
  - pragmatics

- visual context
  - contexts of possible referents
  - depicted actions and relations among characters in a visually presented scene

4 Memory and surprisal in human sentence comprehension

Roger Levy

Introduction

Humboldt famously described language as a system of rules which "makes infinite use of finite means" (Humboldt, 1836; see also Chomsky, 1965), and this is doubly true in the study of language comprehension. On the one hand, the comprehender's knowledge of language must be finitely characterized: the brain itself as a computational device is finite, as is the comprehender's experience of her native language. Hence understanding is an act of generalization: the comprehender must apply the knowledge gleaned from her lifetime of previous linguistic experience to analyze a new sentence and infer what the speaker is likely to have intended to mean. This need for analysis gives rise to the second sense in which Humboldt's aphorism is true: to understand a sentence in real time the comprehender must deploy her limited cognitive resources to analyze input that is potentially unbounded in its complexity. Nowhere are these truths more evident than in the determination of sentence structure during language comprehension, as in (1) below. Before you go on reading, take as much time as you need to fully understand this sentence, and while you are doing so, reflect upon what you find difficult about it. You may even want to write down your reflections on its difficulty so that you can remind yourself of them once you reach the end of the chapter.

(1) Because the girl that the teacher of the class admired didn't call her mother was concerned.

I am confident that you have never encountered this sentence before, but you probably understood it fully with some effort. In order to understand it, you had to correctly construct all the structural relationships it contains: that *girl* is both the subject of *didn't call* and the object of *admired*; that the subject of *admired* is *teacher*; that there is a clause boundary between *call* and *her mother*; that *her mother* is the subject of *was* but not the object of *admired*; and so forth. You have probably encountered few if any sentences with the precise array of structural relationships seen here, but the individual elements are familiar; your ability to understand the sentence at all rests on your ability to put these elements together in novel configurations in real time, despite the occasional difficulty involved.

As this sentence illustrates, although we are generally successful (perhaps remarkably so) in our ability to achieve linguistic understanding in real time, hallmarks of our limited experience and cognitive resources do exist and can be measured: misunderstanding does occur, and even among sentences that are successfully understood, difficulty is differential and localized. That is, not all sentences are equally easy to understand, nor are all parts of a given sentence equally easy to get through. There are two places where you probably found sentence (1) especially difficult: around the word *admired*, where you probably felt uncomfortable with having to keep track of the relationships among the preceding elements *girl*, *teacher*, and *class*; and at the phrase *was concerned*, where you probably were taken aback at encountering the main verb of the sentence without prior warning. By the time we reach the end of this chapter, you will have learned about leading theories of real-time sentence comprehension that account both for your ability to understand sentence (1) and for these sources of difficulty that you may have experienced in doing so.

This chapter thus presents a broad outline of two approaches to understanding these cognitive underpinnings of real-time language comprehension. Each approach is rooted in a deep intuition regarding the nature of limitations in the cognitive resources deployed during sentence understanding. One focuses on *memory*—the use of cognitive resources for storage and retrieval of the representational units used in analysis of linguistic input. The other focuses on *expectations*—the pre-emptive allocation of cognitive resources to various alternatives in the face of uncertainty. In each case, the hypothesis is that the resources in question are sufficiently scarce so as to form a bottleneck in real-time comprehension: over-taxing these resources, either by overloading memory or by presenting the processor with a sufficiently unexpected event, can create measurable disruption in real-time comprehension. Each approach has a rich history in the literature, has been formalized mathematically, and enjoys considerable empirical support. Yet there are cases where the two come into conflict, and their proper resolution remains to be fully understood. In this chapter I begin with memory-based approaches, continue with expectation-based approaches, and then turn to cases where the two come into conflict.

Memory limitations, locality, and interference

The traditional picture of memory limitation in sentence comprehension

The notion of limited memory as a bottleneck on language comprehension dates back to the earliest days of modern psycholinguistics. In the late 1950s, Chomsky introduced the *competence/performance* distinction of knowledge versus patterns of usage of a language, and with it introduced phrase-structure grammars as a formal means of characterizing key aspects of a native speaker's syntactic competence (Chomsky, 1956, 1957). It was immediately recognized, however, that a wide range of sentences generated by linguistically plausible competence grammars could not actually be understood by native speakers, raising questions regarding the relationship between the competence grammars posited by the new generative linguistics and actual linguistic performance. One answer to this problem put forward by George Miller and others (Marks & Miller, 1964; Miller & Chomsky, 1963; Miller & Isard, 1963) was the strong position that competence grammars were essentially faithful characterizations of a speaker's psychological knowledge, but that *performance constraints* interfered with the effective deployment of this competence for some types of sentences. One such type was the *multiply center-embedded* sentence, such as (2) below (Miller & Chomsky 1963; Yngve, 1960):

(2)   This is the malt that the rat that the cat that the dog worried killed ate.

This sentence is simply generated by the repeated application of grammatical rules for forming object-extracted relative clauses, as in (3) below:

(3)   *the dog* worried the cat ⇒ the cat that *the dog* worried

   the cat that the dog worried killed the rat
   ⟺ the rat that *the cat that the dog worried* killed

Despite the straightforwardness of its derivation, however, (2) is extremely difficult to comprehend. That this difficulty cannot be ascribed purely to the complexity of the meaning of the sentence can be seen by comparison with (4) below, which is essentially synonymous but much easier to understand.

(4)   This is the malt that was eaten by the rat that was killed by the cat that was worried by the dog.

The earliest work on this problem (Chomsky & Miller, 1963; Miller & Chomsky, 1963; Yngve, 1960) attributed the difficulty of (2) to the large number of incomplete and nested syntactic relationships that must be maintained partway through the string. Figure 4.1 illustrates the situation for (2), assuming that the comprehender's incremental representation of sentence structure is captured by a left-to-right incrementally expanded context-free tree. After the final instance of *the*, the sentence has reached a fourth level of center-embedding, and a stack of four categories must be kept in memory for faithful completion of the tree when further input is encountered. Yngve (1960) proposed a model in which human incremental language comprehension assigns such incremental structural representations but has severely limited (3 or less) stack depth, making complex center-embedded sentences incomprehensible (see Figure 4.1).

However, it soon became clear that such a straightforward characterization of memory limitation was unworkable (Gibson, 1991; Miller & Chomsky,

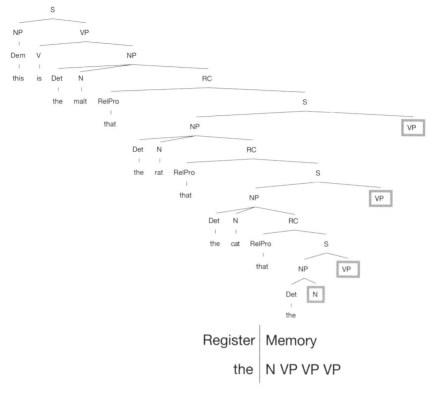

Figure 4.1 Deep inside a multiply center-embedded sentence in the stack-depth model of Yngve (1960).

1963). For one thing, it is empirically the case that processing breakdown seems to happen when the comprehender emerges from the deeply center-embedded structure, around the word *killed*, rather than when the comprehender arrives at the deepest embedding level (Christiansen & MacDonald, 2009; Gibson & Thomas, 1999; Vasishth, Suckow, Lewis, & Kern, 2010). Second, Yngve's strictly top-down model had no good mechanism for explaining how recursively left-branching structures, prevalent in head-final languages such as Japanese, are parsed. Third, the type and arrangement of embedding structures turns out to matter as much as the sheer depth of embedding. A particularly clear example of this latter point can be seen in the contrast of (5) below (the verb–argument dependency arrows drawn in the example will be used later on to describe memory-based analyses of processing difficulty for these examples):

(5)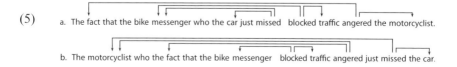

In (5a) an object-extracted relative clause (*who the car just missed*; ORC) is embedded inside a complement clause (*that the bike messenger who the car just missed blocked traffic*; CC). We have the reverse situation in (5b), where a CC is embedded inside an ORC. Gibson and Thomas (1997; see also Cowper, 1976; Gibson, 1991) demonstrated that the CC-inside-ORC variant (5b) is considerably harder to understand than the ORC-inside-CC variant (5a), despite the fact that the depth of phrase-structural center-embedding—two levels—is identical in these cases.

Observations such as these have drawn particular attention to the moments during syntactic comprehension when links between words can be constructed establishing particular aspects of sentence meaning. The key difference between noun-modifying relative and complement clauses is that whereas the former simply involve modification of a noun by a clause that could itself stand alone as an independent sentence, the latter involve **extraction** of a noun phrase (NP), such that proper interpretation requires reconstruction of the relationship between the head noun and the element governing the extraction site (Chomsky, 1981; Pollard & Sag, 1994). Intuitively, an underlying verb–object **dependency** relation needs to be established between *missed* and *bike messenger* in (5a) and between *angered* and *motorcyclist* in (5b), but not between *blocked* and *fact* in either example. Notably, the linear distance between the verb and the object resulting from the extraction is considerably greater for the CC-inside-RC example (*angered* → *motorcyclist* in (5b)) than for the RC-inside-CC example (*missed* → *bike messenger* in (5a)). Furthermore, more noun phrases intervene between the RC verb and its object in (5b) than in (5a).

Two prominent theories of memory in on-line syntactic comprehension have arisen from data of the type described above. One theory is the **dependency locality theory** (DLT, also called syntactic prediction locality theory; Gibson, 1998, 2000; Grodner & Gibson, 2005), which deals with the integrations between elements in a sentence (in practice, usually word–word dependencies), as well as with expectations for those integrations. In DLT, there are two types of costs that can be incurred during processing of part of a sentence: the **integration** cost incurred during the establishment of the dependencies between the currently processed word(s) and earlier parts of the sentence; and the **storage** cost incurred for maintaining representations of incomplete dependencies that will be completed later in the sentence. In the theory, integration costs are larger (i) the more new dependencies are constructed at once and (ii) the more material intervening between the governor and governed elements of each dependency. Hence DLT is able to capture the pattern seen in (5). At the word *angered* in (5b), two dependencies must be constructed simultaneously: one between *angered* and its object, *motorcyclist* (with three intervening nouns—*fact*, *bike messenger*, and *traffic*), and another between *angered* and its subject, *fact* (with two intervening nouns—*bike messenger* and *traffic*). In (5a), there is no corresponding word requiring such a complex set of simultaneous integrations: at each verb where two integrations are required, at least one of the governed NPs is linearly adjacent.

A range of other evidence has also been adduced in support of the integration component of DLT, particularly from the comprehension of different types of relative clauses (e.g., Warren & Gibson, 2002; Hsiao & Gibson, 2003; Gordon, Hendrick, & Johnson 2004; and see below). One of the best-known examples is the asymmetry in comprehension difficulty of SRCs versus ORCs in English when both the head noun and the RC-internal NP are animate, as in (6) below:

(6) a. The reporter who attacked the senator left the room.
     b. The reporter who the senator attacked left the room.

The integration cost at the RC verb *attacked* is greater in the ORC (6b) than in the SRC (6a), since in the ORC there are two preceding dependents that must simultaneously be integrated, one of which is not adjacent to the verb; whereas in the SRC the dependents are integrated one by one—in (6a), the dotted line reflects the fact that when *attacked* is processed *the senator* has not yet been seen and thus is not yet integrated—and each is adjacent to the verb. The greater processing difficulty of such ORCs has been demonstrated empirically in many studies (Ford, 1983; Gordon, Hendrick, & Johnson, 2001; Grodner & Gibson, 2005; King & Just, 1991; Wanner & Maratsos, 1978; inter alia). Evidence for the storage component is scarcer, though see Chen, Gibson, and Wolf (2005); Gibson, Desmet, Grodner, Watson, and Ko (2005); Grodner, Gibson, & Tunstall (2002); and Nakatani and Gibson (2010) for published studies. We will return to the study of Grodner et al. (2002) shortly.

The second theory has many qualitative similarities to DLT, but differs in focusing more exclusively on the integration component of comprehension, and in placing greater emphasis on grounding the content of integration operations in influential theories of working memory within cognitive psychology, specifically theories of **content-addressable** memory with **cue-based recall**. In the most explicit instantiations of such a theory (Lewis & Vasishth, 2005; Lewis, Vasishth, & Van Dyke, 2006), the parser has no explicit representation of linear order of preceding input, including the relative priority of preceding sites of potential syntactic attachment (contrasting with theories such as Yngve's; Figure 4.1). Rather, an incremental, tree-structured representation of the sentence thus far is stored in content-addressible memory, and in order to construct new dependencies between the currently processed word and preceding content, the current word serves as a cue for recall of the appropriate integration site(s). In the SRC of (6a) above, for example, upon reading the word *attacked* the parser must retrieve the representation of *reporter* from content-addressable memory in order to link it as the argument of the current word.

One crucial component of the cue-based recall theory is that representations of all preceding syntactic items stored in working memory compete with one another during retrieval. Two factors affect the ease of retrieval of the correct (**target**) unit. First, retrieval is easier the better the match between the features of the cue and target, relative to the degree of match between the features of the cue and other, non-target, items in working memory. Second, in some variants (Lewis & Vasishth, 2005; Lewis et al., 2006), retrieval is easier the greater the **activation level** of the target item relative to the activation level of other, non-target items: items have a high activation level when first encoded in memory, and while that activation decays over time, every retrieval boosts the item's activation. The theory thus predicts the same differential difficulty effect observed in the English SRC/ORC contrast of (6) and predicted by the DLT. In (6b), as in (6a), one of the operations that has to take place at the RC verb *attacked* is retrieval of the representation of the head noun *reporter* and construction of a dependency of the appropriate type between it and the verb. In (6b), however, unlike in (6a), another noun—*senator*—is already encoded in memory, and successful retrieval requires correct association of these nouns with the subject and object roles for *attacked* respectively. The semantic similarity of the two nouns leads to high retrieval interference, slowing processing and even creating the possibility of misretrieval—that is, interpreting the RC as semantically reversed (as *the reporter attacked the senator*). The predictions of the cue-based recall theory in terms of on-line processing effects thus match those of the DLT, with greater reading times predicted at *attacked* in (6b) than in (6a).

Predictions of the cue-based theory and the DLT diverge, however, for cases such as below:

(7)   The movie that the director watched received a prize.

For the DLT, the RC verbs in (7) and (6b) incur exactly the same integration costs, since they both involve integrating two dependents with the same distances. In the cue-based recall theory, however, two factors make argument retrieval at the RC verb easier in than in (7): first, *movie* and *director* are less semantically similar than *reporter* and *senator*, making their memory representations more distinct; second, the properties of *movie* do not match the retrieval cues for the subject position of *watched*, since only animate entities can perform watching. This difference in predicted processing difficulty was confirmed by Traxler, Morris, and Seely (2002).

Applications beyond center-embedding difficulty

Although the study of memory limitation in on-line sentence comprehension has its roots in processing difficulty and breakdown effects associated with unambiguous center-embedding and retrieval difficulty, the resulting theories have been applied to a considerably wider variety of phenomena. Gibson (1991), for example, introduced the idea that syntactic ambiguity resolution in on-line comprehension might attempt to minimize memory storage costs due to unfulfilled syntactic expectations of the sort encoded in the DLT. One study exploring such an idea is Grodner et al. (2002), who examined sentences like (8) below.

(8) a. The river which the valley (that was) captured by the enemy contains has its source at a glacier. **[RC]**

 b. The commander knows that the valley (that was) captured by the enemy contains a river. **[SC]**

According to DLT in both cases, when *the valley* is processed there is an expectation generated for an upcoming verb for which it is the subject. Further downstream, when the words *that was* are absent (the **ambiguous** variants) there is a temporary syntactic ambiguity at *captured* between a finite-verb interpretation (e.g., *The river which the valley captured the sunlight reflecting off of was flowing quickly*) and a reduced-relative interpretation (as in (8a)). On the finite-verb interpretation, *captured* completes the upcoming-verb expectation generated earlier, but on the reduced-relative interpretation this expectation remains unmet. Hence the reduced-relative interpretation imposes a higher memory-storage cost than the finite-verb interpretation. But as we already saw in analysis of (5), the RC context of itself is more memory-intensive than the SC context of (8b). Thus, if comprehenders avoid especially memory-intensive interpretations—as the RC context combined with the reduced-relative interpretation would lead to—the finite-verb interpretation should be more strongly preferred in the ambiguous variant of (8a) than in the ambiguous variant of (8b). Indeed, Grodner et al. found an interaction between ambiguity and embedded-clause type at the critical region *by the enemy*, which disambiguates the structure toward a reduced relative interpretation; reading times were superadditively greatest in the ambiguous RC condition, suggesting that the RC context may indeed induce comprehenders to entertain a finite-verb analysis of *captured* (though see further discussion under "Conflicting predictions between expectations and memory").

Let us turn now to interference-based theories and a distinctive type of prediction they make, involving cases where preceding context may make retrieval of preceding dependents at a verb not only difficult but even inaccurate. Here I briefly outline two examples. Wagers, Lau, and Phillips (2009) have applied interference-based theory in the study of agreement attraction in on-line comprehension. To explain the phenomenon of agreement attraction, which has been studied primarily in the sentence production literature, consider example (9) below.

(9) a. The key to the cabinets were rusty from many years of disuse. **[ungrammatical, +attractor]**

(9) b. The key to the cabinet were rusty from many years of disuse. **[ungrammatical, −attractor]**

Each of these sentences contains an agreement "error" in which the number marking on the finite verb *were* fails to match the number of the subject NP, which is determined by the head noun of the subject, in this case *key*. Agreement attraction is the phenomenon of errors of the type in sentence (9a), where the verb's number marking matches the number of some noun (the **attractor**, here *cabinets*) other than the true head of the subject, being more common than errors of the type in sentence (9b) (Bock & Miller, 1991; Eberhard, 1999; Eberhard, Cutting, & Bock, 2005; Franck, Vigliocco, & Nicol, 2002; Vigliocco & Nicol, 1998; inter alia). One of the leading theories from the field of language production is that attraction effects arise from **percolation** of agreement features from within a complex NP (here, plural number from *cabinets*) up to the NP head, leading to incorrect representation of the subject NP's number.

In the comprehension literature, Pearlmutter, Garnsey, and Bock (1999) had previously found that plural attractors effectively weakened the precision of comprehenders' on-line assessment of subject–verb agreement. Reading times immediately after the verb in both (9a) and (9b) are inflated compared with singular-verb variants (*was* instead of *were*), but plural attractors reduce the reading-time penalty. The percolation theory of the sentence-production literature can explain the results of Pearlmutter et al. in comprehension: if the comprehender misrepresents the number of the complex NP *the key to the cabinets*, then this might lead to failure to identify the agreement anomaly when the correct syntactic relationship between *were* and the preceding subject NP is constructed. Wagers et al. (2009), however, showed that attraction can equally affect comprehension of verbs inside relative clauses, using sentences such as (10) below:

(10) a. The musician who the reviewer praise so highly will probably win a Grammy.

b. The musicians who the reviewer praise so highly will probably win a Grammy.

Reading times immediately after the RC verb *praise* in (10b) are deflated relative to those in (10a), suggesting that plural marking on the RC head noun can reduce the strength of the anomaly experienced at a singular verb whose subject is an RC-internal singular NP (a similar acceptability pattern was first reported by Kimball and Aissen, 1971). This result is not explained by the percolation theory, because the plural noun (*musicians*) is not inside the RC subject (*the reviewer*), and thus upward percolation of the plural feature would not lead to an incorrect representation of the RC subject's number. As Wagers et al. describe, in an interference-based framework this pattern could arise from the possibility of incorrect retrieval of the RC head for the subject slot of the RC verb, which would result in failure to detect the subject–verb number mismatch. That is, under the interpretation of Wagers et al. the number mismatch may lead to an incorrect syntactic relationship being entertained or even established between *praise* and *reviewers*. Although these results cannot themselves adjudicate completely between theories in which the true subject's number features are incorrectly represented and theories in which the wrong NP is retrieved for the verb's subject slot, they speak to the ability of interference-based theories to make testable predictions regarding on-line comprehension difficulty ranging over a wide variety of syntactic configurations.[1]

A second example relates to the understanding of local coherence effects, where a grammatical analysis that would be available for a substring of a sentence only when that substring is taken in isolation seems to compete with the global grammatical analysis:

(12) a. The coach smiled at the player *tossed* the frisbee.

b. The coach smiled at the player *thrown* the frisbee.

In (12a), *the player tossed* would be analyzable in isolation as the onset of an independent clause with *the player* as the subject and *tossed* as the main verb, but that analysis is inconsistent with the grammatical context set up by the rest of the sentence. This is not an issue in (12b) as the *thrown* does not have the part-of-speech ambiguity that allows it to serve as a finite verb. Tabor, Galantucci, and Richardson (2004) showed that reading times were greater starting at this critical verb in sentences like (12a) as compared with (12b), and argued for a model in which bottom-up and top-down syntactic analysis took place simultaneously and could thus come into conflict (see also Bicknell & Levy, 2009, for a Bayesian variant of such a model).[2]

Van Dyke (2007), however, points out that an interference-based model such as that of Lewis and Vasishth (2005) can accommodate local-coherence effects, since *the player* might sometimes be incorrectly picked out by the subject-retrieval cues of *tossed*. Van Dyke goes on to show examples where a match between a verb's retrieval cues and an NP that is not immediately adjacent can induce similar processing difficulty, as in (13) (see also Van Dyke & Lewis, 2003, for related studies):

(13) The worker was surprised that the resident who said that *the warehouse/neighbor* was dangerous was complaining about the investigation.

Here, differential processing difficulty begins at the region *was complaining*, with greater difficulty when the sentence contains *the neighbor* than when it contains *the warehouse*. This result suggests that when the preceding NP matches the semantic requirements made by the main-clause verb on its subject, it is sometimes entertained as the subject of the main-clause verb even though neither the global nor the local syntactic context would license such an analysis.

Expectation-based comprehension and surprisal

Equally fundamental as the intuition that memory limitations affect on-line sentence comprehension is the intuition that a language user's context-derived expectations regarding how a sentence may continue can dramatically affect how language comprehension unfolds in real time. Among the best-known early demonstrations of this phenomenon are the shadowing studies pioneered by Marslen-Wilson (1975), who demonstrated that listeners continuously repeating back speech they hear with lags as short as a quarter-second are biased to correct disrupted words; for example, when shadowing *He's departing the day after tomorrane* the listener might correct the final word to *tomorrow*, but only when the corrected form of the word was syntactically and semantically consistent with context. This result indicated the extreme rapidity with which comprehenders use context to constrain the interpretation of new linguistic input—in this case, recognition of a word's identity.

Since then, the known empirical scope of this biasing effect of context-derived expectation has expanded in two key respects. First, it is now known that correct expectations increase the *rate* at which novel input is processed. Ehrlich and Rayner (1981) demonstrated that words which are strongly predicted by their preceding context, as measured by the "fill in the blank" Cloze completion method (Taylor, 1953), are read more quickly than unpredictable words. Hence, of the two contexts

(14) a. The boat passed easily under the _____

 b. Rita slowly walked down the shaky _____

the word strongly predicted for context (14a) is read more quickly in that context than in (14b).[3] Analogous signatures of correctly matched expectations can also be found in EEG responses during on-line sentence comprehension (Kutas & Hillyard, 1980, 1984; see also Van Berkum, Brown, Zwitserlood, Kooijman, & Hagoort, 2005; DeLong, Urbach, & Kutas, 2005; and Wicha, Moreno, & Kutas, 2004, for more recent evidence). Second, it is now known that incremental discrimination among alternative analyses of structurally ambiguous input is exquisitely sensitive to both linguistic and non-linguistic context. To take a well-known example, as the sentence onset *Put the apple on the towel . . .* is uttered, the listener's interpretation of *on the towel* (is it describing which apple to move, or where to put the apple?) is strongly influenced by how many apples are present in a visible physical array (Tanenhaus, Spivey-Knowlton, Eberhard, & Sedivy, 1995; see also Altmann & Kamide, 1999; MacDonald, 1993; Trueswell, Tanenhaus, & Garnsey, 1994, among others; see also Spivey, Anderson, & Farmer, this volume). In the 1990s, two classes of computational models were proposed which had a lot to say about how diverse information sources influenced ambiguity resolution: constraint-based models inspired by neural networks (McRae, Spivey-Knowlton, & Tanenhaus, 1998; Spivey & Tanenhaus, 1998; and Tabor & Tanenhaus, 1999; see also McRae & Matsuki, this volume) and probabilistic grammar-based disambiguation models (Crocker & Brants, 2000; Jurafsky, 1996; Narayanan & Jurafsky, 1998, 2002). Because these models covered only resolution of ambiguity in the grammatical analysis of input that had already been seen, however, they had little to say about expectation-derived processing speedups in examples like (14) above, or about the rich set of syntactic-complexity effects found in what are for the most part structurally unambiguous situations (see above, "Memory limitations, locality, and interference").

Surprisal

In 2001, however, Hale, drawing inspiration from Attneave (1959), proposed a quantification of the cognitive effort required to process a word in a sentence—the **surprisal** of the word in the context it appears—which has raised prospects for a unified treatment of structural ambiguity resolution and prediction-derived processing benefits. Surprisal (sometimes called "Shannon information content" in the information theory literature) is defined simply as the log of the inverse of the probability of an event; in the case of a word w_i in a sentence following words $w_1, \ldots, w_{i-1}$) and in extra-sentential context C, the surprisal is thus simply

$$\log \frac{1}{P(w_i | w_1, \ldots, w_{i-1}, C)} \qquad (1)$$

Hale focused on the framing of incremental sentence comprehension as the step-by-step disconfirmation of possible phrase-structural analyses for the sentence, leading to an interpretation of the cognitive load imposed by a word as "the combined difficulty of disconfirming all disconfirmable structures at a given word." On that view, surprisal emerges as a natural metric of word-by-word cognitive load on the assumption that more probable structures are more work to disconfirm (see below, "Theoretical justifications for surprisal," for greater discussion of this assumption).

Surprisal and garden-path disambiguation

Hale (2001) and Levy (2008a) cover a range of psycholinguistic phenomena which can be successfully analyzed within the surprisal framework ranging from classic instances of garden-path disambiguation (*the horse raced past the barn fell*; Bever, 1970) to processing benefits when ambiguity is left unresolved (Traxler, Pickering, & Clifton, 1998; Van Gompel & Pickering, 2001; Van Gompel, Pickering, Pearson, & Liversedge, 2005) to syntactic-expectation-based facilitation in unambiguous contexts (see section on "Constrained syntactic contexts").To give the reader a more concrete picture of how surprisal can simultaneously account for both empirically observed syntactic-processing effects which involve disambiguation and effects which do not, I provide here a novel and fairly explicit illustration of how probabilistic grammatical analysis can be combined with surprisal to derive predictions for a well-studied construction which turns out to exhibit both types of effects. Example (15) from Staub (2007) below serves as a starting point:

(15) When the dog scratched the vet and his new assistant removed the muzzle.[4]

Garden-path disambiguation is an important feature of this sentence: the phrase *the vet and his new assistant* creates a temporary structural ambiguity: this phrase could be the object NP of the subordinate-clause verb *scratched*; or it could be the subject NP of the main clause, in which case *scratched* would have no overt object (Adams, Clifton, & Mitchell, 1998; Clifton, 1993; Ferreira & Henderson, 1990; Frazier & Rayner, 1982; Mitchell, 1987; Pickering & Traxler, 1998; Staub, 2007; Sturt, Pickering, & Crocker, 1999; Van Gompel & Pickering, 2001). Intuitively, the preferred initial interpretation is as the object of *scratched*, which is globally incorrect; the strongest disambiguatory evidence comes at the main-clause verb *removed*. The measurable real-time correlate of this disambiguation effect was first demonstrated by Frazier and Rayner (1982), who showed that the amount of time that the eyes linger upon the disambiguating material is elevated in cases like (15) when compared with cases such as (16), below, in which the presence of either an overt NP object of *scratched* (*its owner* in (16a)) or a comma marking the end of the subordinate clause (16b) facilitates the initial interpretation of the following NP as the main-clause subject:

(16) a. When the dog scratched its owner the vet and his new assistant removed the muzzle.

b. When the dog scratched, the vet and his new assistant removed the muzzle.

How can the relative difficulty of (15) be captured in a framework of sentence comprehension as probabilistic grammar-based inference? Table 4.1, below, illustrates a small probabilistic context-free grammar (PCFG; Booth, 1969; Manning & Schütze, 1999) which includes the grammatical rules necessary to cover both the garden-path and globally correct interpretations of examples (15) and (16). Intuitively, a PCFG both states what grammatical structures are possible (determined by the set of rules in the grammar) and distinguishes the relative likelihood of different possible grammatical structures (with more likely grammatical structures given higher probability values).[5] The syntactic categories and style of phrase structure rule used here are chosen to roughly conform to those used in the Penn Treebank (Marcus, Santorini, & Marcinkiewicz, 1994), the most widely used syntactically annotated corpus in computational linguistics. The probabilities in this grammar are chosen by hand for expository purposes, but they reflect two important facts about the distributions of the relevant constructions in naturalistic English text: first, verb phrases can be either transitive or intransitive (reflected in the presence of both VP → V NP and VP → V rules); second, most but not all sentence-initial subordinate clauses are delimited on the right by a comma (reflected in the high probability of the SBAR → COMPL S COMMA rule).

To understand how probabilistic syntactic knowledge and incremental comprehension interact to yield garden-path disambiguation effects within the surprisal framework, let us consider the probability distribution over incremental parses of the pre-disambiguation sentence prefixes shown in (17) below:

(17) a. When the dog scratched the vet and his new assistant . . .

b. When the dog scratched its owner the vet and his new assistant . . .

In (17a), the PCFG of Table 4.1 makes two incremental parses available, shown in Figure 4.2. These trees are "incremental" in the sense that, aside from nodes strictly dominating input that have already been seen, only nodes that can be inferred with probability 1 are indicated. To explain how inference about a sentence's syntactic structure arises from the application of probabilistic grammars, we introduce a bit of notation: let $w_{1...i}$ denote the sentence thus far (up to the current word w_i) and let the variable T denote some incremental syntactic parse that is logically possible given the grammar and the sentence thus far. The probability of each incremental parse T can be computed using Bayes's Rule, a basic theorem of probability theory, according to which we can say that

$$P(T|w_{1...i}) = \frac{P(T)}{P(w_{1...i})} \qquad (2)$$

That is, the probability of a particular parse T given the string observed thus far is equal to the probability assigned to the parse by the grammar, divided by the total probability of the partial sentence seen thus far.[6] Thus, only parses consistent with the grammar are permitted, and among them, those with higher probability given by the grammar are preferred over those with lower probability. When these computations are applied to the examples in Figure 4.2, we find that the tree in which *the vet and his new assistant* is interpreted as the direct object of *scratched* has probability 0.826, and the tree in which it is interpreted as the main-clause subject has probability 0.174.[7] In (17b), by contrast, only the main-clause subject interpretation is available (with probability 1) for *the vet and his new assistant*, due to the presence of *its owner* as the direct object of *scratched*. With respect to the probabilities assigned to incremental interpretations of a sentence, surprisal theory is thus quite similar to the pruning and attention-shift theories of garden-path disambiguation (Jurafsky, 1996; Narayanan & Jurafsky, 1998, 2002; and Crocker & Brants, 2000).

Table 4.1 A small PCFG for the sentences in section on surprisal and garden-path disambiguation

Rule			Prob.	Rule			Prob.	Rule			Prob.
S	→	SBAR S	0.3	Conj	→	and	1	Adj	→	new	1
S	→	NP VP	0.7	Det	→	the	0.8	VP	→	V NP	0.5
SBAR	→	COMPL S	0.3	Det	→	its	0.1	VP	→	V	0.5
SBAR	→	COMPL S COMMA	0.7	Det	→	his	0.1	V	→	scratched	0.25
COMPL	→	When	1	N	→	dog	0.2	V	→	removed	0.25
NP	→	Det N	0.6	N	→	vet	0.2	V	→	arrived	0.5
NP	→	Det Adj N	0.2	N	→	assistant	0.2	COMMA	→	,	1
NP	→	NP Conj NP	0.2	N	→	muzzle	0.2				
				N	→	owner	0.2				

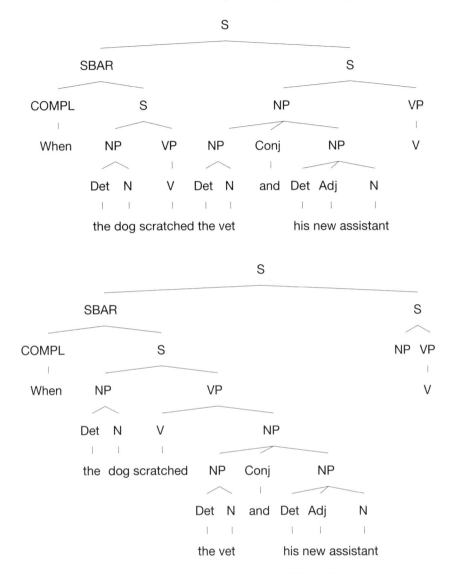

Figure 4.2 The two incremental analyses for sentence (15) pre-disambiguation.

Within the simplest version of surprisal theory, however, the garden-path disambiguation effect itself arises not from complete loss of the correct analysis but from the comprehender's need to hedge her predictive bets regarding how the sentence may continue. Let us ask, given that after processing the word *assistant* the two structures of Figure 4.2 are maintained with the probabilities just stated, how likely is it that the next word of the sentence is the word *removed*? According to the laws of probability theory, both structures contribute

94 Roger Levy

to predicting how likely *removed* is to be the next word in the sentence, but the more likely structure plays a larger role in determining the strength of the prediction. Under the main-clause subject analysis, the conditional probability of *removed* being the next word is 0.2^8; under the direct-object analysis, the conditional probability is 0 since a verb cannot appear until after a main-clause subject has been encountered. The surprisal of *removed* is simply the weighted average of these two probabilities:[9]

$$P(w_{11} = \text{removed} | w_{i...10}) = 0.2 \times 0.174 + 0 \times 0.826 \quad (3)$$
$$= 0.0348$$

so the surprisal is $\log_2 0.0348 = 4.85$ bits. The corresponding surprisal for (17b), in which the incremental syntactic analysis was unambiguously main-clause subject, is $\log_2 0.2 = 2.32$ bits (Table 4.2). Hence surprisal theory correctly predicts the difference in processing difficulty due to this case of garden-pathing.

It is worth noting in this example grammar that no distinction is made between transitive and intransitive verbs. However, Mitchell (1987) and Van Gompel and Pickering (2001) (see also Staub, 2007) provided relevant evidence by comparing reading of sentences like (15) with sentences like (18) with intransitive subordinate-clause verbs.

(18)   When the dog arrived the vet and his new assistant removed the muzzle.

These studies in fact revealed two interesting effects. First, early reading times at the main-clause verb (*removed* in this case) were elevated for transitive as compared with intransitive subordinate-clause verb sentences. This is precisely the effect predicted by incremental disambiguation models in which fine-grained information sources are used rapidly: before encountering the main-clause verb, the comprehender is already much more committed to a main-clause analysis when the subordinate-clause verb is intransitive. Equally interesting, however, early reading times at the onset of the potentially ambiguous NP (*the vet* in this case) were lower for transitive as compared with intransitive subordinate-clause verb sentences. This effect is not obviously predicted by all incremental disambiguation models using fine-grained information sources; the constraint-based model of Spivey and Tanenhaus (1998) and McRae et al. (1998), for example, which predict processing slow-downs when a structural ambiguity is encountered and relative preferences for the alternative interpretations need to be determined, might well predict greater difficulty at the ambiguous-NP onset in the transitive case, since there is a true structural ambiguity only when the preceding verb is transitive.[10]

To understand the predictions of surprisal in this situation, let us refine our grammar very slightly by explicitly distinguishing between transitive and intransitive verbs. We do so by replacing the portion of the grammar of Table 4.1 that mentions the verb category (V) with a finer-grained variant:

VP	→	V NP	0.5		VP	→	Vtrans NP	0.45
VP	→	V	0.5	Replaced by ⇒	VP	→	Vtrans	0.05
V	→	scratched	0.25		VP	→	Vintrans	0.45
V	→	removed	0.25		VP	→	Vintrans NP	0.05
V	→	arrived	0.5		Vtrans	→	scratched	0.5
					Vtrans	→	removed	0.5
					Vintrans	→	arrived	1

In essence, the revision to the grammar says that verbs come in two varieties: transitive (*scratched* and *removed*) and intransitive (*arrived*); transitive verbs usually have a right-sister NP (but not always); intransitive verbs rarely have a right-sister NP (but not never; e.g., *arrived the night before*). For this revised grammar, surprisals at the ambiguous-NP onset and the disambiguating verb can be found in Table 4.2. The disambiguating verb is more surprising when the subordinate-clause verb was transitive (*scratched*) than when it was intransitive (*arrived*), reflecting the stronger preceding commitment to the incorrect analysis held in the transitive case. Furthermore, the ambiguous-NP onset is more surprising in the *intransitive* case. This latter effect may be less intuitively obvious: it reflects the fact in the intransitive case, the comprehender must resort to a low-probability grammatical rule to account for the ambiguous-NP onset—either the intransitive verb has an NP right sister or a subordinate clause without a final comma. Hence under surprisal theory the simple act of encoding verb transitivity into a probabilistic grammar accounts for both of the processing differentials observed by Staub (2007).

Of course, one may reasonably object that this result obtained by a hand-constructed PCFG might not generalize once a **broad-coverage** grammar with rule probabilities reflecting naturalistic usage is adopted—contemporary probabilistic parsers have rules numbering in the tens of thousands, not in the dozens as in the small PCFGs here (Charniak, 1996). Thus Figure 4.3 reports region-by-region surprisals alongside the first-pass time results of Staub (2007) using a grammar obtained from the entire parsed Brown corpus (Kučera & Francis, 1967; Marcus et al., 1994) using "vanilla" PCFG estimation (Charniak,

Table 4.2 Surprisals at ambiguity resolution in (16) and (16a), and at ambiguity onset and resolution in (17), using small PCFG

Original PCFG		*Transitivity-distinguishing PCFG*		
Condition	Resolution	Condition	Ambiguity onset	Resolution
NP absent	4.85	Intransitive (arrived)	2.11	3.20
NP present	2.32	Transitive (scratched)	0.44	8.04

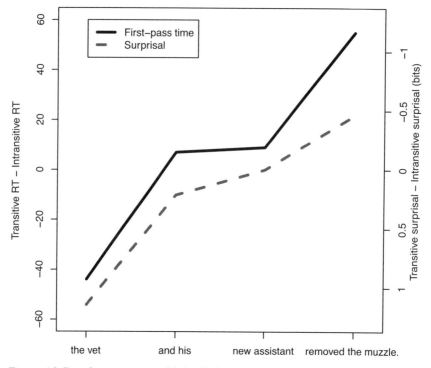

Figure 4.3 Broad-coverage transitivity-distinguishing PCFG assessed on (17).

1996; Levy, 2008a). Because the parsed Brown corpus does not mark verb transitivity, I added the single refinement of distinguishing between verbs which do and do not have an immediate right-sister NP; the resulting grammar has 11,984 rules. With such a grammar there are a huge number of incremental parses that are possible for most partial-sentence inputs, so exact analysis is not as simple as for the small grammar of Table 4.1. Nevertheless, algorithms from computational linguistics can be used to compute word-by-word surprisals for such a large grammar (Jelinek & Lafferty, 1991; Stolcke, 1995). As can be seen in Figure 4.3, broad-coverage surprisal correctly predicts the two reliable differences in first-pass times: those at the onset of the main-clause subject NP, which does not itself involve garden-path disambiguation; and those at the main-clause verb, which does.[11]

Theoretical justifications for surprisal

Another development since Hale's (2001) original proposal has been work justifying surprisal as a metric for on-line processing difficulty within the context of rational cognitive models (Anderson, 1990; Shepard, 1987; Tenenbaum & Griffiths, 2001). Here I briefly describe three such justifications in the literature. First, Levy (2008a) posed the view of surprisal as a measure of **re-ranking cost**. In this approach, the problem of incremental disambiguation is framed as one of allocating limited resources (which correspond to probability mass in probabilistic frameworks) to the possible analyses of the sentence. In this view, the processing difficulty of a word w could be taken to be the size of the shift in the resource allocation (equivalently, in the conditional probability distribution over interpretations) induced by w. Levy (2008a) showed that under highly general conditions in which possible joint word-sequence/interpretation structures are specified by a generative probabilistic grammar, the size of this shift induced by w, as measured by the **relative entropy** (Cover & Thomas, 1991) between the conditional distributions over interpretations before and after seeing w is also the surprisal of w. This re-ranking-cost interpretation is extremely close to Hale's original intuition of processing difficulty as being the work done in disconfirming possible structures.

The other two justifications are distinctive in explicitly modeling the comprehender as a **rational** agent—that is, one which makes decisions which optimize its expected effectiveness in operating in its environment—and in directly confronting the problem of how much *time* a rational agent would spend processing each word of a sentence in its context. One justification involves a focus on **optimal perceptual discrimination**, and is particularly well suited to the problem of analyzing motor control in reading. In many theories of reading (Engbert, Nuthmann, Richter, & Kliegl, 2005; Reichle, Pollatsek, Fisher, & Rayner, 1998; Reilly & Radach, 2006), **lexical access**—identifying the word currently attended to, retrieving its representation from memory, and integrating it into the context—is posited to be a key bottleneck in the overall process of reading a sentence. Formalizing this notion of a lexical-access bottleneck turns out to lead naturally to surprisal as an index of incremental processing difficulty. A simple formalization is given for the isolated word-recognition case by Norris (2006, 2009): before encountering any word, the reader has a set of expectations as to what that word may be. What it means to process a word is to accrue noisy perceptual samples from the word; in general, these samples will gradually guide the reader toward correctly recognizing the word. A simple decision rule for the comprehender is to collect input samples until some predetermined threshold of certainty is surpassed, after which the comprehender can confidently commit to the word's identity and move on. This formulation casts word recognition as a **sequential probability ratio test**, an old problem whose psychological applications date back to Stone (1960; see also Laming, 1968). Mathematical analysis reveals that it is equivalent to a directed random walk in the space of possible word identities, with the average step size toward the correct word identity being approximately constant in log-probability. The starting position of this random walk is simply the word's surprisal, hence the expected time to decision threshold is linear in log-probability. Figure 4.4 illustrates example outcomes of this random walk for different surprisal values; note that as word surprisal increases (smaller values on the y-axis), smaller changes in raw starting probability are needed to obtain similar changes in the amount

(a) Single instance of a random walk

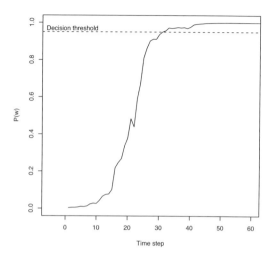

(b) Average posterior probability

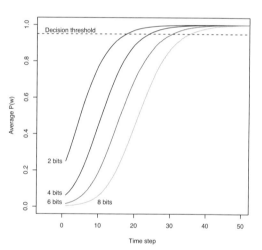

(c) Distribution of times to decision threshold

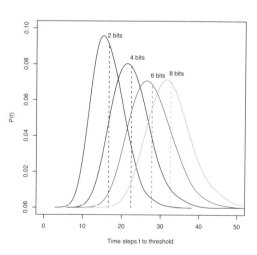

of time needed to reach threshold. The only enhancement to this model required to account for sentence-level reading is to make the comprehender's prior expectations for a word's identity depend on context, as we saw how to do in the previous section (see Bicknell & Levy, 2010, 2012, for recent work using such a model).

The other rational-analysis justification is of **optimal preparation**, introduced by Smith and Levy (2008, submitted). In this approach, one makes the assumption that *some* time-consuming mental computations are required to integrate a word into its context during comprehension; specific commitments as to the type of computation are not required. The time required for a computation is a quantity that can be chosen by the rational agent; it is assumed that shorter times require greater investment of some kind of cognitive resources (these could range from short-term attention to the long-term devotion of specialized neural pathways), but are also of benefit to the agent in comprehension. This sets up a cost–benefit tradeoff between, on the one hand, investment of resources in the possible inputs that could be encountered in a sentence, and on the other hand, the uncertain payoff obtained from greater processing efficiency on the input that is actually encountered. When this tradeoff is combined with a *scale-free* assumption that the optimal cost–benefit balance is independent of the granularity (e.g., at the level of phrases, words, or syllables) at which investments are made, it results in the prediction that the optimal resource allocation will lead to processing times linear in the log-probability of the event.

Conflicting predictions between expectations and memory

Because memory- and expectation-based approaches to comprehension difficulty are each supported by deep intuition, theoretical formalization, and a range of empirical results, it is of great interest to examine the degree of overlap in their empirical coverage. In many types of syntactic configurations investigated in the sentence-processing literature, the two approaches make similar predictions regarding differential processing difficulty. As just one example, the pattern of garden-path disambiguation observed by Grodner et al. (2002) in examples like (8) was explained under DLT as a stronger preference to avoid syntactically complex analysis of new input (a reduced relative clause) when memory load is already high (inside a relative clause) than when memory load

---

Figure 4.4 (facing page) Surprisal as optimal perceptual discrimination. As time accrues and the word-recognition system accrues more perceptual samples from the current word, the probability of the correct word rises gradually until a decision threshold is reached; changes to raw posterior log-probability accrue more slowly when far from the decision boundary (a). A word's average posterior probability follows a smooth curve (b), and increase in mean time to recognition (c, dashed lines) is nearly constant in the word's surprisal. Note that since recognition times are skewed (c, solid lines), mean recognition time is greater than modal time.

is lower (inside a sentential complement). This pattern turns out to be predicted under expectation-based disambiguation accounts such as surprisal for two reasons. First, in English RC postmodifiers of embedded-clause subjects (*the valley* in (8)) are simply less common when the embedded clause itself is an RC (the conditional probabilities are less than 0.5 percent versus 1–2 percent respectively based on estimates from the Penn Treebank). This consideration leads to the same predictions as do memory-based theories for processing of these structures. Second, the head noun (*valley*) in the RC structure creates a source of expectation for the embedded-clause verb, but in this case the expectation is violated in the RC variant relative to the SC variant (in essence, *captured* is not the verb one expects to have both *river* as its object and *valley* as its subject). Hence *captured* is especially surprising in the ambiguous variant of (8a), which could account for the processing difficulty observed by Grodner et al. (2002).[12] More generally, syntactic configurations which place a heavy load on working memory according to the theories covered in the section on "Memory limitations, locality, and interference" seem to be rare—especially in English (Gildea & Temperley, 2007)—so expectation-based theories predict that they are surprising and thus hard to process.

Constrained syntactic contexts

There are also situations where the two approaches can be put into fairly stark conflict. Particular attention has been paid in this regard to **syntactically constrained contexts**. These are contexts which allow a comprehender to infer that a grammatical event of some type X will occur at some point in future input, but the comprehender is uncertain about exactly when X will occur, and by what surface input (e.g., which word) X will be instantiated. This situation is schematized in Figure 4.5b. Consider a situation with more dependents preceding X (Figure 4.5b), as compared with a situation with fewer dependents preceding X (Figure 4.5a). For memory-based theories, processing of X should be more difficult in the case with more dependents, due to the greater number of integrations, greater distance from X of early dependents, and/or potential interference among dependents during retrieval. For expectation-based theories, on the other hand, the additional information obtained from more preceding dependents implies that the expectations of the comprehender regarding when X will be encountered and what input will instantiate it will generally be sharper and more accurate; thus there should on average be less processing difficulty at X than in the situation with fewer preceding dependents. By looking at processing behavior (e.g., reading times) when the comprehender reaches X, we can hope to gain insight into the relative roles of expectations and memory in on-line language comprehension.

However, experimental work on such syntactically constrained contexts using different languages and different construction types has not yielded a fully consistent picture: in some cases, the picture looks like that predicted by expectation-based accounts; in other cases, it looks like that predicted by

Figure 4.5 Syntactically constrained contexts with preceding dependents.

memory-based accounts. Let us begin with some of the clearest evidence of expectation-based processing patterns. In obligatorily head-final language/construction combinations such as the verbal dependency structure of Japanese, Hindi, and German (excepting in the last case main-clause finite verbs), there is little to no evidence that adding pre-verbal dependents makes processing of the final verb more difficult—rather, these additional dependents seem to make the final verb easier to process! To take one example, Konieczny and Döring (2003) examined obligatorily verb-final German subordinate clauses such as in (19) below.

(19) a. ... dass   [der Freund]   [dem Kunden]   [das Auto]   [aus Freude]
        ... that   [the friend]   [the client]   [the car]   [of plastic]
                   NOM   **DAT**   **ACC**
    verkaufte ...
    bought ...
    "The insight that the friend bought the client the plastic car ..."

  b. ... dass   [der Freund]   [des Kunden]   [das Auto]   [aus Freude]
       ... that   [the friend]   [the client]   [the car]   [of plastic]
                  NOM   **GEN**   **ACC**
    verkaufte ...
    bought ...
    "The insight that the friend of the client bought the plastic car ..."

In this elegant study, the two variants of the sentence differ only in a single letter, but this character determines whether the second NP of the subordinate clause is dative and thus a dependent of an as-yet-unseen verb or is genitive and thus a postmodifier of the immediately preceding noun. Regression-path durations on the clause final verb *verkaufte* ("bought") were reliably longer in the genitive-NP variant, suggesting that the dative NP facilitated processing of the verb (see also Konieczny, 1996, 2000; and Levy & Keller, 2013, for additional related experimental data; and Levy, 2008a, for surprisal-based analysis). Similar qualitative effects have been found in Hindi (Vasishth & Lewis, 2006) and Japanese (Nakatani & Gibson, 2008, 2010).

At the same time, there are situations where it seems that it is the predictions of memory-based theories, not expectation-based theories, which are borne out. Postnominal relative clauses with overt relative pronouns are in general syntactically constrained contexts, because the comprehender knows that an

RC verb must appear. Levy, Fedorenko, and Gibson (2013, in press), for example, parametrically varied the number of intervening constituents between a relative pronoun and the verb in subject-extracted RCs in Russian, such as:

(20)   a.   ... ofitsant,   kotoryj   zabyl   prinesti   bljudo   iz teljatiny
            ... waiter,   who   forgot   to_bring   dish   of veal
                            NOM   **ACC**

            posetitelju   v   chernom kostjume ...
            customer   in   black   suit ...
            DAT

"... the waiter, who forgot to bring the veal dish to the customer in the black suit ..."

       b.   ... ofitsant,   kotoryj   bljudo   iz teljatiny   zabyl   prinesti
            ... waiter,   who   dish   of veal   forgot   to_bring
                            NOM   **ACC**

            customer   in   black   suit ...
            posetitelju   v   chernom   kostjume ...
            DAT

       c.   ... ofitsant,   kotoryj   bljudo   iz teljatiny   posetitelju   v
            ... waiter,   who   dish   of veal   customer   in
                            NOM   **ACC**   **DAT**

            chernom   kostjume   zabyl   prinesti ...
            black   suit   forgot   to_bring ...

Because Russian clause structure has free word order—all logically possible orderings of subject, verb, object, and indirect object are acceptable under some circumstances (Krylova & Khavronina, 1988, inter alia)—all three linear orderings in (20) retain the same basic truth-conditional meaning. In (20a), the RC verb complex (*forgot to bring*) immediately follows the relative pronoun; in (20b) the direct object (*the dish of veal*) precedes it; in (20c) both the direct object and the indirect object (*the customer in the black suit*) precede it. Hence expectation-based theories predict that each additional intervener should increase the sharpness of the comprehender's expectations regarding the RC verb complex's argument structure and identity—there are fewer things that a waiter can do to a dish of veal that a waiter can do in general, and even fewer things that a waiter can do to a dish of veal that implicate a customer as an indirect object. Yet there is no trace of expectation-based facilitation at the verb in these cases: instead, reading times at the RC verb complex increase monotonically with the number of intervening constituents. (Levy et al. (2013, in press) did find expectation-based effects at the processing of the accusative NP, *dish of veal*, which was read more slowly in the RC-initial position, which is a rare position for an accusative NP in Russian RCs, than in the post-verbal position, which is a more common position in corpora.) Similar results were obtained for French in a less exhaustive manipulation of RC-internal word order by Holmes and O'Regan (1981).

Finally, let us return to the best-studied syntactically constrained context of all: English SRCs and ORCs with a full, definite RC-internal NP:

(21) a. The reporter that the senator attacked admitted the error.
 b. The reporter that attacked the senator admitted the error.

Using a small PCFG, Hale (2001) showed that surprisal predicts greater overall difficulty for the ORC due to the lower frequency in general of ORCs. Under surprisal, however, this greater difficulty should in principle show up as soon as the possibility that the RC is subject-extracted is ruled out—at the onset of the RC subject *the senator*. At the RC verb, in contrast, one would expect the ORC to have the advantage, given that the RC verb's argument structure and identity are more tightly constrained than for the SRC. The empirical facts in this respect are worth careful attention. It is quite clear from self-paced reading studies that the ORC verb is the site of considerable processing difficulty (Grodner & Gibson, 2005). At the same time, however, Staub (2010) has recently shown that the onset of the ORC is also the site of processing difficulty, by comparing sentences like (21) with similar CC sentences such as (22) below:

(22) The reporter hoped that the senator attacked the chairman of the committee.

In eye-tracking studies, Staub replicated the well-established finding that processing is disrupted at the ORC verb relative to the SRC verb; but at the same time, he also found more regressive eye-movements from the very first word of the ORC—the word *the*—than from the same word in the CC of (22). Surprisal predicts this effect because a comprehender's expectation for an NP initiating a CC is considerably stronger than that for an NP initiating a relative clause, since the majority of RCs are subject-extracted. Thus we find some suggestion that effects of both expectation and memory can be observed even in this well-studied construction.

Broad-coverage evaluation of surprisal and DLT

A critical new development over the past several years is **broad-coverage evaluations** of both expectation-based and memory-based theories by a number of researchers, through analysis of word-by-word reading-time datasets collected using eye-tracking or self-paced reading (Boston, Hale, Kliegl, Patil, & Vasishth, 2008; Demberg & Keller, 2008; Frank, 2009; McDonald & Shillcock, 2003; Roark, Bachrach, Cardenas, & Pallier, 2009; Smith & Levy, 2008). These broad-coverage evaluations differ from traditional controlled studies in that the materials being read are complete texts rather than the isolated sentences typically used in sentence-processing research, they are *naturalistic* (the texts are not constructed for the experiment but are everyday reading materials such as newspaper articles), the potential reading-behavior predictors of theoretical interest are therefore *not balanced*, and the datasets to be analyzed are typically much larger, since every word in every sentence has a conditional probability and (according to most linguistic theories) must be integrated into a syntactic representation. These datasets therefore pose special challenges both in quantifying the processing difficulty predicted by a given theory and in analyzing the predictive value of each such quantification. Nevertheless, these efforts have been consistent in finding significant contributions of surprisal as a predictor in multiple-regression analysis of reading times, even when correlated factors widely known to affect reading behavior such as word length and word frequency (Mitchell, 1984; Rayner, 1998, inter alia) are included as controls. Several of these efforts tested specifically syntax-based estimates of surprisal (Boston et al., 2008; Demberg & Keller, 2008); Frank and Bod (2011) compared surprisal estimates based on PCFGs (specifically, the limited-parallel implementation of Roark 2001, 2004) with those based on simple recurrent networks (SRNs; Elman, 1990) and, based on the result that the estimates given by the SRN achieved greater predictive accuracy of word-by-word reading times than those given by the PCFG, suggested that SRNs better describe human sentence-processing performance. Since the estimation of high-quality PCFGs is an open research problem to which a large amount of effort in the field of computational linguistics continues to be devoted, it is clear that an answer to the important question of which models are most psychologically faithful—as assessed by their fit to human reading-time and other comprehension data—is only in its infancy (see Fossum & Levy, 2012; Monsalve, Frank, & Vigliocco, 2012, for related analyses illustrating that the picture remains incomplete). Demberg and Keller (2008) also constructed a broad-coverage variant of DLT and found that it had predictive value for reading times at nouns and at auxiliary verbs, though curiously not for other words, including open-class verbs. Another broad-coverage analysis, by Smith and Levy (2008, in press), posed a different question: what is the shape of the relationship between conditional word probability and reading time? Surprisal theory assumes a log-linear relationship —that is, reading times should be linear in *log* probabilities, so that a difference between word probabilities of 0.0001 and 0.0099 should have the same effect as that between word probabilities of 0.01 and 0.99. Traditional psycholinguistic practice, on the other hand, implicitly assumes something closer to a linear relationship, with words with in-context Cloze probabilities above 0.6 to 0.7 thought of as "predictable" and those below roughly 0.01 to 0.05 are uniformly categorized as "unpredictable." In non-parametric multiple regression analyses, Smith and Levy recovered a reliable log-linear effect of conditional word probability on reading times in both eye-tracking and self-paced reading datasets, over six orders of magnitude—ranging from probability 1 to 0.000001. In addition to its theoretical value, this result has crucial methodological ramifications, since predictability differences well below 0.01—which could not be reliably recovered from traditional Cloze studies with participants numbering in the dozens—could have large effects on real-time comprehension behavior.

Conclusion

This overview of memory and surprisal in human sentence comprehension both sheds light on a wide variety of sentence-processing phenomena and highlights some outstanding questions which require further research. To illustrate what we have learned, turn back to the opening example of the chapter, sentence (1). As I said before, you probably found this sentence most confusing at two places: around the word *admired* and around the phrase *was concerned*. The first source of confusion can be understood as a memory-based integration effect like those discussed in the section on "Applications beyond center-embedding difficulty": to process *admired*, you need to simultaneously integrate it with *girl* and *teacher*, neither of which is adjacent to *admired* and both of which share many relevant retrieval cues. The second source of confusion can be understood as an expectation-based surprisal effect like the one we saw in the section on "Surprisal and garden-path disambiguation": you probably placed your syntactic bets on *her mother* being the object of *call* and thus were surprised to discover, as *was* indicates, that *her mother* was actually the main-clause subject. Thus the two theories we have covered in this chapter resolve the mysteries of why a typical reader finds sentence (1) difficult where she does.

On the other hand, many open questions remain. Why, for example, do we see the discrepancies in incremental processing costs in syntactically constrained contexts across language and construction type described in the section on "Conflicting predictions between expectations and memory"? It is notable that the cases in which the evidence for memory-based processing costs and against expectation-based costs is clearest involves relativization, which as we saw quite early on in this chapter have long been considered to be the basis for canonical examples demonstrating the limitations of human memory capacity in on-line language comprehension. It is also notable that the clearest evidence for expectation-based patterning in verbal processing comes from obligatorily verb-final languages, in which the comprehender presumably has much more experience with long-distance dependency integrations (see also the comparisons of dependency distances between English and German by Gildea & Temperley, 2010, and Park & Levy, 2009, for more evidence of this connection). Some researchers have taken initial steps toward constructing models which integrate notions of expectation and memory limitation. Demberg and Keller (2009) have introduced an incremental parsing model that contains both *prediction* and *verification* components, which respectively yield surprisal-like and DLT-like processing difficulty gradients. In addition, the model of Lewis and Vasishth (2005) can achieve some types of expectation-derived processing benefits, as processing of multiple preceding dependents can boost the activation level of a governor before it is encountered (see Vasishth & Lewis, 2006, for more discussion).

It is clear that considerably more work—both empirical and theoretical—needs to be done before we have any definitive answers. On the empirical side, coverage of a wider variety of languages and syntactic construction types is required to expand the fundamental knowledge base on which we build theories. On the theoretical side, a number of questions remain outstanding. First, why do we see expectation-based patterning in some situations and memory-based patterns in others? What features of the language, construction type, and potentially even comprehension task induce each type of pattern? Second, what features of context are used—and how, and why—to determine a comprehender's expectations in on-line comprehension? This has been referred to as the **grain-size** problem (Mitchell, Cuetos, Corley, & Brysbaert, 1995), and while we know that the answer is in general "potentially very fine-grained," we are still a long way from truly precise answers. Finally: expectation-based models can be understood as the consequence of optimization in comprehension, situating them within frameworks of rational cognition (Anderson, 1990; Shepard, 1987; Tenenbaum & Griffiths, 2001; see also the section above, "Theoretical justifications for surprisal"). To what extent can memory-based models be understood in a similar light?

Acknowledgments

I would like to express my gratitude to Ted Gibson, Rick Lewis, and Shravan Vasishth for numerous conversations over the past several years that have improved my understanding of the memory-oriented theories of syntactic complexity described here. All mistakes remain my own, of course; and with luck, I have not misrepresented these theories too badly.

Notes

1. As Roger van Gompel points out, interference-based theories make an incorrect prediction for the pattern of verbal agreement processing for grammatical sentences as in (11) below:

   (11) a. The key to the cabinet was rusty from many years of disuse.
        [**grammatical, –attractor**]
        b. The key to the cabinets was rusty from many years of disuse.
        [**grammatical, +attractor**]

   Interference-based theories predict that the verb should be more difficult when both nouns inside the subject NP are singular, as in (11a), since both nouns match the verb's target cue, whereas in (11b) only the true subject matches this cue. But no trace of this pattern was found by either Pearlmutter et al. (1999) or Wagers et al. (2009).

2. Although the local-coherence effect seems difficult to accommodate in a model where syntactic analysis is entirely top-down, Levy (2008b) presents such a model in which the effect arises from uncertainty about the representation of preceding context; Levy, Bicknell, Slattery, and Rayner (2009) confirm predictions made by this model.

3. You have probably already guessed: the vast majority of native English speakers fill in the blank with the word *bridge* (Arcuri, Rabe-Hesketh, Morris, & McGuire, 2001).
4. To keep the grammar used for exposition small, I have substituted *removed* for the phrase *took off* actually used by Staub, to avoid verb–particle constructions. None of the analyses are qualitatibely affected by this change.
5. More technically, a PCFG is a collection of context-free grammatical rules of the form $X \rightarrow \alpha$, where X is a single non-terminal symbol (syntactic category) and α is a sequence of symbols (syntactic categories and/or words), each of which has a probability. The probabilities are constrained such that for every non-terminal symbol X in the grammar, the probabilities of all rules with X on the left-hand side sum to 1: $\Sigma_\alpha P(X \rightarrow \alpha) = 1$. The product of a tree T is the product of the probability of each rule used in the derivation of T (if a rule is used more than once, its probability is multiplied in each time it is used), and the product of a string $w_{1...n}$ is the sum of the products of all trees whose yield (the leaves of the tree, read from right to left) equals $w_{1...n}$. The interested reader is encouraged to consult Jurafsky and Martin (2008) or Manning and Schütze (1999) for more details.
6. To be more technically precise, Bayes Rule tells us that

$$P(T|w_{1...i}) = \frac{P(w_{1...i}|T) P(T)}{P(w_{1...i})}$$

but by definition $P(w_{1...i}|T)$ is 1 when the yield of T is $w_{1...i}$ and 0 otherwise, so if we limit ourselves to considering parses consistent with the input sentence we can just drop the first term in the numerator, giving us equation (2) on p. 91.
7. This difference in conditional probability between the two analyses arises from three differences between the two incremental trees, namely, in the main-clause analysis:
   1. the subordinate-clause VP rewrites to V rather than to V NP;
   2. there is a commitment that only one subordinate-clause SBAR node initiates the sentence;
   3. there is a commitment that there is no comma between the subordinate clause and the main clause.
8. This conditional probability reflects the fact (i) that the subject must not continue with another NP conjunct and (ii) that the main-clause verb must turn out to be *removed*.
9. In probability theory, the determination of this weighted average is called **marginalization**; in its general form for this example we would write that:

$$P(w_{11} = \text{removed}|w_{i...10}) = \sum_T P(w_{11} = \text{removed}|w_{i...10}, T) P(T|w_{i...10})$$

and we would say that the probability of the upcoming word is computed "marginalizing over the possible structural analyses of the sentence thus far."
10. Mitchell (1987) and Van Gompel and Pickering (2001) originally argued that the differential difficulty effect seen at *the vet* was evidence that transitivity information is initially ignored, but the analysis presented here demonstrates that this effect arises under surprisal when transitivity information is *taken into account*. A related piece of evidence is provided by Staub (2007), who shows that the absence of a comma preceding *the vet* increases processing difficulty; the account here is also generally consistent with this result, since most such subordinate clauses do in fact end in commas.
11. This simple model fails to capture the empirical result that the garden-path disambiguation effect is larger in magnitude than the surprise effect at the onset of

the ambiguous NP. Among other reasons, this failure is due to the fact that specific verb–noun preferences are not encoded in the model. *Arrived* can occasionally have an NP right sister; humans know that *vet* is not a good head for such an NP, but our model does not. Thus our model has not disconfirmed the incorrect analysis before the disambiguating region as fully as a model with finer-grained information sources would have.
12. One weakness of this second account for the data of Grodner et al. (2002) is that it predicts a processing difficulty reversal further downstream: the greater implausibility of the finite-verb analysis for the RC context should guide the comprehender toward a reduced-relative analysis, which would lighten the processing burden at the disambiguating region *by the enemy*. However, no such processing reversal was found by Grodner et al. Under surprisal, it is possible that the first consideration (the structural-frequency difference) could eliminate this difficulty reversal. Grodner, Comer, and Gibson (2011) present further data bearing on these issues.

References

Adams, B. C., Clifton, Jr., C., & Mitchell, D. C. (1998). Lexical guidance in sentence processing? *Psychonomic Bulletin & Review, 5(2)*, 265–270.

Altmann, G. T., & Kamide, Y. (1999). Incremental interpretation at verbs: Restricting the domain of subsequent reference. *Cognition, 73(3)*, 247–264.

Anderson, J. R. (1990). *The adaptive character of thought*. Hillsdale, NJ: Lawrence Erlbaum.

Arcuri, S. M., Rabe-Hesketh, S., Morris, R. G., & McGuire, P. K. (2001). Regional variation of Cloze probabilities for sentence contexts. *Behavior Research Methods, Instruments, and Computers, 33(1)*, 80–90.

Attneave, F. (1959). *Applications of information theory to psychology: A summary of basic concepts, methods and results*. New York: Holt, Rinehart and Winston.

Bever, T. (1970). The cognitive basis for linguistic structures. In Hayes, J. (Ed.), *Cognition and the development of language* (pp. 279–362). Chichester: John Wiley & Sons.

Bicknell, K., & Levy, R. (2009). A model of local coherence effects in human sentence processing as consequences of updates from bottom-up prior to posterior beliefs. In *Proceedings of the North American chapter of the Association for Computational Linguistics–Human Language Technologies (NAACL-HLT) conference*.

Bicknell, K., & Levy, R. (2010). A rational model of eye-movement control in reading. In *Proceedings of the Annual Meeting of the Association for Computational Linguistics* (pp. 1168–1178).

Bicknell, K., & Levy, R. (2012). Word predictability and frequency effects in a rational model of reading. In *Proceedings of the 34th Annual Meeting of the Cognitive Science Conference*.

Bock, K., & Miller, C. A. (1991). Broken agreement. *Cognitive Psychology, 23*, 45–93.

Booth, T. L. (1969). Probabilistic representation of formal languages. In *IEEE Conference Record of the 1969 Tenth Annual Symposium on Switching and Automata Theory* (pp. 74–81).

Boston, M. F., Hale, J. T., Kliegl, R., Patil, U., & Vasishth, S. (2008). Parsing costs as predictors of reading difficulty: An evaluation using the Potsdam sentence corpus. *Journal of Eye-Movement Research, 2(1)*, 1–12.

Charniak, E. (1996). Tree-bank grammars. Technical report, Department of Computer Science, Brown University.

Chen, E., Gibson, E., & Wolf, F. (2005). On-line syntactic storage costs in sentence comprehension. *Journal of Memory and Language, 52*, 144–169.
Chomsky, N. (1956). Three models for the description of language. *IRE Transactions on Information Theory, 2(3)*, 113–124.
Chomsky, N. (1957). *Syntactic structures*. Oxford: Mouton.
Chomsky, N. (1965). *Aspects of the theory of syntax*. Cambridge, MA: MIT Press.
Chomsky, N. (1981). *Lectures on government and binding*. Berlin and New York: Mouton de Gruyer.
Chomsky, N., & Miller, G. A. (1963). Introduction to the formal analysis of natural languages. In R. D. Luce, R. R. Bush, & E. Galanter (Eds.), *Handbook of mathematical psychology*, Vol. II (pp. 269–321). Chichester: John Wiley & Sons.
Christiansen, M. H., & MacDonald, M. C. (2009). A usage-based approach to recursion in sentence processing. *Language Learning, 51(1)*, 126–161.
Clifton, C. Jr. (1993). Thematic roles in sentence parsing. *Canadian Journal of Experimental Psychology, 47(2)*, 224–246.
Cover, T., & Thomas, J. (1991). *Elements of information theory*. Chichester: John Wiley.
Cowper, E. A. (1976). Constraints on sentence complexity: A model for syntactic processing. Ph.D. thesis, Brown University, Providence, RI.
Crocker, M., & Brants, T. (2000). Wide-coverage probabilistic sentence processing. *Journal of Psycholinguistic Research, 29(6)*, 647–669.
DeLong, K. A., Urbach, T. P., & Kutas, M. (2005). Probabilistic word pre-activation during language comprehension inferred from electrical brain activity. *Nature Neuroscience, 8*, 1117–1121.
Demberg, V., & Keller, F. (2008). Data from eye-tracking corpora as evidence for theories of syntactic processing complexity. *Cognition, 109(2)*, 193–210.
Demberg, V., & Keller, F. (2009). A computational model of prediction in human parsing: Unifying locality and surprisal effects. In Proceedings of CogSci.
Eberhard, K. M. (1999). The accessibility of conceptual number to the processes of subject–verb agreement in English. *Journal of Memory and Language, 41*, 560–578.
Eberhard, K. M., Cutting, J. C., & Bock, K. (2005). Making syntax of sense: Number agreement in sentence production. *Psychological Review, 112(3)*, 531–559.
Ehrlich, S. F., & Rayner, K. (1981). Contextual effects on word perception and eye movements during reading. *Journal of Verbal Learning and Verbal Behavior, 20*, 641–655.
Elman, J. (1990). Finding structure in time. *Cognitive Science, 14*, 179–211.
Engbert, R., Nuthmann, A., Richter, E. M., & Kliegl, R. (2005). SWIFT: A dynamical model of saccade generation during reading. *Psychological Review, 112(4)*, 777–813.
Ferreira, F., & Henderson, J. (1990). Use of verb information in syntactic parsing: Evidence from eye-movements and word-by-word self-paced reading. *Journal of Experimental Psychology: Learning, Memory, & Cognition, 16(4)*, 555–568.
Ford, M. (1983). A method for obtaining measures of local parsing complexity throughout sentences. *Journal of Verbal Learning and Verbal Behavior, 22*, 203–218.
Fossum, V., & Levy, R. (2012). Sequential versus hierarchical syntactic models of human incremental sentence processing. In *Proceedings of the 3rd annual workshop on cognitive modeling and computational linguistics*.
Franck, J., Vigliocco, G., & Nicol, J. (2002). Subject–verb agreement errors in French and English: The role of syntactic hierarchy. *Language & Cognitive Processes, 17(4)*, 371–404.

Frank, S. L. (2009). Surprisal-based comparison between a symbolic and a connectionist model of sentence processing. In *Proceedings of the 31st annual conference of the Cognitive Science Society* (pp. 1139–1144).

Frank, S. L., & Bod, R. (2011). Insensitivity of the human sentence-processing system to hierarchical structure. *Psychological Science, 22(6)*, 829–834.

Frazier, L., & Rayner, K. (1982). Making and correcting errors during sentence comprehension: Eye-movements in the analysis of structurally ambiguous sentences. *Cognitive Psychology, 14*, 178–210.

Gibson, E. (1991). A computational theory of human linguistic processing: Memory limitations and processing breakdown. Ph.D. thesis, Carnegie Mellon.

Gibson, E. (1998). Linguistic complexity: Locality of syntactic dependencies. *Cognition, 68*, 1–76.

Gibson, E. (2000). The dependency locality theory: A distance-based theory of linguistic complexity. In A. Marantz, Y. Miyashita, & W. O'Neil (Eds.), *Image, language, brain* (pp. 95–126). Cambridge, MA: MIT Press.

Gibson, E., Desmet, T., Grodner, D., Watson, D., & Ko, K. (2005). Reading relative clauses in English. *Language & Cognitive Processes, 16(2)*, 313–353.

Gibson, E., & Thomas, J. (1997). Processing load judgements in English: Evidence for the Syntactic Prediction Locality Theory of syntactic complexity. Manuscript, MIT, Cambridge, MA.

Gibson, E., & Thomas, J. (1999). The perception of complex ungrammatical sentences as grammatical. *Language & Cognitive Processes, 14(3)*, 225–248.

Gildea, D., & Temperley, D. (2007). Optimizing grammars for minimum dependency length. In Proceedings of ACL.

Gildea, D., & Temperley, D. (2010). Do grammars minimize dependency length? *Cognitive Science, 34*, 286–310.

Gordon, P. C., Hendrick, R., & Johnson, M. (2001). Memory interference during language processing. *Journal of Experimental Psychology: Learning, Memory, & Cognition, 27*, 1411–1423.

Gordon, P. C., Hendrick, R., & Johnson, M. (2004). Effects of noun phrase type on sentence complexity. *Journal of Memory and Language, 51(1)*, 97–114.

Grodner, D., Comer, K., & Gibson, E. (2011). Non-local syntactic influences in structural ambiguity resolution. In preparation.

Grodner, D., & Gibson, E. (2005). Some consequences of the serial nature of linguistic input. *Cognitive Science, 29(2)*, 261–290.

Grodner, D., Gibson, E., & Tunstall, S. (2002). Syntactic complexity in ambiguity resolution. *Journal of Memory and Language, 46*, 267–295.

Hale, J. (2001). A probabilistic Earley parser as a psycholinguistic model. In *Proceedings of the second meeting of the North American chapter of the Association for Computational Linguistics* (pp. 159–166).

Holmes, V. M., & O'Regan, J. K. (1981). Eye fixation patterns during the reading of relative-clause sentences. *Journal of Verbal Learning and Verbal Behavior, 20*, 417–430.

Hsiao, F., & Gibson, E. (2003). Processing relative clauses in Chinese. *Cognition, 90(11)*, 3–27.

Humboldt, W. (1988/1836). *On language*. Cambridge University Press. Translated from the German by Peter Heath. Originally published as *Über die Verschienheit des Menschlichen Sprachbaues*, 1836, Berlin.

Jelinek, F., & Lafferty, J. D. (1991). Computation of the probability of initial substring generation by stochastic context free grammars. *Computational Linguistics*, *17(3)*, 315–323.

Jurafsky, D. (1996). A probabilistic model of lexical and syntactic access and disambiguation. *Cognitive Science*, *20(2)*, 137–194.

Jurafsky, D., & Martin, J. H. (2008). *Speech and language processing: An introduction to natural language processing, computational linguistics, and speech recognition*. Second Edition. Englewood Cliffs, NJ: Prentice-Hall.

Kimball, J., & Aissen, J. (1971). I think, you think, he think. *Linguistic Inquiry*, *2*, 241–246.

King, J., & Just, M. A. (1991). Individual differences in syntactic processing: The role of working memory. *Journal of Memory and Language*, *30(5)*, 580–602.

Konieczny, L. (1996). *Human sentence processing: A semantics-oriented parsing approach*. Ph.D. thesis, Universität Freiburg.

Konieczny, L. (2000). Locality and parsing complexity. *Journal of Psycholinguistic Research*, *29(6)*, 627–645.

Konieczny, L., & Döring, P. (2003). Anticipation of clause-final heads: Evidence from eye-tracking and SRNs. In *Proceedings of ICCS/ASCS*.

Krylova, O., & Khavronina, S. (1988). *Word order in Russian*. Moscow: Russky Yazyk Publishers.

Kučera, H., & Francis, W. N. (1967). *Computational analysis of present-day American English*. Providence, RI: Brown University Press.

Kutas, M., & Hillyard, S. A. (1980). Reading senseless sentences: Brain potentials reflect semantic incongruity. *Science*, *207(4427)*, 203–205.

Kutas, M., & Hillyard, S. A. (1984). Brain potentials during reading reflect word expectancy and semantic association. *Nature*, *307*, 161–163.

Laming, D. R. J. (1968). *Information theory of choice-reaction times*. Academic Press.

Levy, R. (2008a). Expectation-based syntactic comprehension. *Cognition*, *106*, 1126–1177.

Levy, R. (2008b). A noisy-channel model of rational human sentence comprehension under uncertain input. In *Proceedings of the 13th conference on empirical methods in natural language processing* (pp. 234–243).

Levy, R., Bicknell, K., Slattery, T., & Rayner, K. (2009). Eye-movement evidence that readers maintain and act on uncertainty about past linguistic input. In *Proceedings of the National Academy of Sciences*, *106(50)*, 21086–21090.

Levy, R., Fedorenko, E., & Gibson, E. (2013). The syntactic complexity of Russian relative clauses. Under review.

Levy, R., & Keller, F. (2013). Expectation and locality effects in German verb-final structures. *Journal of Memory and Language*, *68(2)*, 199–222.

Lewis, R. L., & Vasishth, S. (2005). An activation-based model of sentence processing as skilled memory retrieval. *Cognitive Science*, *29*, 1–45.

Lewis, R. L., Vasishth, S., & Van Dyke, J. (2006). Computational principles of working memory in sentence comprehension. *Trends in Cognitive Science*, *10(10)*, 447–454.

Luce, R. D., Bush, R. R., & Galanter, E., editors (1963). *Handbook of mathematical psychology*, Vol. II. Chichester: John Wiley & Sons.

MacDonald, M. C. (1993). The interaction of lexical and syntactic ambiguity. *Journal of Memory and Language*, *32*, 692–715.

Manning, C. D., & Schütze, H. (1999). *Foundations of statistical natural language processing*. Cambridge, MA: MIT Press.

Marcus, M. P., Santorini, B., & Marcinkiewicz, M. A. (1994). Building a large annotated corpus of English: The Penn Treebank. *Computational Linguistics, 19(2)*, 313–330.

Marks, L., & Miller, G. A. (1964). The role of semantic and syntactic constraints in the memorization of English sentences. *Journal of Verbal Learning and Verbal Behavior, 3*, 1–5.

Marslen-Wilson, W. (1975). Sentence perception as an interactive parallel process. *Science, 189(4198)*, 226–228.

McDonald, S. A., & Shillcock, R. C. (2003). Low-level predictive inference in reading: The influence of transitional probabilities on eye-movements. *Vision Research, 43*, 1735–1751.

McRae, K., Spivey-Knowlton, M. J., & Tanenhaus, M. K. (1998). Modeling the influence of thematic fit (and other constraints) in on-line sentence comprehension. *Journal of Memory and Language, 38(3)*, 283–312.

Miller, G. A., & Chomsky, N. (1963). Finitary models of language users. In R. D. Luce, R. R. Bush, & E. Galanter (Eds.), *Handbook of mathematical psychology*, Vol. II (pp. 419–491). Chichester: John Wiley & Sons.

Miller, G. A., & Isard, S. (1963). Some perceptual consequences of linguistic rules. *Journal of Verbal Learning and Verbal Behavior, 2*, 217–228.

Mitchell, D. C. (1984). An evaluation of subject-paced reading tasks and other methods for investigating immediate processes in reading. In D. Kieras & M. A. Just (Eds.), *New methods in reading comprehension*. Hillsdale, NJ: Erlbaum.

Mitchell, D. C. (1987). Lexical guidance in human parsing: Locus and processing characteristics. In M. Coltheart (Ed.), *Attention and Performance XII: The psychology of reading* (pp. 601–618). London: Erlbaum.

Mitchell, D. C., Cuetos, F., Corley, M., & Brysbaert, M. (1995). Exposure-based models of human parsing: Evidence for the use of coarse-grained (nonlexical) statistical records. *Journal of Psycholinguistic Research, 24*, 469–488.

Monsalve, I. F., Frank, S. L., & Vigliocco, G. (2012). Lexical surprisal as a general predictor of reading time. In *Proceedings of the 13th conference of the European chapter of the Association for Computational Linguistics*.

Nakatani, K., & Gibson, E. (2008). Distinguishing theories of syntactic expectation cost in sentence comprehension: Evidence from Japanese. *Linguistics, 46(1)*, 63–87.

Nakatani, K., & Gibson, E. (2010). An on-line study of Japanese nesting complexity. *Cognitive Science, 34(1)*, 94–112.

Narayanan, S., & Jurafsky, D. (1998). Bayesian models of human sentence processing. In *Proceedings of the twelfth annual meeting of the Cognitive Science Society*.

Narayanan, S., & Jurafsky, D. (2002). A Bayesian model predicts human parse preference and reading time in sentence processing. *Advances in Neural Information Processing Systems, 14*, 59–65.

Norris, D. (2006). The Bayesian Reader: Explaining word recognition as an optimal Bayesian decision process. *Psychological Review, 113(2)*, 327–357.

Norris, D. (2009). Putting it all together: A unified account of word recognition and reaction-time distributions. *Psychological Review, 116(1)*, 207–219.

Park, Y. A., & Levy, R. (2009). Minimal-length linearizations for mildly context-sensitive dependency trees. In *Proceedings of the North American chapter of the Association for Computational Linguistics—Human Language Technologies (NAACL-HLT) conference*.

Pearlmutter, N., Garnsey, S., & Bock, K. (1999). Agreement processes in sentence comprehension. *Journal of Memory and Language, 41*, 427–456.

Pickering, M. J., & Traxler, M. J. (1998). Plausibility and recovery from garden paths: An eye-tracking study. *Journal of Experimental Psychology: Learning, Memory, & Cognition, 24(4)*, 940–961.

Pollard, C., & Sag, I. (1994). *Head-driven phrase structure grammar.* Chicago, IL: University of Chicago Press and Stanford, CA: CSLI Publications.

Rayner, K. (1998). Eye-movements in reading and information processing: 20 years of research. *Psychological Bulletin, 124(3)*, 372–422.

Reichle, E. D., Pollatsek, A., Fisher, D. L., & Rayner, K. (1998). Toward a model of eye-movement control in reading. *Psychological Review, 105(1)*, 125–157.

Reilly, R. G., & Radach, R. (2006). Some empirical tests of an interactive activation model of eye-movement control in reading. *Cognitive Systems Research, 7*, 34–55.

Roark, B. (2001). Probabilistic top-down parsing and language modeling. *Computational Linguistics, 27(2)*, 249–276.

Roark, B. (2004). Robust garden path parsing. *Natural Language Engineering, 10(1)*, 1–24.

Roark, B., Bachrach, A., Cardenas, C., & Pallier, C. (2009). Deriving lexical and syntactic expectation-based measures for psycholinguistic modeling via incremental top-down parsing. In *Proceedings of EMNLP.*

Shepard, R. N. (1987). Toward a universal law of generalization for psychological science. *Science, 237(4820)*, 1317–1323.

Smith, N. J., & Levy, R. (2008). Optimal processing times in reading: A formal model and empirical investigation. In *Proceedings of the 30th annual meeting of the Cognitive Science Society.*

Smith, N. J., & Levy, R. (In press). The effect of word predictability on reading time is logarithmic. Manuscript, UC San Diego.

Spivey, M. J., & Tanenhaus, M. K. (1998). Syntactic ambiguity resolution in discourse: Modeling the effects of referential content and lexical frequency. *Journal of Experimental Psychology: Learning, Memory, & Cognition, 24(6)*, 1521–1543.

Staub, A. (2007). The parser doesn't ignore intransitivity, after all. *Journal of Experimental Psychology: Learning, Memory, & Cognition, 33(3)*, 550–569.

Staub, A. (2010). Eye-movements and processing difficulty in object relative clauses. *Cognition, 116*, 71–86.

Stolcke, A. (1995). An efficient probabilistic context-free parsing algorithm that computes prefix probabilities. *Computational Linguistics, 21(2)*, 165–201.

Stone, M. (1960). Models for choice-reaction times. *Psychometrika, 25(3)*, 251–260.

Sturt, P., Pickering, M. J., & Crocker, M. W. (1999). Structural change and reanalysis difficulty in language comprehension. *Journal of Memory and Language, 40*, 136–150.

Tabor, W., Galantucci, B., & Richardson, D. (2004). Effects of merely local syntactic coherence on sentence processing. *Journal of Memory and Language, 50(4)*, 355–370.

Tabor, W., & Tanenhaus, M. K. (1999). Dynamical models of sentence processing. *Cognitive Science, 23(4)*, 491–515.

Tanenhaus, M. K., Spivey-Knowlton, M. J., Eberhard, K., & Sedivy, J. C. (1995). Integration of visual and linguistic information in spoken language comprehension. *Science, 268*, 1632–1634.

Taylor, W. L. (1953). A new tool for measuring readability. *Journalism Quarterly, 30*, 415.

Tenenbaum, J. B., & Griffiths, T. L. (2001). Generalization, similarity, and Bayesian inference. *Behavioral & Brain Sciences, 24*, 629–640.

Traxler, M. J., Morris, R. K., & Seely, R. E. (2002). Processing subject and object relative clauses: Evidence from eye-movements. *Journal of Memory and Language, 47*, 69–90.

Traxler, M. J., Pickering, M. J., & Clifton, C. (1998). Adjunct attachment is not a form of lexical ambiguity resolution. *Journal of Memory and Language, 39*, 558–592.

Trueswell, J. C., Tanenhaus, M. K., & Garnsey, S. M. (1994). Semantic influences on parsing: Use of thematic role information in syntactic ambiguity resolution. *Journal of Memory and Language, 33*, 285–318.

Van Berkum, J. J. A., Brown, C. M., Zwitserlood, P., Kooijman, V., & Hagoort, P. (2005). Anticipating upcoming words in discourse: Evidence from ERPs and reading times. *Journal of Experimental Psychology: Learning, Memory, & Cognition, 31(3)*, 443–467.

Van Dyke, J. A. (2007). Interference effects from grammatically unavailable constituents during sentence processing. *Journal of Experimental Psychology: Learning, Memory, & Cognition, 33(2)*, 407–430.

Van Dyke, J. A., & Lewis, R. L. (2003). Distinguishing effects of structure and decay on attachment and repair: A retrieval interference theory of recovery from misanalyzed ambiguities. *Journal of Memory and Language, 49(3)*, 285–316.

Van Gompel, R. P. G., & Pickering, M. J. (2001). Lexical guidance in sentence processing: A note on Adams, Clifton, and Mitchell (1998). *Psychonomic Bulletin & Review, 8(4)*, 851–857.

Van Gompel, R. P. G., Pickering, M. J., Pearson, J., & Liversedge, S. P. (2005). Evidence against competition during syntactic ambiguity resolution. *Journal of Memory and Language, 52*, 284–307.

Van Gompel, R. P. G., Pickering, M. J., & Traxler, M. J. (2001). Reanalysis in sentence processing: Evidence against current constraint-based and two-stage models. *Journal of Memory and Language, 45*, 225–258.

Vasishth, S., & Lewis, R. L. (2006). Argument-head distance and processing complexity: Explaining both locality and anti-locality effects. *Language, 82(4)*, 767–794.

Vasishth, S., Suckow, K., Lewis, R. L., & Kern, S. (2010). Short-term forgetting in sentence comprehension: Crosslinguistic evidence from verb-final structures. *Language & Cognitive Processes, 25(4)*, 533–567.

Vigliocco, G., & Nicol, J. (1998). Separating hierarchical relations and word order in language production: Is proximity concord syntactic or linear? *Cognition, 68(1)*, B13–29.

Wagers, M. W., Lau, E. F., & Phillips, C. (2009). Agreement attraction in comprehension: Representations and processes. *Journal of Memory and Language, 61*, 206–237.

Wanner, E., & Maratsos, M. (1978). An ATN approach to comprehension. In M. Halle, J. Bresnan, & G. A. Miller (Eds.), *Linguistic theory and psychological reality*. Cambridge, MA: MIT Press.

Warren, T., & Gibson, E. (2002). The influence of referential processing on sentence complexity. *Cognition, 85(1)*, 79–112.

Wicha, N. Y. Y., Moreno, E. M., & Kutas, M. (2004). Anticipating words and their gender: An event-related brain potential study of semantic integration, gender expectancy, and gender agreement in Spanish sentence reading. *Journal of Cognitive Neuroscience, 16(7)*, 1272–1288.

Yngve, V. (1960). A model and and hypothesis for language structure. In *Proceedings of the American Philosophical Society* (pp. 444–466).

5 Putting syntax in context

*Michael J. Spivey, Sarah E. Anderson,
and Thomas A. Farmer*

Where to put syntax?

Syntax has loomed large in linguistics and psycholinguistics for decades. But it was not always like that. Before Noam Chomsky's (1957) anointing of syntactic structures, most linguists, including his advisor Zelig Harris (1954), defined the goal of linguistics as one of analyzing the distributional statistics of language use to determine the meanings of words. Before Miller and McKean's (1964) psycholinguistic tests of transformational grammar, Osgood, Suci, and Tennenbaum (1957) were busy measuring the meanings of words as locations in a multi-dimensional space.

Since the ascendancy of syntax in these fields as the primary subject of research, there have been multiple attempts to shift attention away from structure and form and back toward content and meaning. Some of these proposals have involved linguistic analyses that emphasize the grammatical consequences of word meanings (Ford, Bresnan, & Kaplan, 1982; Lakoff, 1971). Others have involved psycholinguistic experiments that reveal real-time interactions between syntax and semantics (Marslen-Wilson, 1975; Trueswell, Tanenhaus, & Garnsey, 1994; see also McRae & Matsuki, this volume). And still others have involved computational models that force the syntax and semantics to coexist in the same medium of statistical patterns (Elman, 1991; Hale, 2001; Levy, 2008; St. John & McClelland, 1990; Tabor & Hutchins, 2000; see also Levy, this volume).

These theoretical proposals that renewed an emphasis on semantics were at times (mis)interpreted as suggesting that syntax was unimportant, or even that it did not play a role in sentence comprehension. Rather than having to choose between form and content, and thus encourage the theory pendulum to continue swinging from one extreme to the other, perhaps it would be best to clearly state that the existing evidence makes an unmistakable case that form and content are both equally crucial for sentence processing. Rather than putting syntax on its own pedestal, and rather than putting it unceremoniously in the dustbin, perhaps we can agree to put syntax where it belongs: in context.

By putting syntax in context, we intend to emphasize syntax as a psychologically real constraint in sentence processing, but one that coexists on the same level with equally real semantic constraints (McRae & Matsuki, this volume), statistical constraints (Levy, this volume), and situational context constraints. Even if these abstract syntactic constraints emerge as coarse-grain regularities that derive from the fine-grain statistical patterns accumulated over lexical statistics (e.g., Tabor & Hutchins, 2000; Tabor, Juliano, & Tanenhaus, 1997; see also Culicover & Nowak, 2003), that doesn't make them any less real.

The importance of syntax is especially clear when we feel ourselves "led down the garden path" to parse a sentence in a way that turns out to be grammatically or semantically untenable. In this chapter, we review a range of syntactic processing experiments that explore how non-syntactic context (from intra-sentential, to extra-sentential, to visual/situational) can influence syntactic processing during garden-path-like events. By subtly adjusting our conception of what a garden-path event actually is, we can accommodate a wide range of experimental findings in the sentence-processing literature, and recognize that syntax, semantics, lexical statistics, and even visual/situational context all have to interact fluidly to formulate our real-time understanding of sentences.

What exactly is the garden-path effect?

A great deal of the research that has explored the role of context in syntactic parsing has taken advantage of the fact that readers and listeners process their linguistic input incrementally and therefore frequently encounter temporary syntactic ambiguities. How and when non-syntactic contextual forces influence the resolution of those temporary ambiguities is the focus of this chapter. The term garden-path effect refers to a reader's feeling of being led astray by syntactic preferences while reading a sentence. In reading a garden-path sentence, a participant reaches a point where her understanding of the sentence up until that point no longer makes sense with the syntactic and/or semantic constraints. Take, for example, the sentence, "The horse raced past the barn fell" (Bever, 1970). This famous example lulls readers into feeling that they are understanding the sentence just fine until they reach the final word of the sentence. Many readers often protest that it is simply ungrammatical, even after being told that "raced past the barn" is a reduced relative clause describing *which* horse fell. The investigation of what gives rise to this effect, and the manner in which context can influence it, has led to several different theories about the nature of sentence processing.

Syntax-first models of syntactic ambiguity resolution suggest that syntactic heuristics dictate a single structure to initially pursue (Frazier, this volume). Only if this first analysis is incorrect do semantic and contextual information sources play a role in comprehending the sentence (Ferreira & Clifton, 1986; Frazier, 1988; Frazier & Rayner, 1982; Rayner, Carlson, & Frazier, 1983). If reanalysis is necessary, participants experience the garden-path effect as the recovery mechanism takes some time to replace the first incorrect syntactic structure with a new one. Hence, a sentence either does not induce a garden-path effect because the syntactic heuristics initially selected the correct alternative to parse, or a sentence does induce a garden-path effect because the initially selected syntactic structure had to be corrected. In this account, the way that context exerts its influence on the eventual selection of syntactic alternatives is via a late-stage reanalysis mechanism.

By contrast, constraint-based models of syntactic ambiguity resolution argue that syntax, semantics, verb-based statistical biases, and even non-linguistic context interact immediately and simultaneously during the resolution of a syntactic ambiguity (MacDonald, Pearlmutter, & Seidenberg, 1994; Spivey & Tanenhaus, 1998; Tanenhaus & Trueswell, 1995; see also McRae & Matsuki, this volume). In fact, in the constraint-based account of sentence processing, even syntactically forbidden parses that have strong lexical-statistical support can influence the resolution process (Tabor, Galantucci, & Richardson, 2004). When multiple syntactic parses receive partial support, those multiple structural alternatives are maintained as partially activated representations that compete with one another over time. When the alternatives are somewhat equal in their relative activations, or nearly perfectly equal in their relative activations, or when an untenable alternative initially wins and subsequent information is forced to laboriously overturn that result, the competition process takes longer and longer to settle. In constraint-based accounts, it is that settling process that causes garden-path effects during sentence comprehension. The settling process can be fast, as when the syntactic, semantic, and other contextual biases all generally support the correct syntactic alternative. The settling process can be slightly slow, such as when a moderate majority of the biases support the correct syntactic alternative. The settling process can be significantly slow, such as when the various biases provide near equal support for both syntactic alternatives. And the settling process can be pathologically slow or even reach a "stalemate," such as when most of the constraints support one alternative early on in the sentence, and then later on a new constraint comes to bear that very strongly opposes the adopted alternative. As a result, this class of theories predicts only one population of responses for syntactically ambiguous sentences: a single continuum from fast to slow reading times. In this account, a garden-path is not something that either happens or does not happen. A garden-path is a competition among alternative parses that can produce big slow-downs in comprehension, medium-sized ones, and very small ones. In this account, the way that context exerts its influence on the selection of syntactic alternatives is by participating in the initial resolution process precisely because that initial selection process involves parallel partial-activation of the alternatives. That is, context has a much easier time influencing the salience of a syntactic alternative when that syntactic alternative already has non-zero activation.

Recently, a constructive combination of the syntax-first and constraint-based accounts has been offered, in the form of a probabilistic-selection account. Traxler, Van Gompel, and colleagues proposed the unrestricted-race model of sentence processing (Traxler, Pickering & Clifton, 1998; Van Gompel, Pickering, Pearson, & Liversedge, 2005; Van Gompel, Pickering, & Traxler,

2001), which posits that certain sources of contextual information are simultaneously integrated with syntactic constraints immediately when they become available in the input, and that an instantaneous probabilistic selection process chooses a single syntactic structure to pursue among the weighted alternatives. Similar to constraint-based accounts, this means that many sources of context have an early influence on syntactic parsing. Similar to syntax-first accounts, this means that only one syntactic alternative is pursued at any one time because the selection process is instantaneous and the unchosen alternative is discarded. If the selected alternative turns out to be syntactically untenable or implausible, a reanalysis stage takes over to replace the initially considered syntactic structure with a new one, resulting in the garden-path effect. Therefore, while the unrestricted race model extends syntax-first models substantially by proposing that multiple sources of information can influence initial processing, it is still the case that only a single alternative is considered at any point in time.

Intra-sentential context constrains syntactic parsing

The constraint-based model of sentence processing predicts that lexical and semantic biases converge immediately to guide sentence processing (MacDonald et al., 1994; McRae & Matsuki, this volume; Trueswell et al., 1994), rather than syntactic biases acting in isolation. In contrast, syntax-first models of sentence processing posit that the consideration of an initial syntactic structure is guided solely by syntactic heuristics. Let's again consider Bever's famous example, "The horse raced past the barn fell," and the following sentence, "The suspect detained for questioning was later released." Both of these sentences have the exact same syntactic construction, and if syntactic heuristics alone guide initial parsing decisions, then these two sentences should be parsed with equal difficulty. However, this is not the case because the second sentence is judged to be much easier to understand than the first (Hare, Tanenhaus, & McRae, 2007). Of course, syntax-first accounts place non-structural factors in a late-stage of processing (Frazier & Clifton, 1996), which allows them to influence off-line judgments of difficulty. Thus, off-line judgments of difficulty are not the ideal method of comparing sentences. As we will see, real-time measures of on-line comprehension are crucial for identifying and understanding differences between sentences like these.

The difference between these two example sentences is the verb used in the reduced relative clause, and verbs have been shown to induce graded preferences for particular argument structures that guide sentence processing (Ford, Bresnan, & Kaplan, 1982; Mitchell & Holmes, 1985; Pollard & Sag, 1994; Trueswell, Tanenhaus, & Kello, 1993). The first example uses the verb *raced*, an often-intransitive verb (frequently used in the active voice), combined with the subject *horse*, a semantically appropriate subject for the action of the verb. In this example, then, the semantic and lexical biases of the noun–verb pair converge to promote a main clause interpretation of the sentence, which becomes clearly incorrect when the final word of the sentence is reached. The second example, on the other hand, uses the verb *detained*, an obligatorily transitive verb (frequently used in the passive voice), combined with the subject *suspect*, a semantically appropriate direct object of the detaining event. In the second sentence, the lexical and semantic biases converge to encourage readers to pursue the correct relative clause interpretation of the sentence. Therefore, what appears to be syntactic heuristics may actually be the convergence of lexical and semantic preferences created by the verb argument structure. Redefining so-called syntactic heuristics as lexical and semantic biases obviates the need for a special encapsulated syntactic parser to handle syntactic ambiguity resolution (MacDonald et al., 1994). Note, however, that explaining away syntactic heuristics does not result in the explaining away of syntax itself. In fact, it is arguable that, in this constraint-based framework, the rules of syntax are able to exist in a purer fashion, adhering to a strong competence approach rather than being altered by parsing heuristics (see Hale, 2001, for discussion).

Despite the parsimony of this explanation and evidence in support of it, questions remain regarding the utility of these lexical and semantic cues. For example, the animacy of a noun should influence verb argument structure preferences. Take the following sentence for example, "The landmine buried in the sand exploded." Because the noun is inanimate, the landmine performing the action of burying is unlikely, encouraging readers to pursue the relative clause interpretation of the sentence. However, when Ferreira and Clifton (1986) manipulated the animacy of the first noun of a sentence, the data suggested that such thematic information did not influence initial processing of garden-path sentences in both eye-tracking and self-paced reading experiments. Whether the initial noun was inanimate, and thus an unlikely agent for the action of the verb, or animate, and thus a likely agent, did not appear to alter initial parsing of temporarily ambiguous sentences. These data were used to support the existence of a syntactic module relying on syntactic heuristics only.

Nearly a decade later, these experiments were repeated with several slight changes. By using a slightly different display, in which line breaks did not interfere with the disambiguating region of the sentence, and using slightly different materials, in which the semantic constraints were stronger, Trueswell et al. (1994) reported data suggesting that the animacy of the noun does significantly influence initial processing of a temporarily ambiguous sentence. Processing difficulties in this experiment were related to the thematic fit of the noun–verb pairs. Sentences that contained an inanimate noun with a strong semantic fit with the verb showed no processing difficulty when compared to unambiguous control sentences, and nouns with a weak semantic fit to the verb showed processing difficulties similar to those observed by Ferreira and Clifton (1986). These data, then, suggest that carefully controlling experimental stimuli is crucial for observing the influence of any single source of information during sentence processing.

According to both probabilistic-selection theories (Van Gompel et al., 2001) and constraint-based theories (MacDonald et al., 1994), multiple sources of information are used immediately to bias the reader toward one or another of the syntactic alternatives. However, with so many sources of information available to influence this resolution process, it is rare that a single source of information can be manipulated in such a way that it single-handedly sways the resolution a particular way. Unless the situation is perfectly balanced, the other available sources of information are likely to converge toward one or another alternative. So, any single source of information may only slightly influence processing because the other sources of information converge on another interpretation, and the influence of that single cue under observation is outvoted. With this in mind, it may not be surprising that some studies have had trouble finding statistically significant evidence for the immediate influence of an individual cue on sentence processing (Ferreira & Clifton, 1986; Rayner, Carlson, & Frazier, 1983), even when the data show trends supporting this conclusion (Clifton et al. 2003). When these other sources of information are controlled sufficiently to investigate a single cue, that cue can be observed to immediately influence comprehension of garden-path sentences (MacDonald et al., 1994; McRae, Spivey-Knowlton, & Tanenhaus, 1998; Tanenhaus & Trueswell, 1995; for in-depth review, see McRae & Matsuki, this volume).

Extra-sentential context constrains syntactic parsing

One crucial piece of evidence for distinguishing among different models of syntactic processing is the degree to which information from outside of the current sentence can exert an immediate influence on the presence or magnitude of a garden-path effect. As far back as 1985, Crain and Steedman argued that syntactic ambiguity resolution rests not solely upon structural criteria, but also on the referential properties of the discourse context. Sentences do not typically occur in isolation, divorced from any relevant linguistic context, but are often embedded within a larger discourse, such that language comprehension likely depends, in part, on the ability to integrate incoming information with a pre-existing discourse model.

In a compelling demonstration of the effect of discourse context on the processing of syntactically ambiguous sentences, Altmann, Garnham, and Dennis (1992) investigated the manner in which discourse context influenced processing of the Sentential Complement/Relative Clause ambiguity (1).

(2a) SC-Resolved: He told the woman / that he'd misunderstood / the nature / of her / question.

(2b) RC-Resolved: He told the woman / that he'd misunderstood / to repeat / her last / question.

The fragment *that he'd misunderstood* contains a syntactic ambiguity because *told* can be followed by either a sentential complement (a simplex analysis of the noun phrase (NP), as in (2a)) or a relative clause (the complex NP analysis, as in (2b)). In the first case, *that* is processed as a complementizer, thus resulting in a sentential complement (SC) interpretation. In the second case, *that* becomes a relative pronoun leading to a relative clause (RC) interpretation. Disambiguation occurs in the segment of the sentence occurring after *misunderstood*.

When this type of ambiguity appears outside of any relevant linguistic context, there exists a strong bias in favor of SC-resolution, such that a garden-path arises at disambiguation when the sentence is resolved in accordance with the RC interpretation of the ambiguity. As noted by Crain and Steedman (1985), the combination of a definite noun phrase and a relative clause presupposes two related entities within a wider discourse model, one of which is being singled out by the relativized NP. Consequently, if the discourse context provides only one such referent (or a null context tacitly assumes one referent), then a syntactically ambiguous clause that could be an RC or an SC will be parsed as an SC because the RC's referential presuppositions are not being met by the context. However, according to referential theory, when the referential presuppositions of an RC are met by the discourse context (because it contains two referents for the preceding NP), then the garden-path effect so often observed in RC sentences can be avoided because the syntactically ambiguous clause will be initially parsed as an RC.

Indeed, Altmann et al. (1992) presented both versions of the ambiguity in a multi-sentence context containing either two distinct or two related referents:

SC-Supporting Context

>A bank manager was giving financial advice to **a man** and **a woman**. They were asking about the benefits of a high-interest savings account. The bank manager had misunderstood **the woman's** question about the account but understood **the man** perfectly.

RC-Supporting Context

>A bank manager was giving financial advice to **two women**. They were asking about the benefits of a high interest savings account. The bank manager had misunderstood **one of the women's** questions about the account but understood **the other** perfectly.

Patterns of eye-movements during reading the temporarily ambiguous sentences revealed that context exerted a strong effect on the presence of the garden-path effects traditionally observed with this type of ambiguity. When the discourse-context contained two similar referents (*the two women*), the garden-path effect was significantly attenuated. Additionally, when the discourse-context contained two distinct entities (*the man and the woman*), the SC interpretation was facilitated. The attenuation of the garden-path effect associated with the more complex RC-resolved sentences was attributed to the fact that encountering two very similar entities within a discourse set up an expectation that the entities would be differentiated, and a relative clause is one primary way for that differentiation to occur. The complement analysis, on the other hand, was supported when it appeared in a context containing only one possible referent for the referring expression, *the woman*.

Since these early experiments, the effect of discourse context on the presence of a garden-path effect when an ambiguity is resolved in accordance with the dis-preferred interpretation has become one of the most highly replicated effects in the domain of sentence processing, replicating across language, ambiguity type, modality, and with a wide variety of psychological and psychophysiological testing methods (Altmann et al., 1992; Altmann, Garnham, & Henstra, 1994; Altmann & Steedman, 1988; Altmann, van Nice, Garnham, & Henstra, 1998; Brown, Van Berkum, & Hagoort, 2000; Farmer, Christiansen, & Kemtes, 2005; Hoeks, Vonk, & Schriefers, 2002; Spivey & Tanenhaus, 1998; Spivey-Knowlton, Trueswell, & Tanenhaus, 1993; Van Berkum, Brown, & Hagoort, 1999a, 1999b). A few other experiments, however, have failed to find commensurate effects of discourse-based context (Ferreira & Clifton, 1986; Mitchell, Corley, & Garnham, 1992; Rayner, Garrod, & Perfetti, 1992). And still others have found immediate discourse-context effects with certain types of syntactic ambiguities and delayed effects of discourse context with other types of syntactic ambiguities (Britt, Perfetti, Garrod, & Rayner, 1992).

Of course, in order to discriminate between models that predict immediate context effects and those that predict delayed context effects, it is crucial to operationalize what one means by "immediate." Self-paced reading and eye-tracking during reading can provide on-line measures of sentence processing, but they are necessarily recording motor output that is the result of a substantial amount of perceptual and cognitive processing. To demonstrate immediacy, one must show that the effect of the extra-sentential context influences the initial parsing process of the ambiguity, otherwise syntax-first models can always account for the influence of non-syntactic factors as attributable to a rapid second-stage reanalysis mechanism instead of to the mechanism responsible for first-stage processing. Indeed, ERP research has demonstrated that the effect of ambiguity on the EEG signal is modulated by the presence or absence of a biasing context, and that the onset of such an effect occurs very shortly after perceptual processing.

Van Berkum et al. (1999a) investigated the degree to which discourse-context can influence the initial processing of Dutch sentences containing an SC/RC ambiguity, as in examples (3–4), below:

(3a) **SC-resolved ambiguous sentence**

David vertelde / het meisje / dat / er / visite kwam.
David told / the girl$_{neu}$ / that$_{comp}$ / there / would be some visitors.

(3b) **RC-resolved ambiguous sentence**

David vertelde / het meisje / dat / had / zitten bellen op te hangen.
David told / the girl$_{neu}$ / that$_{RelPro}$ / had / been phoning to hang up.

In Dutch, nouns with the neuter gender can be followed by a lexically ambiguous version of *dat* (3); *dat* might either be a complementizer, thus signifying the onset of a complement clause, or it could be a relative pronoun, thus denoting the onset of a relative clause. The presence of an expletive pronoun (like *er* in (3a)) after *dat* strongly supports the complement clause interpretation of the ambiguity, whereas an auxiliary (like *had* in (3b)) after *dat* signals that it is indeed a relative pronoun, thus supporting the relative clause interpretation of the ambiguity. In the absence of any additional constraining information, there exists a strong preference for the SC interpretation of this ambiguity. As such, when it is subsequently resolved with the RC interpretation, a garden-path effect occurs at disambiguation (Altmann et al., 1992).

Sentences like (3) were presented to participants as the final sentence in short (2–3 sentence) vignettes containing either one unique referent for the referring expression (*the girl* in example (3)) of the ambiguous target sentence (*the boy and the girl* both mentioned in the context), or two potential referents (*the two girls*), neither of which could be a unique referent for the referring expression in (3). On the SC-resolved sentences, they found that a P600/SPS (a positive ERP wave associated with structural anomalies) occurred at the disambiguating word when two referents were present in the discourse-context, relative to the condition in which only one possible referent for the referring expression existed. Conversely, for the RC-resolved sentences, a P600/SPS occurred at the disambiguating word in the one-referent condition relative to the two-referent condition.

The results above demonstrate that when no unique referent can be established for a referring expression (as in the two-referent context), the comprehension system is much more amenable to the RC interpretation, given that it affords the possibility that a unique referent will be specified (or that the two similar referents will be differentiated amongst somehow). The P600/SPS on the disambiguating word when context does not support the ultimately correct resolution of the ambiguity can be seen as a reflection of the garden-path effect, occurring early enough to manifest itself during the processing of the first disambiguating word. Although this effect demonstrates that, very early on, discourse context has already created the expectation for one syntactic resolution over the other, the authors also included an additional condition showing that disambiguating gender information was much less influential than the discourse context in a sentence where no ambiguity should have been present.

(4a) SC-immediate unambiguous sentence
David vertelde / de vrouw / dat / er / visite kwam.
David told / the woman$_{common}$ / that$_{comp}$ / there / would be some visitors.

(4b) RC-forced unambiguous sentence
David vertelde / de vrouw / die / had / zitten bellen op te hangen.
David told / the woman$_{common}$ / that$_{RelPro}$ / had / been phoning to hang up.

Although nouns with neuter gender can be followed by the lexically ambiguous version of *dat* in Dutch, thus providing psycholinguists with an ambiguity to exploit, when *dat* occurs after nouns that are assigned a common gender, it can not be interpreted as the beginning of a relative clause. As such, in (4a), the common gender associated with *de vrouw* forces a complemetizer interpretation of *dat*, thereby eliminating any structural ambiguity. If the common gendered noun is the head of a relative clause, however, then the relative pronoun with which it is associated must be *die* (as in (4b)), once again eliminating the presence of any ambiguity.

Of interest however, van Berkum, Brown, and Hagoort (1999a) found that in the two-referent context, sentences with immediate SC-resolution (due to the common gendered noun) elicited a P600 on the unambiguous complementizer *dat* relative to the same word-position in the one-referent context. So, even though the presence of the common gender noun required a complementizer interpretation of *dat*, the two-referent condition caused participants to garden-path momentarily. The authors then argue that the analysis gets checked against the gender marking of the noun in the previous NP and that, during that check, the misanalysis is noted and a garden-path-like effect gets observed (the P600). The evidence for such a claim comes from the fact that on the following word *er*, no P600 emerges, suggesting that the parse had already been recovered.

The take-home message from the manipulation in example (4) is that the effect of context was so strong that it caused an early and strong expectation for an RC, a bias formidable enough to cause the system to ignore purely syntactic information (at least momentarily), while in pursuit of referential support for the under-specified common-gendered noun (specifically in the two-referent condition). Stated alternatively, discourse-context mattered first. The effects reported above have been replicated, both with the same experimental presentation parameters (van Berkum et al., 1999b) and in the auditory modality with natural speech (Brown, van Berkum, & Hagoort, 2000). The presence and reliability of the P600 in response to the violation of expectations that were created, at least in part, by the discourse-context presents a strong challenge to any model assigning an initial temporal superiority to syntactic heuristics.

Van Berkum et al. (1999b) also used the main experimental manipulation above to explore the nature of referential processing as it relates to the assignment of reference to definite NPs upon interception. Collapsing across all four sentence-conditions ((3) and (4)), they demonstrated that a negative ERP component (with a post-stimulus onset of ~300 ms) occurred at the noun in the post-verbal definite NP ("the girl/the woman") in the two-referent contexts as compared to the one-referent contexts. That is, when no one unique referent can be assigned to the definite NP, the systems subserving referential processing treat the referential ambiguity as something like a semantic or pragmatic anomaly. They did note, however, that as compared to the well-established characteristics of the N400 (a negative ERP wave associated with semantic anomalies), the component elicited by the referential ambiguity had a later onset, lacked a clear peak, and was sustained longer by the anterior (as opposed to posterior) scalp sites.

Van Berkum, Brown, Hagoort, and Zwitserlood (2003) made the bolder claim that the N400-like component they had observed in previous studies, time-locked to the presence of referential ambiguity, was not related to the N400 component and was not an index of semantic and/or pragmatic processing. Instead, they argued that this component is functionally and morphologically distinct from the N400 and can be seen instead as an ERP component that is related to referential processing. By administering the same materials (albeit with a slightly faster SOA and in the auditory modality) as those in van Berkum et al. (1999b), van Berkum et al. (2003) once again elicited a negative component beginning at ~320–370 ms post definite NP onset in the two-referent as compared to the one-referent context. This negativity occurred initially at both anterior and posterior scalp sites, but disappeared quickly in the posterior recording sites (by ~600 ms post NP onset) relative to the anterior recording sites, where it was much more sustained.

In a crucial alternative condition, participants heard sentences that contained a *discourse-dependent* semantic anomaly (like, "John ate a sandwich with salami") in a context that introduced John as a vegetarian. Relative to the control condition (where no discourse-dependent anomaly existed), a classic N400 (originating ~200 ms post-stimulus onset, peaking clearly at ~400 ms, and with a centro-parietal distribution) occurred on the sentence-final words in response to the discourse-dependent semantic anomaly. Thus, their (unnamed) N400-like component is related to referential processing, and is elicited, according to van Berkum et al. (2003), when a unique reference for a definite NP cannot be established – importantly, they do not consider it the same as an N400 resulting from a discourse-dependent anomaly. This referentially induced negativity has more recently been shown to be sensitive even to highly specific types of referential information. For example, it disappears in contexts where two potential referents for a referring expression were initially present but, subsequently, one becomes unavailable (e.g. one of the referents dies), demonstrating immediate sensitivity to the detailed properties of the mental model that get constructed during longer multi-sentence passages (Nieuwland, Otten, & van Berkum, 2007).

ERP studies involving the Discourse Context × Syntactic Ambiguity manipulation suggest that referential context can bias the system to expect particular information downstream. The garden-path effects reported above, then, can be viewed as arising by way of expectation violation, and it is this expectation violation that is indexed by the P600 effects reported. The overwhelming importance of the context manipulation is highlighted further by the fact that the contextual information dominates at least certain types of lower-level syntactic cues (like gender) in determining which of multiple potential parses the comprehension system will initially entertain. Moreover, the early onset (~500 ms after the onset of the first disambiguating word) of the ERPs

126 *Michael J. Spivey et al.*

that index the garden-path effect on trials where a mismatch exists between the context-produced expectations and the ultimate resolution of the ambiguity support the very early use of referential information during processing (especially when factoring out the time taken for perceptual processing).

Visual situational context constrains syntactic parsing

Demonstrating that some sentences that precede a target sentence can influence its syntactic parsing in real-time is important evidence for our proposal of "putting syntax in context." Apparently the non-syntactic linguistic information in those referential contexts can influence the initial resolution of a syntactic ambiguity. However, even more striking evidence for non-syntactic information influencing parsing comes from *non-linguistic* visual contexts. Can information that isn't even part of the language processing system tell syntax what to do? A great deal of evidence now shows that while listening to a spoken instruction that contains a temporary syntactic ambiguity, information from a different sensory modality (visual perception) can immediately influence the resolution of that syntactic ambiguity.

For example, if participants are presented with a display of real objects like that in Figure 5.1a, and are then instructed to "Put the spoon on the napkin in the bowl," they tend to initially fixate the spoon and then fixate the upper right napkin (as if it were potentially relevant as a destination of the putting event), before finally fixating the bowl and placing the spoon in it (Spivey, Tanenhaus, Eberhard, & Sedivy 2002; Tanenhaus, Spivey-Knowlton, Eberhard, & Sedivy, 1995; Trueswell, Sekerina, Hill, & Logrip, 1999). This eye-movement pattern suggests that participants are often initially parsing "on the napkin" as syntactically attached to the verb phrase, i.e., temporarily treating it as the destination for the spoon's "putting" event. The brief fixation of the irrelevant napkin is evidence of this incorrect parse because it very rarely happens in the control condition, where the spoken instruction is syntactically unambiguous (e.g., "Put the spoon that's on the napkin in the bowl"). The critical demonstration that visual/situational context can intervene during on-line syntactic processing comes from the condition where the same syntactically ambiguous instruction was delivered with the visual display in Figure 5.1b. In this context, participants rarely ever looked at the irrelevant destination (e.g., the other napkin). Since there are two spoons in this context (introducing a referential ambiguity, à la Altmann & Steedman, 1988), upon hearing "the spoon," the participant does not yet know which spoon is being referred to, and both spoons tend to get fixated upon briefly. Then, upon hearing "on the napkin," the referential uncertainty introduced by having two potential spoons encourages the system to parse "on the napkin" as syntactically attached to the noun phrase rather than to the verb phrase, thus discriminating which spoon is being referred to and thereby minimizing any syntactic garden-path effect.

Subsequent work shows that this influence of visual/situational context interacts with information about the verb's argument-structure biases (Snedeker

Figure 5.1 When instructed to "Put the spoon on the napkin in the bowl," participants often mis-parse the syntactic attachment of the initial prepositional phrase when there is only one visible referent for "spoon" (a), but not when there are two such referents (b).

Source: Figure adapted from Spivey and Richardson (2009).

& Trueswell, 2004). For example, when under rushed time constraints (Novick, Thompson-Schill, & Trueswell, 2008), adults' eye-movement patterns indicate a greater reliance on lexical-statistical biases than on the visual/situational context – just as seen in children (Trueswell et al., 1999; see also Snedeker, this volume). The visual/situational context also interacts with information about the motor affordances that exist between the listener and the objects in the scene (Chambers, Tanenhaus, & Magnuson, 2004). For example, consider a display like Figure 5.1b, except that it contains a cracked egg in a bowl in the upper left corner, another (cracked) egg in a glass in the lower left corner, an empty bowl in the upper right corner, and a pile of flour in the lower right corner. When instructed to "pour the egg in the bowl onto the flour," participants tended to initially look at both liquid eggs, settle their eyes on the one in the bowl, then look at the flour, and then carry out the correct action. Since the noun phrase, "the egg," was referentially ambiguous, listeners quickly incorporated the syntactically ambiguous prepositional phrase "in the bowl," as attached to the noun phrase to resolve that referential ambiguity, and that caused them to minimize the garden-path interpretation of thinking the bowl in the upper right corner was a potentially relevant destination – much like in the previous experiments (Spivey et al., 2002; Tanenhaus et al., 1995). However, with a subtle manipulation of the affordances of the objects, Chambers et al. were able to make that garden-path effect come back! When the extra cracked egg in the glass was replaced by an uncracked egg in its shell, that extra egg no longer afforded a pouring action, and thus for the purposes of this particular verb, the display was equivalent to a one-referent context. When participants heard, "pour the egg," they tended to look only at the liquid egg, and when they then heard, "in the bowl," they frequently fixated the empty bowl as a potential destination, thus exhibiting the garden-path effect.

Garden-path sentences are not the only place where visual context can influence parsing. Since syntactic processing is so continuously incremental and anticipatory (e.g., Marslen-Wilson, 1975), there are always moments in time when a syntactic constituent can be confidently projected before it has been received, and sentence interpretation can take advantage of this anticipation. For example, Altmann and Kamide (1999) presented participants with line drawings of scenes containing a potential agent (e.g., a boy) and several possible direct objects (only one of which was edible, e.g., a cake). When participants heard "The boy will move the cake," they moved their eyes from the boy to the cake soon after the word "cake." However, when they heard "The boy will eat the cake," many of the participants were already fixating the cake before the word "cake" was even heard! Thus, the situational context combined with the syntax and the verb's thematic role preferences (e.g., direct objects that are edible) to make people able to comprehend the full sentence before it was finished being spoken (see also Kamide, Altmann, & Haywood, 2003).

In fact, even recent memory of a visual context can be combined with syntax to achieve rapid interpretation of a sentence. Altmann (2004) replicated some of the anticipatory eye-movement results from Altmann and Kamide (1999) with a display that initially presented the potential Subjects and Direct Objects and then took them away. With the screen totally blank, eye-movement data were still informative about how listeners were comprehending the incoming linguistic input. Participants made anticipatory eye-movements to the corresponding locations of the appropriate entities (which were now empty) while the spoken sentence was being understood. (See also Huette, Winter, Matlock, & Spivey, 2011; and Spivey & Geng, 2001, for similar blank-screen eye-tracking studies of verbal aspect and of visual imagery, respectively.)

Knoeferle and Crocker (2006) then pitted the visual/situational context against the semantic and thematic role biases at the same time to see how these two different forms of context influence syntactic processing when they disagree with one another. For example, what if your thematic role knowledge of verbs tells you that hexing is typically performed by wizards and spying is typically performed by detectives, but the visual/situational context shows you a detective holding a magic wand and a wizard using a pair of binoculars? *In situ*ations like that, participants make anticipatory eye-movements that are consistent with using the *visual context* as the guide for likely agents of spying events and hexing events (see also Knoeferle, Habets, Crocker, & Münte, 2008, for confirmation of the strong role of visual context in influencing parsing in a related ERP study). Thus, similar to what was observed with garden-path sentences, it looks as though verb-based preferences are indeed still active during spoken language comprehension in a visual context, but when the situational context conflicts with them and is visually co-present, the situational information tends to outweigh the stored lexical biases.

But what about when the situational information is no longer visually co-present, as when Altmann and Kamide (2004) removed the images from the display and then played the spoken sentence with a blank screen? Who will "tell syntax what to do," situational context or semantic/thematic roles? To explore this question, Knoeferle and Crocker (2007) presented their depicted event (of detectives and wizards, etc.) and then removed it to have a blank screen during delivery of the spoken sentence. With longer and longer delays between removal of the display and onset of the spoken sentence, the preference for depicted-event biases over thematic-role biases waned over time. Thus, internally stored thematic-role biases drove comprehension more and more as the visual memory of the situation decayed.

While these eye-movement data from the visual-world paradigm compellingly demonstrate that non-syntactic information can quickly influence parsing decisions in the face of syntactic uncertainty, they cannot easily speak to the issue of *how* context exerts that influence. For example, on an individual event of hearing a sentence in a visually constraining situation, does context wind up instantaneously flipping the parser's choice to selecting the situationally appropriate alternative and summarily discarding the semantically appropriate alternative? Or does context instead combine with other constraints in a quantitative fashion to make both alternatives partially active and then gradually settle over time toward one or the other alternative? Due to the ballistic nature of saccadic eye-movements, on any given trial in these eye-tracking experiments, a participant either looks at the incorrect destination object, indicating a sizeable garden-path event, or she doesn't. To test for graded proclivities toward attending to one object or another, as an index of partial activation of the syntactic parse associated with that object, our experiments need to record something other than saccadic eye-movements and fixations – something that can exhibit a graded spatial attraction toward objects in the field of view.

For example, the streaming x,y coordinates of computer-mouse movements were used by Spivey, Grosjean, and Knoblich (2005) to explore real-time spoken word recognition and demonstrate a graded spatial attraction toward "cohort" objects whose names have overlapping acoustic/phonetic properties (for quantitative simulations of the potential underlying mechanisms, see Spivey, Dale, Knoblich, & Grosjean, 2010, and van der Wel, Eder, Mitchel, Walsh, & Rosenbaum, 2009). Farmer, Anderson-Cargill, Hindy, Dale, and Spivey (2007b) extended this paradigm to test for context effects in syntactic parsing and to measure graded spatial attraction toward the incorrect destination object in syntactically ambiguous sentences like, "Put the spoon on the napkin in the bowl." In these computer-mouse trajectories, Farmer et al. were able to observe what can be seen as a continuous index of the degree to which one syntactic representation was active, relative to another, across time. In some trials (especially in the two-referent context, Figure 5.1b), participants click-grabbed the spoon and dragged it nearly straight to the bowl, but in other trials their trajectory curved slightly toward the irrelevant napkin, and in still other trials the trajectory curved substantially toward the napkin (especially in the one-referent context, Figure 5.1a). Farmer et al. replicated the previous effects of visual/situational context, whereby the visual co-presence of two potential referents causes the listener to veer away from parsing the prepositional phrase (e.g., "on the napkin") as syntactically attached to the verb phrase and instead attach it to the noun phrase – thus avoiding the garden-path. Moreover, through a series of extensive distributional analyses, Farmer, Anderson, and Spivey (2007a) were also able to explore the trial-by-trial curvature magnitudes of each movement trajectory. They interpreted these analyses, and accompanying simulations, as consistent with the idea that the very reason context can influence parsing is because the alternatives of a syntactic ambiguity are simultaneously partially-active (not discarded), and thereby amenable to having their non-zero activation modulated by contextual constraints.

Thus, results from a variety of experiments and methodologies suggest that visual/situational context can rapidly influence syntactic ambiguity resolution during real-time sentence comprehension. Moreover, it may be that this contextual influence is made possible precisely because multiple syntactic alternatives are simultaneously available and active. Indeed, if only one syntactic alternative was being considered by the language processing system at any given time then it would be exceptionally difficult for context that supported an unconsidered syntactic alternative to bring that support to bear.

Conclusion

In dozens and dozens of syntactic processing experiments, there is a great deal of accumulating evidence for immediate effects of intra-sentential context, extra-sentential context, and even visual/situational context. In fact, this body of evidence for "putting syntax in context" has grown so much that syntax-first models of sentence processing (Frazier & Fodor, 1978; Frazier & Clifton, 1996) have been modified to accommodate some of these immediate effects of context while preserving the serial processing of syntactic structures (Britt et al., 1994; Van Gompel et al., 2005; see also Traxler & Frazier, 2008). In a probabilistic-selection account of syntactic ambiguity resolution (Van Gompel et al., 2005), certain sources of non-syntactic information can influence which syntactic alternative is selected, and the non-selected alternative is then discarded. If the discarded alternative turns out to be the correct one, a reanalysis mechanism (much like that used in the original syntax-first models) must re-build that syntactic structure. This type of model can accommodate many of the effects of non-syntactic context, and it also predicts a bimodal distribution of garden-path magnitudes (i.e., only full-fledged garden-paths and non-garden-paths; nothing in between). Current research continues to examine whether context exerts its influence on syntax by selecting one alternative and discarding another, or whether the various linguistic and contextual constraints combine and compete over time in a more continuous dynamical process (see Farmer et al., 2007a; Van Gompel et al., 2005).

The theoretical framework for sentence processing that predicts both the wide array of observed context effects and also the gradation in garden-path magnitudes is the constraint-based account (MacDonald et al., 1994; Tanenhaus

& Trueswell, 1995). This account integrates various sources of non-syntactic information to support multiple simultaneously active syntactic alternatives, and uses a dynamic competition process (e.g., Bates & MacWhinney, 1989) to settle toward one of those alternatives. The adjudication among these different theoretical accounts of sentence processing is far from over. In addition to needing more empirical tests and data analyses for resolving the theoretical debate, we will also need more computational simulations of the competing models. Progress in this field will be greatly advanced by more simulations that make quantitative predictions of reading times (Green & Mitchell, 2006; Spivey & Tanenhaus, 1998) of computer-mouse movements (Farmer et al., 2007a) and of eye-movements (Scheutz, Eberhard, & Andronache, 2004). Building a computational implementation of one's theory is the safest way to avoid positing intuitive predictions that one's theory may actually be incapable of making, or missing out on predictions that one's model actually forces itself to make. What are especially useful are simulations that can have their parameters adjusted to become versions of the alternative models, thus allowing the different theories to compete on a level playing field (Farmer et al., 2007a; McRae et al., 1998; Tanenhaus, Spivey-Knowlton, & Hanna, 2000).

References

Altmann, G. T. M. (2004). Language-mediated eye-movements in the absence of a visual world: The 'blank screen paradigm'. *Cognition*, *93*, 79–87.

Altmann, G. T. M., Garnham, A., & Dennis, Y. (1992). Avoiding the garden-path: Eye-movements in context. *Journal of Memory and Language*, *31*, 685–712.

Altmann, G. T. M., Garnham, A., & Henstra, J. (1994). Effects of syntax in human sentence parsing: Evidence against a structure-based proposal mechanism. *Journal of Experimental Psychology: Learning, Memory, and Cognition*, *20*, 209–216.

Altmann, G. T. M., & Kamide, Y. (1999). Incremental interpretation at verbs: Restricting the domain of subsequent reference. *Cognition*, *73*, 247–264.

Altmann, G. T. M., & Kamide, Y. (2004). Now you see it, now you don't: Mediating the mapping between language and the visual world. In J. Henderson & F. Ferreira (Eds.), *The interface of language, vision, and action: Eye-movements and the visual world* (pp. 347–386). New York: Psychology Press.

Altmann, G. T. M., van Nice, K., Garnham, A., & Henstra, J. A. (1998). Late closure in context. *Journal of Memory and Language*, *38*, 459–484.

Altmann G. T. M., & Steedman, M. (1988). Interaction with context during human sentence processing. *Cognition*, *30*, 191–238.

Bates, E., & MacWhinney, B. (1989). Functionalism and the competition model. In B. MacWhinney & E. Bates (Eds.), *The crosslinguistic study of sentence processing* (pp. 3–73). Cambridge: Cambridge University Press.

van Berkum, J. J. A., Brown, C. M., & Hagoort, P. (1999a). Early referential context effects in sentence processing: Evidence from event-related potentials. *Journal of Memory and Language*, *41*, 147–182.

van Berkum, J. J. A., Brown, C. M., & Hagoort, P. (1999b). Semantic integration in sentences and discourse: Evidence from the N400. *Journal of Cognitive Neuroscience*, *11*, 657–671.

van Berkum, J. J. A., Brown, C. M., Hagoort, P., & Zwitserlood, P. (2003). Event-related brain potentials reflect discourse-referential ambiguity in spoken-language comprehension. *Psychophysiology, 40,* 235–248.
Bever, T. G. (1970). The cognitive basis for linguistic structures. In J. R. Hayes (Ed.), *Cognition and the growth of cognition* (pp. 279–362). New York: Wiley.
Britt, M., Perfetti, C., Garrod, S., & Rayner, K. (1992). Parsing in discourse: Context effects and their limits. *Journal of Memory and Language, 31,* 293–314.
Britt, M. A. (1994). The interaction of referential ambiguity and argument structure in the parsing of prepositional phrases. *Journal of Memory and Language, 33,* 251–283.
Brown, C. M., van Berkum, J. J. A., & Hagoort, P. (2000). Discourse before gender: An event-related brain potential study on the interplay of semantic and syntactic information during spoken language understanding. *Journal of Psycholinguistic Research, 29,* 53–68.
Chambers, C. C., Tanenhaus, M., & Magnuson, J. (2004). Actions and affordances in syntactic ambiguity resolution. *Journal of Experimental Psychology: Learning, Memory, and Cognition, 30,* 687–696.
Chomsky, N. (1957). *Syntactic structures.* Oxford: Mouton.
Clifton, C., Traxler, M. J., Mohamed, M. T., Williams, R. S., Morris, R. K., & Rayner, K. (2003). The use of thematic role information in parsing: Syntactic processing autonomy revisited. *Journal of Memory and Language, 49,* 317–334.
Crain, S., & Steedman, M. (1985). On not being led down the garden path. In D. R. Dowty, L. Karttunen, & A. M. Zwicky (Eds.), *Natural language parsing: Psychological, computational and theoretical perspectives* (pp. 320–358). Cambridge: Cambridge University Press.
Culicover, P., & Nowak, A. (2003). *Dynamical grammar.* New York: Oxford University Press.
Elman, J. (1991). Distributed representations, simple recurrent networks, and grammatical structure. *Machine Learning, 7,* 195–224.
Farmer, T., Anderson, S., & Spivey, M. J. (2007a). Gradiency and visual context in syntactic garden-paths. *Journal of Memory and Language, 57,* 570–595.
Farmer, T., Anderson-Cargill, S., Hindy, N., Dale, R., & Spivey, M. J. (2007b). Tracking the continuity of language comprehension: Computer-mouse trajectories suggest parallel syntactic processing. *Cognitive Science, 31,* 889–909.
Farmer, T. A., Christiansen, M. H. & Kemtes, K. A. (2005). Sentence processing in context: The impact of experience on individual differences. In *Proceedings of the 27th annual meeting of the Cognitive Science Society* (pp. 642–647). Mahwah, NJ: Lawrence Erlbaum.
Ferreira, F., & Clifton, C. (1986). The independence of syntactic processing. *Journal of Memory and Language, 25,* 248–368.
Ford, M., Bresnan, J. W., & Kaplan, R. M. (1982). A competence-based theory of syntactic closure. In J. W. Bresnan (Ed.), *The mental representation of grammatical relations* (pp. 727–796). Cambridge, MA: MIT Press.
Frazier, L. (1988). Getting there (slowly). *Journal of Psycholinguistic Research, 27,* 123–146.
Frazier, L., & Clifton, C. (1996). *Construal.* Cambridge, MA: MIT Press.
Frazier, L., & Fodor, J. (1978). The sausage machine: A new two-stage parsing model. *Cognition, 6,* 291–325.
Frazier, L., & Rayner, K. (1982). Making and correcting errors during sentence comprehension: Eye-movement in the analysis of structurally ambiguous sentences. *Cognitive Psychology, 14,* 179–210.

Green, M., & Mitchell, D. (2006). Absence of real evidence against competition during syntactic ambiguity resolution. *Journal of Memory and Language*, *55*, 1–17.

Hale, J. (2001). A probabilistic Earley parser as a psycholinguistic model. In *Proceedings of the 2nd conference of the North American chapter of the Association for Computational Linguistics*, Vol. 2, (pp. 159–166), Pittsburgh, PA.

Hare, M., Tanenhaus, M., & McRae, K. (2007). Understanding and producing the reduced relative construction: Evidence from ratings, editing, and corpora. *Journal of Memory and Language*, *56*, 410–435.

Harris, Z. (1954). Transfer grammar. *International Journal of American Linguistics*, *20*, 259–270.

Hoeks J. C. J., Vonk W., Schriefers, H. (2002). Processing coordinated structures in context: The effect of topic-structure on ambiguity resolution. *Journal of Memory and Language*, *46*, 99–119.

Huette, S., Winter, B., Matlock, T., & Spivey, M. (2011, March). *Spatiotemporal fixation differences on a blank screen during aspect comprehension.* Talk presented at the *24th Annual CUNY Conference on Human Sentence Processing*, 24–26 March, Stanford, CA.

Kamide, Y., Altmann, G. T. M., & Haywood, S. L. (2003). The time-course of prediction in incremental sentence processing: Evidence from anticipatory eye-movements. *Journal of Memory and Language*, *49*, 133–159.

Knoeferle, P., & Crocker, M. W. (2006). The coordinated interplay of scene, utterance, and world knowledge: Evidence from eye-tracking. *Cognitive Science*, *30*, 481–529.

Knoeferle, P., & Crocker, M. W. (2007). The influence of recent scene events on spoken comprehension: Evidence from eye-movements. *Journal of Memory and Language*, *57*, 519–543.

Knoeferle, P., Habets, B., Crocker, M. W., & Münte, T. F. (2008). Visual scenes trigger immediate syntactic reanalysis: Evidence from ERPs during situated spoken comprehension. *Cerebral Cortex*, *18*, 789–95.

Lakoff, G. (1971). On generative semantics. In D. Steinberg & L. Jakobovitz (Eds.), *Semantics: An interdisciplinary reader in philosophy, linguistics and psychology*. Cambridge: Cambridge University Press.

Levy, R. (2008). Expectation based syntactic comprehension. *Cognition*, *106*, 1126–1177.

MacDonald, M., Pearlmutter, N., & Seidenberg, M. (1994). The lexical nature of syntactic ambiguity resolution. *Psychological Review*, *101*, 676–703.

McRae, K., Spivey-Knowlton, M. J., & Tanenhaus, M. K. (1998). Modeling the influence of thematic fit (and other constraints) in on-line sentence comprehension. *Journal of Memory and Language*, *38*, 283–312.

Marslen-Wilson, W. (1975). Sentence perception as an interactive parallel process. *Science*, *189*, 226–228.

Miller, G., & McKean, K. (1964). A chonometric study of some relations between sentences. *Quarterly Journal of Experimental Psychology*, *16*, 197–308.

Mitchell, D., Corley, M., & Garnham, A. (1992). Effects of context in human sentence parsing: Evidence against a discourse-based proposal mechanism. *Journal of Experimental Psychology: Learning, Memory, and Cognition*, *18*, 69–88.

Mitchell, D., & Holmes, V. (1985). The role of specific information about the verb in parsing sentences with local structural ambiguity. *Journal of Memory and Language*, *24*, 542–559.

Nieuwland, M. S., Otten, M., & van Berkum, J. J. A. (2007). Who are you talking about? Tracking discourse-level referential processes with ERPs. *The Journal of Cognitive Neuroscience, 19,* 1–9.

Novick, J. M., Thompson-Schill, S. L., & Trueswell, J. C. (2008). Putting lexical constraints in context into the visual-world paradigm. *Cognition, 107*(3), 850–903.

Osgood, C., Suci, G., & Tennenbaum, P. (1957). *The measurement of meaning.* Champaign, IL: University of Illinois Press.

Pollard, C., & Sag, I. (1994). *Head-driven phrase structure grammar.* Chicago, IL: University of Chicago Press.

Rayner, K., Carlson, M., & Frazier, L. (1983). The interaction of syntax and semantics during sentence processing: Eye-movements in the analysis of semantically biased sentences. *Journal of Verbal Learning and Verbal Behavior, 22,* 358–374.

Rayner, K., Garrod, S., & Perfetti, C. A. (1992). Discourse influences during parsing are delayed. *Cognition, 45,* 109–139.

Scheutz, M., Eberhard, K., & Andronache, V. (2004). A parallel, distributed, realtime, robotic model for human reference resolution with visual constraints. *Connection Science, 16,* 145–167.

Snedeker, J., & Trueswell, J. (2004). The developing constraints on parsing decisions: The role of lexical-biases and referential scenes in child and adults sentence processing. *Cognitive Psychology, 49,* 238–299.

Spivey, M. J., Dale, R., Knoblich, G., & Grosjean, M. (2010). Do curved reaching movements emerge from competing perceptions? *Journal of Experimental Psychology: Human Perception and Performance, 36,* 251–254.

Spivey, M. J., & Geng, J. (2001). Oculomotor mechanisms activated by imagery and memory: Eye-movements to absent objects. *Psychological Research, 65,* 235–241.

Spivey, M., Grosjean, M., & Knoblich, G. (2005). Continuous attraction toward phonological competitors. In *Proceedings of the National Academy of Sciences, 102,* 10393–10398.

Spivey, M. & Richardson, D. (2009). Language embedded in the environment. In P. Robbins and M. Aydede (Eds.), *The Cambridge Handbook of Situated Cognition.* (pp. 382–400). Cambridge: Cambridge University Press.

Spivey, M. & Tanenhaus, M. (1998). Syntactic ambiguity resolution in discourse: Modeling the effects of referential context and lexical frequency. *Journal of Experimental Psychology: Learning, Memory, and Cognition, 24,* 1521–1543.

Spivey, M., Tanenhaus, M., Eberhard, K. & Sedivy, J. (2002). Eye-movements and spoken language comprehension: Effects of visual context on syntactic ambiguity resolution. *Cognitive Psychology, 45,* 447–481.

Spivey-Knowlton, M., Trueswell, J. & Tanenhaus, M. (1993). Context effects in syntactic ambiguity resolution. *Canadian Journal of Experimental Psychology, 47,* 276–309.

St. John, M. F., & McClelland, J. L. (1990). Learning and applying contextual constraints in sentence comprehension. *Artificial Intelligence, 46,* 217–257.

Tabor, W., Galantucci, B., & Richardson, D. (2004). Effects of merely local syntactic coherence on sentence processing. *Journal of Memory and Language, 50,* 355–370.

Tabor, W., & Hutchins, S. (2000). Mapping the syntax/semantics coastline. In L. Gleitman & A. Joshi (Eds.), *Proceedings of the 22nd annual meeting of the Cognitive Science Society* (pp. 511–516), Mahwah, NJ: Lawrence Erlbaum Associates.

Tabor, W., Juliano, C., & Tanenhaus, M. K. (1997). Parsing in a dynamical system: An attractor-based account of the interaction of lexical and structural constraints in sentence processing. *Language and Cognitive Processes, 12,* 211–271.

Tanenhaus, M., Spivey-Knowlton, M., Eberhard, K., & Sedivy, J. (1995). Integration of visual and linguistic information in spoken language comprehension. *Science, 268*, 1632–1634.

Tanenhaus, M., Spivey-Knowlton, M., & Hanna, J. (2000). Modeling the effects of discourse and thematic fit in syntactic ambiguity resolution. In M. Crocker, M. Pickering, & C. Clifton (Eds.), *Architectures and mechanisms for language processing* (pp. 90–118). Cambridge: Cambridge University Press.

Tanenhaus, M., & Trueswell, J. (1995). Sentence comprehension. In J. Miller & P. Eimas (Eds.), *Handbook of cognition and perception*. New York: Academic Press.

Traxler, M., & Frazier, L. (2008). The role of pragmatic principles in resolving attachment ambiguities: Evidence from eye-movements. *Memory & Cognition, 36*, 314–328.

Traxler, M., Pickering, M. J., & Clifton, C. (1998). Adjunct attachment is not a form of lexical ambiguity resolution. *Journal of Memory and Language, 39*, 558–592.

Trueswell, J. C., Sekerina, I., Hill, N. M. & Logrip, M. L. (1999). The kindergarten path effect: Studying on-line sentence processing in young children. *Cognition, 73*, 89–134.

Trueswell, J., Tanenhaus, M., & Garnsey, S. (1994). Semantic influences on parsing: Use of thematic role information in syntactic disambiguation. *Journal of Memory and Language, 39*, 102–123.

Trueswell, J., Tanenhaus, M., & Kello, C. (1993). Verb-specific constraints in sentence processing: Separating effects of lexical preference from garden-paths. *Journal of Experimental Psychology: Learning, Memory, and Cognition, 19*, 528–553.

Van Gompel, R. P. G., Pickering, M. J., Pearson, J., & Liversedge, S. P. (2005). Evidence against competition during syntactic ambiguity resolution. *Journal of Memory and Language, 52*, 284–307.

Van Gompel, R., Pickering, M. J., & Traxler, M. (2001). Reanalysis in sentence processing: Evidence against current constraint-based and two-stage models. *Journal of Memory and Language, 52*, 284–307.

Van der Wel, R. P. R. D., Eder, J., Mitchel, A., Walsh, M., & Rosenbaum, D. (2009). Trajectories emerging from discrete versus continuous processing models in phonological competitor tasks. *Journal of Experimental Psychology: Human Perception and Performance, 32*, 588–594.

6 Syntactic constraints on referential processing

Patrick Sturt

Introduction

One of the characteristics of natural language is the prevalence of referential expressions, such as pronouns (e.g. *he* or *she*) and reflexives (e.g. *himself* or *herself*). The interpretation of these expressions requires reference resolution – it is not enough to know simply that *he* refers to a male individual; we need to know *which* male individual it refers to. Although there is usually little or no intuitive difficulty in interpreting referential expressions in natural language, in reality, the mental processes involved are extremely complex, requiring the use of many different kinds of knowledge, including semantic and discourse-level information, but also syntactic constraints. For example, imagine that you are reading Joseph Heller's novel *Catch 22*, and you come across the sentence in (1):[1]

(1) Colonel Cathcart pledged eternal gratitude to Colonel Korn for the ingenious moves **he** devised and was furious with **him** afterward when **he** realized **they** might not work.

This example includes four pronouns, which are highlighted in bold in the example. There is a strong intuition that the first pronoun (labelled *he* in the example) refers to *Colonel Korn*. Part of the reason for this preference comes from the meaning of the sentence. Cathcart is grateful to Korn because of 'ingenious moves' that one of the two men devised. In this context, it would make little sense for Cathcart to be grateful for his own (i.e. Cathcart's own) ingenious moves.

The second pronoun, *him*, must refer to *Colonel Korn*, but the situation here is slightly different. In this case, the pronoun refers to Colonel Korn, because this is the only grammatically possible male referent within the context. According to many syntactic theorists, this is due to Principle B of binding theory (see, e.g. Chomsky, 1981). If the intended referent had been *Colonel Cathcart*, then a reflexive, *himself*, would have to be used, as is the case in a slightly later sentence in the same passage of the book:

(2) Colonel Cathcart was jealous of Colonel Korn's intelligence and had to remind **himself** often that Colonel Korn was still only a lieutenant

colonel, even though **he** was almost ten years older than Colonel Cathcart, and that Colonel Korn had obtained **his** education at a state university.

In (2), the reflexive *himself* has to refer to *Colonel Cathcart*, and cannot refer to *Colonel Korn*, even though the latter is closer to the reflexive in the string. This is because of Binding Principle A (Chomsky, 1981). Notice that if the reflexive is changed to a pronoun (*him*), then the reverse is true: the pronoun has to refer to Colonel Korn (*Colonel Cathcart was jealous of Colonel Korn's intelligence and had to remind* **him** *often that . . .*).

The scope of this chapter

Even from a brief consideration of the examples above, we can see that the processing of reference requires access to a number of different types of knowledge. In some cases, grammatical binding constraints are relevant; they can force a pronoun to refer to a particular referent or rule out another referent. In other cases, non-syntactic factors such as semantics, discourse prominence, or world-knowledge play an important role. The current chapter will focus on the way in which reference assignment is affected by syntactic constraints, namely binding phenomena, as illustrated in the examples above. Before proceeding, it is important to point out that, despite the current chapter's focus on binding constraints, there are, of course, many other ways in which referential processing interacts with sentence processing (see, for example, Spivey, Anderson, & Farmer; this volume).

Background to binding constraints

Many syntactic theories posit three separate principles, which constrain the distribution of different types of anaphoric expressions. Principle A governs the distribution of reflexives (e.g. *himself*) and reciprocals (e.g. *each other*) (which are often called 'anaphors' in Chomskyan theories (Chomsky, 1981)). Principle A explains the contrasts in (3a):[2]

(3a)   John thinks that Peter's brother hates himself.

In (3a), the reflexive *himself* can take *Peter's brother* as an antecedent, but both *Peter* and *John* would make ungrammatical antecedents. This is because, according to Principle A, the antecedent of a reflexive must *locally bind* the reflexive; in other words, the antecedent must not only be in the same local domain as the reflexive, but must also be in an appropriate configurational relationship with the reflexive, and co-refer with it.[3] We will not be concerned here with the details of the appropriate definition of the local domain, but as a first approximation, we can define it as the minimal clause that contains the reflexive[4]; for example, in (3a), it would be the complement clause (*Peter's brother hates himself*). The appropriate configurational relationship is often defined in terms of the requirement that the antecedent *c-commands* the reflexive.[5] In (3a), *John* and *Peter's brother* both c-command *himself*, but *Peter* does not. Therefore, Principle A allows only *Peter's brother* to be the antecedent of *himself*; because this is the only antecedent that satisfies both the locality requirement and the c-command requirement.

Principle B deals with the distribution of pronouns (such as *he*, *she*, etc.), which are in many cases in complementary distribution to reflexives (though there are exceptions, which we will discuss later). Therefore, the possibilities for the antecedent of *him* in (3b) are the reverse of those for the reflexive in (3a):

(3b)   John thinks that Peter's brother hates him.

Principle B captures this by requiring that pronouns must *not* be locally bound; in other words, the antecedent may not c-command the pronoun in the relevant local domain.

Finally, Principle C deals with referential expressions other than those covered by Principles A and B. According to this requirement, the referential expression (or R-expression) may not be bound, either locally or non-locally. For example, in (4), the R-expressions *Peter* and *John* may not be co-referential with *He*, because *He* c-commands both of the R-expressions:

(4)   He thinks that Peter hates John.

Within syntactic theory, the study of binding principles has been informed by intuitive judgements about the possibilities of co-reference. However, although the intuitive judgements can tell us about the constraints at an abstract level, they do not tell us about how the constraints are used in the interpretation of sentences. In order to answer this question, experimental techniques are required.

Binding as a filter

Consider again example (3a) repeated below:

(3a)   John thinks that Peter's brother hates himself.

It is intuitively clear that *himself* can only refer to *Peter's brother*, and not to either *John* or *Peter*, but what are the cognitive mechanisms that allow us to arrive at this interpretation? Presumably, when the reflexive, or other pronoun, has been processed, a suitable antecedent is sought, and it is often assumed that the choice is made from a set of candidate alternatives known as the *initial candidate set* (see Kennison, 2003, for example). In what ways do binding constraints influence the formation of this candidate set? According to one view, the binding constraints (Principle A, in this case) act as a *filter* on the initial candidate set. So, according to the *Binding as initial filter* account, the candidate set for the reflexive *himself* in (3) would include only *Peter's brother*, while *Peter* or *John* would never be considered as antecedents. Alternative accounts are possible, in which potential antecedents can be considered even if they are not sanctioned by the binding principles. For example, Badecker and Straub (2002) proposed a *constraint-based* account, in which the relevant binding principle is only one of many constraints that simultaneously act on the choice of antecedent. According to such accounts, the initial candidate set can include antecedents that are not grammatical in terms of binding theory. These antecedents may be quickly ruled out during processing.

Initial support for the binding-as-initial-filter model came from a cross-modal priming study reported by Nicol and Swinney (1989), in which participants had to make a lexical decision to a visually presented word while listening to sentences like (5):

(5) The boxer told the swimmer that the doctor for the team would blame him for the recent injury.

In (5), Principle B of the binding theory allows the pronoun *him* to refer to *the boxer* or *the swimmer*, but not *the doctor*. Thus, if binding principles act as an initial filter, then *the doctor* would never be considered in the initial candidate set. To test this, Nicol and Swinney (1989) presented a probe word at the pronoun offset in sentences like (5), and this probe word could be either related or unrelated to *boxer*, *swimmer*, or *doctor*. Lexical decision times showed priming facilitation for probe words that were related to the two antecedents that were legal in terms of binding theory, but no such facilitation for probe words that were related to the illegal antecedent *doctor*. Nicol and Swinney (1989) interpreted this as evidence for the binding-as-initial filter model. However, one drawback of the cross-modal priming technique is that it is informative about processing that occurs at a certain defined point in the sentence (i.e. where the probe word is presented), but does not give us information about other points in time. Thus, although the evidence from this study is indeed consistent with the notion that only grammatically licit antecedents were included in the initial candidate set, it is also possible that non-grammatically licensed antecedents may have been considered at some point that could not be measured using the methodology. For example, it is possible that non-grammatical antecedents may have been considered at a later point than was measured, or, perhaps, even at an extremely early point following the onset of the pronoun. If the latter is the case, then such antecedents would need to have been ruled out very quickly, in order not to affect reaction times to the probe word. Also, as pointed out by Badecker and Straub (2002), if the activation of alternative candidates is affected by both excitatory and inhibitory mechanisms, then the cross-modal priming methodology may not be able to rule out the possibility that an ungrammatical antecedent is being considered, given the design used by Nicol and Swinney (1989). This is because an antecedent could simultaneously receive both excitatory activation (due to semantic factors) and inhibition, due to being an ungrammatical antecedent, leading to a net result of no priming. However, this lack of priming does not necessarily imply that the relevant antecedent has not been considered.

Clifton, Kennison, and Albrecht (1997) also reported evidence consistent with the *binding as filter* account. They recorded participants' reading times as they read sentences like (6) in a self-paced reading task:[6]

(6)   a.   The supervisors paid him yesterday to finish typing the manuscript.

        b.   The supervisor paid him yesterday to finish typing the manuscript.

        c.   The supervisors paid his assistant to finish typing the manuscript.

        d.   The supervisor paid his assistant to finish typing the manuscript.

In (6c) and (6d), *the supervisor(s)* is a grammatically possible antecedent for the possessive pronoun *his*, but this antecedent matches the pronoun in grammatical number in (6d) only. In (6a) and (6b), in contrast, *the supervisor(s)* is not a binding-accesible antecedent for the accusative pronoun *him*, because it is ruled out by Principle B. If binding theory acts as an initial filter on subsequent processing, then *the supervisor(s)* should be in the initial candidate set for the pronoun in (6c, d), but not in (6a, b). In (6d), *his* matches in number with *the supervisor* (i.e. they are both plural), whereas in (6c), there is a number mismatch (i.e. *his* is singular, but *the supervisors* is plural), meaning that *his* does not have a valid antecedent in the sentence. Assuming that Principle B acts as an initial filter on the set of potential referents, then this number mismatch should lead to increased processing difficulty in (6c) relative to (6d), while no such difference should be found between (6a) and (6b). In fact, this is exactly the pattern that Clifton et al. (1997) obtained. Reading times were slower in (6c) than in (6d) at the word immediately following the pronoun, but no such difference was observed between (6a) and (6b).

Thus the study of Clifton et al. (1997) is consistent with the idea that the initial candidate set contains only those antecedents that are licit in terms of binding theory. However, using a similar design, Kennison (2003) showed that processing can be affected by antecedents that are ungrammatical in terms of binding theory. In her Experiment 2, Kennison used stimuli similar to the following, again using self-paced reading.

(7)   a.   Susan/Carl/They watched his classmate during the open rehearsals of the school play.

        b.   Susan/Carl/They watched him yesterday during the open rehearsals of the school play.

Similarly to Clifton et al. (1997), Kennison (2003) manipulated the form of the pronoun, such that the subject of the sentence was either an antecedent that was allowed by Principle B (7a), or not (7b). Moreover, the subject was either a gender-matching name (*Carl*), a gender-mismatching name (*Susan*), or a plural pronoun (*They*). In the cases where the subject was a binding-compatible antecedent (i.e. 7a) Kennison (2003) found that reading times were long when the gender of the name mismatched the pronoun, compared to when it matched, in the region immediately following the pronoun. In contrast, when the subject was ruled out by Principle B (7b), the reverse effect was found, with longer reading times when the subject *matched* in gender than when it did not. Kennison (2003) interpreted this result as evidence against the initial filter view, arguing that the initial candidate set for the pronoun must have included all and only those antecedents that matched the pronoun in number, irrespective of whether the potential antencedent was licit in terms of binding principles. This means that both *Carl* and *Susan* would be included in the initial candidate set, for both (7a) and (7b). In (7a), where binding constraints allow co-reference, it is relatively easy to link the pronoun with the gender matching antecedent *Carl*, and also easy to rule out the gender mismatching antecedent *Susan*. In contrast, when binding constraints do not allow co-reference, in (7b), the only grammatical solution is for *him* to refer to an entity not mentioned in the sentence. According to Kennison (2003), this requires cancelling the search for an antecedent, and this can be done more quickly when potential candidate antecedents mismatch in features, so *Susan*, which mismatches the pronoun in gender, can be eliminated from consideration more quickly than *Carl*.

Interestingly, Kennison (2003) also found that reading times in both (7a) and (7b) were relatively fast when the subject was the plural pronoun *They*. Kennison (2003) interpreted this as evidence that the initial candidate set contained only those potential antecedents that matched in number. According to this proposal, as *They* does not match *him* in number, it is not included in the initial candidate set. Therefore, it leads to no extra processing load, either when a binding accessible antecedent is available (7a) or not (7b).

Taken together, the results of Clifton et al. (1997) and Kennison (2003) present a rather complicated picture. In Clifton et al.'s study, the mismatch cost found in (6c) relative to (6d) would be consistent with the claim that the initial candidate set can include elements that mismatch the pronoun in number, while in Kennison's study, the lack of a similar cost for the *They* condition in (7a) suggests that the candidate set does not contain number-mismatching elements. Conversely, in Clifton et al.'s study, the lack of a difference between (6a) and (6b) suggests that the candidate set does not include elements that are ruled out as antecedents by binding theory, while in Kennison's study, the cost for matching gender in (7b) suggests that such binding-inaccessible antecedents may in fact be included. This shows that when we ask which types of elements might or might not be included in an initial candidate set, we need to pay attention to detailed features, such as whether the element is a pronoun (e.g. *They* in Kennison's study) or a definite noun phrase (e.g. *the supervisors* in Clifton et al.'s study). It might also be the case that the degree to which ungrammatical antecedents affect processing could be affected by individual differences.

Further experimentation is needed in order for us to gain a better understanding of the factors that influence the initial candidate set.

The experiments of Clifton et al. (1997) and Kennison (2003) are similar in that their stimuli included only one noun phrase that could potentially act as a pronominal antecedent, any given condition. In contrast, we have seen that Nicol and Swinney (1989) used stimuli that contained multiple potential antecedents, some of which were legal, and some not legal, in terms of binding theory. Although Nicol and Swinney (1989) did not observe processing effects arising from non-binding-compatible antecedents, this might have been because the cross-modal priming method did not allow observations at multiple points in time following the onset of the pronoun. In contrast, other authors, including Badecker and Straub (2002) and Sturt (2003b), have used methods that allow for the continuous measurement of processing effects at and following the appearance of the pronoun in the input. This, as well as the possibility of manipulating features of the potential antecedents independently (both those that are legal and not legal in terms of binding theory), gives further scope for observing how potential antecedents might affect processing.

Badecker and Straub (2002) examined word-by-word self-paced reading times for sentences like (8):

(8) a. *multiple match*
John thought that Bill owed him another chance to solve the problem.

b. *accessible match*
John thought that Beth owed him another chance to solve the problem.

c. *inaccessible match*
Jane thought that Bill owed him another chance to solve the problem.

d. *no match*
Jane thought that Beth owed him another chance to solve the problem.

In each experimental condition, two named characters were introduced, of which one (the *accessible antecedent*) was a grammatical antecedent for a subsequent pronoun in terms of binding theory (e.g. *John* is a grammatical antecedent for *him* in 8a), and the other (the *inaccessible antecedent*, e.g. *Bill* in (8a)) was not. The design orthogonally manipulated the gender of the accessible and inaccessible antecedents, such that either (a) both of them matched in gender with the pronoun (the *multiple match* condition), (b) the accessible antecedent matched but the inaccessible antecedent did not (the *accessible match* condition), (c) only the inaccessible antecedent matched (the *inaccessible match* condition), or (d) neither of the two antecedents matched (the *no match* condition).

There were two main results of this experiment. First, conditions (8c) and (8d) showed longer reading times than (8a) and (8b) respectively, in the two words immediately following the pronoun. This result is expected because in (8c) and (8d), there is no gender-matching name that can act as a grammatically permissible antecedent for the pronoun in terms of Principle B. Theoretically more interesting was the contrast between the *multiple match* condition (8a) and the *accessible match* condition (8b), where the multiple match condition showed longer reading times than the accessible match condition, again, at the word immediately following the pronoun. This result is unexpected on the binding-as-filter view, because in each of the two conditions (8a) and (8b), there is only one name that can grammatically act as an antecedent of the pronoun (i.e. *John*). Therefore, the entity corresponding to this name should be the only member of the initial candidate set of the pronoun, and since the name matches the pronoun in gender in both conditions, there should be no difference in processing. The reading time differences between (8a) and (8b) indicate that the gender of the *inaccessible* antecedent was affecting processing soon after the pronoun was read, which is consistent with the claim that this (ungrammatical) antecedent is included in the initial candidate set for the pronoun. In fact, Badecker and Straub (2002) argued for an *interactive-constraint* view, whereby

> the initial stages of interpreting referentially dependent expressions are governed not only by structural constraints imposed by the binding theory but also by the focus status of candidate antecedents and by the morphosyntactic properties of the pronoun or reflexive that is in need of an interpretation.
>
> (p. 750)

Up to this point, we have been assuming that the earliest effects on reading time reported by Badecker and Straub (2002), and by Kennison (2003), are a true reflection of the state of the initial candidate set that is created as soon as the anaphoric expression is processed. However, in order to be sure that we are dealing with the *initial* candidate set, we also need to be sure that we are dealing with the *initial* stage of processing. In the self-paced reading studies of Badecker and Straub (2002) and Kennison (2003), effects of ungrammatical antecedents began to be detected one or two words after the pronoun. This effect might directly reflect processing events that occur in the initial stages of anaphor resolution, and thus be informative about the content of the initial candidate set. However, there remains a possibility that the effects observed by Badecker and Straub (2002) and Kennison (2003) may be indicative of processing that occurs some time *after* the initial candidate set has been formed. If this is the case, the candidate set may initially have included only grammatical antecedents, but the experimental methodology used in the studies (self-paced reading) might not have been sensitive enough to detect this.

Sturt (2003b) reported two eye-tracking experiments with a design similar to Experiment 1 of Badecker and Straub (2002). Eye-tracking during reading was chosen as the methodology because it offers a greater possibility to distinguish late from early effects of processing. For example, if an experimental manipulation has an effect on the time spent on the first fixation in a region, this indicates that the relevant variable has an extremely early influence on processing, while if the effect of the variable is found only on the time spent re-reading that region after fixating subsequent regions, then it can be concluded that the influence of that variable is delayed. The study reported by Sturt (2003b) specifically aimed to establish the earliest point at which referential processing occurred. The study also sought to detect whether any influence of ungrammatical antecedents could be found. The idea of the study was that if such influences could be found, it would be possible to determine whether the ungrammatical antecedent should be considered to be part of the initial candidate set. This could be determined by looking at the point in time at which such an effect emerges, relative to the point where the anaphoric processing begins.

In the first experiment reported by Sturt (2003b), participants' eye movements were recorded while they read discourses such as the following (alternatives separated by slashes represent orthogonal manipulations of the experimental factors):

(9) a. Jonathan/Jennifer was pretty worried at the City Hospital. He/She remembered that the surgeon had pricked himself with a used syringe needle. There should be an investigation soon.

b. Jonathan/Jennifer was pretty worried at the City Hospital. He/She remembered that the surgeon had pricked herself with a used syringe needle. There should be an investigation soon.

The design included an entity that was a grammatical antecedent for the reflexive in terms of Principle A (the 'accessible antecedent': *the surgeon*), and one that was not (the 'inaccessible antecedent': *Jonathan/Jennifer*). The gender matching was manipulated orthogonally between (a) the reflexive and the accessible antecedent, and (b) the reflexive and the inaccessible antecedent (gender stereotypes were used for the accessible antecedent to avoid the presentation of ungrammatical sentences). The idea of this design is that by comparing effects associated with the accessible antecedent with those associated with the inaccessible antecedent, we can determine whether each of these types of antecedent affects processing at the same time, or whether one type of antecedent has its effect earlier than the other. This in turn can lead to inferences about the contents of the initial candidate set in reference resolution.

The results showed that there was an effect of the gender of the accessible antecedent in very early measures of processing, including the duration of the first fixation on the reflexive. This showed that initial fixations were longer on the reflexive when it mismatched the stereotypical gender of the accessible antecedent (*surgeon – herself*) than when it matched it (*surgeon – himself*).

This early effect was not accompanied in early measures by any effect related to the inaccessible antecedent, which Sturt (2003b) interpreted as evidence consistent with the binding as filter hypothesis. At first sight, this appears to be inconsistent with the findings reported by Badecker and Straub (2002) and Kennison (2003). However, it is possible that the effects of inaccessible antecedents that these authors reported emerged some time after the formation of the initial candidate set, and were not indicative of the very earliest points of processing. Indeed, in Sturt's study, in eye-movement measures indicative of later processing, such as second-pass time at and before the reflexive (i.e. the time spent re-reading these regions), or initial fixations on later regions of the sentence, there were effects of the inaccessible antecedent. These effects were generally of two types. First, for the accessible match conditions (i.e. where the stereotypical gender of the accessible antecedent matched the gender of the reflexive, as in *surgeon – himself*) reading times were longer when the inaccessible antecedent (*Jonathan/Jennifer*) mismatched the gender of the reflexive than when it matched. Note that the direction of this effect is opposite to that reported by Kennison (2003) and Badecker and Straub (2002), who found instead that there was evidence of difficulty when an inaccessible antecedent *matched* in gender with the anaphoric expression. The second type of effect was that, for the accessible mismatch conditions (i.e. where the stereotypical gender of the accessible antecedent did not match the gender of the reflexive: *surgeon – herself*), reading times were longer when the inaccessible antecedent *matched* the gender of the reflexive than when it mismatched. Taken together, these results can be intepreted in terms of a model in which the initial candidate set contains only binding-compatible antecedents (i.e. consistent with the binding-as-filter view), but where later interpretative processes can access antecedents that lie outside this set. Sturt (2003b) called this the *defeasible filter* account.

Other work using *Event Related Potentials* has failed to find any effects of binding-inaccessible antecedents for reflexives (Xiang, Dillon, & Phillips, 2009). However, unlike the Sturt (2003b) study mentioned above, Xiang et al.'s study did not include a context sentence, and the inaccessible antecedent might not have been salient enough in the discourse representation to affect processing. In addition, the Event Related Potential method is not well suited to investigating processing at multiple words following the critical reflexive, and so the study may have been unable to detect delayed effects of the inaccessible antecedent.

Before concluding this section, it is worth pointing out that the initial filter view does not appear to be true of skilled speakers of English as a second language. Although such speakers often show evidence of being aware of the appropriate English binding constraints in their performance in off-line tasks, analysis of reading time data reveals a tendency to link reflexives with discourse-prominent, but structurally inaccessible, antecedents during on-line processing (see Roberts, this volume). This is true both for Japanese speakers of English (Felser, Sato, & Bertenshaw, 2009), and German speakers of English

(Felser & Cunnings, 2012). This is consistent with the claim that non-native speakers have difficulty in constructing structural representations on-line, and that they rely on non-structural, or discourse factors instead (Clahsen & Felser, 2006).

Binding and interpretation

In the preceding paragraphs, we have reviewed a number of studies that sought to investigate the effect of syntactic constraints on the initial stages of reference resolution. However, in order to obtain a full picture, it is necessary also to consider what factors influence the final interpretations that people make when they process sentences. For example, given that there is some evidence that people consider potential antecedents that are ungrammatical in terms of binding theory, it is important to consider the extent to which these ungrammatical antecedents affect the final interpretation. According to constraint-based accounts (e.g., Badecker & Straub, 2002; Runner, Sussman, & Tanenhaus, 2003, 2006), the extent to which ungrammatical antecedents influence the final interpretation is presumably a function of the relative importance of grammatical information in relation to other constraints. If other constraints, such as discourse prominence, are strong enough, they may outweigh the grammatical binding constraints, leading to a final interpretation in which the antecedent of the anaphoric expression is not grammatical. In contrast, the defeasible filter account (Sturt, 2003b) would predict that there is a stage of early anaphoric processing during which binding principles are applied faithfully, but where the final interpretation is not necessarily faithful to the grammar. In contrast, according to the strict view of the binding-as-filter account, there is no possibility for binding-inaccessible antecedents to participate in the final interpretation. Ultimately, however, the comprehension system must have some way of allowing our interpretations to violate binding theory. One reason for this is that it is quite easy to find real-life examples of binding violations, which are quite easy to interpret. For example Zribi Hertz (1989) gives a number of examples from literary texts, many of which require binding principles to be abandoned in order for interpretation to be successful. One of the examples quoted by Zribi Hertz (1989) is:

(10) Maggie looked at him. Did he mean herself – herself and the baby?

In (10), *herself* is intended to refer to *Maggie*. However, according to Principle A, *he* is the only possible antecedent. If (as intuition suggests) people interpret (10) in the intended way, it must be the case that either we are capable of forming interpretations that violate binding constraints, or otherwise, that Principle A should be revised to allow for the intended co-reference in (10). However, according to most theoretical accounts, (10) is a very canonical configuration for the application of Principle A, so it is arguably more appropriate to retain Principle A, and take (10) as an example in which the final interpretation is not faithful to the principle (see also arguments in Sturt, 2003a). According to the defeasible filter account, for example, the initial processing of *herself* in (10) would involve an attempted link between the reflexive and *he*, which would result in a gender mismatch, causing processing difficulty that would in principle be detectable using experimental techniques, but not necessarily available to conscious introspection. At a later stage of processing, the reference of the reflexive would be re-assigned to *Maggie*.

Despite the theoretical importance of examining the interplay between intial anaphoric assignment and final interpretations, rather few experimental studies have tackled this issue. To the author's knowledge, the only published experiments that have combined an interpretation task with on-line measurement of referential preferences have been the visual-world studies reported by Runner et al. (2003), Runner et al. (2006) and Kaiser, Runner, Sussman, and Tanenhaus (2009). These studies all used tasks in which participants are required to indicate their interpretation of a referential expression; for example, the Runner et al. studies used an *act-out* task in which participants manipulated a doll in response to spoken stimuli like (11) (example taken from Runner et al. (2006)):

(11) Look at Joe. Pick up Ken. Have Ken touch Harry's picture of himself.

The participants' response to (11) would involve picking up one of three named dolls, and making the doll touch the appropriate picture in a visual-world display. An implicit measure of interpretation is therefore available by recording the doll (or doll's picture) that participants choose in the act-out task. However, by tracking eye movements, during the spoken sentence, it is also possible to examine the referents that are being considered as a function of time. This is based on the observation that looks to potential referents in this task are closely time-locked to the spoken input (Tanenhaus, Spivey-Knowlton, Eberhard, & Sedivy, 1995), so the relative frequencies of looks to the dolls (or pictures of dolls) can be used to draw inferences about which item is being considered as a referent of an anaphoric expression. Moreover, because the implicit measure of interpretation is being recorded on every trial, this also means that the fixation behavior can be analysed as a function of the eventual interpretation choice, giving the opportunity to test theories that make predictions about the relation between the initial consideration of a referent and the final interpretation.

The motivation for the visual-world studies reported by Runner et al. (2003), Runner et al. (2006), and Kaiser et al. (2009) was broader than that of the reading-based studies described above, in that the visual-world studies aimed to test theoretical claims about binding theory at a competence level, as well as claims about the role of binding constraints in processing. All of these studies examined interpretations for reflexives and pronouns in *Picture Noun Phrases*, where it is well known that the complementarity of distribution of reflexives and pronouns can break down.

For example, consider (12) (taken from Kuno, 1987, p.127):

(12)　John told Mary that [there was a picture of himself in the morning paper].

In (12), the standard definition of Principle A does not predict that co-reference should be possible between *himself* and *John*. This is because the local domain within which *himself* should be bound corresponds to the complement clause (bracketed in (12)). However, intuitions suggest that co-reference is in fact possible in this case. Moreover, intuitively, *himself* can be replaced by *him* in (12), maintaining the co-indexation between the pronoun and *John*.

It has been claimed (see especially Kuno, 1987, Zribi Hertz, 1989) that semantic and discourse factors are needed to explain the possibilities for co-reference in examples that use picture noun phrases, like (12). Reflexives in such environments are often called *logophors*, and are often assumed to be exempt from Principle A (see Pollard & Sag, 1994, Reinhart & Reuland, 1993, for example).

Now, compare (13) and (14) below:

(13)　Have Ken touch Harry's picture of himself

(14)　Have Ken touch the picture of himself.

Example (13), which repeats one of Runner et al.'s (2006) critical conditions from (11), includes a possessor in the picture noun phrase (i.e. *Harry's*), while (14) does not. According to nearly all syntactic theories, the presence of a possessor in the specifier position of the picture noun phrase means that the noun phrase should act as the relevant local domain for the anaphor. Therefore, according to such theories, Principle A requires *Harry* to be the antecedent of *himself* in (13). In contrast, the lack of a possessor in (14) means that *himself* would be treated as a logophor, exactly as in (12), in most syntactic theories, allowing *Ken*, or even noun phrases outside the clause, to act as the antecedent. Part of the motivation for the studies reported by Runner et al. (2003) and Runner et al. (2006) was to test the claim that reflexives in picture noun phrases are interpreted as logophors, even when the phrase contains a possessor, as in (13). And, in fact, Runner et al.'s participants did show a relatively high proportion of interpretations in violation of Principle A for reflexives in sentences like (13), suggesting that reflexives in such syntactic contexts are logophors. However, rather different results were found for the interpretation of pronouns in sentences like (15):

(15)　Have Ken touch Harry's picture of him.

Here, assuming standard theoretical accounts of binding principles, *him* can only refer to *Ken*, due to Principle B. In contast to the results for reflexives,

Runner et al. (2006) found that their participants' interpretations were much more faithful to the relevant binding principles for pronouns (15) than for reflexives (13). Therefore, Runner et al. (2006) assumed that pronouns were indeed constrained by Principle B, even in picture noun phrases with possessors.

The visual-world method employed by Runner et al. (2006) also gave them an opportunity to test how the initial consideration of potential antecedents can relate to the final interpretation. On the assumption that pronouns in their stimuli were constrained by binding theory, Runner et al. (2006) tested whether the early stages of referential processing were constrained by binding principles. If this is the case, then, following the pronoun in a sentence like (15), participants should not look at the picture of the doll corresponding to *Harry* any more than they look at the picture of a third, unmentioned doll, since both of these correspond to ungrammatical antecedents. Instead, if binding constraints work as an initial filter, then, even during the earliest stages of pronoun resolution, they should look at the picture corresponding to the grammatical antecedent (i.e. *Ken* in 15). However, Runner et al. (2006) found that, during the earliest stages immediately following the processing of the pronoun, people looked equally often at the picture corresponding to the the possessor *Harry*, and to the picture corresponding to the grammatical antecedent (*Ken*), while they looked much less often at an unmentioned doll. As mentioned above, however, participants' final interpretations for the pronoun sentences were strongly in line with the predictions of Principle B. Given that ungrammatical antecedents were initially considered, this result is inconsistent with the view of binding as an initial filter. Instead, the results are more in line with Badecker and Straub's (2002) claim that the initial candidate set may contain antecedents that are later ruled out by binding principles. For their reflexive conditions, Runner et al. (2006) also showed that participants briefly considered antecedents that would be ruled out by Principle A as standardly defined. However, given that Runner et al. (2006) argue that the reflexives in their stimuli are exempt from Principle A (in their terms, the reflexives are *logophors*), the on-line reflexive results do not bear decisively on the question of whether binding constraints act as an initial filter.

Like Runner et al.'s (2006) studies, the visual-world experiments reported by Kaiser et al. (2009) also examined the interpretation of reflexives and pronouns inside picture noun phrases. Here, the authors were interested in the effect of verb meaning on reference, in sentences like (16):

(16) a. Peter told John about a picture of himself/him on the wall.

b. Peter heard from John about a picture of himself/him on the wall.

Kaiser et al. (2009) assumed that reference resolution for the reflexive (*himself*) and the pronoun (*him*) in (16) would be affected by structural preferences – the reflexive should prefer to refer to the subject (*Peter*) and the pronoun should prefer to refer to the internal argument of the verb (*John*). On top of this, the authors assumed that the preferences would be modulated by the semantic roles assigned by the verbs *told* and *heard*, and their aim was to examine how the structural and semantic biases would interact. As for the semantic biases, Kuno (1987) claimed that reflexives in sentences like (16) have a preference to refer to an antecedent that provides the *source* of information (e.g. *Peter* in (16a), or *John* in (16b)). However, a contrasting prediction can be made for pronouns, based on theoretical arguments by Tenny (2003), namely that the pronoun has a preference to refer to the *perceiver* of information (e.g. *John* in (16a), or *Peter* in (16b)). Kaiser et al.'s results showed that people's interpretations of sentences like (16) were affected by the structural preference as well as by the semantic bias both in the final interpretation, and in the earlier stages of reference resolution. However, the two factors were weighted differently for the two referential expressions, with the structural preference having a stronger effect than the semantic bias for the reflexives, but a more equal weighting of the two factors for pronouns.

Based on these results Kaiser et al. (2009) argued for a *form-specific multiple constraints* approach to reference resolution, whereby different types of referential expression can be differentially sensitive to different constraints. This differential sensitivity may in fact be an instance of a more general phenomenon, applying not only in Picture noun phrases, but also in more 'canonical' sentence types, where binding constraints are commonly assumed to apply, and this might be related to differences in the speed of acquisition of the structural constraints on different referential forms. In fact, there is evidence that children acquire Principle B (the constraint applying to pronouns) later than they acquire Principle A (the constraint applying to reflexives) (see Chien & Wexler, 2009; Guasti, 2002). This delay in the acquisition of Principle B may be one particular facet of the lesser sensitivity of pronouns to structural constraints relative to reflexives, even in adults.

Some evidence consistent with this view is given by Clackson, Felser, and Clahsen (2011), who reported a visual-world study comparing the on-line use of Binding Principles A and B in adults and 6–9-year-old children. Rather than using Picture noun phrases, the experimental stimuli used sentence forms that are uncontroversially subject to binding principles (e.g. *He watched as Mr. Jones bought a huge box of popcorn for himself/him over the counter*). The results showed that in the pronoun conditions, both adults and children were temporarily affected by the presence of a gender-matching antecedent that was not licit under binding principles. However, for the reflexive conditions, this competition effect was reliable only for the children. Moreover, children performed at ceiling levels in their final interpretation of the reflexive sentences, but often selected an ungrammatical referent for the pronoun (adults performed at ceiling for both pronouns and reflexives). Taken together, Clackson et al.'s results are consistent with the claim that pronouns are generally less sensitive than reflexives to structural constraints.

Backwards anaphora

In the previous sections, we have discussed cases in which the anaphoric expression (e.g. *him* or *himself*) follows the antecedent. In such cases, it is natural to think of the anaphoric expression triggering a search, or other retrieval process of previously processed information from memory. However, consider the case of cataphora (or backwards anaphora) in (17) (example from Van Gompel & Liversedge, 2003):

(17)   When he was at the party, the boy cruelly teased the girl during the party games.

In (17), the pronoun *he* does not have an antecedent in the preceding context, but the subsequent context does contain an appropriate gender-matching antecedent (i.e. *the boy*). What kind of process governs the formation of the dependency between the pronoun and the subsequent antecedent? In such cases of backwards anaphora, it does not seem appropriate to talk about a initial candidate set of antecedents for the pronoun as discussed for the cases of forwards anaphora discussed above. This is because, at the point where the pronoun is first encountered, there may not be any candidate antecedents, and the candidate set, if anything, has to be constructed dynamically as the rest of the sentence is processed.

So, it is important to ask how this dynamic process of antecedent identification takes place. Van Gompel and Liversedge (2003) argued for a two-stage account of referential assignment, on the basis of a gender mismatch cost that they obtained in eye tracking, for cases like (17); reading times at (or immediately after) the main clause subject (*the boy*) were longer when the pronoun mismatched in gender (*she*) than when it matched (*he*). They argued that, when the potential antecedent is processed, an initial attempt is made to link the antecedent to the pronoun before the relevant gender and number features of the antecedent have been retrieved. Van Gompel and Liversedge (2003) claimed that the mismatch difficulty was due to the subsequent retrieval of the (mismatching) gender feature, and the need to revoke the previous referential assignment.

However, Kazanina, Lau, Lieberman, Yoshida, and Phillips (2007) point out that Van Gompel and Liversedge's (2003) results could also be explained if we assume a more dynamic process involving prediction. Specifically, in examples like (17), the subject noun phrase might be predicted ahead of time, while the initial subordinate clause is being processed. If this is the case, the predicted subject noun phrase could be provisionally assigned as the antecedent of the pronoun, even before this phrase is recognised bottom-up in the input. The mismatch cost can then be explained in terms of the clash between the gender feature that is predicted, and the gender feature of the actual noun phrase when it is encountered in the bottom-up input. This type of predictive process, which Kazanina et al. (2007) call 'active search', shares some similarities with the processes involved in *wh* filler-gap dependencies, where studies have shown that gaps corresponding to filler phrases are posited before bottom-up evidence appears in the input, as evidenced by filled-gap effects (Aoshima, Phillips, & Weinberg, 2004; Stowe, 1986) (see also Kreiner, Sturt, and Garrod (2008) for a related proposal involving the prediction of the antecedent of cataphora).

One important question that was addressed by Kazanina et al. (2007) is the extent to which backward anaphoric dependencies are constrained by binding principles. The choice of antecedent for backwards anaphora can be constrained by Principle C of binding theory. Compare (18a) and (18b), for example (from Kazanina et al., 2007, Experiment 3):

(18) a. He/She continued drinking cheap American beer while the creepy, old bachelor hit on every woman in the bar . . .

b. His/Her coworkers continued drinking cheap American beer while the creepy, old bachelor hit on every woman in the bar . . .

In (18a), Binding Principle C prevents the pronoun *he/she* from referring to *the creepy old bachelor*, because the pronoun c-commands the phrase. In (18b), by contrast, there is no such c-command relation (since the pronoun (*his/her*) is embedded inside the subject of the sentence, and co-reference is possible). Kazanina et al. (2007) manipulated gender using a logic analogous to that of Van Gompel and Liversedge (2003) to determine whether the dependencies of backwards anaphora would be constrained by binding principles. Specifically, if Principle C prevents the initial formation of the dependency between the pronoun and *the creepy old bachelor* in (18a), then there should be no attempt to make *he/she* refer to *the creepy old bachelor*. Thus, processing difficulty should not differ as a function of the gender matching between the pronoun and the antecedent. In contrast, in (18b), Principle C does not rule out the dependency, so such a mismatch cost should indeed be observed, because *her* will mismatch in gender with *the creepy old bachelor*, leading to extra difficulty relative to the matching condition *his*. In fact, this was exactly the pattern that Kazanina et al. (2007) observed. Thus, the dynamic search process for finding an antecedent of a cataphoric pronoun appears to be constrained by Principle C, though which part of this search process is constrained is not yet known. If it is true that cataphoric dependencies are often constructed via prediction, in advance of the appearance of the antecedent in the input, as suggested by Kazanina et al. (2007), then one possibility is that the predictive dependency formation itself is sensitive to the binding principles. In other words, when a potential antecedent position has been predicted following the appearance of the cataphoric pronoun, an anaphoric link is posited only in cases where this link would be sanctioned by the relevant binding principles.

Given that Principle C appears to act as an absolute filter on the formation of backward anaphoric dependencies, a further question is whether all constraints might act in a similar manner. Kazanina and Phillips (2010) compared

Principle C with the *poka-constraint* in a Russian study. The *poka-constraint* is a Russian-specific condition on backwards anaphora that applies to sentences that include adverbial clauses using the connective *poka* ('while'). In such sentences, 'an agentive pronoun subject of an embedded clause cannot co-refer with an agentive main clause subject' (Kazanina & Phillips, 2010).

The constraint is illustrated by the contrast between (19a) and (19b):

(19) a. Posle togo kak on čital knigu, Ivan s'el jabloko.
after he read book, Ivan ate apple
('After he read the book, Ivan ate an apple.')

b. *Poka on čital knigu, Ivan s'el jabloko.
while he read book, Ivan ate apple
('While he read the book, Ivan ate an apple.')

In example (19a), co-reference is possible between *on* ('he') and *Ivan*, just as it is in the English translation. However, because (19b) uses the connective *poka*, and both the subject of the main clause and that of the subordinate clause are agentive, co-reference is not possible between the two subjects.

In their self-paced reading experiment, Kazanina and Phillips (2010) manipulated the gender matching between a cataphoric pronoun and a subsequent noun phrase antecedent. In one pair of conditions, the dependency was grammatically licit; in the second pair of conditions, the dependency was ruled out by Principle C; and in the third pair of conditions, the dependency was ruled out by the poka-constraint. The first two pairs of conditions effectively replicated the findings of Kazanina et al. (2007), showing a gender mismatch cost for the cases where the backward anaphoric dependency was licit in terms of Principle C, but not where the dependency was ruled out by the Principle C. Thus, in Russian as well as English, Principle C appears to act as an absolute filter on the formation of backward anaphoric dependencies. However, the results for the *poka*-constraint were different. In these conditions, reading times following the antecedent were longer when the gender of the preceding pronoun *matched* the antecedent, compared with when it did not. This cost for gender matching conditions under the poka-constraint is reminiscent of the effects reported by Badecker and Straub (2002) and Kennison (2003), discussed above, and is consistent with an initial attempt to form the dependency, followed by a period of competition during which the gender matching makes it more difficult to eliminate the ungrammatical element from consideration as an antecedent.

The role of binding constraints in processing: reflections

As the preceding sections have shown, there is now a growing body of work that investigates the role of syntactic constraints on referential processing. Most of this work has sought to evaluate the role that binding constraints have in the on-line formation of referential dependencies, some of it focusing on the extent to which syntactic constraints act as a filter on the interpretation of anaphoric expressions, and some focusing on the question of exactly how the constraints should be defined at the competence level.

The available evidence does not give a very consistent answer to the question of whether binding constraints act as an initial filter on the formation of a candidate set of antecedents. Some studies have demonstrated intrusive effects of antecedents that are not licensed by the binding theory (Badecker & Straub, 2002; Kennison, 2003; Runner et al., 2006), while others have shown no such effects (Nicol & Swinney, 1989; Clifton et al., 1997), or have shown such effects only after a certain delay (Sturt, 2003b). It is possible that the degree to which syntactic constraints act as an initial filter depends on the referential expression in question. Clackson et al.'s (2011) study, mentioned above, is consistent with the idea that reflexives are more tightly constrained by structural principles than pronouns are, and indeed, most of the studies that have shown intrusive effects of binding-inaccessible antecedents have involved pronouns, and (temporary) violations of Principle B (Badecker & Straub, 2002; Kennison, 2003; Runner et al., 2006), while Sturt (2003b), who found evidence only of relatively *late* intrusive effects, used reflexives, which are subject to Principle A. In keeping with this, Xiang et al. (2009) found no evidence for intrusive effects in an Event Related Potential study looking at the interpretation of reflexives, while in the same study, intrusive effects were found for a different type of linguistic dependency, namely negative polarity licensing. Moreover, although Runner et al. (2003) and Runner et al. (2006) did find intrusive effects of ungrammatical antecedents for reflexives, their reflexives occured in syntactic positions which, according to their arguments, may not have been subject to Principle A. In addition, although Badecker and Straub (2002) showed an intrusive effect of an ungrammatical antecedent for reflexives in one of their experiments, the effect for reflexives was not replicated in other experiments that they report, even in experiments that also showed intrusive effects for pronouns in the same design. It seems likely, therefore, that some types of linguistic dependencies may be more prone to intrusive effects than others. The question of why this may be so is a complex one that takes us beyond the scope of this chapter, but see Phillips, Wagers, and Lau (2011) for some interesting observations and arguments on this topic.

Another source of variability is the experimental methods that have been used, including eye tracking during reading (Sturt, 2003b), self-paced reading (Badecker & Straub, 2002; Clifton et al., 1997; Kennison, 2003), visual-world eye tracking (Kaiser et al., 2009; Runner et al., 2003, 2006), and Event Related Potentials (Xiang et al., 2009). Although it may be premature to make claims about the effect of different methodologies, some methodological cautions are worth considering. In studies that use a methodology based on reading time (i.e. self-paced reading, or eye tracking during reading) it may be difficult to distinguish between effects that genuinely reflect the consideration of an anaphoric relationship, on the one hand, and lower level effects of lexical activation on the other. For example Banaji and Hardin (1996) demonstrated lexical priming between gender stereotype words and gender-marked pronouns. Reaction times to a pronoun were faster if the pronoun was preceded by a gender-matching stereotype word compared with a mismatching word. Since the task involved only isolated words, it is likely that the participants did not attempt to make an anaphoric link between the pronoun and the stereotyped noun. If no anaphoric link was made, then it implies that reaction times (and therefore reading times) at or following a pronoun could be affected by priming of gender features associated with a noun, irrespective of the structural relationship between them, and irrespective of the status of the noun as an antecedent. Thus, reading time effects of mismatch cost, associated with both accessible and inaccessible antecedents need to be interpreted with this in mind.

A second methodological caution for methods that rely on reading time is related to the apparent variability in the nature of the effects associated with binding-inaccessible antecedents. The direction of such effects has not been consistent across a range of studies. For example, Badecker and Straub (2002) found a multiple-match cost: reading times were relatively slow when both accessible and inaccessible antecedents matched the gender of a pronoun, relative to when only the accessible antecedent matched. However, Sturt (2003b) found the opposite effect, where an inaccesibe antecedent could lead to slower reading times, when the accessible antecedent matched in gender. The source of such variabilty is not currently known. However, one difference between the stimuli of Badecker and Straub (2002) and Sturt (2003b) is that while Badecker and Straub (2002) used proper names for both accessible and inaccessible antecedents, Sturt (2003b) used a proper name for the inaccessible antecedent (e.g. *Jonathan*) and a stereotype noun phrase for the accessible noun phrase (e.g. *the surgeon*). Because the two potential antecedents were of a similar type in the Badecker and Straub (2002) study, this might have led to *similarity-based interference*. This phenomenon, which is well-known in the memory literature, can also affect sentence processing (Gordon, Hendrick, & Levine, 2002; Levy, this volume; Lewis & Vasishth, 2005), and appears to affect retrieval in particular (Van Dyke & McElree, 2006). In the case of the Badecker and Straub (2002) study, the similarity of the two potential antecedents could have caused interference during retrieval, given that they both also match the gender cue of the pronoun.

These considerations suggest that the intrusive effects associated with inaccessible antecedents in reading-time studies may reflect a number of different types of processes, including priming, memory retrieval, and other factors. Moreover, given that there is variability in the direction of the effect, it might even be the case that two different processes have a simultaneous effect in opposite directions, leading to no observable difference. Modelling should be a focus of future work in this area, in order to help us understand the relevant phenomena more fully. It will also help our understanding if we use a number of different techniques to look at the same problem. For example, Event Related Potentials (e.g. Harris, Wexler, & Holcomb, 2000; Xiang et al.,

2009) may allow us to separate out different types of effects, assuming that lexical priming, memory interference, and other processes have different electrophysiological signatures.

In contrast to techniques based on reading-time, the visual-world paradigm has the advantage that inferences do not need to be made about the relative differences in duration between conditions. However, as in reading-time studies, it is not always possible to be sure that the data are reflecting anaphoric processes. In the visual-world paradigm, inferences are made about the consideration of potential antecedents in terms of the relative proportion of looks to various objects in a scene, as a function of time. However, in order to make such inferences, the researcher needs to be very careful to ensure that any differences in proportion of looks are really due to the consideration of an item as a referent of an anaphor. As Runner et al. (2006, p.226) point out, in some cases, increases in looks to an object may occur due to other factors, such as whether the object has recently been mentioned, and this effect could make it appear that an ungrammatical antecedent is being considered as a referent, when this might not actually be the case. In many cases, such difficulties in interpreting the data could be resolved by including extra control conditions in the design (Runner et al., 2006, p. 238, n. 10), or, possibly, by analysing the data using a more complex statistical model incorporating some measure of previous looks as a co-variate.

Conclusions

Despite the rather variable nature of the studies discussed above, several conclusions can now be made about the role of binding constraints in sentence interpretation. The first is that binding constraints operate on-line, and are available extremely quickly following the processing of a referential expression. Given that binding constraints are defined in terms of structural information, this is consistent with the idea that syntactic structure is also built very quickly in response to the input (see Sturt & Lombardo, 2005, for related arguments). The second conclusion is that binding constraints are often violated – not only can people settle on a final interpretation of a sentence that does not satisfy binding constraints, but also antecedents that are not accessible in terms of the binding constraints can affect processing on-line. Third, and related to the last point, binding constraints do not pose an absolute filter on the possibilities for antecedent selection. Though we have not fully resolved the question of whether such a filter might be operative at the very earliest stages of processing, the balance of evidence is that it is, at least some types of anaphoric expressions, such as co-argument reflexives.

What are the priorities for future work in this area? As is clear from this chapter, binding constraints have a very complex effect on sentence processing, and explicit models are needed to help us understand the phenomena involved. Such models will need to combine syntactic and referential processing, and provide an account of the relevant aspects of the syntax–discourse interface (see Dubey, 2010, for a recent example). In addition, it seems likely that memory retrieval will become an important focus of future work in referential processing,[7] and computational models should be able to account for the various types of interference effects (or lack of such effects) that are found in experimental studies. In future work, it will also be important to compare different types of referential expressions using the same experimental method, but it will also be instructive to combine methods so that the advantages of one method can compensate for the disadvantages of another. If such modelling and experimental work is successful, it will provide a valuable window on the inner workings of the human language processing system.

Notes

1. *Catch 22*, Vintage, Random House, London, p.217.
2. We use subscripts to indicate the possible coindexing. The star "*" indicates an ungrammatical coindexing.
3. In this chapter we ignore the distinction between co-reference (two elements referring to the same entity) and co-indexation (two elements receiving the same index in interpretation). Although this distinction is theoretically important, it will not be germane to the discussion here.
4. For slightly different proposals, see Reinhart and Reuland (1993), or Pollard and Sag (1994), for example.
5. C-command (Reinhart, 1976) defines a structural relation between two nodes in a phrase structure tree, which is similar to the relationship between an operator and its scope in logical languages. A typical definition is: α c-commands β if and only if α does not dominate β, and every branching node that dominates α also dominates β.
6. See Van Gompel (this volume) for a description of the self-paced reading method.
7. See Phillips, Wagers, and Lau (2011) and Martin, Nieuwland, and Carreiras (2012) for illuminating discussions concerning the relation between referential dependency formation and retrieval in content-addressable memory frameworks.

References

Aoshima, S., Phillips, C., & Weinberg, A. (2004). Processing filler-gap dependencies in a head-final language. *Journal of Memory and Language, 51*, 23–54.

Badecker, W., & Straub, K. (2002). The processing role of structural constraints on the interpretation of pronouns and anaphora. *Journal of Experimental Psychology: Learning Memory and Cognition, 28(4)*, 748–769.

Banaji, M. R., & Hardin, C. (1996). Automatic stereotyping. *Psychological Science, 7*, 136–141.

Chien, Y. C., & Wexler, K. (2009). Children's knowledge of locality conditions in binding as evidence for the modularity of syntax and pragmatics. *Language Acquisition, 1*, 225–295.

Chomsky, N. (1981). *Lectures on government and binding.* Dordrect, The Netherlands: Foris.

Clackson, K., Felser, C., & Clahsen, H. (2011). Children's processing of reflexives and pronouns in english: Evidence from eye-movements during listening. *Journal of Memory and Language, 65*, 128–144.

Clahsen, H., & Felser, C. (2006). Grammatical processing in language learners. *Applied Psycholinguistics*, *27*, 3–42.

Clifton, C., Kennison, S. M., & Albrecht, J. E. (1997). Reading the words *him* and *her*: Implications for parsing principles based on frequency and on structure. *Journal of Memory and Language*, *36*, 276–292.

Dubey, A. (2010). The influence of discourse on syntax: A psycholinguistic model of sentence processing. In *Proceedings of the 48th annual meeting of the Association for Computational Linguistics* (pp. 1179–1188), 11–16 July, Uppsala, Sweden.

Felser, C., & Cunnings, I. (2012). Processing reflexives in a second language: The timing of structural and discourse level cosntraints. *Applied Psycholinguistics*, *33(3)*, 571–603.

Felser, C., Sato, M., & Bertenshaw, N. (2009). The on-line application of binding principle A in English as a second language. *Bilingualism: Language and Cognition*, *12*, 485–502.

Gordon, P. C., Hendrick, R., & Levine, W. H. (2002). Memory load interference in syntactic processing. *Psychological Science*, *13*, 425–430.

Guasti, M. (2002). *Language acquisition: The growth of grammar.* Cambridge, MA: MIT Press.

Harris, T., Wexler, K., & Holcomb, P. (2000). An ERP investigation of binding and co-reference. *Brain and Language*, *75*, 313–346.

Kaiser, E., Runner, J., Sussman, R. S., & Tanenhaus, M. K. (2009). Structural and semantic constraints on the resolution of pronouns and reflexives. *Cognition*, *112*, 55–80.

Kazanina, N., Lau, E., Lieberman, M., Yoshida, M., & Phillips, C. (2007). The effect of syntactic constraints on the processing of backwards anaphora. *Journal of Memory and Language*, *56*, 384–409.

Kazanina, N., & Phillips, C. (2010). Differential effects of constraints on the processing of Russian cataphora. *Quarterly Journal of Experimental Psychology*, *63(2)*, 371–400.

Kennison, S. M. (2003). Comprehending the pronouns *her*, *him*, and *his*: Implications for theories of referential processing. *Journal of Memory and Language*, *49*, 335–352.

Kreiner, H., Sturt, P., & Garrod, S. (2008). Processing definitional and stereotypical gender in reference resolution: Evidence from eye-movements. *Journal of Memory and Language*, *58*, 239–261.

Kuno, S. (1987). *Functional syntax: Anaphora discourse and empathy.* Chicago, IL: University of Chicago Press.

Lewis, R., & Vasishth, S. (2005). An activation-based model of sentence processing as skilled memory retrieval. *Cognitive Science*, *29*, 1–45.

Martin, A., Nieuwland, M., & Carreiras, M. (2012). Event-related brain potentials index cue-based retrieval interference during sentence comprehension. *Neuroimage*, *59*, 1859–1869.

Nicol, J., & Swinney, D. (1989). The role of structure in co-reference assignment during sentence comprehension. *Journal of Psycholinguistic Research*, *18*, 5–19.

Phillips, C., Wagers, M., & Lau, E. (2011). *Grammatical illusions and selective fallibility in real-time language comprehension.* In J. Runner (Ed.), *Experiments at the Interfaces*, Syntax and Semantics, Vol. 37, (pp. 153–186), Bingley, UK: Emerald Publications.

Pollard, C., & Sag, I. (1994). *Head-driven phrase structure grammar.* Stanford, CA, and Chicago, IL: CSLI and University of Chicago Press.

Reinhart, T. (1976). The syntactic domain of anaphora. Unpublished doctoral dissertation, Massachussetts Institute of Technology.

Reinhart, T., & Reuland, E. (1993). Reflexivity. *Linguistic Inquiry*, *24*, 657–720.
Runner, J. T., Sussman, R. S., & Tanenhaus, M. K. (2003). Assignment of reference to reflexives and pronouns in picture noun phrases: Evidence from eye-movements. *Cognition*, *81*, B1–13.
Runner, J. T., Sussman, R. S., & Tanenhaus, M. K. (2006). Assigning referents to reflexives and pronouns in picture noun phrases. Experimental tests of binding theory. *Cognitive Science*, *30*, 1–49.
Stowe, L. A. (1986). Parsing *wh*-constructions: Evidence for on-line gap location. *Language and Cognitive Processes*, *1*, 227–245.
Sturt, P. (2003a). A new look at the syntax-discourse interface: The use of binding principles in sentence processing. *Journal of Psycholinguistic Research*, *32(2)*, 125–139.
Sturt, P. (2003b). The time-course of the application of binding constraints in reference resolution. *Journal of Memory and Language*, *48(3)*, 542–562.
Sturt, P., & Lombardo, V. (2005). Processing coordinate structures: Incrementality and connectedness. *Cognitive Science*, *29*, 291–305.
Tanenhaus, M. K., Spivey-Knowlton, M. J., Eberhard, K. M., & Sedivy, J. C. (1995). Integration of visual and linguistic information in spoken language comprehension. *Science*, *268*, 1632–1634.
Tenny, C. (2003). *Short distance pronouns in representational noun phrases and a grammar of sentiece*. Manuscript available at: www.linguist.org.
Van Dyke, J. A., & McElree, B. (2006). Retrieval interference in sentence processing. *Journal of Memory and Language*, *55*, 157–166.
Van Gompel, R. P. G., & Liversedge, S. P. (2003). The influence of morphological information on cataphoric pronoun assignment. *Journal of Experimental Psychology: Learning Memory and Cognition*, *29*, 128–139.
Xiang, M., Dillon, B., & Phillips, C. (2009). Illusory licensing effects across dependency types. *Brain and Language*, *108*, 40–55.
Zribi Hertz, A. (1989). Anaphor binding and narrative point of view: English reflexive pronouns in sentence and discourse. *Language*, *65*, 695–727.

7 Semantic interpretation of sentences

Steven Frisson and Matthew J. Traxler

Introduction

To satisfy the main goal of language processing, comprehenders need to understand the message conveyed by the text. Syntax and lexical semantics represent crucial components of this endeavor. To interpret *The man bit the blind bat* correctly, comprehenders must know how English syntax works (e.g., that the subject usually is the first phrase in the sentence) and what is meant by *bat*. While a lot has been learned about syntactic and lexical processing of text, this does not tell the whole story of sentence interpretation, because sentence interpretation is not the same as merely reading out the lexical information associated with specific words presented in a specific order. For example, the sentence *The man started the dish* is usually interpreted as *started eating the dish*. However, there is nothing in the syntactic structure that evokes or forces this interpretation. Similarly, nothing in the lexical representation of the words in the sentence makes such an interpretation inevitable (e.g., *The cook started the dish* is usually interpreted as *started making the dish*).

This chapter discusses aspects of semantic interpretation that go beyond the mere activation of lexical meaning. While a number of well-developed theories describe syntactic processing (mainly serial, modular versus constraint-based, interactive), comparable theories describing sentence-semantics are still in the developmental stages. Generally speaking, diverse semantic phenomena have been investigated in isolation, and hardly any attempts have been made to relate them to each other to construct more encompassing views of semantic processing. Although we do not intend to propose such a theory in the present chapter, we hope to highlight some common themes that connect different topics.

Incrementality

When does interpretation start? It is generally accepted that we interpret sentences incrementally, i.e., that we start interpreting the linguistic input as soon as it becomes available (Just & Carpenter, 1980). While this seems evident, this was not the prevalent view in the early years of psycholinguistics when it was assumed that much of the processing was delayed until the end of a clause or sentence was reached (see Fodor, Bever, & Garrett, 1974). Good evidence that semantic and syntactic parsing is not delayed comes from shadowing and eye-tracking experiments which show immediate corrections of an incorrect input in the case of shadowing and immediate inflated fixation times when a sentence becomes implausible (Marslen-Wilson, 1975; Pickering & Traxler, 1998; Steedman, 1989; Rayner, Warren, Juhasz, & Liversedge, 2004). In the case of syntactic processing it makes sense to immediately select a specific syntactic structure because (a) the number of constructions at a given point is usually very restricted, (b) holding multiple parses in working memory might be costly, and (c) multiple syntactic constructions come with multiple and possibly contradictory semantic analyses. (But see Christianson, Hollingworth, Halliwell, & Ferreira, 2001, for evidence that sometimes multiple syntactic constructions are kept active.) In the case of lexical processing, incrementality seems to be the norm as well, with immediate selection of one meaning of a lexically ambiguous word (e.g., Rayner & Duffy, 1986).

However, this does not necessarily imply that *all* processing is immediate. With respect to lexical processing, the resolution of noun–verb (*The trains* versus *He trains*) and verb–verb (e.g., *dock the boat* versus *dock the wages*) ambiguities does not seem to be immediate (Frazier & Rayner, 1987; Pickering & Frisson, 2001; see also Folk & Morris, 2003). More generally, higher-order semantic and pragmatic effects tend to show up in somewhat later eye-movement measures (Clifton, Staub, & Rayner, 2007; see also Rayner & Clifton, 2009; Staub & Rayner, 2007), though as will be shown below, this is not necessarily the case. Occasional non-immediacy in semantic processing also makes sense intuitively. Misinterpreting *bat* in *The man bit the bat* or *pitcher* in *Steinbrenner liked the pitcher* results in drastically different interpretations, while misunderstanding *book* in *Steinbrenner liked the book* as referring to its content rather than the object (or vice versa) does not seem to be hugely disruptive (see Frazier & Rayner, 1990; Frisson, 2009; Pickering & Frisson, 2001, for a discussion of how words with multiple meanings like *bat* or *pitcher* are processed differently from words with multiple senses like *book*).

If it is indeed the case that semantic interpretation does not always occur immediately and fully, then locally supported interpretations (e.g., within one noun phrase (NP)) should be preferred over globally supported interpretations (those depending on integrating across different phrases). This is indeed what was found by Frisson, Pickering, and McElree (2003). They contrasted the processing of intersective adjectives (in which a simple intersection is made between the denotation of the adjective and the denotation of the noun, as in *The strong fireman*) to subsective adjectives (in which the adjective picks out a subset of the set denoted by the noun, as in *The strong candidate*). In their first experiment they found that in a sentence like (1a/b), the "strong applicant" was initially interpreted subsectively as evidenced by longer reading times on the disambiguating following context.

(1a/b) Sam is a strong applicant/fireman because he can easily lift 250 pounds, and much more.

In their second experiment they used strongly constraining preceding contexts like (2):

(2)   Even though he had lifted weights for years, the strong . . .

If contextual information were used immediately, *strong* would be interpreted as physically strong, and, thus, *strong applicant* as a physically strong person (an intersective interpretation that would fit perfectly well with the rest of the sentence). Eye-tracking data showed, however, that readers needed extra processing effort to interpret *strong applicant* compared to *strong fireman* following (2), indicating that the preceding context had not overridden the inherent subsective bias in the interpretation of the adjective–noun combination and thus that the local interpretation took priority over the global interpretation.

Other evidence showing that some semantic processing is delayed comes from so-called *clausal* and *sentential wrap-up effects*. Readers tend to fixate longer at the end of a clause or sentence than at other positions in a sentence (Just & Carpenter, 1980; Mitchell & Green, 1978; Rayner, Kambe, & Duffy, 2000). Wrap-up effects are typically explained as resulting from additional integrative processing, e.g., the need to relate clauses and sentences to each other and update the evolving discourse model. While we do not currently have good, detailed explanations of what exactly these operations include (cf. Frazier, 1999), intuitively the end of a sentence seems to be a place to "take stock" and reflect on what has, and has not yet, been processed. However, this interpretation of the effect has recently been called into question. Hirotani, Frazier, and Rayner (2006) contrasted semantically simple sentences like (3a/b/c/d) to complex sentences like (4) in which the direct object (*the marinade for the venison* steaks) was more elaborate. They manipulated whether "fish" or "venison steaks" was clause final or clause internal, followed by a comma, or by a full stop.

(3a)   The mother cooked the fish yesterday, after the boy caught it.
       He was excited.
       (clause-internal)

(3b)   The mother cooked the fish after the boy caught it. He was excited.
       (clause-final, no comma)

(3c)   The mother cooked the fish, after the boy caught it. He was excited.
       (clause-final, comma-marked)

(3d)   The mother cooked the fish. After the boy caught it he was excited.
       (sentence-final)

(4)   Jeremy prepared the marinade for the venison steaks . . .

They found that having a comma (3c) slows down processing on the direct object compared to the clause-internal (3a) and clause-final, no comma (3b) conditions. Having a full stop (3d) slowed down processing even more. However, and crucially, the amount of slow-down was comparable for the simple and complex sentences, which does not fit with the idea that more complex sentences should result in longer wrap-up effects. Hirotani et al. instead suggest that wrap-up effects reflect implicit prosody effects. When reading aloud, people pause upon encountering a comma or full stop, and something similar might happen when reading silently, without the need to "reflect" (see also Warren, White, & Reichle, 2009, for a more complicated picture).

Incrementality is at least as important when listening to speech. Unlike what happens during reading, in listening the pace is set by somebody else and one never knows when one has the chance to "catch up." In addition, while one can go back in a text to *re-re*ad something if necessary, the linear speech stream does not allow this (although opportunities for interaction and feedback during dialogue provide similar opportunities for repetition and clarification). Hence, interpreting the unfolding speech stream as soon as possible seems to be the most obvious way to deal with spoken input. Indeed, research using the "visual world" paradigm, in which participants look at a scene while listening to speech has shown that listeners use auditory information as soon as it becomes available to pick out a referent in a scene (e.g., Sedivy, Tanenhaus, Chambers, & Carlson, 1999; Tanenhaus, Spivey-Knowlton, Eberhard, & Sedivy, 1995) and even use it to predict what the next referent will be (e.g., Altmann & Kamide, 1999).

In short, incremental processing in which information is processed as soon as it becomes available seems to be the default mode in sentence comprehension. However, an immediate, full-blown interpretation at every level is unlikely, and the depth of processing can be influenced, at the least, by the likelihood that helpful, e.g., semantically disambiguating, information will follow (e.g., Frazier & Rayner, 1987; Pickering & Frisson, 2001), and by task requirements (e.g., Christianson et al., 2001; Ferreira & Patson, 2007).

Thematic roles

One of the most important tasks in sentence comprehension is understanding who did what to whom, i.e., which role each noun and verb plays in the sentence. In some languages, like English, the order in which the words appear is usually a good source of information of who did what (in languages like German and Russian, which have a freer word order, case marking and other morphological cues indicate how thematic roles should be assigned). However, word order in itself can only provide biases rather than definitive assignment of a thematic role. For example, grammatical subjects tend to be agents or doers (e.g., *the publisher* in (5)), but they can also be recipients (as in (6)) or themes (in (7)).

(5)   The publisher sent an email to the author.

(6)   The publisher received an email from the author.

(7)   The publisher was sent an email by the author.

As is clear from the examples, both the syntactic structure (e.g., active versus passive) and the semantics of the verb influence what roles the participants play. A lot of research has gone into determining when this semantic information is used in on-line processing and whether it affects the building of the syntactic sentence structure (for overviews, see Jackendoff, 2002; Trueswell & Tanenhaus, 1994). Other research has concentrated on how semantically specified these thematic roles are, going from very general (e.g., *doer* versus *undergoer*, Bornkessel & Schlesewsky, 2006) to very specific conceptual content (e.g., the likely agent for a verb like *pay* is someone who is a customer, while *customer* is a likely patient for a verb like *serve*; Ferretti, McRae, & Hatherell, 2001).

Work by Boland and colleagues (e.g., Boland, Tanenhaus, Garnsey, & Carlson, 1995) showed that thematic roles are assigned to linguistic candidates early during processing. Boland et al. (1995) had participants read sentences word by word and for each word indicate whether the unfolding sentence still made sense. In one experiment, they used dative constructions like (8) and (9) which contain three thematic roles: agent, recipient, and theme.

(8)   Which uneasy pupils did Harriet distribute the science exams to_ in class?

(9)   Which car salesmen did Harriet distribute the science exams to_ in class?

Upon reading the verb *distribute*, the agent role is assigned to the subject (*Harriet*). While in theory the *wh*-filler phrase could be assigned either the theme or the recipient role, only the recipient role is plausible (people are unlikely themes to be distributed). The remaining theme role is then assigned to the direct object (*exams*). Evidence for the view that these roles are assigned even before the syntax unambiguously indicates role assignment (by means of *to_* signaling the gap location) comes from the finding that readers started to reject (9) already upon reading the object NP (*the science exams*). Hence, thematic roles are assigned without appreciable delay and before the entire syntactic construction is known (see also Pickering, Traxler, & Tooley, 2010). Altmann (1999) extended this research and showed that thematic role expectancies can be created on the basis of preceding context. For example, if in the prior context something drinkable was mentioned, then the sentence fragment "He drank" was judged to be more sensible than when nothing drinkable had been introduced.

Upon reading a verb, its subcategorization frame is activated describing the syntactic arguments it can take (e.g., direct object, indirect object). These arguments are then assigned thematic roles. One question is whether thematic roles need explicitly expressed arguments before they can be assigned or whether implicit, "open" roles are generated during on-line reading. Good evidence that readers indeed go beyond the information gathered from expressed arguments comes from Mauner, Tanenhaus, and Carlson (1995; see also Carlson & Tanenhaus, 1988). They constructed sentences with optionally intransitive verbs. When the verbs were used intransitively, they only have one slot (e.g., the experiencer slot in *The ship sank*). When used transitively, the verbs have two slots (typically an agent and a theme or experiencer, as in *The pirates sank the ship*). Comprehenders constructed or projected an implicit agent (e.g., *the captain*, *the owners* . . .) when the verbs were used in implicitly transitive constructions, such as (10), but not in intransitive constructions, such as (12). As a result, the purpose clause (*to collect* . . .) of sentences with an implicit agent (10) were processed as fast as sentences with an explicitly stated agent (11) because both satisfied the requirement that *to collect* needs an agent, but sentences without a possible implicit agent (12) were processed slower:

(10)   The ship was sunk to collect a settlement from the insurance company.

(11)   The ship was sunk by the owners to collect a settlement from the insurance company.

(12)   The ship sank to collect a settlement from the insurance company.

Hence, readers make on-line inferences about the likely participants in a scenario (e.g., that someone sank the ship in order to collect insurance money), and this is done on the basis of a verb's argument structure.

Argument structures of verbs can affect processing difficulty in other contexts as well. Both in linguistic and in processing terms it is possible to make a distinction between arguments and adjuncts. While arguments are specified by the subcategorization of their head (verb or noun), adjuncts are not (for more detailed discussion, see Frazier & Clifton, 1996; Schütze & Gibson, 1999; Traxler & Tooley, 2007). The interpretation of an argument is closely dependent on its head, while an adjunct can be used in many distinct constructions with basically the same semantic interpretation. Only arguments are thought to specify thematic roles while adjuncts do not (but see Grimshaw, 1990). For example, in (13), *to Harry* is an argument as its interpretation depends on the verb, while *to Harry* in (14) is an adjunct (examples taken from Boland & Blodgett, 2006):

(13)   The bully sent a threatening letter to Harry.

(14)   The bully stapled a threatening letter to Harry.

Reading experiments (e.g., Clifton, Speer, & Abney, 1991; see also Traxler, 2008) have shown a strong preference for argument interpretation (when both argument and adjunct interpretations are possible), and faster processing when a phrase must be interpreted as an argument rather than an adjunct. At an interpretative level, this suggests that readers have a bias to relate the elements in a sentence directly to each other, rather than assume that they are not a fundamental part of the syntactic construction.

The previous discussion suggests that thematic role assignment is a largely passive process in that (explicit or implicit) arguments "receive" their role once they become available. However, research by Altmann and colleagues using the visual world paradigm has shown that the processor does not need to wait for linguistic material in order to set up predictions about the likely referent to fill a projected thematic role (e.g., Altmann & Kamide, 1999; Kamide, Altmann, & Haywood, 2003; see Altmann & Mirković, 2009, for an in-depth discussion; see also Knoeferle, Crocker, Scheepers, & Pickering, 2005, for evidence in German). In one series of experiments, participants looked at a scene including a boy, a cake, and a number of inedible distractors while they heard a sentence like (15). Their eye-movements were recorded during listening.

(15) The boy will eat the cake.

They found that participants already started fixating the plausible referent of *eat* (i.e., the cake) while hearing the verb. As these fixations were made before hearing the theme (*the cake*), they are considered anticipatory eye-movements and indicate that, upon hearing the verb, listeners already start to restrict their attention to those objects in the visual scene that can take the (projected) thematic (theme) role.

The discussion of thematic role assignment shows that language users very quickly start to determine which elements in a sentence belong together and how, in order to understand which function each one is associated with. The subcategory information of the verb (and possibly other heads) determines the number of arguments that receive a thematic role. The speed at which this assignment happens, together with the finding that arguments can already receive their role before the syntax specifies the right role (cf. Boland et al., 1995), or even before they have been presented (cf. Altmann & Kamide, 1999), again points towards fast incremental processing.

Coercion

In order to understand a sentence, the different elements in that sentence need to be related to each other. This is achieved by *semantic compositionality* (Frege, 1892), which is the idea that sentence interpretation involves both the activation of the words' meaning and the syntactic combination of them in a larger structure (for an excellent description of compositionality and the different versions of it, see Pylkkänen & McElree, 2006). Subcategorization schemes are an important tool in establishing what goes with what (e.g., a verb and two arguments), and thematic role assignment (e.g., an agent and a theme) helps determine how constituents are semantically related to each other. However, a straightforward compositional process, in which the meaning of a complex expression depends entirely on the meaning of its constituents, is sometimes not possible. For example, certain verbs like *begin* and *finish* require an event-denoting complement (one begins or finishes doing something). Nevertheless, sentences (15) and (16) are perfectly fine in English even though the complements (*novel, sandwich*) are not events in themselves:

(15) The teenager began the novel as soon as he got to his room upstairs.

(16) The gentleman finished the sandwich as soon as he came into the office.

Constructions like these are called *complement coercions*. In order to satisfy the requirements from the verb, the complement is thought to be type-coerced into the appropriate (event) type (for in-depth discussions, see Jackendoff, 1997, 2002; Pustejovsky, 1995). In other words, the complement, which is an entity-denoting object, is transformed or coerced into an event. The way this is done is by *enriched composition*, or the addition of unexpressed semantic content. Concretely, in order to arrive at the required event type for the complement, the object is interpreted in an event-like way: *began reading the novel* or *finished eating the sandwich*. This process of reinterpretation changes the complement noun from an entity to an event.

Is this semantic operation costly, and, if so, exactly which part of the interpretation process imposes the cost? Different lines of research have shown that complement coerced constructions are indeed more taxing to interpret than non-coerced constructions. Compared to non-coerced constructions in which the event is spelled out (17) or in which the complement already refers to an event (e.g., *fight* in 18), coerced constructions take longer to process, and rely on different brain processes, as evidenced by eye-tracking, self-paced reading, speed-accuracy trade-off, and brain imaging experiments (e.g., Kuperberg, Choi, Cohn, Paczynski, & Jackendoff, 2010; Lapata, Keller, & Scheepers, 2003; McElree, Traxler, Pickering, Seely, & Jackendoff, 2001; Pylkkänen & McElree, 2007).

(17) The teenager began reading the novel . . .

(18) The teenager began the fight . . .

A lot of progress has been made in determining where the coercion cost comes from (for an overview, see Frisson & McElree, 2008; Pylkkänen & McElree, 2006), or at least in ruling out certain potential sources of processing difficulty. First, the need to generate or activate a suitable coerced-event interpretation does not seem to be costly in itself, because spelling out the intended activity in the immediately preceding sentence does not eliminate the cost (Traxler,

McElree, Williams, & Pickering, 2005). Second, the coercion cost does not seem to be related to having to select one interpretation amongst several candidates, nor to competition between possible interpretations (Frisson & McElree, 2008; Scheepers, Keller, & Lapata, 2008). For example, an expression like *The man began the novel* can be interpreted as *began reading/writing/ editing/printing/binding/...* and so on. Frisson and McElree (2008), using eye tracking, showed that expressions with several possible interpretations were not more difficult to process than expressions with only one frequent interpretation. This suggests that the coercion cost is more like a constant operational cost associated with the need to come up with an enriched interpretation. Third, the difficulty does not seem to come from constructing an alternative sense (or deferred interpretation; Nunberg, 2004), as other constructions with a deferred interpretation like the metonymy in *read Dickens* are processed as fast as non-deferred interpretations as in *met Dickens* and faster than a coerced construction like *started Dickens* (McElree, Frisson, & Pickering, 2006). Fourth, it does not seem to be related to the detection of a semantic anomaly between the verb and the complement as a coerced construction activates a different part of the brain than a semantic anomaly (Pylkkänen, Llinás, & McElree, submitted; but see Kuperberg et al., 2010). The coercion cost, as argued by McElree and colleagues, reflects the operation needed to generate additional semantic structure (e.g., *started [VERBing the book]*), i.e., enriched composition, so that the complement can become of the required semantic type.

An alternative explanation for the enriched composition effect has been offered by Kuperberg et al. (2010). They propose that the coercion cost points towards a mismatch between the properties of the verb and the complement. More specifically, they suggest that the argument structure stored with a verb is more specific than is often assumed and includes a description of the expected semantic type of the arguments. Hence, upon processing a possibly coercing verb like *begin*, a projection or prediction is made that the following argument will be of the semantic type *event*. When this prediction is not confirmed, a semantic anomaly is recorded, as indexed by an N400 effect. At present, no evidence conclusively favors either hypothesis, though results reported by Frisson, McElree, and Thyparampil (2005) seem to be more compatible with the enriched composition hypothesis. Using eye tracking, they investigated constructions which engender an enriched interpretation though do not require type-shifting (see 19):

(19)   The court reporter completed the testimony about the gruesome murder.

The argument (*the testimony*) refers to an event, so there is no need to type-shift, and there is no violation of the projected semantic argument structure. Nevertheless, most people do not interpret the sentence in a simple compositional way (that the court reporter testified herself). Rather, because the subject (*court reporter*) is an unlikely agent for the straightforward, non-coerced interpretation, people compute an enriched interpretation (e.g., *completed [recording the testimony]*). In line with the idea that the coercion cost is related to the generation of additional semantic content (enriched interpretation), Frisson et al. found a coercion cost very similar to the cost detected in type-shifted coerced constructions.

There are other types of construction that involve coercion (see Pylkkänen & McElree, 2006, for an overview). One that has received a good deal of attention is aspectual coercion, in which a bounded, telic verb like *belched* needs to be reinterpreted in an unbounded, iterative way (see (20); from Pickering, McElree, Frisson, Chen, & Traxler, 2006):

(20) Until well into the evening, the boy belched loudly just to annoy his mother.

While this type of construction is typically seen as a case of coercion (Jackendoff, 1997, 2002; Pustejovsky, 1995), not everyone agrees. One difference, as pointed out by Pylkkänen and McElree (2006), is that a transparent semantic composition is, while unlikely, possible in the case of aspectual coercion (i.e., it could be one really long belch). Interestingly, the existing evidence on how these constructions are processed is not entirely unambiguous. A number of studies involving a secondary task (e.g., the stop-making-sense task) have shown differential processing between aspectual coercion and control sentences (e.g., Todorova, Straub, Badecker, & Frank, 2000; Piñango, Winnick, Ullah, & Zurif, 2006; Piñango, Zurif, & Jackendoff, 1999; see also Brennan & Pylkkänen, 2008). However, eye-tracking experiments have failed to show such an effect (Pickering et al., 2006). Whether this is related to item selection (with some being more likely to be interpreted in a non-coerced, straightforward way), to a difference in methodology, to the fact that hardly any semantic content needs to be generated in the case of aspectual coercion (merely a change from non-iterative to iterative), or to the fact that the type-shifting is instigated by an adverb rather than the argument structure, is still unclear.

Finally, coercion-like operations also seem to operate at the phrasal level:

(21) The athlete is convinced that the difficult mountain will require all his strength.

In (21), the adjectival phrase, *difficult mountain*, cannot be interpreted as a simple intersection between the denotation of the adjective and the denotation of the noun. Rather, people interpret this construction something like *a [difficult to climb] mountain*. The adjective *difficult* requires an event to combine with, though *mountain* refers to an object. At first sight, this looks very much like a sort of complement coercion (cf. *The climber started the mountain*); however, an important difference is that type-shifting is not applicable in adjective–noun coercions. Specifically, *mountain* in (21) does not change type in the sentence interpretation, it remains referring to an object. Pustejovsky (1995) called the adjective–noun coercion a form of *selective binding*, in which the adjective "binds" with a typical property in the word's lexical representation (e.g., that mountains can be climbed).

Frisson, Pickering, and McElree (2011) showed that coerced adjective–noun constructions like (21) were fixated for longer than non-coerced adjective–noun constructions, like (22):

(22)   The athlete is convinced that the difficult exercise will require all his strength.

(As the noun *exercise* already refers to an event, semantic composition is straightforward.) Hence, these results indicate that costly enriched interpretation can occur without type-shifting, and that coercion-like operations are not restricted to interactions between verbs and their arguments. (An alternative explanation based on the co-occurrence frequencies of the adjective–noun combinations could not account for the results either, see Frisson et al., 2011.)

Coercion effects indicate that when semantic composition is not straightforward, and extra semantic content needs to be generated, processing slows down. Discussion continues regarding the time-course of the effect. Most eye-tracking experiments show somewhat delayed coercion effects, with the effect coming out either on the words following the complement noun or in eye-movement measures that normally index later processing events (e.g., regression-path duration). This pattern has led some researchers to suggest that semantic effects are usually delayed compared to syntactic effects. While semantic effects may be more delicate than syntactic effects, we do not think that they are necessarily delayed. In fact, Frisson and McElree's (2008) experiment on complement coercion, which had a substantially larger number of datapoints per participant than other eye-tracking experiments, did find significant early (first-pass) effects.

Plausibility

At a very general level, difficulty in interpretation, like coercion cost, may reflect the degree of (im)plausibility of a sentence's most likely interpretation. For example, *he started the book* takes longer to understand because the simple composition (putting the book in motion) is not very plausible. However, we think this is an unlikely explanation, at least in the case of complement coercion, as plausibility or acceptability ratings of coerced and control constructions (e.g., the spelled-out version: *he started reading the book*) are usually very comparable. It is true that non-coerced control constructions tend to get slightly higher acceptability scores than coerced constructions in pretests, though this might just reflect the fact that scorers need to put in extra work to come up with a coerced interpretation. Besides, the coerced constructions tend to be scored as very acceptable.

A more interesting line of research on plausibility looks at what type of semantic manipulations lead to plausibility effects, how fast the effects appear, how they relate to selectional restrictions and argument structure, and how the larger sentence context can affect them. Rayner et al. (2004; see also Murray, 1998) contrasted sentences like (23–25):

(23)   John used a knife to chop the large carrots for dinner.

(24)   John used a pump to chop the large carrots for dinner.

(25)   John used an axe to chop the large carrots for dinner.

They found that, compared to perfectly acceptable sentences like (23), sentences that contained an *inappropriate* theme (like (24)) showed an early (gaze duration) effect on the target word (*carrots*) itself. When the sentence contained only an *unlikely* theme (like (25)), readers spent more time reading the target word as well, though the effect only started showing up on the post-target region and was not immediate but only when (some) re-reading was taken into account as well. In short, a sentence containing a clear semantic anomaly—concretely, an impossible relationship between the theme and the verb/complement—is immediately noticed. When the incongruity is less severe, readers seem to temporarily hold off judgment. This difference in processing profile could be linked to a difference in the use of semantic and world-knowledge information; when the semantic clash is related to a semantic mismatch (e.g., due to selection restrictions), disruption is immediate, but when the mismatch is mainly because it contrasts with how we know the world operates (e.g., that people usually don't use an axe to chop carrots), the effect is delayed. (See also the discussion of Urbach & Kutas, 2010, below.)

Warren and McConnell (2007) extended this research by demonstrating that these types of context effects show up immediately (in first-fixation duration) when the semantic clash is between the verb and its object (see 26), but are delayed when the incongruity is between other parts of the sentence (see 27).

(26)   The man used a photo to blackmail the thin spaghetti yesterday evening.

(27)   The man used a blow-dryer to dry the thin spaghetti yesterday evening.

In (26), the thematic relation between the verb (*to blackmail*) and its argument (*spaghetti*) indicates that spaghetti cannot be blackmailed as one tends not to blackmail inanimate objects; in contrast, (27) expresses a possible though improbable state of affairs.

Whether this difference in processing between improbable and impossible sentences is caused by lexical-semantic information becoming available before world-knowledge or by semantic interpretation going from coarser- to finer-grained (Sanford & Garrod, 2005), was addressed by Warren, McConnell, and Rayner (2008). They reasoned that it should be possible to annul violations of general world-knowledge: if a context is used in which the improbable relation becomes plausible (e.g., in a fantasy context), the plausibility effect should disappear. In contrast, if the early plausibility effect is related to more automatic, lexical processing, then different contexts should not eliminate the effect. This is indeed what was found: the early disruption (due to the impossibility noticed from the assignment of thematic roles) was still present in the fantasy context, but the later, more integrative costs had disappeared.

While these results are intriguing, the conclusion is not necessarily shared by all. First, recent findings from Matsuki et al. (2011) indicate that plausibility effects can show up as fast as selection restrictions effects, which casts doubt on a strict distinction between world-knowledge and lexical-semantic knowledge. Second, while Ferguson and Sanford's (2008) data on counterfactuals in context are in line with Warren et al.'s (2008) pattern of results, Filik's (2008) eye-tracking data are not. She used sentences expressing a semantic–pragmatic anomaly (see 28) and manipulated the preceding context.

(28) He picked up the lorry and carried on down the road.

This sentence was preceded either by a neutral context (29) or a fictional context (30):

(29) Terry was very annoyed at the traffic jam on his way to work.

(30) The Incredible Hulk was annoyed that there was a lot of traffic in his way.

Filik found that the implausibility effect that was present in the neutral prior context condition disappeared when the prior context introduced a fictional character or setting. These results suggest that context can have a very early effect on plausibility. However, as also pointed out by Warren et al. (2008), Filik did not systematically contrast impossible to improbable constructions, and it is therefore difficult to conclude much about the time-course of semantic information versus world-knowledge. (As an aside, things are likely to be more complicated than a clear semantic versus pragmatic opposition. We would expect that (28) will not lead to disruption if the preceding context introduces a non-fictional account of a little boy playing with his toys. In this case, the referential knowledge of the object *lorry* is changed rather than a change in the appropriateness of the subject in carrying out the action of the verb.) Third, by no means all (psycho)linguists agree that there is such a strong division between semantic and world knowledge (for some discussion, see Pylkkänen & McElree, 2006). In fact, a number of experiments using event-related potential (ERP) and functional magnetic resonance imaging (fMRI) by Hagoort and colleagues (e.g., van Berkum, Hagoort, & Brown, 1999; Hagoort, Hald,

Bastiaansen, & Petersson, 2004; Nieuwland & van Berkum, 2005, 2006) have questioned the idea of distinct non-overlapping semantic and pragmatic (world-knowledge) processing. In their famous *train* experiment, Hagoort et al. (2004) examined the processing of sentences with a semantic violation (*The Dutch trains are sour*) to sentences with a world-knowledge violation (*The Dutch trains are white*; Dutch trains are distinctively yellow). Both violations showed a similar N400 effect compared to a control sentence (*The Dutch trains are yellow*), though the oscillatory brain activity, arguably reflecting post-integration processes, showed a dissimilarity between the two types of violation. They concluded that, temporally, semantic and pragmatic interpretation occurs in parallel. However, their conclusion that the oscillatory differences indicate that language users keep track of what makes a sentence hard to interpret is less clear and leaves open the possibility that semantic and world-knowledge information is at some level unique. (See also Sereno & Rayner, 2003, for an argument that eye-tracking data might more directly reflect processing than ERPs do.)

To conclude, the plausibility experiments suggest a distinction between processing something that sounds "strange" and something that sounds "wrong." A strong case can also be made that thematic role assignment occurs very quickly (see also 2 above) and is evaluated immediately. Whether semantic and pragmatic interpretation is used discretely or in parallel is at present an unresolved issue.

Quantifiers

Quantifiers do more than just provide some kind of quantification of a term, they can also affect how other parts of a sentence will be interpreted. For example, the reason why a sentence like *Five ships appeared on the horizon; two were sunk and four were damaged* sounds infelicitous is related to the tendency to assign a subset interpretation to cardinals when possible ("four out of the ships previously introduced" rather than four new ones). We will briefly discuss three types of quantifier constructions: cardinal quantifiers, single quantifier expressions, and quantifier scope ambiguities in doubly quantified sentences. For interesting work on how quantifiers affect discourse focus, see work by Moxey and colleagues (see Paterson, Filik, & Moxey, 2009, for an overview). One of the questions to address is how quickly the semantic information of the quantifier is integrated in the rest of the sentence.

Bare cardinal quantifiers are arguably the easiest case (everyone agrees on what *three* means, though the meaning of *most* can be quite discourse dependent, and idiosyncratic: e.g., see the difference in percentage for *most people* in *most people voted for Gore* versus *most people like sweets*). Off-line data suggest that, when confronted with a cardinal that can be interpreted as either a specification of a new set of entities or as a subset of a previously introduced set, people prefer the subset interpretation. For example, given a sentence fragment like *Five players make over £100,000 a week, three* . . . , participants are more likely to continue with *three (of them) are not worth it* rather than *three (other players) make less than £50,000*. In an eye-tracking study, Frazier and colleagues (2005) found processing difficulties for sentences that were not compatible with the subset interpretation (31a) compared to sentences that were (31b):

(31a/b) Five ships appeared on the horizon. Three ships sank. [Six/Two] were bombarded by enemy fire.

The disruption appeared quite quickly, in the first-pass reading measure on the region immediately following the quantifier (*were bombarded*), indicating that the subset interpretation is set up (almost) immediately upon reading the cardinal. However, ERP data by Kaan, Dallas, and Barkley (2007) point to a possibly different source of this effect. Using sentences like (32), Kaan et al. found no differences between the subset compatible and incompatible interpretation until about 900–1500 ms after quantifier onset, half a second or more later than in the eye-tracking data by Frazier et al. (2005).

(32) [Twelve/Four] flowers were put in the vase. Six had broken stems and were put in the trash.

They argue that this divergence in the ERP signal is related to the need to introduce a new referent in the discourse context (see also Burkhardt, 2006) rather than something directly triggered by the semantics of the quantifier. In any case, research on the processing of bare cardinals points to relatively fast integration of the quantifier interpretation into the unfolding sentence interpretation, though what exactly causes the disruption in the subset incompatible sentences remains unclear.

Single quantifier expressions seem to behave similarly, though their final interpretation might be more delayed than is the case for cardinals. In a recent study, Urbach and Kutas (2010) examined to what extent quantifier expressions like *most* and *few*, and *often* and *rarely*, are interpreted incrementally. They used sentences like (32a/b) to establish that *growing worms* led to an N400 effect in ERP recording:

(32a/b) Farmers grow crops/worms as their primary source of income.

They then added a quantifier to the sentence (see 33a/b) and established that this reversed the off-line acceptability ratings (in that *Few farmers grow worms* now becomes more acceptable than *Few farmers grow crops*).

(33a/b) Most/Few farmers grow crops/worms as their primary source of income.

They reasoned that if the meaning of the quantifier is immediately and fully integrated in the context (and world-knowledge is immediately used to interpret the unfolding sentence), the N400 effect on *worms* should disappear when preceded by *Few farmers*. While they did find a (small but significant) modulation of the N400 effect in these cases, the effect did not reverse at all. The authors argue that this indicates that while some part of the quantifier's meaning (a partial or underspecified interpretation, see also Frisson, 2009) is integrated in the context, a fully contextually specified interpretation (consistent with the off-line ratings) is delayed.

Finally, Filik, Paterson, and Liversedge (2004; see also Kurtzman & MacDonald, 1993; Paterson, Filik, & Liversedge, 2008) used eye tracking to examine quantifier scope ambiguities as can be found in (34a/b; double object construction) and (35a/b; dative construction):

(34a/b) The celebrity gave [an/every] in depth interview to [every/a] reporter from the newspaper, but the [interview(s)/reporter(s)] [was/were] not very interesting/interested.

(35a/b) The celebrity gave [a/every] reporter from the newspaper [every/an] in depth interview, but the [interview(s)/reporter(s)] [was/were] not very interesting/interested.

(Only the *a–every* and *every–a* conditions were tested, not the *a–a* or *every–every* conditions.) The problem the reader is confronted with is whether the quantifiers need to be interpreted with wide or narrow scope, for example, if *an in depth interview* is assigned wide scope, then one single interview is given to all the reporters, but if *every reporter* is given wide scope, then *an in depth interview* will, in fact, be interpreted as many different in-depth interviews (e.g., Fodor & Sag, 1982). The results showed that *every–a* double object sentences (34b) required more processing than *a–every* double object sentences on the region containing the direct and indirect objects, while dative constructions showed the opposite pattern. They argued that this result indicates that two strategies interact with each other (see Ioup, 1975), a quantifier hierarchy principle which spells out which quantifier takes wide scope over another quantifier in a sentence (e.g., *every* is higher in the hierarchy than *a* and therefore takes wide scope) and a grammatical hierarchy principle, which ranks the syntactic positions in order of scope (e.g., *indirect object* takes scope over *direct object*). More interesting for the present discussion is that the effects only showed up in "late" eye-movement measures (total time spent reading a region, which included re-reading). Hence, while readers seem to calculate "an" interpretation of the sentence in line with those principles, it does not occur instantaneously; and the depth at which this interpretation is formed remains unclear. In this sense, the data are in line with Urbach and Kutas (2010), who proposed a somewhat impoverished early interpretation of the quantifier (see also Paterson et al., 2008).

To summarize, data from experiments investigating quantifier expressions demonstrate that their interpretation takes time to compute and that resolution might not be immediate. Given that, in theory, it is possible to immediately assign an interpretation, this pattern of results argues against a strict incremental processing view in which each word is immediately interpreted to its fullest, contextually appropriate, extent.

Non-literal language

A sentence can express a literal meaning, which can be computed using standard compositional processes, but the exact same sentence can express a variety of non-literal meanings as well. For example, in the context of the sentence *The animals were grazing on the hillside*, the target sentence *The sheep followed their leader over the cliff*, will be assigned a literal meaning (Ortony, 1979; see also Inhoff, Lima, & Carroll, 1984; Shinjo & Myers, 1987). In the literal interpretation, referring expressions, like *sheep*, *leader*, and *cliff*, will be assigned default, literal meanings ("animal," "ram," and "steep drop-off," respectively). By contrast, in the context of the sentence *The Wall Street banker advised the clients to buy more shares*, comprehenders assign the same target sentence a non-literal interpretation. In this case, the referring expressions *sheep*, *leader*, and *cliff* are all assigned non-default, non-literal interpretations ("not-too-bright investors," "Wall Street banker," and sudden, "large decrease in stock prices," respectively). One question in research on non-literal language concerns how and when comprehenders compute non-literal interpretations for sentences such as the example above.

According to the *standard pragmatic view*, computation of literal meaning is an obligatory step in sentence interpretation that occurs temporally prior to the computation of non-literal meaning (Clark & Lucy, 1975; Glucksberg, 1998; Searle, 1979). One basic prediction that falls out of the standard pragmatic view is that sentences that require non-literal interpretations to make sense or to fit well with the preceding context should be more difficult to understand than sentences whose literal interpretations make sense and fit easily with preceding context. However, with almost no exceptions, the published literature indicates that comprehenders compute non-literal meanings as quickly as they compute literal meanings (Blasko & Connine, 1993; Gibbs, 1979; Harris, 1976; Pollio, Fabrizi, Sills, & Smith, 1984). McElree and Nordlie (1999), using a speed–accuracy-tradeoff paradigm, addressed the possibility that reading time and cross-modal priming studies may have masked temporal differences with differential accuracy across literal and metaphor conditions. While asymtotic accuracy was lower for non-literal sentences (e.g., *some mouths are sewers*) than for literal sentences, the timing parameters showed that accuracy diverged from chance at the same point in time for both literal and non-literal sentences. McElree and Nordlie concluded that, "The ... temporal dynamics for interpreting figurative and literal strings are incompatible with any viable formulation of a serial processing model in which figurative processing is delayed until the string has been interpreted in a literal fashion" (pp. 491–492). Other studies have shown that, under some circumstances, literal expressions can take longer to understand than non-literal expressions (Glucksberg, 1998, 2003). The bulk of the research suggests that non-literal interpretations are computed in the same timeframe as literal interpretations, and this seems to apply generally to a variety of non-literal expressions.

Non-literal meaning can be packed into units as small as a single word, which happens in the case of *metonymy* (Frisson & Pickering, 1999, 2001, 2007; McElree et al., 2006; see also Frazier & Rayner, 1990). In a metonym, a word is used in such a way that its default interpretation does not apply, but there is a connection between the default sense and the contextually appropriate sense. This occurs in statements such as producer-for-product metonymies, as in *My grandmother read Dickens* (compare to *My grandmother met Dickens*), place-for-event metonymies, as in *The students protested during Vietnam* (compare to *The students traveled around Vietnam*), and place-for-institution metonymies, as in *John talked to the convent yesterday* (compare to *John walked to the convent yesterday*). Eye-tracking experiments involving expressions such as *The students protested during/traveled around Vietnam* show that metonymic expressions are just as easy to process as comparable literal expressions. What makes a metonymic expression difficult to process is whether an individual has encountered the expression before. That is, familiar metonymic expressions are easy to understand, but novel ones, such as *The students protested during Finland*, are not. Thus, the ready availability of a metonymic interpretation seems to be the critical factor. This conclusion was supported by experiments involving a contextual manipulation. If context supports a metonymic interpretation of a novel metonymic expression, the novel metonymic expressions are processed almost just as quickly as equivalent literal expressions (Frisson & Pickering, 2007). Thus, comprehenders are able to use context to quickly establish a non-literal interpretation for expressions that have previously been used only in a literal fashion.

The "when" question for non-literal interpretation has been largely laid to rest, but the "how" question remains a topic of ongoing discussion. Early accounts in the two-stage tradition had non-literal interpretations being computed for sentences only if the literal interpretation proved faulty in some way (Clark & Lucy, 1975; Miller, 1979; Searle, 1979; Stern, 2000). Because some literally true statements are assigned non-literal or metaphoric meanings ("No man is an island," "I'm not the wreck of the Hesperus"), literal falsehood does not represent an obligatory prerequisite to non-literal interpretation. Later accounts appealed to Gricean principles as a replacement for the literal falsehood criterion (Stern, 2000; cf. Grice, 1989). On this account, if a literal interpretation violated one of the "rules" of conversation, such as overstating the obvious, being off-topic, and so on, then comprehenders would seek a non-literal interpretation. However, as with all "literal first" hypotheses, the Gricean violation hypothesis fails to account for the rapid computation of non-literal meanings. It also fails to account for effects of non-literal interpretations in task contexts where only a literal interpretation is required, as in *semantic stroop* experiments (Glucksberg, 1998, 2003; Glucksberg, Gildea, & Bookin, 1982; Keysar, 1989;

see also Kazmerski, Blasko, & Dessalegn, 2003; Wolff & Gentner, 2000). In these experiments, participants are asked to say whether a statement is literally true or not. Apt metaphoric statements like *My job is a jail* take longer to reject than inapt metaphoric statements like *My job is a hamper*. Because both statements are literally false, they both should require a "no" response. If literal meanings were computed before metaphoric meanings, response times should be equivalent for apt and inapt (literally false) metaphoric statements. The results of semantic stroop tasks are taken as evidence against the primacy of literal interpretations.

The *dual-reference* and *career of metaphor* hypotheses have been proposed as replacements for the literal-falsehood and Gricean violation hypotheses (Bowdle & Gentner, 2005; Glucksberg & Haught, 2006a, b), at least for the interpretation of metaphoric expressions. According to the dual-reference hypothesis, a metaphoric expression such as *my lawyer is a shark* sets up a mental representation in which the *vehicle* "shark" simultaneously refers to a literal shark as well as a superordinate category, such as "dangerous animals." It is this dual reference that makes expressions such as "my lawyer is a *well-paid* shark" felicitous. Lawyers can be "sharks," because "shark" serves as a pointer to the ad hoc category "dangerous animals." Similarly, the expression "well-paid shark" can be felicitous, even though it is literally nonsensical, because "lawyer" fits into this ad hoc category. The career-of-metaphor hypothesis proposes that metaphors first appear as literal comparisons, as in "The photocopier was like a roadblock," and later transition to metaphoric statements, as in "The photocopier was a roadblock." However, contrary to career-of-metaphor predictions, recent studies have shown that aptness, rather than novelty, predicts how subjects will respond to metaphoric statements (Glucksberg & Haught, 2006a, b).

Finally, just because non-literal and literal meanings appear to be computed within the same time frame, this does not mean that they are computed using the same mechanisms and processes. Some theorists proposed a special role for the right hemisphere in computing non-literal interpretations (Bottini et al., 1994). This conclusion was based on early investigations of right-hemisphere-damaged patients, who performed poorly on sentence-picture matching experiments (see Johns, Tooley, & Traxler, 2008). In these instances, patients appeared to assign literal meanings to expressions such as *he had a heavy heart*, because they were more likely to select a picture of a man holding a large heart than a picture of a man weeping. However, follow-up studies indicated that right-hemisphere patients did know the meanings of non-literal expressions. They just had difficulty performing sentence–picture matching. Further, although different patterns of neural activation are observed for non-literal expressions compared to literal expressions, imaging studies do not consistently show greater right-hemisphere activity for non-literal compared to literal expressions, and some studies show greater right-hemisphere activity for literal than for non-literal expressions (Coulson & van Petten, 2002; Eviatar

& Just, 2006; Rapp, Leube, Erb, Grodd, & Kircher, 2004, 2007; Saygin, McCullough, Alac, & Emmorey, 2010; Shibata, Abe, Terao, & Miyamoto, 2007; Stringaris, Medford, Giampietro, Brammer, & David, 2007) . As a result, some theorists argue that lateralization is governed more by whether a particular meaning is salient, rather than by whether a particular meaning is literal or non-literal (Giora, 2003; Mashal, Faust, & Hendler, 2005; Mashal, Faust, Hendler, & Jung-Beeman, 2007). The more often an individual encounters a metaphoric expression, the more salient will be its metaphoric meaning, relative to any literal interpretations.

Perceptual simulation and embodied sentence interpretation

One fundamental question, whether the topic relates to word-, sentence-, or discourse-level processes is: What kinds of semantic representations do comprehenders build? Traditional approaches to word- and sentence-level semantics have appealed to abstract symbolic representations as the substrate of interpretation (Burgess & Lund, 1997; Chomsky, 1990; Landauer & Dumais, 1997). By contrast, models of discourse interpretation have appealed more to models or simulations that are grounded in experience, perception, and action (Barsalou, 1999; Glenberg & Robertson, 2000; Johnson-Laird, 1983; Zwaan, Madden, Yaxley, & Aveyard, 2004).

A variety of this latter type of model falls within the developing embodied language tradition. According to embodied language theorists, the interpretation of linguistic expressions calls upon the same neural systems that are used in perception and action-planning. To support such claims, advocates point to behavioral experiments showing that real-world plausibility, rather than mere association, predicts people's behavior on a variety of language tasks (Glenberg & Robertson, 2000). Participants judge statements like "she made a pillow by filling up her sweater with leaves" as more plausible than ". . . by filling up her sweater with water," even though "leaves" and "water" are equally associated with the preceding context. Behavioral demonstrations of action-compatibility effects (ACE) also suggest that perceptual simulations play a role in sentence comprehension. The embodied language hypothesis views action planning as playing a critical role in language understanding, because comprehenders are thought to interpret linguistic expressions by running covert simulations of the actions that they describe. That is, participants imagine themselves undertaking the actions that the text describes (Willems, Hagoort, & Casasanto, 2010; Zwaan & Taylor, 2006). In fact, embodiment accounts go further by assuming that meaning can only be accessed via action-based representations.[1] Thus, embodied semantics advocates are happy to note that the same parts of motor and pre-motor cortex become active when participants imagine themselves performing an action and when they read about someone else performing the same action (Buccino et al., 2005). In fact, activity in the motor cortex appears to differ depending on which body part is associated with an action

(Hauk, Johnsrude, & Pulvermuller, 2004). When participants read sentences that contain verbs referring to leg-related actions (e.g., kick), the pattern of activity in the motor cortex is different from when they read sentences containing verbs that refer to arm- or mouth-related actions (e.g., throw, chew). Some advocates go one step further and assert that mirror neurons, neurons that have been found to become active in monkeys when they perform an action or watch someone else perform the same action, provide the neural substrate for action-simulation, and hence for language understanding in humans (Gallese & Lakoff, 2005; Rizzolatti & Arbib, 1998; Rizzolatti & Craighero, 2004).

The embodied language hypothesis, and the mirror-neuron variant, are not without their critics, however. For example, a recent meta-analysis of fMRI studies shows that patterns of activation are not as neat as would be predicted by the embodied semantics hypothesis (Kemmerer & Gonzalez-Castillo, 2010). When different fMRI studies involving the comprehension of action verbs were compared, the results showed little or no consistency in the areas of the brain that were activated. Further, there are considerable discrepancies in both the fMRI literature and the transcranial magnetic stimulation (TMS) literature across studies. TMS involves stimulating the cortex of the brain with magnetic pulses. At different degrees of intensity, TMS can either disrupt or enhance neural firing. Results in TMS studies differ based on the secondary task that is used, the timing of the application of TMS, as well as stimulus onset (Tomasino, Fink, Sparing, Dafotakis, & Weiss, 2008). Patterns of activation in fMRI studies also seem to be heavily task-dependent, with the clearest motor activations coming in studies where participants are engaged in explicit stimulus-comparison tasks (i.e., are two consecutive stimuli identical or different?). Finally, the TMS research enterprise has produced some truly anomalous results. For example, one experiment by Liuzzi and colleagues showed that applying TMS to the leg motor cortex affected participants' responses on a speech-perception task (Liuzzi et al., 2008). They explained this result by asserting that leg-movement plays a communicative function, and that therefore leg movement was part of the speech planning process. An alternative conclusion could have been that the legs have little or nothing to do with speech and that, therefore, the results of the TMS paradigm should be generally viewed with extreme caution.

Finally, language contains a whole variety of words that do not have a perception or action counterpart in the external world, such as abstract words, determiners, and prepositions and words that are relational in nature (e.g., *it has grown colder* does not necessarily mean that it is cold, for example, one can say this at the end of a heat wave when the temperature has dropped to a bearable 90 °F). Furthermore, how non-literal language is interpreted in this model remains unresolved: does one activate the motor cortex when reading *The old man kicked the bucket* and if so, does that mean that a literal interpretation was attempted first (which would go against the behavioral findings of faster processing of the idiomatic meaning, e.g., Swinney & Cutler, 1979)?

Summary and conclusions

In this chapter, we have reviewed research on a variety of sentence interpretation processes. The basic work of sentences is describing who did what to whom. Early research showed that many aspects of sentence interpretation, including syntactic structure-building and basic semantic interpretation occur very rapidly in speech processing (within 200 ms of stimulus onset; Marslen-Wilson, 1973, 1975). Thus, comprehenders must rapidly use cues available in the sentence to make thematic assignments. More recent research suggests that comprehenders are flexible in their interpretive processing, and are capable of assigning non-default interpretations to strings of words when contextual information overrides default lexical-semantic values. Such effects can be observed in the processing of non-literal expressions (e.g., *my wife is an animal*) as well as expressions whose default interpretations violate semantic or world knowledge. Comprehenders also use cues from quantifiers rapidly to identify groups or sets of entities to place in focus. Other cues, including verb argument structures, are used to anticipate mention of likely role-players. The preceding should not be read as implying that all aspects of sentence interpretation take place immediately and to the fullest extent possible, however. For example, some aspects of non-literal language interpretation may be deferred in the case of metonymies, especially when different senses of a metonymic expression are not central to the ongoing discourse. Aside from questions of when various aspects of interpretation are completed, researchers have focused on how sentence-semantics are mentally represented. Recently, many theorists have advocated for perceptual simulation and embodied representations as a critical component of sentence interpretation. More work needs to be done, however, to connect hypothesized simulation activity to its neural substrate, and to clarify whether perceptual simulation is obligatory or optional.

Acknowledgments

This project was supported in part by awards from the National Science Foundation (# 1024003) and the National Institutes of Health (1R01-HD048914–01A2) to the second author.

Note

1. We thank Christoph Scheepers for pointing this out.

References

Altmann, G. T. M. (1999). Thematic role assignment in context. *Journal of Memory and Language*, *41*, 124–145.

Altmann, G. T. M., & Kamide, Y. (1999). Incremental interpretation at verbs: Restricting the domain of subsequent reference. *Cognition*, *73*, 247–264.

Altmann, G. T. M., & Mirković, J. (2009). Incrementality and prediction in human sentence processing. *Cognitive Science*, *33*, 583–609.

Barsalou, L. W. (1999). Perceptual symbol systems. *Behavioral and Brain Sciences*, *22*, 577–660.

van Berkum, J. J. A., Hagoort, P., & Brown, C. M. (1999). Semantic integration in sentences and discourse: Evidence from the N400. *Journal of Cognitive Neuroscience*, *11*, 657–671.

Blasko, D. G., & Connine, C. M. (1993). Effects of familiarity and aptness on metaphor processing. *Journal of Experimental Psychology: Learning, Memory, and Cognition*, *19*, 295–308.

Boland, J. E., & Blodgett, A. (2006). Argument status and PP-attachment. *Journal of Psycholinguistic Research*, *35*, 385–403.

Boland, J. E., Tanenhaus, M. K., Garnsey, S. M., & Carlson, G. N. (1995). Verb argument structure in parsing and interpretation: Evidence from *wh*-questions. *Journal of Memory and Language*, *34*, 774–806.

Bornkessel, I. & Schlesewsky, M. (2006). Generalised semantic roles and syntactic templates: A new framework for language comprehension. In I. Bornkessel, M. Schlesewsky, B. Comrie, & A.D. Friederici (Eds.), *Semantic role universals and argument linking: Theoretical, typological and psycholinguistic perspectives* (pp. 327–353). Berlin and New York: Mouton de Gruyter.

Bottini, G., Corcoran, R., Sterzi, R., Paulescu, E., Schenone, P., Scarpa, P., Frackowiak, R. S. J., & Frith, C. D. (1994). The role of right hemisphere in the interpretation of figurative aspects of language: A positron emission tomography study. *Brain*, *117*, 1241–1253.

Bowdle, B. F., & Gentner, D. (2005). The career of metaphor. *Psychological Review*, *112*, 193–216.

Brennan, J., & Pylkkänen, L. (2008). Processing events: Behavioral and neuromagnetic correlates of aspectual coercion. *Brain & Language*, *106*, 132–143.

Buccino, G., Riggio, L., Melli, G., Binkofski, F., Gallese, V., & Rizzolatti, G. (2005). Listening to action-related sentences modulates the activity of the motor system: A combined TMS and behavioral study. *Cognitive Brain Research*, *24*, 355–363.

Burgess, C., & Lund, K. (1997). Modelling parsing constraints with high-dimensional context space. *Language and Cognitive Processes*, *12*, 177–210.

Burkhardt, P. (2006). Inferential bridging relations reveal distinct neural mechanisms: Evidence from event-related brain potentials. *Brain & Language*, *98*, 159–168.

Carlson, G., & Tanenhaus, M. (1988). Thematic roles and language comprehension. In W. Wilkins (Ed.), *Thematic relations* (pp. 263–300). New York: Academic Press.

Chomsky, N. (1990). Formalization and formal linguistics. *Natural Language and Linguistic Theory*, *8*, 143–147.

Christianson, K., Hollingworth, A., Halliwell, J. F., & Ferreira, F. (2001). Thematic roles assigned along the garden path linger. *Cognitive Psychology*, *42*, 368–407.

Clark, H. H., & Lucy, P. (1975). Understanding what is meant from what is said: A study in conversationally conveyed requests. *Journal of Verbal Learning and Verbal Behavior*, *14*, 56–72.

Clifton, C. Jr., Speer, S., & Abney, S. P. (1991). Parsing arguments: Phrase structure and argument structure as determinants of initial parsing decisions. *Journal of Memory & Language*, *30*, 251–271.

Clifton, C. Jr., Staub, A., & Rayner, K. (2007). Eye-movements in reading words and sentences. In R. Van Gompel, R., M. H. Fischer, W. S. Murray, & R. L. Hill (Eds.), *Eye-movements: A window on mind and brain* (pp. 341–372). New York: Elsevier.

Coulson, S., & van Petten, C. (2002). A special role for the right hemisphere in metaphor comprehension? ERP evidence from hemifield presentation. *Brain Research*, *1146*, 128–145.

Eviatar, Z., & Just, M. A. (2006). Brain correlates of discourse processing: An fMRI investigation of irony and conventional metaphor comprehension. *Neuropsychologia*, *44*, 2348–2359.

Ferguson, H. J., & Sanford, A. J. (2008). Anomalies in real and counterfactual worlds: An eye-movement investigation. *Journal of Memory and Language*, *58*, 609–626.

Ferreira, F., & Patson, N. D. (2007). The "Good Enough" approach to language comprehension. *Language and Linguistics Compass*, *1(1–2)*, 71–83.

Ferretti, T. R., McRae, K., & Hatherell, A. (2001). Integrating verbs, situations schemas, and thematic role concepts. *Journal of Memory and Language*, *44*, 516–547.

Filik, R. (2008). Contextual override of pragmatic anomalies: Evidence from eye-movements. *Cognition*, *106*, 1038–1046.

Filik, R., Paterson, K. B., & Liversedge, S. P. (2004). Processing doubly quantified sentences: Evidence from eye-movements. *Psychonomic Bulletin & Review*, *11*, 953–959.

Fodor, J. D., Bever, T., & Garrett, M. (1974). *The psychology of language*. New York: McGraw-Hill.

Fodor, J. D., & Sag, I. (1982). Referential and quantificational indefinites. *Linguistics & Philosophy*, *5*, 355–398.

Folk, J. R., & Morris, R. K. (2003). Effects of syntactic category assignment on lexical ambiguity resolution in reading: An eye-movement analysis. *Memory and Cognition*, *31*, 87–99.

Frazier, L. (1999). *On sentence interpretation*. Dordrecht: Kluwer Academic Publishers.

Frazier, L., & Clifton, C. Jr. (1996). *Construal*. Cambridge, MA: MIT Press.

Frazier, L., Clifton, C., Rayner, K., Deevy, P., Koh, S., & Bader, M. (2005). Interface problems: Structural constraints on interpretation? *Journal of Psycholinguistic Research*, *34*, 201–231.

Frazier, L., & Rayner, K. (1987). Resolution of syntactic category ambiguities: Eye-movements in parsing lexically ambiguous sentences. *Journal of Memory and Language*, *26*, 505–526.

Frazier, L., & Rayner, K. (1990). Taking on semantic commitments: Processing multiple meanings versus multiple senses. *Journal of Memory and Language*, *29*, 181–200.

Frege, G. (1952/1892). On sense and reference. In P. Geach & M. Black (Eds.), *Translations from the philosophical writings of Gottlob Frege*. Oxford: Blackwell.

Frisson, S. (2009). Semantic underspecification in language processing. *Language and Linguistics Compass*, *3*, 111–127.

Frisson, S., & McElree, B. (2008). Complement coercion is not modulated by competition: Evidence from eye-movements. *Journal of Experimental Psychology: Learning, Memory, and Cognition*, *34*, 1–11.

Frisson, S., McElree, B., & Thyparampil, P. (2005). Coercion without type-shifting: The role of the subject in enriched interpretations. In *Proceedings of the 11th annual conference on architectures and mechanisms for language processing* (p. 108). University of Ghent, Belgium, September 5–7.

Frisson, S., & Pickering, M. J. (1999). The processing of metonymy: Evidence from eye-movements. *Journal of Experimental Psychology: Learning, Memory, and Cognition*, *25*, 1347–1365.

Frisson, S., & Pickering, M. J. (2001). Figurative language processing in the Underspecification Model. *Metaphor and Symbol*, *16*, 149–171.

Frisson, S., & Pickering, M. J. (2007). The processing of familiar and novel senses of a word: Why reading Dickens is easy but reading Needham can be hard. *Language and Cognitive Processes, 22*, 595–613.

Frisson, S., Pickering, M. J., & McElree, B. (2003). The influence of local and global context on the interpretation of adjective-noun combinations. In Alonso-Ovalle, L. (Ed.), *On semantic processing.* UMOP, 27. University of Massachusetts, Amherst: GLSA.

Frisson, S., Pickering, M. J., & McElree, B. (2011). The difficult mountain: Enriched composition in adjective-noun phrases. *Psychonomic Bulletin & Review, 6*, 1172–1179.

Gallese, V., & Lakoff, G. (2005). The brain's concepts: The role of the sensory-motor system in reason and language. *Cognitive Neuropsychology, 22*, 455–479.

Gibbs, R. W. (1979). Contextual effects in understanding indirect requests. *Discourse Processes, 2*, 1–10.

Giora, R. (2003). *On our mind: Salience, context, and figurative language.* New York: Oxford University Press.

Glucksberg, S. (1998). Understanding metaphors. *Current Directions in Psychological Science, 7*, 39–43.

Glucksberg, S. (2003). The psycholinguistics of metaphor. *Trends in Cognitive Sciences, 7*, 92–96.

Glucksberg, S., Gildea, P., & Bookin, H. B. (1982). On understanding nonliteral speech: Can people ignore metaphors? *Journal of Verbal Learning and Verbal Behavior, 21*, 85–98.

Glucksberg, S., & Haught, C. (2006a). On the relation between metaphor and simile: When comparison fails. *Mind and Language, 21*, 360–378.

Glucksberg, S., & Haught, C. (2006b). Can Florida become like the next Florida? When metaphoric comparisons fail. *Psychological Science, 17*, 935–938.

Glenberg, A. M., & Robertson, D. A. (2000). Symbol grounding and meaning: A comparison of high-dimensional and embodied theories of meaning. *Journal of Memory and Language, 43*, 379–401.

Grice, H. P. (1989). *Studies in the way of words.* Cambridge, MA: Harvard University Press.

Grimshaw, J. (1990). *Argument structure.* Cambridge, MA: MIT Press.

Hagoort, P., Hald, L., Bastiaansen, M., & Petersson, K. M. (2004). Integration of word meaning and world knowledge in language comprehension. *Science, 304*, 438–441.

Harris, R. J. (1976). Comprehension of metaphors: A test of the two-stage processing model. *Bulleting of the Psychonomic Society, 8*, 312–314.

Hauk, O., Johnsrude, I., Pulvermuller, F. (2004). Somatotopic representation of action words in human motor and premotor cortex. *Neuron, 41*, 301–307.

Hirotani, M., Frazier, L., & Rayner, K. (2006). Punctuation and intonation effects on clause and sentence wrap-up: Evidence from eye-movements. *Journal of Memory and Language, 54*, 425–443.

Inhoff, A. W., Lima, S. D., & Carroll, P. J. (1984). Contextual effects on metaphor comprehension during reading. *Memory & Cognition, 12*, 558–567.

Ioup, G. (1975). Some universals for quantifier scope. In J. Kimball (Ed.), *Syntax and semantics*, Vol. 4 (pp. 37–58), New York: Academic Press.

Jackendoff, R. (1997). *The architecture of the language faculty.* Cambridge, MA: MIT Press.

Jackendoff, R. (2002). *Foundations of language.* New York: Oxford University Press.

Johns, C. L., Tooley, K. M., & Traxler, M. J. (2008). Right hemisphere language disorders. *Language and Linguistics Compass, 2,* 1038–1062.

Johnson-Laird, P. N. (1983). *Mental models.* Cambridge: Cambridge University Press.

Just, M. A., & Carpenter, P. (1980). A theory of reading: From eye fixations to comprehension. *Psychological Review, 85,* 109–130.

Kaan, E., Dallas, A. C., & Barkley, C. M. (2007). Processing bare quantifiers in discourse. *Brain Research, 1146,* 119–209.

Kamide, Y., Altmann, G. T. M., & Haywood, S. L. (2003). The time-course of prediction in incremental sentence processing: Evidence from anticipatory eye-movements. *Journal of Memory and Language, 49,* 133–159.

Kazmerski, V., Blasko, D., & Dessalegn, B. (2003). ERP and behavioral evidence of individual differences in metaphor comprehension. *Memory & Cognition, 31,* 673–689.

Kemmerer, D., & Gonzalez-Castillo, J. (2010). The two-level theory of verb meaning: An approach to integrating the semantics of action with the mirror neuron system. *Brain & Language, 112,* 54–76.

Keysar, B. (1989). On the functional equivalence of literal and metaphoric interpretations in discourse. *Journal of Memory and Language, 28,* 275–285.

Knoeferle, P., Crocker, M. W., Scheepers, C., & Pickering, M. J. (2005). The influence of the immediate visual context on incremental thematic role-assignment: Evidence from eye-movements in depicted events. *Cognition, 95,* 95–127.

Kuperberg, G. R., Choi, A., Cohn, N., Paczynski, M., & Jackendoff, R. (2010). Electrophysical correlates of complement coercion. *Journal of Cognitive Neuroscience, 22,* 2685–2701.

Kurtzman, H. S., & MacDonald, M. C. (1993). Resolution of quantifier scope ambiguities. *Cognition, 48,* 243–279.

Landauer, T. K., & Dumais, S. T. (1997). A solution to Plato's problem: The latent semantic analysis theory of acquisition, induction, and representation of knowledge. *Psychological Review, 104,* 211–240.

Lapata, M., Keller, F., & Scheepers, C. (2003). Intra-sentential context effects on the interpretation of logical metonymy. *Cognitive Science, 27,* 649–668.

Liuzzi, G., Ellger, T., Flöel, A., Breitenstein, C., Jansen, A., & Knecht, S. (2008). Walking the talk: Speech activates the leg motor cortex. *Neuropsychologia, 46,* 2824–2830.

Marslen-Wilson, W. D. (1973). Linguistic structure and speech shadowing at very short latencies. *Nature, 244,* 522–523.

Marslen-Wilson, W. D. (1975). Sentence perception as an interactive parallel process. *Science, 189,* 226–228.

Mashal, N., Faust, M., & Hendler, T. (2005). The role of right hemisphere in processing nonsalient metaphorical meanings: Application of principal components analysis to fMRI data. *Neuropsychologia, 43,* 2084–2100.

Mashal, N., Faust, M., Hendler, T., & Jung-Beeman, M. (2007). An fMRI investigation of the neural correlates underlying the processing of novel metaphoric expressions. *Brain & Language, 100,* 115–126.

Matsuki, K., Chow, T., Hare, M., Elman, J. L., Scheepers, C., & McRae, K. (2011). Event-based plausibility immediately influences on-line language comprehension. *Journal of Experimental Psychology: Learning, Memory, and Cognition, 37,* 913–934.

Mauner, G., Tanenhaus, M. K., & Carlson, G. N. (1995). Implicit arguments in sentence processing. *Journal of Memory & Language, 34,* 357–382.

McElree, B., Frisson, S., & Pickering, M. J. (2006). Deferred interpretations: Why starting Dickens is taxing but reading Dickens isn't. *Cognitive Science, 30,* 181–192.

McElree, B., & Nordlie, J. (1999). Literal and figurative interpretations are computed in equal time. *Psychonomic Bulletin & Review, 6,* 486–494.
McElree, B., Traxler, M., Pickering, M. J., Seely, R., & Jackendoff, R. (2001). Reading time evidence for enriched composition. *Cognition, 78,* B17–25.
Miller, G. A. (1979). Images and models, similes and metaphors. In A. Ortony (Ed.), *Metaphor and thought* (pp. 202–250). Cambridge: Cambridge University Press.
Mitchell, D. C., & Green, D. W. (1978). The effects of context and content on immediate processing in reading. *Quarterly Journal of Experimental Psychology, 30,* 609–636.
Murray, W. S. (1998). Parafoveal pragmatics. In G. Underwood (Ed.), *Eye guidance in reading and scene perception* (pp. 181–200). Oxford: Elsevier.
Nieuwland, M. S., van Berkum, J. (2005). Testing the limits of the semantic illusion phenomenon: ERPs reveal temporary semantic change deafness in discourse comprehension. *Cognitive Brain Research, 24,* 691–701.
Nieuwland, M. S., & van Berkum, J. J. A. (2006). When peanuts fall in love: N400 evidence for the power of discourse. *Journal of Cognitive Neuroscience, 18,* 1098–1111.
Nunberg, G. (2004). The pragmatics of deferred interpretation. In L. Horn & G. Ward (Eds.), *Handbook of pragmatics* (pp. 344–364). Oxford: Blackwell.
Ortony, A. (1979). Beyond literal similarity. *Psychological Review, 86,* 161–180.
Paterson, K. B., Filik, R., & Liversedge, S. P. (2008). Competition during the processing of quantifier scope ambiguities: Evidence from eye-movements during reading. *Quarterly Journal of Experimental Psychology, 61,* 459–473.
Paterson, K. B., Filik, R., & Moxey, L. M. (2009). Quantifiers and discourse processing. *Language and Linguistics Compass, 3,* 1390–1402.
Pickering, M. J., & Frisson, S. (2001). Processing ambiguous verbs: Evidence from eye-movements. *Journal of Experimental Psychology: Learning, Memory, and Cognition, 27,* 556–573.
Pickering, M. J., McElree, B., Frisson, S., Chen, L., & Traxler, M. J. (2006). Underspecification and aspectual coercion. *Discourse Processes, 42,* 131–155.
Pickering M. J., & Traxler M. J. (1998). Plausibility and the recovery from garden paths: An eyetracking study. *Journal of Experimental Psychology: Learning, Memory, and Cognition, 24,* 940–61.
Pickering, M. J., Traxler, M. J., & Tooley, K. M. (2010). Thematic processing during sentence comprehension. Paper submitted for publication.
Piñango, M. M., Winnick, A., Ullah, R., & Zurif, E. (2006). Time-course of semantic composition: The case of aspectual coercion. *Journal of Psycholinguistic Research, 35,* 233–244.
Piñango, M. M., Zurif, E., & Jackendoff, R. (1999). Real-time processing implications of enriched composition at the syntax–semantics interface. *Journal of Psycholinguistic Research, 28,* 395–414.
Pollio, H. R., Fabrizi, M. S., Sills, A., & Smith, M. K. (1984). Need metaphoric comprehension take longer than literal comprehension? *Journal of Psycholinguistic Research, 13,* 195–214.
Pustejovsky, J. (1995). *The generative lexicon.* Cambridge, MA: MIT Press.
Pylkkänen, L., & McElree, B. (2006). The syntax-semantics interface: On-line composition of sentence meaning. In M. Traxler & M. A. Gernsbacher (Eds.), *Handbook of psycholinguistics* (2nd ed.). New York: Elsevier.
Pylkkänen, L., & McElree, B. (2007). An MEG study of silent meaning. *Journal of Cognitive Neuroscience, 19,* 126–149.

Pylkkänen, L., Llinás, R., & McElree, B. (submitted). Distinct effects of semantic plausibility and semantic composition in MEG.

Rapp, A. M., Leube, D. T., Erb, M., Grodd, W., & Kircher, T. T. J. (2004). Neural correlates of metaphor processing. *Cognitive Brain Research*, *20*, 395–402.

Rapp, A. M., Leube, D. T., Erb, M., Grodd, W., & Kircher, T. T. J. (2007). Laterality in metaphor processing: Lack of evidence from functional magnetic resonance imaging for the right hemisphere theory. *Brain & Language*, *100*, 142–149.

Rayner, K., & Clifton, C. Jr. (2009). Language processing in reading and speech perception is fast and incremental: Implications for event related potential research. *Biological Psychology*, *80*, 4–9.

Rayner, K., & Duffy, S. A. (1986). Lexical complexity and fixation times in reading: Effects of word frequency, verb complexity, and lexical ambiguity. *Memory & Cognition*, *14*, 191–201.

Rayner, K., Kambe, G., & Duffy, S. A. (2000). The effect of clause wrap-up on eye-movements during reading. *The Quarterly Journal of Experimental Psychology*, *53A*, 1061–1080.

Rayner, K., Warren, T., Juhasz, B. J., & Liversedge, S. P. (2004). The effect of plausibility on eye-movements in reading. *Journal of Experimental Psychology: Learning, Memory, and Cognition*, *30*, 1290–1301.

Rizzolatti, G., & Arbib, M. A. (1998). Language within our grasp. *Trends in Neurosciences*, *21*, 188–194.

Rizzolatti, G., & Craighero, L. (2004). The mirror-neuron system. *Annual Review of Neuroscience*, *27*, 169–192.

Sanford, A. J., & Garrod, S. C. (2005). Memory-based approaches and beyond. *Discourse Processes*, *39*, 205–223.

Saygin, A. P., McCullough, S., Alac, M., & Emmorey, K. (2010). Modulation of BOLD response in motion-sensitive lateral temporal cortex by real and fictive motion sentences. *Journal of Cognitive Neuroscience*, *22*, 2480–2490.

Scheepers, C., Keller, F., & Lapata, M. (2008). Evidence for serial coercion: A time-course analysis using the visual-world paradigm. *Cognitive Psychology*, *56*, 1–29.

Schütze, C. T., & Gibson, E. (1999). Argumenthood and English prepositional phrase attachment. *Journal of Memory and Language*, *40*, 409–431.

Searle, J. (1979). Metaphor. In A. Ortony (Ed.), *Metaphor and Thought* (pp. 92–123). Cambridge: Cambridge University Press.

Sedivy, J. C., Tanenhaus, M. K., Chambers, C. G., & Carlson, G. N. (1999). Achieving incremental semantic interpretation through contextual representation. *Cognition*, *71*, 109–147.

Sereno, S., & Rayner, K. (2003). Measuring word recognition in reading: Eye-movements and event-related potentials. *Trends in Cognitive Sciences*, *7*, 489–493.

Shibata, M., Abe, J., Terao, A., & Miyamoto, T. (2007). Neural bases of metaphor comprehension: An fMRI study. *Cognitive Studies Bulletin of the Japanese Cognitive Science Society*, *14*, 339–354.

Shinjo, M., & Myers, J. L. (1987). The role of context in metaphor comprehension. *Journal of Memory and Language*, *26*, 226–241.

Staub, A., & Rayner, K. (2007). Eye-movements and on-line comprehension processes. In G. Gaskell (Ed.), *The Oxford handbook of psycholinguistics* (pp. 327–342). Oxford: Oxford University Press.

Steedman, M. J. (1989). Grammar, interpretation and processing from the lexicon. In W. Marslen-Wilson (Ed.), *Lexical representation and process* (pp. 463–504). Cambridge, MA: MIT Press.

Stern, J. (2000). *Metaphor in context*. Cambridge, MA: MIT Press.
Stringaris, A. K., Medford, N. C., Giampietro, V., Brammer, M. J., & David, A. S. (2007). Deriving meaning: Distinct neural mechanisms for metaphoric, literal, and non-meaningful sentences. *Brain & Language, 100*, 150–162.
Swinney, D., & Cutler, A. (1979). The access and processing of idiomatic expressions. *Journal of Verbal Learning and Verbal Behaviour, 18*, 523–534.
Tanenhaus, M. K., Spivey-Knowlton, M. J., Eberhard, K. M., & Sedivy, J. C. (1995). Integration of visual and linguistic information in spoken language comprehension. *Science, 268*, 1632–1634.
Todorova, M., Straub, K., Badecker,W., & Frank, R. (2000, August). Aspectual coercion and the on-line computation of sentential aspect. In *Proceedings of the 22nd Annual Conference of the Cognitive Science Society* (pp. 3–8), 13–15 August, Philadelphia, PA.
Tomasino, B., Fink, G. R., Sparing, R., Dafotakis, M., & Weiss, P. H. (2008). Action verbs and the primary motor cortex: A comparative TMS study of silent reading, frequency judgments, and motor imagery. *Neuropsychologia, 46*, 1915–1926.
Traxler, M. J. (2008). Structural priming among prepositional phrases: Evidence from eye-movements. *Memory & Cognition, 36*, 659–674.
Traxler, M., McElree, B., Williams, R. S., & Pickering, M. J. (2005). Context effects in coercion: Evidence from eye-movements. *Journal of Memory and Language, 53*, 1–25.
Traxler, M. J., & Tooley, K. M. (2007). Lexical mediation and context effects in sentence processing. *Brain Research, 1146*, 59–74.
Trueswell, J. C., & Tanenhaus, M. K. (1994). Towards a lexicalist framework of constraint-based syntactic ambiguity resolution. In C. Clifton, L. Frazier, & K. Rayner (Eds.), *Perspectives on sentence processing* (pp. 155–179). Hillsdale, NJ: Erlbaum.
Urbach, T. P., & Kutas, M. (2010). Quantifiers more or less quantify on-line: ERP evidence for partial incremental interpretation. *Journal of Memory and Language, 63*, 158–179.
Warren, T., & McConnell, K. (2007). Investigating effects of selectional restriction violations and plausibility violation severity on eye-movements in reading. *Psychonomic Bulletin & Review, 14*, 770–775.
Warren, T., McConnell, K., & Rayner, K. (2008). Effects of context on eye-movements when reading about possible and impossible events. *Journal of Experimental Psychology: Learning, Memory, and Cognition, 34*, 1001–1010.
Warren, T., White, S. J., & Reichle, E. D. (2009). Investigating the causes of wrap-up effects: Evidence from eye-movements and E-Z Reader. *Cognition, 111*, 132–137.
Willems, R. M., Hagoort, P., & Casasanto, D. (2010). Body-specific representations of action verbs: Neural evidence from right- and left-handers. *Psychological Science, 21(1)*, 67–74.
Wolff, P., & Gentner, D. (2000). Evidence for role-neutral initial processing of metaphors. *Journal of Experimental Psychology: Learning, Memory, & Cognition, 26*, 529–541.
Zwaan, R. A., Madden, C. J., Yaxley, R. H., & Aveyard, M. E. (2004). Moving words: Dynamic representations in language comprehension. *Cognitive Science, 28*, 611–619.
Zwaan, R. A., & Taylor, L. J. (2006). Seeing, acting, understanding: Motor resonance in language comprehension. *Journal of Experimental Psychology: General, 135*, 1–11.

8 Children's sentence processing

Jesse Snedeker

Abe (4 years, 3 months) and his father having a meal:

Father:	What do you want on your toast?
Abe:	The same thing I had on the first toast.
Abe:	Except this time cut it into four pieces.
Father:	I haven't heard anybody ask for anything . . .
Abe:	Please. Is that better?
Father:	That's better.
Abe:	Daddy, did you throw that yellow sled away?
Father:	What sled?
Abe:	It was paper and it was long and it had a line.
Father:	I don't remember it.
Abe:	Well, it was a paper one that I made.
Father:	Oh, I don't think I threw it away.
Abe:	Well, I never saw it again.
Abe:	Maybe, Mommy throwed it away.
Father:	Maybe. When did you make it?
Abe:	A day when you weren't home.

(Kuczaj, 1976; MacWhinney, 2000)

Interchanges like this are common in households with preschool-aged children. Long before they develop manners or tact, young children are full participants in conversational exchanges. Each of Abe's responses suggests that he understood precisely what his father had just said and what his intentions were in saying it. For example, in the second line, Abe indicates not just what he would like, but what he would like on his toast. Later he picks up on his father's indirect request for politeness (line 5) and subtly expresses some skepticism about his father's ignorance about the fate of his sled (line 11). Experiences like this lead most parents to assume that by 4 years of age a child will understand most of what is said to them and a little too much of what they overhear.

Underlying this everyday accomplishment is a complex set of processes. To understand what he is hearing, Abe must: transform the acoustic input into a phonological representation, identify each word that is spoken, integrate these words into a structured syntactic representation and then use that representation to determine what the speaker intended to convey. The field of sentence processing examines the cognitive processes that depend upon word identification and give rise to higher-level combinatorial representations. These higher-level representations include not only syntactic and semantic structures, but also representations that are not always thought of as linguistic (e.g., conceptual representations, pragmatic inferences and the referential implications of utterances). The number of representational levels, their nature and their relations to one another are matters of theoretical dispute both in linguistics and psycholinguistics. The necessity of these processes, however, is indisputable. For example, to properly answer his father's question (line 1), Abe had to form a dependency between the *wh*-word at the beginning of the sentence (*what*) and the direct-object position of the verb (*want*).

Sentence processing is often defined as the study of how comprehenders build these higher-level representations, on a moment-to-moment basis, as a sentence unfolds. This definition is problematic in two ways. First, it implicitly suggests that comprehension and production are separate systems that should be studied independently. However, there are logical reasons that the two processes must be linked (e.g., we learn a language by hearing it and then produce it ourselves) and strong evidence that they are tightly coupled (Pickering & Garrod, 2007). Second, by placing such a strong emphasis on time, this definition can create an artificial division between "online" and "offline" processing. Every mental process unfolds over time, including our judgments about the meaning or acceptability of a sentence. Thus a complete theory of language comprehension must explain not only the initial processes that occur as a sentence is unfolding but how these processes constrain and explain the interpretation that we ultimately arrive at.

Nevertheless, this chapter will focus on research which uses temporally sensitive methods to study language comprehension, for reasons both practical and intellectual. All research on language development necessarily involves comprehension, production or both, and thus there are thousands of studies measuring children's off-line language comprehension. The vast majority of these studies focus on what children know about language and how this changes during development. There is very little work on language comprehension processes in children and how these processes unfold over chronometric time. This chapter reviews this small literature with an emphasis on research that has been directly informed by the field of adult sentence processing.

There are several reasons for studying children's sentence processing. First, it is a critical but poorly understood aspect of child development. By four, children have mastered the basics of their native language, amassed an impressive vocabulary, and appear to understand much of what is said to them, but we know little about how they employ their knowledge as they are listening. Are young children able to understand sentences as rapidly as adults or should we slow down when we talk to them? Do they reliably arrive at the same interpretations as we do, or is our communication with children jeopardized by systematic differences in how we resolve linguistic ambiguity? Are there qualitative changes in language comprehension strategies across the development?

Second, the tools and knowledge that we gain from studying typically developing children could be employed to explore atypical development and disordered language in adults. Many clinical populations have deficits with language comprehension which are poorly characterized and poorly understood. For example, many high-functioning children with autism perform well on static standardized tests of grammar, yet they appear to have great difficulty following conversations and contributing to them. Sensitive measures of moment-to-moment language comprehension could provide insight into these difficulties. While work in this area has just begun, the initial findings are promising and provocative (Brock, Norbury, Einav & Nation, 2008; Diehl, Friedberg, Paul & Snedeker, under review; Nation, Marshall & Altmann, 2003).

Third, studies of children's sentence processing can help us understand language development. Some language processing studies provide information about the scope of children's linguistic representations and thus directly constrain our theory of language acquisition. Other studies provide us with information about how children interpret the utterances that they hear and the kinds of errors that they make. This information is critical because presumably children learn a language based on their own internal representation of the input (Fodor, 1998).

Finally, if we understand how sentence processing develops in childhood it will constrain our understanding of the adult end-state. Language comprehension in adults is an intricate and highly practiced skill, in which many sources of information are rapidly integrated. Some theories take this as evidence that comprehension involves continuous interaction between levels of representation, resulting in real-time predictions that approximate those of an ideal observer (McRae & Matsuki, this volume). Other theories propose that the initial flow of information through the system is more constrained (or modular), with the integration of other information occurring only after this initial analysis (see Frazier, this volume). Data from children could inform this debate by documenting which features of the system emerge early (and thus might reflect the basic building blocks of comprehension) and which appear later as children acquire speed, knowledge, and greater cognitive flexibility. Developmental data is also relevant to theories that claim that efficiency of sentence processing depends upon domain-general cognitive processes, such as working memory (Just & Carpenter, 1992) or domain-specific knowledge and experience (MacDonald & Christiansen, 2002). For example, capacity-based theories predict that there should be close associations between changes in working memory and changes in sentence processing across development. Similarly experience-based theories predict that differences in the type or amount of input across development should be associated with change in language comprehension.

In the first section, I provide a bird's eye view of adult sentence processing, to ground our discussion of how the system develops. Then, I discuss the methods that are used to study children's moment-to-moment language comprehension. This is followed by a quick tour of some of the topics that have been explored in young children, and, finally, a summary of the conclusions that can be drawn from this research and the questions that remain.

The end-state: language comprehension in adults

Half a century of systematic exploration has led to a rich (albeit incomplete) understanding of how adult listeners interpret spoken language. While there is still considerable controversy in this field, there is broad agreement on three basic issues (see Altmann, 2001; Elman, Hare & McRae, 2005; Treiman, Clifton, Meyer & Wurn, 2003, for reviews).

First, language comprehension involves a series of processes which are ordered with respect to one another. Phonological processing must begin before words can be recognized. Lexical representations must be accessed to identify the meaning(s) of the word and its syntactic properties, which are needed to generate the syntactic and semantic structure of the utterance. The semantic structure is then enriched and disambiguated by pragmatic inferences that are guided by information about communication and the context of language use.

Second, each of these processes is incremental. This means that processing at higher levels begins before processing at the lower levels is completed. Many theorists use the metaphor of spreading activation (or cascading water) to capture this relation. As soon as activation (information) begins to accumulate at one level of analysis, it is propagated on to the next level, initiating the higher-level process while the lower one is still in progress. Thus word recognition is underway by the time the first phoneme has been heard, syntactic and semantic processing begin as soon as candidate word forms become active (often leading to expectations about words that have yet to be heard), and pragmatic inferences can be made before a clause is completed.

Third, processing at a given level can be rapidly influenced by information from other levels, both higher and lower, in the linguistic system. For example, word identification is rapidly influenced by top-down information about the syntactic and semantic context in which that word appears, as well as bottom-up information about the phonological and prosodic form of the word.

At the syntactic level, interactivity in adult parsing has been explored by examining the way readers initially interpret, and misinterpret, syntactically ambiguous phrases. For example, consider the sentence fragment (1):

(1)   Mothra destroyed the building with . . .

At this point in the utterance the prepositional phrase (PP) beginning with *with* is ambiguous because it could be linked to the verb *destroyed* (VP-attachment), indicating an instrument (e.g., *with her awesome powers*); or it could be linked to the definite noun phrase *the building* (NP-attachment) indicating a modifier (e.g., *with many balconies*). In adults, several different kinds of information rapidly influence the interpretation of ambiguous phrases.

For example, knowledge about the particular words in the sentence constrains on-line interpretation of ambiguous phrases (Taraban & McClelland, 1988; Trueswell, Tanenhaus & Kello, 1993). For instance, the sentence in (1) favors the instrument analysis but if we change the verb from *destroyed* to *liked*, the preference flips and the modifier analysis, or NP-attachment, is favored. This kind of information is often called *lexical bias* or *verb bias*. The observed change in preferences could reflect knowledge about the kinds of structures in which each verb is likely to appear (information accessed during word retrieval and then passed on to the syntactic parser), it could reflect semantic knowledge about the arguments of the verb (accessed during word retrieval and passed on to semantic analysis), or it could reflect a more global analysis of the plausibility of different events (pragmatic processing), which influences the relations posited during semantic analysis, which in turn constrains syntactic parsing.

Adults can also use intonation or prosody to resolve attachment ambiguities. If we hear a pause before the preposition (*destroyed the building ... with the tower*), we are more likely to assume that the prepositional phrase is attached to the verb phrase and interpret it as an instrument. In contrast, a pause or intonational break before the direct object (*destroyed ... the building with the tower*) favors NP-attachment (Pynte & Prieur, 1996; Schafer, 1997).

Finally, the situation in which the utterance is used can influence our interpretation (Crain & Steedman, 1985). For example, if only one building is under consideration, VP-attachment is likely to be preferred, but if multiple buildings are available then we are more likely to initially interpret the ambiguous phrase as a modifier specifying the building in question (Altmann & Steedman, 1988; Spivey, Anderson & Farmer, this volume). This type of information is often called *referential context*. In a reading task, the referential context depends upon the information provided in the passage and the reader's knowledge of the world. In some studies of spoken language comprehension, the referential context is a set of objects that the participant can act on.

The bulk of the evidence suggests that adults rapidly integrate these different information sources to arrive at the analysis that best meets the constraints they have encountered. But disputes continue about the details of this process: Do some sources of information establish the candidate analyses while other sources of information weigh in at a later stage?

Methods for studying children's sentence processing and their limitations

Early work on the development of language comprehension was hampered by a lack of appropriate paradigms for testing young children. Until the 1990s, research on adult language comprehension relied on reading-time methods and paradigms that involved switching between a primary task and secondary task (dual-task paradigms). Because these paradigms have proven useful for studying adults, creative experimenters adapted them for use with children (see Clahsen, 2008, for review). Reading-time paradigms have been used primarily with children between the ages of eight and thirteen (Joseph et al., 2008; Traxler, 2002). Dual-task paradigms using auditory language may provide a somewhat wider window into development. The auditory moving window paradigm—in which children push a button to hear segments of an utterance—has been used successfully in children as young as 7 (Felser, Marinis & Clahsen, 2003; Kidd & Bavin, 2007), while the cross-modal picture priming paradigm (described below) has been used with children 4 to 6 years of age (Love, 2007; McKee, Nicol & McDaniel, 1993).

Taken together this body of work provides ample evidence that children engage in incremental interpretation, assigning a structural analysis to a sentence as it unfolds and determining the dependencies between words. For example, Love's (2007) cross-modal picture priming study demonstrates that children interpret filler-gap constructions, such as relative clauses, in much the same way as adults. In this study, children listened to sentences like (2) below, while making judgments about whether depicted items were alive or inanimate.

(2)   The zebra that the hippo had kissed on the nose ran far away.

In these sentences the head of the relative clause (*the zebra*) is also the object of the verb (*kissed*). Syntactic theories capture this relation by positing a structural connection between this noun and the direct-object position (e.g., a trace or index). Children were sensitive to this relationship. When they saw the picture of the zebra immediately after the verb, they were faster to respond to it than the picture of the hippo, suggesting that they had reactivated the noun upon encountering the verb. In contrast, when the pictures appeared earlier in the sentence (right before *hippo*), there was no difference.

While these studies have been informative, it is difficult to know how to interpret children's failures in such tasks, because both reading-time and dual-task paradigms require skills which are unnecessary for spoken language comprehension and which are developing at a furious pace during the school years. As they learn to read, children build a new language input system which allows them to decode orthographic symbols into lexical and phonological representations (Dehaene, 2009). Once decoding has occurred, children can make use of the higher-level processes underlying spoken language comprehension to construct syntactic, semantic and discourse representations (e.g., Kendeou, Savage & van den Broek, 2009). In college-educated adults, the decoding process is rapid and relatively effortless, and thus reading times are generally sensitive to the effects of syntactic, semantic and discourse manipulations (Clifton, Staub & Rayner, 2007). But in young children, decoding is slow and effortful. For example, children take considerably longer to read a 6-letter word than a 4-letter word, (Aghababian & Nazir, 2000; Bijeljac-Babic, Millogo, Farioli & Grainger, 2004; Joseph, Liversedge, Blythe, White & Rayner,

2009). This suggests that young children decode words character by character, while adults and older children process words more holistically (Acha & Perea, 2008). While word-length effects diminish gradually with age, they are still much larger in 11-year-olds than in adults. Similarly, dual-task paradigms require that the child have the ability to rapidly switch between two tasks (e.g., listening to the sentence and pushing the button). While children as young as 6 can engage in task switching, they make more errors than older children (Dibbets & Jolles, 2006). The temporal cost of switching between tasks is considerably greater in children and adolescents than it is in young adults (Cepeda, Kramer & Gonzalez de Sather, 2001).

The difficulties that children face in these paradigms could influence the outcomes of sentence-processing studies in several ways. First, the additional time spent on task switching or decoding could introduce more noise into the data, making it less sensitive to variation related to higher-level language processing (particularly if language processing itself is not particularly difficult for children). Second, the effort expended in decoding text or shifting between tasks could leave children without sufficient cognitive resources to make use of cues and strategies that they might otherwise employ. Finally, task switching could delay the measure of interest (the button press) by a constant amount, independent of linguistic processing. Under these conditions an increase in language processing time could have no apparent effect on reaction times because it would be absorbed into the slack introduced by the sluggish control process (see Sternberg, 1998).

These considerations suggest that children's language comprehension is best studied by looking at their spontaneous responses to spoken language. Auditory word recognition develops rapidly in the second year of life, long before children can spell their names or remember to push a button (Fernald, Pinto, Swingley, Weinberg & McRoberts, 1998). In the past 20 years, two paradigms have been developed which provide information about spoken language processing in young children, without requiring a secondary task.

First, many researchers have studied children's on-line language processing by examining what they look at as they are listening to an utterance. These methods stem from the preferential looking paradigm, which was developed to study intermodal perception (Spelke, 1979) and off-line language comprehension in infants (Golinkoff, Hirsh-Pasek, Cauley & Gordon, 1987), and from the visual-world paradigm that was developed by Michael Tanenhaus and his colleagues to study on-line spoken language comprehension in adults (Tanenhaus, Spivey-Knowlton, Eberhard & Sedivy, 1995). In eye-gaze paradigms, children hear a word or a sentence that refers to the visual scene that accompanies it. The visual scene can be a video, a still picture or a set of objects placed on a tabletop. As the child is listening to the sentence, her gaze direction is recorded. Later the child's eye-movements are analyzed with respect to the accompanying utterance, allowing researchers to make inferences about the child's evolving interpretation of the utterance.

In adults, these methods are sensitive to language processing at multiple levels and have been successfully used to explore such diverse issues as: the time-course of lexical activation (Allopenna, Magnuson & Tanenhaus, 1998); the integration of syntactic and semantic constraints during sentence processing (Kamide, Altmann & Haywood, 2003); and the role of contextual cues in resolving referential and syntactic ambiguities (Chambers, Tanenhaus & Magnuson, 2004). Much of the developmental work has focused on word recognition, demonstrating that 1- and 2-year-old children rapidly and incrementally map phonological input onto lexical entries (Fernald, Perfors & Marchman, 2006; Fernald et al., 1998; Sekerina & Brooks, 2007; Swingley & Aslin, 2002; Swingley & Fernald, 2002). However, as we will see below, researchers have also examined higher-level processes such as syntactic ambiguity resolution, pronoun interpretation and syntactic priming.

Eye-gaze paradigms, as currently employed, have some limitations. They typically depend on a referential link between language and visual scene (e.g., looks to the referent of a pronoun or noun): thus they are less suitable for studying processes that do not directly affect reference (e.g., detection of subject–verb agreement errors). In addition, they rely upon the general tendency for people to shift their eyes toward objects under discussion. These shifts in overt attention appear to be robust and ecologically valid in some discourse contexts (e.g., when a new referent is being introduced) but they may be less useful and robust in other contexts (e.g., when an entity that has been extensively discussed is mentioned once again).

The second method for studying children's spontaneous spoken-language comprehension is to measure neural activity while the child is listening to sentences. Analysis of how this neural activity differs across different utterances or tasks can allow us to draw inferences about the cognitive and neural processes that support language comprehension. Most of the research in developmental psycholinguistics has relied on two brain imaging methods: fMRI (functional magnetic resonance imaging) and ERP (event related potentials). Although, fMRI is the dominant method in cognitive neuroscience, in part because of its good spatial resolution, it has two disadvantages for studying the development of sentence processing. First, fMRI requires that participants spend a long period of time lying still in a very small, dark and noisy space, something few children enjoy. Consequently, fMRI studies of language typically focus on older children (7–12 years) and adolescents (13–18 years). Second, fMRI provides limited information about the relative timing of different neural activations, and, as we noted earlier, sentence processing has largely been concerned with questions about how processes unfold over time. To date, fMRI studies on developmental psycholinguistics have primarily focused on identifying the network of brain regions involved in language processing and documenting differences in the activation of these regions at different ages and in children with developmental disorders (see, e.g., Ahmad, Balsamo, Sachs, Xu & Gaillard, 2003; Booth et al., 2000; Brauer & Friederici, 2007). While many differences across populations have been found, their interpretation is called into question by differences in the signal-to-noise ratio across populations (see McKone, Crookes, Jeffery & Dilks, 2012).

For these reasons, in this chapter we will focus on experiments using ERP to study children's moment-to-moment sentence processing. In ERP studies, electrodes on the scalp are used to measure neural activity related to particular stimulus events that occur repeatedly throughout the study (e.g., the onset of a verb or an anomalous word). This technique provides relatively poor information about the neural regions responsible for the signal, but it provides fine-grained information about when the neural activity occurred. ERP has two additional advantages over fMRI for developmental researchers. First, the cost of the equipment makes the method affordable for many small-scale research programs. Second, although children must remain still during the critical trials and wear the electrode cap or net, they do not have to tolerate darkness, noise or claustrophobia.

Nevertheless there are also limitations to ERP studies, as they are currently designed, that affect what we can learn about the development of sentence processing. Most ERP research designs examine neural responses to anomalous utterances, and thus provide limited information about the evolving interpretation of well-formed utterances. Furthermore, our interpretation of ERP data in children is largely based on what we know about particular ERP effects in adults, and, as we shall see, the interpretation of these effects is often in dispute.

Syntactic ambiguity resolution

The first study to employ eye-gaze paradigms to study on-line syntactic processing was Trueswell, Sekerina, Hill and Logrip's (1999) study of children's interpretation of garden-path sentences. The study examined whether children would commit to an interpretation of a locally ambiguous phrase, and whether their interpretation would be shaped by the referential context in which the sentence occurred. Children were given spoken instructions to move objects about on a table while their eye-movements were recorded. The critical trials contained a temporary PP-attachment ambiguity, see (3) below. The verb (*put*) was one that typically appears with a PP argument encoding the destination of the action, thus supporting an initial analysis of the phrase *on the napkin* as VP-attached.

(3)   Put the frog on the napkin in the box.

In contexts with just one frog, adults initially looked over to the incorrect destination (the empty napkin) suggesting that they were misanalysing the first prepositional phrase (*on the napkin*) as a VP-attached destination (Tanenhaus et al., 1995). But, as mentioned earlier, when two frogs were provided (one of which was on a napkin) the participants were able to immediately use the referential context to avoid this garden-path, resulting in eye-movements similar to unambiguous controls (e.g., *Put the apple that's on the napkin . . .*).

In contrast 5-year-olds were unaffected by this manipulation of referential context. In both one-referent and two-referent contexts, children frequently looked at the incorrect destination, suggesting that they pursued the VP-attachment analysis regardless of the number of frogs. In fact, the children's actions suggested that they often failed to revise this misanalysis. On over half of the trials, their actions involved the incorrect destination. For example, for the utterance in (3) many children put the frog onto the napkin and then placed it in the box. By age 8, most children acted like adults in this task, using referential context to guide their parsing decisions about ambiguous phrases. These findings have been replicated in subsequent studies (Hurewitz, Brown-Schmidt, Thorpe et al., 2000; Weighall, 2008). Children's failures cannot be attributed to grammatical ignorance: they produce NP-attached prepositional phrases in their spontaneous speech by 2 (Snedeker & Trueswell, 2004) and they appear to understand their discourse function (Hurewitz et al., 2000). Nevertheless, they systematically fail to revise their initial parsing commitments.

There are two plausible explanations for why children have an overwhelming preference for the VP-attachment in this task. First, children's parsing preferences could be driven by their statistical knowledge of the verb *put*, which requires the presence of a PP argument (the destination). Second, children could have a general structural preference for VP-attachment. Such a preference would be predicted by theories that propose that syntax is modular and that simpler syntactic structures are preferred during acquisition (Frank, 1998) and parsing (i.e., a minimal attachment strategy, Frazier & Fodor, 1978). On such a theory, parsing revisions that are based on lexical or referential sources might simply get faster over the course of development (Goodluck & Tavakolian 1982), until the erroneous analyses become undetectable to experimenters measuring adult comprehension.

The modularity hypothesis receives some support from experiments on parsing in older children using reading-time methods (Traxler, 2002) or dual-task paradigms (Felser, Roberts, Gross & Marinis, 2003). For example, Traxler found that children as old as 13 failed to use lexical information or semantic plausibility to resolve temporary ambiguities like those in (4).

(4) a. When Sue tripped *the girl* **fell** over and the vase was broken.

  b. When Sue tripped *the table* **fell** over and the vase was broken.

  c. When Sue fell *the policeman* **stopped** and helped her up.

In all three cases, children slowed down at the second verb (in bold face), suggesting that they had misanalyzed the post-verbal noun (in italics) as the direct object of the first clause even when it was an implausible direct object (4b) or the verb was one which is typically intransitive (4c). However, as we noted earlier, reading-time methods may generally underestimate children's higher-level language processing abilities. In addition, these stimuli may present a parsing problem that children have never encountered before: clause closure ambiguities like these are generally disambiguated by prosodic boundaries in speech (Kjelgaard & Speer, 1999) and by commas in edited text.

Snedeker and Trueswell (2004) explored whether younger children (4.5 to 6) would use lexical information during spoken language comprehension in a simple, common construction. Children and adults heard globally ambiguous prepositional phrase attachments, as in (5). We manipulated both the bias of the verb and the referential context in which the utterance was used. The instructions were presented in contexts that provided distinct referents for the prepositional object under the two analyses. For example in (5c) both a large fan and pig holding a fan were provided (see Figure 8.1).

(5) a. Choose the cow with the fork. (modifier biased)

b. Feel the frog with the feather. (unbiased)

c. Tickle the pig with the fan. (instrument biased)

Both the adults and the children were strongly swayed by the type of verb that was used in the instructions. When the verb was one that frequently appeared with an instrument phrase (5c), participants began looking at the potential instrument (e.g., a large fan) shortly after the onset of the prepositional object. When the verb was strongly biased to a modifier analysis (5a), participants focused in on the animal holding the object instead. Verb biases strongly shaped the ultimate interpretation that the adults and children assigned to the prepositional phrase: instrument-biased verbs resulted in actions involving the target instrument, while modifier-biased verbs resulted in actions on the target animal. In addition, adults also incorporated referential constraints into their analyses, performing more modifier actions in the two-referent conditions and looking at the target instrument less often. In contrast, children showed little sensitivity to the referential manipulation. Although there was a weak effect of referential context on children's eye-movements (with marginally more looks to the target instrument in the one referent context), the children's ultimate interpretation of the prepositional phrase was based exclusively on verb bias. These effects of verb bias on children's interpretation of PP-attachment ambiguities have been replicated by other researchers using a variety of paradigms (see Kidd & Bavin, 2005, 2007), including a training paradigm in which 5-year-olds developed biases for neutral verbs on the basis of just a few unambiguous examples for each verb (Qi, Yuan & Fisher, 2011).

Snedeker and Yuan (2008) built upon these findings by using the same sentences and paradigm to explore young children's and adults' use of prosody in on-line parsing. While prior studies of adult comprehension had found rapid effects of prosody on ambiguity resolution (Kjelgaard & Speer, 1999; Snedeker & Trueswell, 2003), prior studies with young children had found that they did not use prosody to resolve syntactic ambiguity (Choi & Mazuka, 2003). For our study, two prosodic variants of each sentence were created. The modifier

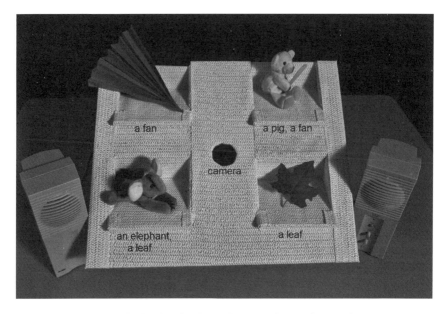

Figure 8.1 Example of a display for the verb bias and prosody experiments (Snedeker & Trueswell, 2004; Snedeker & Yuan, 2008). Printed words are for illustration only. The target sentence was: *Tickle the pig with the fan.*

prosody had an intonational phrase (IP) break after the verb (*You can tap . . . the frog with the flower*) while the instrument prosody had an IP break after the noun (*You can tap the frog . . . with the flower*). The prosody of the sentence was fully crossed with the verb-bias manipulation described above, resulting in six different conditions.

We found that both the children and the adults made rapid use of prosody to interpret the ambiguous phrase. By 200 ms after the critical word began, adults who heard instrument prosody were already looking at the instrument more than those who heard modifier prosody. In children these effects were smaller and emerged a bit later (500 ms after the onset of the critical word). The effects of verb bias were also robust and rapid, indicating that lexical information plays a central role even when strong prosodic cues are present. In children the effect of verb bias appeared as soon as the critical word began. Since eye-movements take approximately 200 ms to program and execute, this indicates that the children were using information about the verb to guide syntactic analysis immediately after encountering the preposition.

Taken together these studies demonstrate that young children can use multiple cues to resolve syntactic ambiguity. Why then do they fail to use referential context? Two explanations have been proposed. First, Trueswell and Gleitman (2004) have pointed out that the number of possible referents in a scene is only a weak predictor of syntactic structure, while the verb in the sentence is a stronger predictor (see Brown-Schmidt & Tanenhaus, 2008; Kidd & Bavin,

2007, for relevant data). If children acquire parsing constraints by learning about the correlations of different features in the input, then we might expect that more robust cues would be acquired before less robust cues. Second, referential context may be more difficult for children to acquire or use because it is a top-down cue relative to syntactic parsing. Top-down cues, by their nature, involve representations that are more central and further away from perception. Thus they can only be tracked if lower-level processes have led the child to encode the situation in the relevant manner. Furthermore, to use a top-down cue during processing, the child must activate the relevant syntactic representations, evaluate them at a higher level, and send that information back down to the parser. Given their slower processing speed (Kail, 1991), children may have difficulty completing these steps fast enough to influence their interpretation of the utterance.

To disentangle these two possibilities, we tested children's ability to use another top-down cue to syntactic ambiguity, semantic plausibility (Snedeker, Worek & Shafto, 2009). Unlike referential context, plausibility is a highly valid cue; events that are more plausible are more likely to have happened in the past and thus more likely to have been discussed. Furthermore, we know that young children are sensitive to plausibility. Like adults, they know which objects are plausible arguments for a given verb and will look to these objects after hearing the verb (Nation, Marshall & Altmann, 2003; Yuan, Fisher, Kandhadai & Fernald, 2011).[1] However, the calculation of sentence-level plausibility requires a semantic or pragmatic analysis of the syntactic structure under consideration, and thus plausibility is a top-down cue for parsing. If children have difficulty using top-down information during on-line language comprehension, then we would expect that they would be less likely to use plausibility information and slower to employ it. To test this, we manipulated the plausibility of sentences with instrument-biased (6a) and modifier-biased verbs (6b) by varying the object of the prepositional phrase, using the same paradigm and age groups as before.

(6) a. You can tickle the bear with the mirror/paintbrush.

(6) b. You can find the bear with the sponge/magnifying glass.

The adult's early eye movements were strongly influenced by plausibility of the utterance, but were not affected by the bias of the verb. In contrast, the children's eye-movements were only sensitive to the bias of the verb: when the sentence had a verb that commonly appears with instruments the children looked at the target instrument regardless of whether it was a plausible instrument for performing the action. Plausibility did have an effect on children's actions, though this effect was smaller than it was in adults. Thus children are not insensitive to the plausibility of an analysis; they are simply slower to use this information during parsing and more likely to rely on lexical biases (see Kidd, Stewart & Serratrice, 2011, for related findings). Taken together, these findings suggest that children's ambiguity resolution incorporates multiple information sources, but children are less likely to use top-down cues perhaps because they have difficulty making the relevant inferences quickly enough to influence syntactic parsing.

Pronoun interpretation

Ambiguity occurs at every level of linguistic representation. In adults, the mechanisms involved in ambiguity resolution are broadly similar across levels: candidate representations are activated on the basis of the input and constraints from several other representational systems influence which analysis is selected. As we saw earlier, children also use multiple sources of information for resolving syntactic ambiguity. Children's lexical processing also appears to share the core features of the adult comprehension system (Huang & Snedeker, 2011; Rabagliati, Pylkkänen & Marcus, 2012).

In addition, there is a growing body of research on how children determine the referent of a pronoun, which can be described as a case of ambiguity resolution at the discourse level. Across contexts, a given pronoun can refer to one of a nearly infinite set of referents, but in a specific context the interpretation of that pronoun is constrained by its gender, its grammatical form and syntactic position in the sentence, and the structure of the discourse in which it occurs. Pronouns are ideally suited for developmental research because they are extremely common in child-directed speech and lend themselves to a variety of visually based paradigms. Research on children's on-line pronoun interpretation has focused on two topics.

First, several studies have explored whether children show immediate sensitivity to the grammatical constraints on co-reference (see Sturt, this volume, for studies on adults). For example, McKee and colleagues (1993) used the cross-model picture priming paradigm to examine the interpretation of pronouns in 4–6-year-olds. Children heard sentences like (7) below in which the object of an embedded clause was either a referential noun (*the nurse*), a reflexive pronoun (*himself*) or a non-reflexive pronoun (*him*).

(7)   The alligator knows that the leopard with green eyes is patting the nurse/himself/him on the head with a soft pillow.

At the end of the object noun phrase, children saw a picture of the character who was the subject of the embedded clause (e.g., the leopard). Both children and adults responded more quickly to this picture after a reflexive pronoun than after a referential noun. This suggests that participants reactivated the subject when they encountered the reflexive pronoun, because reflexives must have a local antecedent while referential nouns do not. When the critical noun was a non-reflexive pronoun, which cannot refer to the local antecedent, the adults responded as slowly as they had in baseline conditions, indicating that they did not reactivate the subject noun. The children's performance, however, varied.

Those children who had demonstrated an adult-like understanding of pronouns in an off-line judgment task also performed like the adults in the on-line task. In contrast, children who accepted local antecedents for non-reflexive pronouns in the judgment task, re-activated these antecedents in the on-line task (responding as quickly to the leopard in the non-reflexive condition as in the reflexive condition). By middle childhood, children's performance in this task appears to be uniformly adult-like (Love, Wallenski & Swinney, 2009).

These findings have been interpreted as evidence that grammatical constraints on pronoun resolution (the binding principles, Chomsky, 1981) act as an initial filter on pronoun resolution, limiting the pool of possible referents to those which are grammatically permissible. Subsequent studies, using the visual-world paradigm, call this interpretation into question. For example, Clackson, Felser and Clahsen (2011) had children and adults listen to sentences like (8a) or (8b) while viewing a picture of the two characters in the story.

(8) a. Susan was waiting outside the corner shop. She watched as Mr. Jones bought a huge box of popcorn for himself/her over the counter.

b. Peter was waiting outside the corner shop. He watched as Mr. Jones bought a huge box of popcorn for himself/him over the counter.

The critical measure was looks to the antecedent of the reflexive (Mr. Jones) or the antecedent of the non-reflexive pronoun (Susan or Peter) after pronoun onset. Both children and adults were quick to close in on the correct character when the gender of the pronoun clearly indicated the intended referent (8a). When gender was uninformative (8b), both groups experienced more interference from the incorrect referent. However, interference was greater for children than adults. Nevertheless, even the youngest children looked more at the correct antecedent than the incorrect one and these effects emerged early in processing. Thus the data suggest that syntax has a rapid but probabilistic influence on pronoun processing; sensitivity to this constraint is present by about 4 years of age, but children's use of this cue improves with age (see also, Sekerina, Stromswold & Hestvik, 2004).

The second topic that has been explored is children's use of discourse structure to interpret non-reflexive pronouns. When given a sentence like (9), about 90 percent of adults will interpret the pronoun as referring to the subject of the previous sentence (Emily).

(9) Emily went to school with Hannah. She read ten books.

Adults use this order of mention (or subject) strategy as rapidly as they use gender information. Within about 300 ms of hearing the pronoun they begin to shift their gaze to the first-mentioned character (Arnold, Eisenband,

Brown-Schmidt & Trueswell, 2000). Children's performance is far less reliable. Some eye-gaze studies find that children as young as 2.5 years already prefer to resolve pronouns to the subject of the prior sentence (Song & Fisher, 2005, 2007), while others find no evidence of a first-mention bias in the eye-movements or the actions of 4- and 5-year-olds (Arnold, Brown-Schmidt & Trueswell, 2007). Our own work suggests that the first-mention bias is present in preschoolers but its effects are much weaker than in adults and it emerges more slowly (Hartshorne, Nappa & Snedeker, 2010). In contrast, gender has similar effects on the off-line performance and early eye-movements of children and adults.

It is tempting to explain this pattern as another example of the priority of bottom-up lexically encoded information (like gender) over higher-level cues (like discourse structure). We suspect that this is not the case. Young children appear to be adept at using discourse structure to constrain their interpretation of a pronoun in many other contexts. For example, in sentences like (10) they can use the repeated mention of a single character (Emily) to determine the referent of the pronoun (Hartshorne et al., 2010), even when the pronoun is separated from this antecedent by two sentences.

(10)   Emily and Hannah are going to Disneyland. Emily has never been to Disneyland. Disneyland has lots of fun activities. It also has great food. She is really excited about going.

But there are two other reasons why children may fail to use the first-mention strategy for utterances like (9). First, children may experience interference from the character in object position who has been most recently mentioned (Hannah). Interference of this kind could reflect the nature of children's memory and the search process used in pronoun resolution, or it could reflect a conflict between a very general strategy (pronouns refer to recently mentioned entities) and a more specific strategy (pronouns generally refer of the subject of the previous sentence). Second, children may acquire cues of pronoun resolution based on their reliability (Arnold et al., 2007). While gender is a highly valid cue, order of mention is not. In fact, in many contexts, adults systematically link pronouns to the object of the previous utterance:

(11)   Gamera dislikes Godzilla because he is so unpleasant.
       (he = Godzilla)

Observations like these have led some theorists to question whether adults actually have a first-mention bias for pronoun resolution or whether these preferences instead reflect complex constraints based on the meaning of the prior utterance and the inferred structure of the discourse (Kehler, Kertz, Rohde & Elman, 2008). This hypothesis radically changes the nature of the acquisition problem.

What representations underlie children's sentence processing?

While on-line methods are typically used to explore the processes that are involved in language comprehension, they can also give us insight into the nature of children's linguistic representations. For example, Malathi Thothathiri and I have used structural priming in an eye-gaze paradigm to explore how children represent argument structure. Languages have systematic correspondences between syntactic relations, such as subject and object, and semantic categories, such as agent and patient or theme. These correspondences allow us to interpret who did what to whom, even when the verb in the sentence is novel. For example, in (12) we all know who the culprit is—even if we never encountered this particular verb and harbor no prejudices against motorists.

(12) The driver doored the cyclist.

Tomasello and colleagues have suggested that young preschoolers use templates based on the behavior of individual verbs to guide comprehension and production (Tomasello, 1992). For example, a young child might have a template for the verb hit that captures the knowledge illustrated in (13) and another template for push, illustrated in (14).

(13) _____$_X$ hit _____$_Y$ (where X = hitter, Y = hittee)

(14) _____$_A$ push _____$_B$ (where A = pusher, B = pushee)

With these templates, children would be able interpret and produce new utterances with the same verb (such as *The taxi hit the delivery van*). But since the item-based templates do not include abstract syntactic and semantic relations, they would provide no guidance for interpreting utterances with novel verbs like that in (12). Thus to evaluate children's linguistic representations, researchers typically examine children's comprehension and production of sentences with novel verbs.

Almost two decades' worth of research has yielded mixed results and contrasting interpretations. Many novel-verb production studies show limited generalization in children under the age of 4 (Tomasello, 2000) but these results are contradicted by novel-verb comprehension studies that demonstrate robust generalization in children under 2 (Fisher, Gertner, Scott & Yuan, 2010). For example, 21-month-old children who hear "the duck is gorping the bunny" will tend to look at videos where the duck is the agent of a novel action and the bunny is the patient, whereas those who hear "the bunny is groping the duck" prefer events where the opposite is true (Gertner, Fisher & Eisengart, 2006). However, both types of findings are open to alternate interpretations. Subtle aspects of verb meaning can constrain the use of verbs in sentence structures. For example, *Give me a cookie* is grammatical while *Pull me a cookie* is not (see Pinker, 1989). Thus, children may fail at a novel-verb generalization task simply because they have failed to grasp the exact meaning of a new verb (Fisher, 2002). Conversely, success at a novel-verb task could reflect the use of problem-solving strategies that are unique to novel stimuli, rather than the use of abstract representations (see Ninio, 2005; Thothathiri & Snedeker, 2008a). For example, children who are flummoxed by the novel verb could substitute in a known verb and interpret the sentence using the template for that form (e.g., translating "daxing" as "pushing" and using the template in (14)).

Most of the concerns about novel-verb studies stem from their placing children in situations where they are faced with unfamiliar linguistic input. Structural priming is a method by which we can circumvent these issues to explore how utterances with known verbs influence one another. This technique has long been used to investigate the representations that underlie language production in adults (Bock, 1986). For example, adult participants are more likely to produce a passive sentence (e.g., *The man was struck by lightening*) after reading a passive sentence (e.g., *The president was confused by the question*) than after reading an active sentence (e.g., *The question confused the president*). Since the two constructions express the same semantic relations, priming can be attributed to syntactic representations or mappings between syntax and semantics. Furthermore, since priming occurs despite the fact that the primes and targets use different nouns and verbs, we can infer that adults have access to abstract representations that capture the similarities between these sentences.

In recent years, production priming has been used to study the nature of children's linguistic abstractions. Some researchers have found evidence for abstract structural priming in 3- and 4-year-old children (Bencini & Valian, 2008; Huttenlocher, Vasilyeva & Shimpi, 2004; Messenger, Branigan & McLean, 2011). Others have not (Goldwater, Tomlinson, Love & Echols, 2011; Savage, Lieven, Theakston & Tomasello, 2003). The paradigm that we have developed combines structural priming and eye-gaze analysis to investigate the effects of priming on on-line comprehension (Thothathiri & Snedeker, 2008a, 2008b). Since production tasks are often more difficult for children than comprehension tasks (Hirsh-Pasek & Golinkoff, 1996), this may provide a more sensitive measure of children's linguistic knowledge. If children have item-specific representations (as assumed under the verb island hypothesis) then we would expect priming within verbs but not between verbs. In contrast, if children have abstract syntactic or semantic categories, then we would expect to see between-verb priming.

The critical sentences in these studies used dative verbs, such as *give*, *bring* or *send*, which typically have three arguments: an agent, a recipient and a theme. In English, there are two ways in which these arguments can be expressed, as shown in (15). In the prepositional-object construction (15a) the theme appears as the direct object, while the recipient is expressed by the prepositional phrase marked by *to*. In the double-object construction (15b) the recipient is the direct object while the theme is expressed as a second noun phrase.

(15) a. The gardener gave the pomegranate to Persephone.

b. The gardener gave Persephone the pomegranate.

Datives are well-suited for developmental studies of priming because both constructions are acquired well before the age of three (Campbell & Tomasello, 2001). The two forms of the dative have essentially the same meaning and differ only in how the semantic roles get mapped onto syntactic elements. Thus, priming using datives offers a reasonably clear case of structural priming independent of conceptual differences.

In our study, children were given sets of trials consisting of two prime sentences followed by a target sentence. The primes were either double-object or prepositional-object datives and the target sentence was also either a double-object or prepositional-object dative. Our goal was to determine whether double-object and prepositional-object datives would prime the interpretation of subsequent utterances that used a different verb and had no common content words. For example, would hearing *Send the frog the gift* facilitate comprehension of *Show the horse the book*?

To link priming to eye movements we made use of a well-studied phenomenon in word recognition, the cohort effect (Marslen-Wilson & Welsh, 1978). As a spoken word unfolds, listeners activate the lexical items that share phonemes with the portion of the word that they have heard. In the visual-world paradigm, this process results in fixations to the referents of words that share phonemes with the target word (Allopenna et al., 1998). These effects are particularly strong at the beginning of a word, when all of the phonological information is consistent with multiple words (the members of this cohort). In our studies we used priming as a top-down constraint which might modulate the activation of different members of a phonological cohort.

(16) a. Bring the monkey the hat.

b. Bring the money to the bear.

The target trials were either double object (16a) or prepositional datives (16b). The set of toys that accompanied the utterance contained two items that were phonological matches to the initial part of the direct-object noun. One was animate and hence a potential recipient (e.g., a monkey) while the other was inanimate and hence a more likely theme (e.g., some money). Thus the overlap in word onsets (e.g., *mon* . . .) created a lexical ambiguity which was tightly linked to a short-lived ambiguity in the argument structure of the verb. We expected that priming of the double-object dative would lead the participants to interpret the first noun as a recipient, resulting in more looks to the animate match, while priming of the prepositional-object dative would lead them to interpret it as a theme resulting in more looks to the inanimate match.

In our initial studies, we used primes and targets that shared the same verb. We found that young 4-year-olds showed robust within-verb priming during the ambiguous region. Young 3-year-olds were slower in interpreting the target sentences, but when we expanded the analysis window based on the timing of their eye-movements, we found a reliable priming effect. Children who had heard double-object primes were more likely to look at the potential recipient (the monkey) than children who had heard the prepositional-object primes.

To examine the nature of the structures that children use, we conducted parallel experiments in which the prime and target utterances had no content words in common (between-verb priming). Under these circumstances the abstract grammars predict priming, while item-based grammars do not. We found that both young 4-year-olds and young 3-year-olds showed between-verb priming. In the 3-year-olds the effect of between-verb priming was almost as large as the effect of within-verb priming, indicating that there was no benefit gained when the two utterances shared a verb. This suggests that abstract representations play a dominant role in on-line comprehension in young children.

Evidence from event-related potentials

ERP research on the development of sentence processing has largely focused on children's response to semantic and syntactic anomalies. In adults, semantic anomalies (see 17 below) are associated with an increase in the N400 component of the ERP waveform. This is a negative going component that becomes detectable about 250 ms after word onset and typically peaks at about 400 ms. Converging evidence from fMRI and magnetoencephalography (MEG) studies suggest that the N400 reflects bilateral activation of the middle and superior temporal gyri and perhaps an additional left-inferior frontal source (Kuperberg et al., 2000).

The N400 component has generally been interpreted as an index of lexical-semantic processing, though there is some disagreement about precisely which aspect or aspects of lexical or semantic processing it measures (Osterhout, Kim & Kuperberg, 2012). Critically, the N400 occurs for all words, not just semantic anomalies, including words presented in isolation. The magnitude of the component has been linked to frequency, cloze probability, and high-level semantic or pragmatic constraints. One interpretation is that the N400 reflects lexical access and that high-level manipulations of semantic and pragmatic factors affect this component indirectly by placing top-down constraints on lexical processes. A second interpretation is that the N400 (or some part of it) reflects the semantic integration of a word into a sentence or a picture into its context.

The N400 appears quite early in development. In picture priming paradigms, infants as young as 14 months show a larger N400 response when they hear an isolated word that does not match a picture that they are viewing ("dog" for a picture of a cat versus "dog" for a dog; Friedrich & Friederici, 2004, 2005a). By 19 months of age, children show a sustained negativity for semantic anomalies in spoken sentences like (17), which has a scalp distribution similar to the N400 (Friederich & Friederici, 2005b).

(17)   The cat drinks the ball/milk.

In both paradigms, the N400-like effects have a later onset in infants than in adults and are more prolonged, suggesting that lexical access becomes faster and less effortful over time. Between 5 and 15 years of age, the N400 to semantic anomalies declines in both amplitude and duration suggesting continued improvements in lexical processing (Holcomb, Coffey & Neville, 1992).

While the anomalous sentence paradigms are generally interpreted as evidence for combinatorial semantic processing in children (see e.g., Friederici, 2006), the validity of this analysis depends on the cognitive processes underlying the N400 and a precise characterization of the stimulus manipulation. For example, if the N400 reflects lexical processing and the effect of the sentential context occurs via word-to-word lexical priming, then this effect would not require the construction of linguistic representations above the level of the word. To date, the developmental studies have used stimuli in which semantic plausibility appears to be confounded with lexical associations (e.g., in (17) *drink* is associated with *milk*, but not *ball*).

ERPs have also been used to study the response to syntactic anomalies in young children. In adults, two ERP components are associated with syntactic anomalies, like those in (18).

(18)   a.   The lion in the zoo roars.

      b.   The lion in the roars.

The first is the P600: a late positivity with a central parietal distribution which is robustly observed for a wide variety of syntactic anomalies, but also appears in garden-path sentences at the point where reanalysis is required (Osterhout et al., 2012). The second is the ELAN, or early left-anterior negativity (named for the area of the scalp where it was detected). The ELAN emerges as early as 150 ms after stimulus onset and has been argued to reflect the construction of syntactic phrases (Friederici, 2002; Neville, Nicol, Barss, Forster & Garrett, 1991).

Oberecker, Friedrich, and Friederici (2005) presented 32-month-old children with sentences that contained syntactic category violations like those in (18). Like adults, the children showed a two-part response consisting of both an ELAN and P600, though both effects emerged slightly later in the children. In contrast, 24-month-olds produced a strong P600 but showed no sign of an ELAN (Oberecker & Friederici, 2006). A similar pattern of findings occurs in studies examining tense violations (19a,b).

(19)   a.   My uncle will watch the movie.

      b.   My uncle will watching the movie.

Adults show a biphasic response to these morphosyntactic violations, consisting of a left-anterior negativity that emerges around 300–500 ms (a LAN) followed by a P600. In contrast, 3- to 4-year-old children show a P600 effect but no LAN (Silva-Pereyra, Rivera-Gaxiola & Kuhl, 2005). ELAN effects for phrase structure violations in passives also emerge later, appearing in 7-year-olds but not in 6-year-olds (Hahne, Eckstein & Friederici, 2004).

Friederici and colleagues have interpreted these results in terms of a model of adult processing, based on ERP findings, which posits a three-stage process of sentence comprehension (Friederici, 2002; Friederici & Weissenborn, 2007). In the first phase, syntactic structures are constructed based solely on information about the syntactic category of the word (150–300 ms, indexed by the ELAN). In the second phase, lexical-semantic and morphosyntactic processes occur in two separate streams, leading to the assignment of thematic roles and other semantic relations between words (300 ms–500 ms, indexed by the N400 and later left-anterior negativities). Then, in the third phase, these two streams of information are integrated (500 ms–1000 ms, indexed by the P600). Thus, this model, like the minimal attachment model (Frazier & Fodor, 1978), posits that structural processing is initially modular with other information sources being integrated later in chronometric time.

This processing model, in concert with the developmental ERP studies described above, led Friederici (2006) to propose that syntactic structure building operations (indexed by the ELAN) first emerge at around 2.5 years and become more automated across development. New, more complex, morphosyntactic operations appear later as the child gains the requisite linguistic experience (Clahsen, Luck & Hahne, 2007; Hahne et al., 2004; Silva-Pereyra et al., 2005). This developmental hypothesis is consistent with theories of acquisition which argue that children's early word combinations (18 to 30 months) are either lexically based (Tomasello, 1992) or semantic rather than syntactic (Schlesinger, 1982).

This developmental account is a radical departure from standard arguments for modularity (Fodor, 1983). Modular theories posit a deep architectural connection between a given module (syntactic processing) and its privileged input (syntactic category information). This connection could result from innate constraints on human development or from systematic patterns in the language input that shape the processing system. In either account, we might expect this privileged connection to be present early in development. Modularity is often motivated by appeals to computational limitations which prevent the immediate integration of information. Because children have slower processing speed than adults, many theorists have suggested that processing is more modular in childhood and becomes more interactive over development (Felser et al., 2003; Joseph et al., 2008; Traxler, 2002). Friederici appears to be making the opposite claim: the privileged-structure building route develops late, while the secondary non-modular system that integrates semantic cues is present even in young children.

These conclusions, however, depend on the assumption that the ELAN indexes early syntactic processing. Recent studies using magnetoencephalography (an imaging technique with the temporal resolution of ERP but superior spatial resolution) have found that this response is generated in sensory cortices—the visual cortex for written words (Dikker, Ragbagliati & Pylkkänen, 2009) and the primary auditory cortex for spoken words (Herrmann, Maess, Hasting & Friederici, 2009). The magnitude of these effects depends upon the degree to which the target word has the form features that would be typical for the expected syntactic category (Dikker, Ragbagliati, Farmer & Pylkkänen, 2010). These findings suggest that ELAN-like effects are caused by the violation of predictions about *word form* that are made on the basis of higher-level syntactic representations. In this account, ELAN-like effects result from top-down, predictive processing. Thus the absence of these effects in young infants (or older children) would be consistent with the findings from the visual-world paradigm suggesting that top-down processing is less robust early in development (see earlier sections).

The top-down hypothesis may help to explain why early effects of syntactic mismatch appear in some infant studies and not others. For example, in a recent study with 24-month-olds, Bernal, Dehaene-Lambertz, Milotte & Christophe (2010) found an early response to syntactic category violations over the left temporal cortex (a positivity emerging 350 ms after word onset). On the basis of source localization and function, they suggest that this component is parallel to the ELAN and reflects preliminary syntactic analysis. However, they provide no explanation for why syntactic analysis would be facilitated in their task relative to Oberrecker and Friederici's (2006), which found no early response to category violations in this age group. Critically, Bernal's task appears to be optimally suited for producing top-down expectations about word forms: each critical word is introduced in the context prior to the test sentences and is used in eight test sentences across the experiment. Thus ongoing syntactic or semantic analysis could result in quite precise expectations about what the speaker is about to say. To illustrate this, a translation of one dialog appears below (20) with the noun violation in bold and the control noun in italics.

(20)   The chicken looks down. She sees a strawberry. But she **strawberries** it without noticing. Now she looks at it with envy. What will she do? She wants to eat the *strawberry*.

Characterizing children's sentence processing

In this chapter I have described a few of the questions that have been explored in the emerging field of children's sentence processing. While this work is really just beginning, the picture that is emerging strongly suggests that by about 4 years of age the child's language processing system is similar to that of adults in several critical ways.

First, children appear to construct representations at multiple levels that have roughly the same content and scope as that of adults. For example, the structural priming studies demonstrate that children who have just turned 3 have abstract grammatical representations which they employ during on-line comprehension.

This parallels the findings from studies of phonological processing and priming which demonstrate that young children represent speech sounds in a format quite similar to adults' (Mani & Plunkett, 2010; Swingley & Aslin, 2002).

Second, like adults, children engage in incremental interpretation of linguistic input. Children make hypotheses about the syntactic and semantic relationships between phrases as these phrases unfold (Trueswell et al., 1999). These initial predictions are generated on the basis of the information that is available early in the sentence (Choi & Trueswell, 2010). When this information turns out to be misleading, children, like adults, experience syntactic garden-paths. But unlike adults, young children do not appear to recover from these misanalyses, and thus they often make errors that are inconsistent with late-arriving grammatical cues. Children's lexical processing is also clearly incremental. For example, as children activate the phonological cohort of an unfolding word, activation spreads to the semantic associates of the cohort members resulting in phonosemantic priming (e.g., priming from log→key by way of lock; Mani, Durrant & Floccia, 2012; Huang & Snedeker, 2011).

Third, like adults, children use multiple sources of information, in concert, to resolve ambiguity at each level of representation. For example, by 4 years of age children employ lexical and prosodic cues to interpret PP-attachment ambiguities (Snedeker & Trueswell, 2004; Snedeker & Yuan, 2008). Similarly, young children use grammatical gender, syntactic constraints and some forms of discourse structure to disambiguate pronominal reference (Clackson et al., 2011; Hartshorne et al., 2010).

Nevertheless, in the preschool and elementary years, children's language comprehension differs from that of adults in systematic ways. First, as we noted earlier, children appear to be unable or unwilling to revise their interpretation of garden-path sentences. Children also appear to have more difficulty switching between interpretations across trials (Snedeker & Yuan, 2008). Both of these patterns have been argued to reflect deficits in executive function, a set of abilities that are subserved by the prefrontal cortex, that are linked to cognitive planning and control, and that develop slowly across childhood (Novick, Trueswell & Thompson-Schill, 2005; Mazuka, Jincho & Oishi, 2009).

In addition to these errors in control, children often fail to make use of information that has a strong and rapid influence on adult comprehension such as: the first-mention bias in pronoun resolution (Arnold et al., 2007); the global plausibility of an interpretation (Snedeker et al., 2009); and the number of referents available in the context (Trueswell et al., 1999). Many of these cues appear to involve top-down constraints on lower-level of linguistic processes. Our review of the ERP literature suggested that top-down prediction is slow to develop: ELAN-like effects, which appear to reflect form-level predictions, are largely absent from developmental studies.

In the past decade, there has been considerable progress in the study of children's on-line language processing. In addition to the phenomena we describe here, other researchers have addressed morphological processing (Clahsen et al., 2007), the calculation of pragmatic inferences (Huang &

Snedeker, 2009), and the use of prosody as a cue to discourse structure (Arnold, 2008; Ito, Jincho, Minai, Yamane & Mazuka, 2012). Cross-linguistic work is gaining momentum (Choi & Trueswell, 2010; Ito et al., 2012). New techniques are being developed. While we still have far more questions than answers, there is every reason to believe that the next 10 years will bring us even closer to understanding how moment-to-moment language comprehension develops.

Acknowledgments

Preparation of this chapter was supported by a grant from the National Science Foundation (NSF-BCS 0921012) and fueled by conversations with Yi Ting Huang, Malathi Thothathiri, Lila Gleitman, John Trueswell, Manizeh Khan, Hugh Rabagliati, and Josh Hartshorne.

Note

1. Young children will also look more at objects that are associated with both the agent and the verb, rather than objects that are merely associated with one or other (Borovsky, Elman & Fernald, 2012). However, it is not clear whether this requires the child to combine their knowledge of both words or merely reflects the summation of two separate constraints.

References

Acha, J., & Perea, M. (2008). The effects of length and transposed-letter similarity in lexical decision: Evidence with beginning, intermediate and adult readers. *British Journal of Psychology*, *99*, 245–264.

Aghababian, V., & Nazir, T. A. (2000). Developing normal reading skills: Aspects of the visual processes underlying word recognition. *Journal of Experimental Child Psychology*, *76(2)*, 123–150.

Ahmad Z., Balsamo L. M., Sachs B. C., Xu B., & Gaillard, W. D. (2003). Auditory comprehension of language in young children: Neural networks identified with fMRI. *Neurology*, *60*, 1598–1605.

Allopenna, P. D., Magnuson, J. S., & Tanenhaus, M. K. (1998). Tracking the time-course of spoken word recognition using eye-movements: Evidence for continuous mapping models. *Journal of Memory & Language*, *38*, 419–439.

Altmann, G. (2001). The language machine: Psycholinguistics in review. *British Journal of Psychology*, *92*, 129–170.

Altmann, G., & Steedman, M. (1988). Interaction with context during human sentence processing. *Cognition*, *30*, 191–238.

Arnold, J. E. (2008). The BACON not the bacon: How children and adults understand accented and unaccented noun phrases. *Cognition*, *108(1)*, 69–99.

Arnold, J. E., Brown-Schmidt, S., & Trueswell, J. (2007). Children's use of gender and order-of-mention during pronoun comprehension. *Language and Cognitive Processes*, *22*, 527–565.

Arnold J. E., Eisenband J., Brown-Schmidt, S., & Trueswell, J. (2000). The rapid use of gender information: Evidence of the time-course of pronoun resolution from eyetracking. *Cognition*, *76*, B13–26.

Bencini, G. M. L., & Valian, V. (2008). Abstract sentence representation in 3-year-olds: Evidence from comprehension and production. *Journal of Memory and Language, 59*, 97–113.

Bernal, S., Dehaene-Lambertz, G., Milotte, S., & Chrisophe, A. (2010). Two-year-olds compute syntactic structure on-line. *Developmental Science, 13(1)*, 69–76.

Bijeljac-Babic, R., Millogo, V., Farioli, F., & Grainger, J. (2004). A developmental investigation of word length effects in reading using a new on-line word identification paradigm. *Reading and Writing, 17*, 411–431.

Bock, J. K. (1986). Syntactic persistence in language production. *Cognitive Psychology, 18*, 355–387.

Booth, J. R., MacWhinney, B., Thulborn, K. R., Sacco, K., Voyvodic, J. T., & Feldman, H. M. (2000). Developmental and lesion effects in brain activation during sentence comprehension and mental rotation. *Developmental Neuropsychology, 18*, 139–169.

Borovsky, A., Elman, J., & Fernald, A. (2012). Knowing a lot for one's age: Vocabulary skill and not age is associated with the timecourse of incremental sentence interpretation in children and adults. *Journal of Experimental Child Psychology, 112(4)*, 417–36.

Brauer, J., & Friederici, A. D. (2007). Functional neural networks of semantic and syntactic processes in the developing brain. *Journal of Cognitive Neuroscience, 19(10)*, 1609–1623.

Brock, J., Norbury, C. F., Einav, S., & Nation, K. (2008). Do individuals with autism process words in context? Evidence from language-mediated eye-movements. *Cognition, 108*, 896–904.

Brown-Schmidt, S., & Tanenhaus, M. K. (2008). Real-time investigation of referential domains in unscripted conversation: A targeted language game approach. *Cognitive Science, 32*, 643–684.

Campbell, A. L., & Tomasello, M. (2001). The acquisition of English dative constructions. *Applied Psycholinguistics, 22*, 253–267.

Cepeda, N. J., Kramer, A. F., & Gonzalez de Sather, J. C. M. (2001). Changes in executive control across the life-span: Examination of task switching performance. *Developmental Psychology, 37*, 715–730.

Chambers, C., Tanenhaus, M., & Magnuson, J. (2004). Actions and affordances in syntactic ambiguity resolution. *Journal of Experimental Psychology: Learning, Memory, and Cognition, 30(3)*, 687–696.

Choi, Y., & Mazuka, R. (2003). Young children's use of prosody in sentence parsing. *Journal of Psycholinguistic Research, 32*, 197–217.

Choi, Y., & Trueswell, J. C. (2010). Children's (in)ability to recover from garden paths in a verb-final language: Evidence for developing control in sentence processing. *Journal of Experimental Child Psychology, 106*, 41–61.

Chomsky, N. (1981). *Lectures on government and binding: The Pisa lectures*. Berlin and New York: Mouton de Gruyter.

Clackson, K., Felser, C., & Clahsen, H. (2011). Children's processing of reflexives and pronouns in English: Evidence from eye-movements during listening. *Journal of Memory and Language, 65*, 128–144.

Clahsen, H. (2008). Behavioral methods for investigating morphological and syntactic processing in children. In I. Sekerina, E. Fernández & H. Clahsen (Eds.), *Developmental psycholinguistics: On-line methods in children's language processing* (pp. 1–27). Amsterdam: Benjamins.

Clahsen, H., Luck, M., & Hahne, A. (2007). How children process over-regularizations: Evidence from event-related brain potentials. *Journal of Child Language, 34*, 601–22.

Clifton, C. Jr., Staub, A., & Rayner, K. (2007). Eye-movements in reading words and sentences. In R. Van Gompel (Ed.), *Eye-movements: A window on mind and brain* (pp. 341–372). Amsterdam: Elsevier.

Crain, S., & Steedman, M. (1985). On not being led up the garden path: The use of context by the psychological parser. In D. R. Dowty, L. Karttunen, & A. M. Zwicky (Eds.), *Natural language parsing: Psychological, computational and theoretical perspectives* (pp. 320–358). Cambridge: Cambridge University Press.

Dehaene, S. (2009). *Reading in the brain*. New York: Penguin Viking.

Dibbets, P., & Jolles, J. (2006). The switch task for children: Measuring mental flexibility in young children. *Cognitive Development, 21*, 60–71.

Diehl, J., Friedberg, C., Paul, R., & Snedeker, J. (under review). The use of prosody during syntactic processing in children and adolescents with autism spectrum disorders.

Dikker, S., Rabagliati, H., & Pylkkänen, L. (2009). Sensitivity to syntax in visual cortex. *Cognition, 110*, 293–321.

Dikker, S., Rabagliati, H., Farmer, T. A., & Pylkkänen, L. (2010). Early occipital sensitivity to syntactic category is based on form typicality. *Psychological Science, 1;21(5)*, 629–634.

Elman, J., Hare, M., & McRae, K. (2005). Cues, constraints, and competition in sentence processing. In M. Tomasello & D. Slobin (Eds.), *Beyond nature–nurture: Essays in honor of Elizabeth Bates* (pp. 111–138), Mahwah, NJ: Lawrence Erlbaum Associates, Publishers.

Felser, C., Marinis, T., & Clahsen, H. (2003). Children's processing of ambiguous sentences: A study of relative clause attachment. *Language Acquisition, 11*, 127–163.

Felser, C., Roberts, L., Gross, R., & Marinis, T. (2003). The processing of ambiguous sentences by first and second language learners of English. *Applied Psycholinguistics, 24*, 453–89.

Fernald, A., Perfors, A., & Marchman, V. (2006). Picking up speed in understanding: Speech processing efficiency and vocabulary growth across the 2nd year. *Developmental Psychology, 42(1)*, 98–116.

Fernald, A., Pinto, J., Swingley, D., Weinberg, A., & McRoberts, G. (1998). Rapid gains in speed of verbal processing by infants in the 2nd year. *Psychological Science, 9*, 228–231.

Fisher, C. (2002). The role of abstract syntactic knowledge in language acquisition: A reply to Tomasello. *Cognition, 82*, 259–278.

Fisher, C., Gertner, Y., Scott, R., & Yuan, S. (2010). Syntactic bootstrapping. *Wiley interdisciplinary reviews: Cognitive science, 1*, 143–149.

Fodor, J. A. (1983). *Modularity of mind: An essay on faculty psychology*. Cambridge, MA: MIT Press.

Fodor, J. D. (1998). Parsing to learn. *Journal of Psycholinguistic Research, 27(3)*, 339–374.

Frank, R. (1998). Structural complexity and the time-course of grammatical development. *Cognition, 66*, 249–301.

Frazier, L., & Fodor, J. D. (1978). The sausage machine: A new two-stage parsing model. *Cognition, 6*, 291–325.

Friederici, A. D. (2002). Towards a neural basis of auditory sentence processing. *Trends in Cognitive Sciences, 6*, 78–84.

Friederici, A. D. (2006). The neural basis of language development and its impairment. *Neuron, 52*, 941–952.

Friederici, A. D., & Weissenborn, J. (2007). Mapping sentence form onto meaning: The syntaxsemantic interface. *Brain Research*, *1146*, 50–58.

Friedrich, M., & Friederici, A. D. (2004). N400-like semantic incongruity effect in 19-month-olds: Processing known words in picture contexts. *Journal of Cognitive Neuroscience*, *16*, 1465–1477.

Friedrich, M., & Friederici, A. D. (2005a). Phonotactic knowledge and lexical-semantic processing in one-year-olds: Brain responses to words and nonsense words in picture contexts. *Journal of Cognitive Neuroscience*, *17*, 1785–1802.

Friedrich, M., & Friederici, A. D. (2005b). Semantic sentence processing reflected in the event-related potentials of one- and two-year-old children. *Neuroreport*, *16*, 1801–1804.

Gertner, Y., Fisher, C., & Eisengart, J. (2006). Learning words and rules: Abstract knowledge of word order in early sentence comprehension. *Psychological Science*, *17*, 684–691.

Goldwater, M. B., Tomlinson, M., Love, B. C., & Echols, C. H. (2011). Structural priming as structure-mapping: Young children use analogies from previous utterances to guide sentence production. *Cognitive Science*, *35*, 156–170.

Golinkoff, R. M., Hirsh-Pasek, K., Cauley, K. M., & Gordon, L. (1987). The eyes have it: Lexical and syntactic comprehension in a new paradigm. *Journal of Child Language*, *14*, 23–45.

Goodluck, H., & Tavakolian, S. (1982). Competence and processing in children's grammar of relative clauses. *Cognition*, *11*, 1–27.

Hahne A., Eckstein K., & Friederici, A. D. (2004). Brain signatures of syntactic and semantic processes during children's language development. *Journal of Cognitive Neuroscience*, *16*, 1302–1318.

Hartshorne, J. K., Nappa, R., & Snedeker, S. (2010). Ambiguous pronoun processing development: Probably not U-shaped. *Proceedings of BUCLD 35* (pp. 272–282), 5–7 November, Boston, MA.

Herrmann, B., Maess, B., Hasting, A. S., & Friederici, A. D. (2009). Localization of the syntactic mismatch negativity in the temporal cortex: An MEG study. *NeuroImage*, *48(3)*, 590–600.

Hirsh-Pasek, K., & Golinkoff, R. M. (1996). *The origins of grammar: Evidence from comprehension*, Cambridge, MA: MIT Press.

Holcomb, P. J., Coffey, S. A., & Neville, H. J. (1992). Visual and auditory sentence processing: A developmental analysis using event-related brain potentials. *Developmental Neuropsychology*, *8*, 203–241.

Huang, Y., & Snedeker, J. (2009). Semantic meaning and pragmatic interpretation in five-year olds: Evidence from real time spoken language comprehension. *Developmental Psychology*, *45(6)*, 1723–1739.

Huang, Y., & Snedeker, J. (2011). Cascading activation across levels of representation in children's lexical processing. *Journal of Child Language*, *38 (3)*, 644–661.

Hurewitz, F., Brown-Schmidt, S., Thorpe, K., Gleitman, L. R., & Trueswell, J. C. (2000). One frog, two frog, red frog, blue frog: Factors affecting children's syntactic choices in production and comprehension. *Journal of Psycholinguistic Research*, *29*, 597–626.

Huttenlocher, J., Vasilyeva, M., & Shimpi, P. (2004). Syntactic priming in young children. *Journal of Memory and Language*, *50*, 182–195.

Ito, K., Jincho, N., Minai, U., Yamane, N., & Mazuka, R. (2012). Intonation facilitates contrast resolution: Evidence from Japanese adults & 6-year olds. *Journal of Memory and Language*, *66 (1)*, 265–284.

Joseph, H. S. S. L., Liversedge, S. P., Blythe, H. I., White, S. J., Gathercole, S. E., & Rayner, K. (2008). Children's and adults' processing of anomaly and implausibility during reading: Evidence from eye-movements. *Quarterly Journal of Experimental Psychology*, *61(5)*, 708–723.

Joseph, H. S. S. L., Liversedge, S. P., Blythe, H. I., White, S. J., & Rayner, K. (2009). Word length and landing position effects during reading in children and adults. *Vision Research*, *49*, 2078–2086.

Just, M. A., & Carpenter, P. A. (1992). A capacity theory of comprehension: Individual differences in working memory. *Psychological Review*, *99*, 122–149.

Kail, R. V. (1991). Development of processing speed in childhood and adolescence. In H. W. Reese (Ed.), *Advances in child development and behavior*, Vol. 25. New York: Academic Press.

Kamide, Y., Altmann, G. T. M., & Haywood, S. L. (2003). The timecourse of prediction in incremental sentence processing: Evidence from anticipatory eye-movements. *Journal of Memory and Language*, *49*, 133–156.

Kehler, A., Kertz, L., Rohde, H., & Elman, J. L. (2008). Coherence and coreference revisited. *Journal of Semantics*, *25*, 1–44.

Kendeou, P., Savage, R., & van den Broek, P. (2009). Revisiting the simple view of reading. *British Journal of Educational Psychology*, *79(2)*, 353–370.

Kidd, E., & Bavin, E. L. (2005). Lexical and referential cues to sentence interpretation: An investigation of children's interpretations of ambiguous sentences. *Journal of Child Language*, *32*, 855–876.

Kidd, E., & Bavin, E. L. (2007). Lexical and referential influences on on-line spoken language comprehension: A comparison of adults and primary school age children. *First Language*, *27*, 29–52.

Kidd, E., Stewart, A., & Serratrice, L. (2011). Children do not overcome lexical biases where adults do: The role of the referential scene in garden path recovery. *Journal of Child Language*, *38*, 222–234.

Kjelgaard, M. M., & Speer, S. R. (1999). Prosodic facilitation and interference in the resolution of temporary syntactic closure ambiguity. *Journal of Memory and Language*, *40*, 153–194.

Kuczaj, S. (1976). -ing, -s and -ed: A study of the acquisition of certain verb inflections. Unpublished doctoral dissertation, University of Minnesota.

Kuperberg, G. R., McGuire, P. K., Bullmore, E. T., Brammer, M. J., Rabe-Hesketh, S., Wright, I. C., Lythgoe, D. J., Williams, S. C., & David, A. S. (2000). Common and distinct neural substrates for pragmatic, semantic, and syntactic processing of spoken sentences: An fMRI study. *Journal of Cognitive Neuroscience*, *12*, 321–341.

Love, T. (2007). Recovery of canonical order by pre-school children: A real-time investigation. *Journal of Psycholinguistic Research*, *36*, 191–206.

Love, T., Walenski, M., & Swinney, D. (2009). Slowed speech input has a differential impact on on-line and off-line processing in children's comprehension of pronouns. *Journal of Psycholinguistic Research*, *38 (3)*, 285–304.

MacDonald, M. C., & Christiansen, M. H. (2002). Reassessing working memory: Comment on Just and Carpenter (1992) and Waters and Caplan (1996). *Psychological Review*, *109*, 35–54.

McKee, C., Nicol, J., & McDaniel, D. (1993). Children's application of binding during sentence processing. *Language and Cognitive Processes*, *8*, 265–290.

McKone, E., Crookes, K., Jeffery, L., & Dilks, D. D. (2012). A critical review of the development of face recognition: Experience is far less important than previously believed. *Cognitive Neuropsychology*, *29*, 174–212.

MacWhinney, B. (2000). *The CHILDES Project: Tools for analyzing talk.* Third Edition. Mahwah, NJ: Lawrence Erlbaum Associates.

Mani, N., Durrant, S., & Floccia, C. (2012). Activation of phonological and semantic codes in toddlers. *Journal of Memory and Language, 66(4),* 612–622.

Mani, N., & Plunkett, K. (2010). In the infant's mind's ear: Evidence for implicit naming in 18-month-olds. *Psychological Science, 21,* 908–913.

Marslen-Wilson, W. D., & Welsh, A. (1978). Processing interactions and lexical access during word recognition in continuous speech. *Cognitive Psychology, 10,* 29–63.

Mazuka, R., Jincho, N., & Oishi, H. (2009). Development of executive control and language processing, *Language and Linguistic Compass, 3(1),* 59–89.

Messenger, K., Branigan, H. P., & McLean, J. F. (2011). Evidence for (shared) abstract structure underlying children's short and full passives. *Cognition, 121,* 268–274.

Nation, K., Marshall, C., & Altmann, G. (2003). Investigating individual differences in children's real-time sentence comprehension using language-mediated eye-movements. *Journal of Experimental Child Psychology, 86,* 314–329.

Neville, H., Nicol, J., Barss, A., Forster, K., & Garrett, M. (1991). Syntactically based sentence processing classes: Evidence from event-related brain potentials. *Journal of Cognitive Neuroscience, 3,* 151–165.

Ninio, A. (2005). Testing the role of semantic similarity in syntactic development. *Journal of Child Language, 32,* 35–61.

Novick, J. M., Trueswell, J. C., & Thompson-Schill, S. L. (2005). Cognitive control and parsing: Reexamining the role of Broca's area in sentence comprehension. *Cognitive Affective & Behavioral Neuroscience, 5,* 263–281.

Oberecker, R., & Friederici, A. D. (2006). Syntactic ERP components in 24-month-olds' sentence comprehension. *Neuroreport, 17,* 1017–1021.

Oberecker, R., Friedrich, M., & Friederici, A. D. (2005). Neural correlates of syntactic processing in two-year-olds. *Journal of Cognitive Neuroscience, 17,* 1667–1678.

Osterhout, L., Kim, A., & Kuperberg, G. (2012). The neurobiology of sentence comprehension. In M. Spivey, M. Joannisse, & K. McRae (Eds.), *The Cambridge handbook of psycholinguistics* (pp. 365–389). Cambridge: Cambridge University Press.

Pickering, M. J., & Garrod, S. (2007). Do people use language production to make predictions during comprehension? *Trends in Cognitive Sciences, 11,* 105–110.

Pinker, S. (1989). *Learnability and cognition: The acquisition of argument structure.* Cambridge, MA: MIT Press.

Pynte, J., & Prieur, B. (1996). Prosodic breaks and attachment decisions in sentence parsing. *Language and Cognitive Processes, 11,* 165–192.

Qi, Z., Yuan, S., & Fisher, C. (2011). Where does verb bias come from? Experience with particular verbs affects on-line sentence processing. In N. Danis, K. Mesh, & H. Sung (Eds.), *Proceedings of the 35th annual Boston University conference on language development* (pp. 500–512), 5–7 November, 2010, Boston, MA: Cascadilla Press.

Rabagliati, H., Pylkkänen, L., & Marcus, G. F. (2012). Top-down influence in young children's lexical ambiguity resolution. *Developmental Psychology,* doi: 10.1037/a0026918.

Savage, C., Lieven, E., Theakston, A., & Tomasello, M. (2003). Testing the abstractness of children's linguistic representations: Lexical and structural priming of syntactic constructions in young children. *Developmental Science, 6,* 557–567.

Schafer, A. J. (1997). Prosodic parsing: The role of prosody in sentence comprehension. Unpublished doctoral dissertation. Amherst, MA: University of Massachusetts.

Schlesinger, I. M. (1982). *Steps to language: Toward a theory of native language acquisition.* Hillsdale, NJ: Erlbaum.

Sekerina, I., & Brooks, P. (2007). Eye-movements during spoken word recognition in Russian children, *Journal of Experimental Child Psychology, 98,* 20–45.

Sekerina, I., Stromswold, K., & Hestvik, A. (2004). How do adults and children process referentially ambiguous pronouns? *Journal of Child Language, 31,* 123–152.

Silva-Pereyra, J., Rivera-Gaxiola, M., & Kuhl, P. K. (2005). An event-related brain potential study of sentence comprehension in preschoolers: Semantic and morpho-syntactic processing. *Brain Research, 23,* 247–258.

Snedeker, J., & Trueswell, J. (2003). Using prosody to avoid ambiguity: Effects of speaker awareness and referential context, *Journal of Memory and Language, 48,* 103–130.

Snedeker, J., & Trueswell, J. C. (2004). The developing constraints on parsing decisions: The role of lexical-biases and referential scenes in child and adult sentence processing. *Cognitive Psychology, 49,* 238–299.

Snedeker, J., Worek, A., & Shafto, C. (2009). The role of lexical bias and global plausibility in children's on-line parsing. Paper presented at the *Boston University conference on language development.* Boston, MA. November 2009.

Snedeker, J., & Yuan, S. (2008). The role of prosodic and lexical constraints in parsing in young children (and adults). *Journal of Memory and Language, 58,* 574–608.

Song, H., & Fisher, C. (2005). Who's "she"? Discourse prominence influences preschoolers' comprehension of pronouns. *Journal of Memory and Language, 52,* 29–57.

Song, H., & Fisher, C. (2007). Discourse prominence effects on 2.5-year-old children's interpretation of pronouns. *Lingua, 117,* 1959–1987.

Spelke, E. S. (1979). Perceiving bimodally specified events in infancy. *Developmental Psychology, 15,* 626–636.

Sternberg, S. (1998). Discovering mental processing stages: The method of additive factors. In D. Scarborough & S. Sternberg (Eds.), *An invitation to cognitive science: Methods, models, and conceptual issues,* Cambridge, MA: MIT Press, pp.703–863.

Swingley, D., & Aslin, R. (2002). Lexical neighborhoods and the word-form representations of 14-month-olds. *Psychological Science, 13(5),* 480–484.

Swingley, D., & Fernald, A. (2002). Recognition of words referring to present and absent objects by 24-month-olds. *Journal of Memory and Language, 46,* 39–56.

Taraban, R., & McClelland, J. (1988). Constituent attachment and thematic role assignment in sentence processing: Influences of content-based expectations. *Journal of Memory and Language, 27,* 1–36.

Tanenhaus, M., Spivey-Knowlton, M., Eberhard, K., & Sedivy, J. (1995). Integration of visual and linguistic information in spoken language comprehension. *Science, 268,* 1632–1634.

Thothathiri, M., & Snedeker, J. (2008a). Syntactic priming during language comprehension in three- and four-year-old children. *Journal of Memory and Language, 58,* 188–213.

Thothathiri, M., & Snedeker, J. (2008b). Give and take: Syntactic priming during spoken language comprehension. *Cognition, 108,* 51–68.

Tomasello, M. (1992). *First verbs: A case study in early grammatical development,* New York: Cambridge University Press.

Tomasello, M. (2000). The item-based nature of children's early syntactic development. *Trends in Cognitive Sciences, 4,* 156–163.

Traxler, M. (2002). Plausibility and subcategorization preference in children's processing of temporarily ambiguous sentences: Evidence from self-paced reading. *Quarterly Journal of Experimental Psychology: Human Experimental Psychology, 55A*, 75–96.

Treiman, R., Clifton, C., Meyer, A., & Wurn, A. (2003). Language comprehension and production. In A. Healy & R. Procter (Eds.), *Handbook of psychology: Experimental psychology*, Vol. 4 (pp. 527–547). Hoboken, NJ: John Wiley & Sons.

Trueswell, J., & Gleitman, L. R. (2004). Children's eye-movements during listening: Evidence for a constraint-based theory of parsing and word learning. In J. M. Henderson & F. Ferreira (Eds.), *Interface of vision, language, and action*. New York: Psychology Press.

Trueswell, J. C., Sekerina, I., Hill, N. M., & Logrip, M. L. (1999). The kindergarten-path effect: Studying on-line sentence processing in young children. *Cognition, 73*, 89–134.

Trueswell, J. C., Tanenhaus, M. K., & Kello, C. (1993). Verb-specific constraints in sentence processing: Separating effects of lexical preference from garden paths. *Journal of Experimental Psychology: Learning, Memory, and Cognition, 19(3)*, 528–553.

Weighall, A. (2008). On still being led down the kindergarten path: Children's processing of structural ambiguities. *Journal of Experimental Child Psychology, 99*, 75–95.

Yuan, S., Fisher, C., Kandhadai, P., & Fernald, A. (2011). You can stipe the pig and nerk the fork: Learning to use verbs to predict nouns. *Proceedings of the 35th annual Boston University conference on language development* (pp. 665–677). Boston, MA: Cascadilla Press.

9 Sentence processing in bilinguals

Leah Roberts

Introduction

It is uncontroversial that native speakers incrementally process the language input, making rapid use of bottom-up, lexical-semantic and syntactic information as well as top-down, discourse-pragmatic information as new material is integrated into the parse during real-time sentence processing. The major question in the field of bilingual[1] sentence processing is to what extent this is the case when processing in one's second language (L2). Most studies examine bilinguals' parsing procedures applied to the L2 input once grammatical knowledge has been independently established, and the predominant debate in the field focuses on whether bilingual sentence processing (in 'late' or post-puberty learners) is qualitatively different from that of native speakers. Clahsen and Felser (2006a, b) argue for this position. Their Shallow Structure Hypothesis (SSH) states that bilinguals' processing of multi-clause constructions is lexically driven, making use of linear parsing heuristics rather than being a structurally determined process, as they assume for L1 (e.g., Pickering, Clifton, & Crocker, 2000; Pritchett, 1992). In other words, while bilinguals can establish local dependencies, such as computing gender agreement within a noun phrase, their processing is fundamentally different from that of native speakers when it comes to the processing of structural dependencies across clauses, because 'the L2 grammar does not provide the type of syntactic information required to process non-local grammatical phenomena in native-like ways' (Clahsen & Felser, 2006b, p. 565). Other researchers assume that bilinguals have access to the same parsing procedures available for monolingual processing, and that performance differences are attributable to factors such as insufficient L2 proficiency and/or cognitive capacity limitations, like speed and working memory (e.g., Dekydtspotter, Schwartz, & Sprouse, 2006; Hopp, 2010). Even at advanced levels of competence, bilingual performance is often more variable and bilinguals are not always able to access and apply their grammatical knowledge as immediately as native speakers (e.g., Hoover & Dwivedi, 1998; Jiang, 2004, 2007) and under some circumstances they perform like native speakers of lower working memory capacity (e.g., Havik, Roberts, van Hout, Schreuder, & Haverkort, 2009). This suggests a quantitative rather than a qualitative or fundamental difference between the two populations (e.g., Hopp, 2006). On the other hand, on-line processing data showing that advanced learners pattern together and differently from native speakers in their use of syntactic information, irrespective of learners' proficiency, cognitive capacity and/or the typological distance between the L1 and the L2 (e.g., Marinis, Roberts, Felser, & Clahsen, 2005; Papadopoulou & Clahsen, 2003; Roberts & Felser, 2011), supports a fundamental difference account between bilingual and native speaker parsing. In sum, there are mixed results. Nevertheless, whether one takes a fundamental difference approach or not, it is consistently observed that differences between bilingual and native speakers – and the greatest observed processing difficulties – lie in the application of grammatical information during real-time sentence comprehension.

In this chapter, an overview of the research findings in bilingual sentence processing is presented, organised around topics familiar from monolingual sentence-processing research, including the extent to which the input is incrementally processed, how misanalyses are handled, and how dependencies are resolved across multi-clause constructions and during referential processing. The chapter ends with a summary of the factors that may account for differences between bilingual and native speaker sentence processing, and suggestions for topics for further research.

Incremental parsing and reanalysis

Processing garden-path sentences

Many studies have investigated (1) whether, or to what extent, bilingual sentence processing is as incremental as native speakers' processing and (2) whether this is the case even when reanalysis of the input must occur. Evidence from studies of the processing of temporarily ambiguous sentences in which 'garden-path' (GP) effects are elicited indicates that under many circumstances bilinguals endeavour to interpret sentences incrementally, attempting to interpret each word of the input as immediately as it is encountered, which causes processing difficulty when it has led to an incorrect analysis, and revision is required for successful interpretation (Dussias & Cramer Scaltz, 2008; Frenck-Mestre & Pynte, 1997; Juffs & Harrington, 1995, 1996; Juffs, 2004, 2005, 2006; Roberts & Felser, 2011). For instance, looking at learners' incremental processing using word-by-word grammaticality judgment tasks, Juffs and Harrington (1995, 1996) found that Chinese–English bilinguals were slower to read the disambiguating verbs (*proved/cheated*) in GP sentences with pre-posed adjunct (1a) and complement (1b) clauses, in comparison to non-GP sentences containing intransitive verbs (e.g., *arrive*) (1c).

(1)   a.   After Bill drank the water proved to be poisoned.

        b.   Sam warned the student cheated on the exam.

        c.   After Sam arrived the guests began to eat.

Thus the bilinguals initially misanalysed the ambiguous noun phrases (NPs; *the water, the student*) in the GP sentences (see also, Juffs, 2004; Frenck-Mestre & Pynte, 1997), and were sensitive on-line to the subcategorisation properties of the verbs used.

Similarly, Dussias and Cramer Scaltz (2008) found that Spanish–English bilinguals' reading times in a self-paced reading study were higher following disambiguation when sentence continuations went against the verb's bias for taking either a direct object (2a) or a sentence complement (2b).

(2)   a.   The CIA director confirmed the rumour could mean a security leak.

        b.   The ticket agent admitted the mistake when he got caught.

The learners patterned like native speakers, except when encountering the few verbs whose biases differed between Spanish and English. In these cases, they appeared to transfer their L1 verb biases to their processing of the L2.

These GP reading-time data show that given the requisite knowledge, bilinguals can incrementally process the input, being able to rapidly access the subcategorisation properties and biases of L2 verbs, and this information can constrain initial parsing decisions. It is not clear from these studies however, that the bilinguals are always ultimately able to recover the correct interpretation following misanalysis (see also Juffs & Harrington 1995, 1996, for evidence that bilinguals may fail to reanalyse). As with monolingual studies, the manipulation of semantic information such as 'pragmatic plausibility' has been used as a diagnostic to investigate the process of recovery from misanalysis (or reanalysis, or re-ranking of favoured analyses) in such temporary ambiguities (e.g., Pickering & Traxler, 1998), and the findings suggest that revision may be more problematic in general for bilinguals. For example, Roberts and Felser (2011) examined the word-by-word reading-time profiles of Greek–English bilinguals for GP sentences as in (3), to investigate the extent to which learners incrementally process the input following misanalysis.

(3)   The journalist wrote the book (the girl) had amazed all the judges.

The authors found that following the initial attempt to integrate the ambiguous NP (*book/girl*) with the main verb (*wrote*) – as shown by higher reading-times when this led to an implausible sentence fragment (*wrote the girl*) in comparison to plausible conditions (*wrote the book*) – the plausibility of this original analysis affected the ease of recovery following disambiguation. That is, on and beyond the disambiguating complement clause verb (*had amazed*), the reading-time patterns reversed, with processing difficulty observed for the plausible condition. Therefore, like native speakers, bilinguals' commitment to a plausible initial analysis is stronger than to an implausible one and so harder to abandon in the face of new evidence.

Given that the learners had equally high scores for the end-of-trial comprehension questions in the plausible and implausible conditions (over 90 per cent), the learners in the Roberts and Felser study had apparently fully recovered on-line from their original misanalyses. However this was not the case in their processing of constructions with fronted adjuncts like (4), although they were again very sensitive to the plausibility of the ambiguous NP (*song/beer*) as potential direct object of the preceding verb (*played*).

(4)   While the band played the song (the beer) pleased all the customers.

Specifically, there was no reversal of the reading-time patterns following disambiguation as was observed for the complement clause ambiguities (3); rather, the implausible condition (*played the beer*) continued to cause elevated reading times up until the end of the sentence. The bilinguals achieved significantly higher accuracy scores on the comprehension questions following the implausible (95 per cent) compared to the plausible preposed adjunct conditions (85 per cent), thus the plausibility of the original analysis indeed affected recovery, but at a much later point in processing in comparison to the complement clause items. Assuming a structurally based parser (e.g., Gorrell, 1995), the authors argue that the bilinguals had more trouble with preposed adjuncts because the revision required for successful interpretation is more substantial than that needed for the complement clause items. That is, although case and theta-role reassignment must take place for both, the hierarchical relations must be changed in the preposed adjunct sentences because the ambiguous NP must be reanalysed as subject of the superordinate clause. This is assumed to be more costly than merely adding a new clause boundary and altering the object to a subject analysis as needed for reanalysis in the complement clause items (cf., Gorrell, 1995; Pritchett, 1992; Sturt & Crocker, 1996; Weinberg, 1999). Thus structural complexity affected the learners' ability to incrementally process the sentence following their initial misanalyses.

Overall, the results of the above garden-path studies show while incrementally processing the input, bilinguals' parsing decisions are often constrained in similar ways to native speakers, but that L1–L2 differences at the semantic level can influence this process (see also Frenck-Mestre & Pynte, 1997). However, recovery from misanalysis may be more difficult to achieve on-line for bilinguals, particularly when this involves structurally more complex input.

Processing filler-gap sentences

Incremental processing and reanalysis has also been examined in studies investigating bilinguals' parsing of filler-gap constructions like *wh*-questions. *Wh*-construction formation differs cross-linguistically, and questions relating to cross-linguistic influence at the grammatical level on L2 processing can be addressed. Furthermore, effects of cognitive capacity can be investigated, since the *wh*-filler must be held in working memory during incremental processing. Like native speakers, bilinguals attempt to link a fronted *wh*-item (*filler*) to its subcategorising head (or lexical licenser) as soon as possible (cf., e.g., active filler strategy, Frazier & Flores d'Arcais, 1989; phrase-structure approach, Gorrell, 1995; minimal chain principle, De Vincenzi, 1991), and this can lead to misanalysis (e.g., Juffs & Harrington, 1995; Juffs, 2005). Plausibility has also been manipulated in such studies in the investigation of the recovery from misanalysis. In monolingual research, there is evidence that the implausibility of a fronted *wh*-constituent does not stop the parser from initially attempting to integrate it with the first potential subcategoriser (or from positing a gap at the first available site) when processing *wh*-dependencies such as *Which food did the children read about ___ in class?* (e.g., Boland, Tanenhaus, Garnsey, & Carlson, 1995). However, again, the plausibility of the resulting sentence fragment affects the relative cost of recovery (e.g., Clifton, 1993; Stowe, 1989), and this too has been observed for bilinguals, even when *wh*-constructions are formed differently in the learners' L1 (e.g., Williams, Möibus, & Kim, 2001). Despite this, differences in cognitive capacity and proficiency may affect bilinguals' incremental processing of such constructions. For example, in a self-paced reading study with an accompanying grammaticality judgment task, Dussias and Piñar (2010) found in general a cost asymmetry in Chinese–English bilinguals' on-line processing of subject and object *wh*-extraction constructions (5), as has been shown in native English speakers (see also Juffs, 2005; Juffs & Harrington, 1995). However, this was only the case for those learners of high working memory, as measured by Waters and Caplan's (1996) reading span test.

(5) a. Who did the police know (declare) ___ killed the pedestrian? (subject extraction)

b. Who did the police know (declare) the pedestrian killed ___ ? (object extraction)

Specifically, in the disambiguating region (with reading times collapsed across three words: *killed the pedestrian/the pedestrian killed*), both the high- and the low working memory bilinguals patterned like the native speakers in that the subject-extraction items (5a) overall were more problematic to process than object extractions (5b). This suggests that all groups were applying a gap-filling strategy which pushed them to attempt to integrate the *wh*-filler into the first clause as object of the main verb, e.g., *Who did the police know?* (cf., parsing constraints explained under various theoretical accounts, e.g., Carlson & Tanenhaus, 1988; De Vincenzi, 1991; Frazier, 1987; Pritchett, 1992). Processing difficulty is arguably caused by having to reanalyse the *wh*-filler as subject of the complement clause verb. However, it was only the bilinguals of high working memory who showed the same reading time profiles as the native speakers in terms of the effect of plausibility of the filler as direct object on the ease of recovery from misanalysis. That is, the high working memory bilinguals and the natives found it more costly to process the disambiguating region when the filler was a plausible direct object (*Who did the police know*) than when it was implausible (*Who did the police declare*), suggesting that a plausible initial misanalysis is more difficult to give up than an implausible one. Although also affected by plausibility, for the low working memory learners the overall processing disadvantage for the subject-extraction items (5a) was driven by the implausible filler condition (*Who did the police declare killed*), which led to very high reading times (915 ms) in comparison to the other three conditions (all approximately 730 ms). In sum, all the bilinguals appeared to have attempted to integrate the filler at the first potential gap site, like the native speakers, but only the high working memory group appeared to attempt reanalysis during the on-line processing of the items, like the native speakers. Despite this difference between the two bilingual groups in their incremental processing procedures, all the bilinguals were less accurate at judging the subject-extraction items with plausible fillers (*Who did the police know killed*) (63 per cent) in comparison to the native speakers (74 per cent) and to the other three conditions (all approximately 75 per cent). Taking the judgment and the reading-time results together, this suggests that the lower working memory bilinguals did ultimately encounter most difficulty with subject-extraction items with plausible fillers, but the effect showed up in off-line measures, rather than during the processing of the experimental items as was the case for native speakers and the higher working memory group. Given the very low accuracy scores for all the bilinguals for this condition however, it would seem that full recovery from misanalysis may not have taken place, whether the process was instigated during on-line processing or not. A similar lack of on-line recovery following misanalysis in subject *wh*-extractions was reported in Jackson and van Hell (2011) for their lower-proficiency group of Dutch-English bilinguals, and for low working memory learners in Williams's (2006) on-line plausibility judgment study.

Incremental processing in verb-final languages

Another question that is applied to bilingual sentence processing is whether it is incremental even if the verb – the head of the structure – is sentence final, or whether analysis is delayed until the lexical information provided by the verb becomes available. Similar findings to those outlined in the garden-path and *wh*-filler-gap studies above have been reported; that is, with the requisite knowledge, bilinguals use morpho-syntactic information like case-marking to incrementally build up the argument structure of a sentence before encountering the thematic verb, as observed with native speakers (e.g., Frazier, 1987; Frazier & Flores d'Arcais, 1989; Friederici & Frisch, 2000; Konieczny, Hemforth, Scheepers, & Strube, 1997). However, this becomes more difficult to achieve on-line for lower-proficiency and/or lower working memory bilinguals.

Jackson (2008) investigated English–German bilinguals' processing of single-clause *wh*-questions (6), specifically asking whether they would show the same processing difficulty as native German speakers for object-first *wh*-questions, given that the preference for subject- over object-extractions differs between the two languages (Schlesewsky, Fanselow, Kliegl, & Krems, 2000;

Bader & Meng, 1999). The participants read items in which the lexical verb appeared early in the construction (past simple, *traf*, (6a)) or at the end of the sentence (present perfect, *hat ... getroffen*, (6b)).

(6)   a. **Past simple**
Welche Ingenieurin traf den/der Chemiker gestern Nachmittag im Café?
Which-NOM/ACC engineer met the-ACC chemist/the-NOM chemist yesterday afternoon in the café?
'Which engineer met the chemist/did the chemist meet yesterday in the café?'

   b. **Present perfect**
Welche Ingenieurin *hat* den/der Chemiker gestern Nachmittag *getroffen*?
Which-NOM/ACC engineer has the-ACC chemist/the-NOM chemist yesterday afternoon in the café met?
'Which engineer met the chemist/did the chemist meet yesterday in the café?'

The experimental items were ambiguous until the case-marking information on the second NP disambiguated towards either a subject-first (*den Chemiker*) or object-first (*der Chemiker*) *wh*-construction. The highly proficient group, as observed for native speakers, slowed down on the critical NP when it was nominative (*der Chemiker*) and thus pushed for an object-first interpretation. However, the less proficient bilinguals displayed higher reading times at the point of disambiguation for dispreferred object-first items only when they had encountered the thematic verb prior to disambiguation, that is, in the past simple (6a). For the present perfect sentences (6b), the effect was visible at the end of the sentence, at the position of the thematic verb (see also Hopp, 2006). This suggests that at lower levels of proficiency, L2 processing is not fully incremental in the absence of lexical–thematic information at the verb, even for single-clause constructions.

As well as proficiency, the extent to which native-like processing occurs may be task-dependent; specifically, it may be more likely to occur when the participants' attention is particularly directed towards the manipulation. For instance, two self-paced reading studies on English–German bilinguals' processing of unambiguous *wh*-extractions (7) found native-like processing patterns only when the participants also undertook a secondary grammaticality judgment task (Jackson & Dussias, 2009) in comparison to the study in which the participants read for comprehension only (Jackson & Bobb, 2009).

(7)   Wer (Wen) denkst du, bewunderte den Sportler nach dem Spiel?
Who-NOM (Who-ACC) think you, admired the athlete after the game
'Who do you think missed the teacher/whom do you think the teacher missed after the game?'

Specifically, in both studies, as for native speakers, the bilinguals' reading times increased for the subject- versus the object-extraction items on processing the matrix verb (*denkst*) and the following NP (*du*), showing their preference for subject- versus object-first constructions. However, only in the judgment task study did the bilinguals' reading time patterns reverse on the complement clause (although delayed by one word, appearing on the complement NP, *den Sportler*), with object extractions being more difficult to process than subject extractions. This is arguably because of the load that is imposed on working memory by the holding of a dislocated object in memory (cf. findings that object extraction is difficult in German, even when the filler is overtly case-marked and thus unambiguous, e.g., Fiebach, Schlesewsky, & Friederici, 2002; Felser, Clahsen, & Münte, 2003). In the parallel study whose participants were required only to read for comprehension (Jackson & Bobb, 2009), there was no difference between the two conditions in the complement clause, and no effects of individual differences of either proficiency or working memory capacity. Given these task-related findings, perhaps the lower proficient L2 learners in the Jackson (2008) study would have incrementally processed the *wh*-constructions, had the secondary task been metalinguistic rather than the comprehension matching task which did not focus their attention on the case-marking information.

Further evidence for a delay in parsing decisions in the absence of lexical-semantic information was found in a self-paced reading study on temporarily ambiguous subject- and object-relative clauses by Havik, Roberts, van Hout, Schreuder, and Haverkort (2009) with advanced German–Dutch bilinguals of different working memory capacities. Despite the fact that Dutch speakers, like German speakers, have a robust subject-first word order preference (e.g., Kaan, 2001; Schlesewsky et al., 2000; Schriefers, Friederici, & Kühn, 1995), the bilinguals showed no on-line preference for subject-first (8a) word order when the task required them to read for comprehension only, irrespective of reading-span capacity, and even though they displayed a subject-first preference in the off-line task.

(8)   a.   Daar is de machinist die de conducteurs *heeft* bevrijd uit het brandende treinstel.
(subject relative)
'That is the engine-driver who has saved the guards from the burning train-carriage.'

       b.   Daar is de machinist die de conducteurs *hebben* bevrijd uit het brandende treinstel.
(object relative)
'That is the engine-driver who the guards have saved from the burning train-carriage.'

However, in the experiment in which participants from the same population made a truth-value judgment after each experimental item (which specifically targeted the argument roles of the ambiguous NPs), the high working memory group showed the processing disadvantage that was observed for the Dutch native speakers in both experiments: slowing down following disambiguation when the number information on the auxiliary verb (*heeft/hebben*, 'has/have') forced the dispreferred object-first (8b) interpretation. Furthermore, the high working memory bilinguals patterned together with the low working memory native speakers in that the effects of the dispreferred object-relative clause were in evidence during the on-line processing of the short items (8a, b), but not with 'long' conditions, in which a padding phrase was inserted (*die de conducteurs na het ongeluk met de trein heeft/hebben* . . . , 'who the guards *after the accident with the train* has/have . . .) to create 'heavier' versions of the subject- (8a) and object-relative conditions (8b). These long conditions (1) elicited lower accuracy scores for both groups, and (2) on-line subject-first preference effects only in the high working memory native speakers.

Therefore, even when L1 and the L2 are maximally comparable, in the absence of biasing lexical-semantic information (both the NPs were animate and equally semantically able to be subjects or objects) or disambiguating case-marking information prior to syntactic disambiguation, bilinguals may fail to build up the argument structure and make an on-line commitment to a particular analysis during real-time processing. However, at least under explicit task conditions, and for those of higher working memory capacity, bilinguals can process the input like (some) native speakers, which argues against a fundamental difference for bilingual processing (cf., Clahsen & Felser, 2006a; see Indefrey, 2006a).

Investigating learners' on-line commitments further, Jackson and Roberts (2010) presented German-Dutch bilinguals with very similar sentences to those in Havik et al. (9) and found that manipulating the animacy of one of the NPs pushed the learners to incrementally assign grammatical/thematic roles during real-time processing.

(9) a. Voor de kinderen is de clown, die de taarten heeft gegooid, het hoogtepunt van de voorstelling.
(SubjRC, animate subject)
'For the children the clown, that threw the pies, was the highlight of the performance.'

b. Voor de kinderen is de clown, die de taarten hebben geraakt, het hoogtepunt van de voorstelling.
(ObjRC, inanimate subject)
'For the children the clown, that the pies hit, was the highlight of the performance.'

As found with the native Dutch speakers (as well as those in an earlier monolingual study, Mak, Vonk, & Schriefers, 2006), there was not an across-the-board parsing preference for subject-first relative clauses, nor did the bilinguals appear to construct relative clauses on the basis of animacy information alone, as might be predicted if bilinguals over-rely on semantic cues (cf., Clahsen & Felser, 2006a). Rather, both groups made parsing decisions on the basis of an interaction between topic-hood and animacy information.[2] Specifically, it was only in the conditions in which the first NP was animate that the participants appeared to build a relative clause: with much higher reading times for an object- (9b) than for a subject-relative (9a) clause, arguably reflecting reanalysis in the former case, suggesting that a subject-relative clause was expected when NP1 was animate, which led to reading-time increases when the dispreferred object relative had to be constructed. This was observed on the auxiliary (*heeft*) and the participle (*gegooid/geraakt*) for the learners, but only on the participle for the native speakers.

In contrast, in the conditions in which the first NP was inanimate, no processing difficulty was observed for either subject (10a) or object constructions (10b) for either group (as also observed in Mak et al., 2006).

(10) a. Voor de kinderen zijn de taarten, die de clown hebben geraakt, het hoogtepunt van de voorstelling.
(SubjRC, inanimate subject)
'For the children the pies, that hit the clown, were the highlight of the performance.'

b. Voor de kinderen zijn de taarten, die de clown heeft gegooid, het hoogtepunt vande voorstelling.
(ObjRC, animate subject)
'For the children the pies, that the clown threw, were the highlight of the performance.'

Bilinguals are, therefore, able to build argument structure in real time in the absence of the lexical (subcategorising) verb and disambiguating case-marking information, if provided with sufficient lexical-semantic biasing information to do so, and arguably applying the same processing procedures to those of native speakers.

Processing relative clause attachment ambiguities

Another construction used to investigate bilingual sentence processing is the relative clause attachment ambiguity (11). Given observed cross-linguistic differences in native speakers' resolution preferences, the construction is used to examine the transfer of parsing preferences. That is, speakers of some languages prefer the first NP of the antecedent complex to host the modifying relative clause (*the servant was on the balcony*, e.g., Greek, German, French, Spanish) and others the second NP (*the actress was on the balcony*, e.g., English, Norwegian) (see Papadopoulou, 2006 for an overview).

(11) Someone shot the servant of the actress who was on the balcony.

In a set of self-paced reading studies with either English or Greek as the target language, no reading-time differences with a genitive complex NP antecedent (12) were found when bilinguals were forced to resolve the ambiguity towards the NP favoured either in their L1 or in the L2 (Felser, Roberts, Marinis, & Gross, 2003; Papadopoulou & Clahsen, 2003).

(12) The dean called to the students of (with) the professor who was (were) in the hall.

This was the case even when the learners' L1 and the L2 exhibited the same (NP1) parsing preference, which is striking given that positive transfer from the L1 to the L2 could have, but did not occur (Spanish–, Russian–, and German–Greek bilinguals, Papadopoulou & Clahsen, 2003). However, when the antecedent complex contained a thematic preposition, then a robust on-line preference (NP2) was obtained (e.g., *with*, Felser, Clahsen et al., 2003; *next to*, Roberts, 2003; *me* 'with', Papadopoulou & Clahsen, 2003). These authors assume that native speakers' parsing of these relative clause adjuncts is guided by structural principles: Predicate Proximity, which states that for NP1 languages, attachment to the host closest to the main predicate is preferred (Gibson, Pearlmutter, Canseco-Gonzalez, & Hickok, 1996); and a locality constraint for NP2 preference languages like English such as Recency (Gibson et al., 1996) or Late Closure (Frazier, 1978) which pushes the parser to attach new material to the most recent and structurally lower attachment sites. These structurally based parsing principles apply in cases only with genitive complex NP antecedents (whether morphologically marked as in Greek or with a case-assigning preposition, such as *of* in English). On the further assumption that a lexical preposition restricts the processing domain to its immediately following constituents thus leaving NP2 as the only option for modification (*with the actress*, cf., Frazier & Clifton, 1996) and that, like native speakers, L2 learners are sensitive to this, the authors argue that bilinguals' processing differs from native speakers' in that they do not employ structural parsing procedures, but are able to make use of lexical–thematic information.

However, there are other studies in which on-line preferences have indeed been observed with genitive constructions, and many indicate an important role for proficiency and/or exposure to the L2 (e.g., Dussias, 2003, 2004; Fernández, 1999; Miyao & Omaki, 2006). For instance, using the eye-tracking methodology, Dussias and Sagarra (2007) found that Spanish–English bilinguals with little exposure (9 months) to the target language transferred their first language NP1 preference to the L2, whereas a group with more extensive exposure (5 years) exhibited an NP2 attachment preference, like native English speakers. Similarly, Frenck-Mestre (2002) found those English– and Spanish–French bilinguals who had been resident in France for 5 years showed native-like NP1 attachment preferences. Furthermore, although experience with the L2 may be important, there is evidence that with a biasing preceding discourse context, target-like preferences can be observed even with low proficient bilinguals (cf., English classroom-learners of French, Dekydtspotter, Donaldson, Edmonds, Liljestrand Fultz, & Petrush, 2008).

Given these findings, it may be that the Greek and German groups in the Felser et al. study were 'on their way' to NP2 target-like parsing preferences (e.g., Hernandez, Bates, & Avila, 1994), as predicted by exposure-based accounts like the Tuning Hypothesis (Mitchell & Cuetos, 1991), thus showing a preference for neither NP1 nor NP2. However, this explanation has more trouble accounting for the findings where both the native and target languages of the bilinguals share the same preferences, as was found in Papadopoulou and Clahsen (2003) (also Havik et al., 2009), particularly as their knowledge of Greek morphology and relative clause constructions was established independently.

The mixed results found for the processing of these relative clause constructions is in stark contrast to the more consistent findings for constructions such as subject–object ambiguities and *wh*-filler-gap sentences, reported above. It may be that what underlies these differences is that the phenomenon focused on in the former is a non-obligatory constituent (a relative clause adjunct) and, as such, is open to more flexible interpretation than obligatory arguments (cf., e.g., the Construal Hypothesis, Frazier & Clifton, 1996). This idea is supported by findings from EEG studies[3] on bilinguals' processing of syntactic versus semantic violations. Specifically, it has been observed that syntax-related components (LAN, P600) – although less in evidence across studies than semantic components (N400) – are more consistently elicited by structural violations involving obligatory constituents in contrast to optional ones (e.g., *Das Eis wurde im ___ gegessen*, 'The ice-cream was in-the eaten', Hahne & Friederici, 2001 versus *Le chauffeur qui est dans la ___ dort*, 'The driver who is in the ___ is sleeping', Isel, 2007). This is most likely because there are stronger parsing expectations in the case of obligatory constituents (Isel, 2007), in contrast to optional constituents, where more factors (discourse-pragmatic, frequency, etc.) contribute to the interpretation, which may make on-line interpretation more problematic for bilinguals.

Applying grammatical knowledge during on-line processing

The data from the above studies show that although bilinguals have little trouble employing on-line lexical-semantic information – like plausibility (e.g., Roberts & Felser, 2011), animacy (e.g., Jackson & Roberts, 2010), subcategorisation (e.g., Juffs & Harrington, 1996), and verb bias information (e.g., Dussias & Cramer Scaltz, 2008) – incremental processing, linking a dislocated constituent with its subcategoriser and recovering from syntactic misanalysis become problematic the more structurally complex the input, the lower the level of proficiency, and the less the comprehenders' attention is drawn to grammatical information by task requirements. This suggests that bilinguals have specific difficulty with grammatical processing, even when the requisite knowledge is in place. Indeed, the central debate in the bilingual sentence processing literature relates to grammatical processing. Specifically, researchers ask whether differences in parsing between native speakers and bilinguals reflect a qualitative or fundamental difference as proposed in the SSH (Clahsen & Felser, 2006a, b), or are such differences better attributed to quantitative factors such as differences in proficiency level, cognitive capacity, and processing speed. This debate parallels that found in the field of L2 acquisition (Slabakova, 2009), where the question centres on whether learners who have acquired their L2 after puberty can ever acquire grammatical knowledge to a native-like level (assuming a critical period for language acquisition, cf., Lenneberg, 1967). Many researchers in the L2 sentence-processing field (tacitly or overtly) assume a structurally based processor with a modular architecture. A distinction is made between the grammar and the parser, and researchers focus on the extent to which bilinguals have access to and make use of (abstract) syntactic information during on-line processing, once they have shown evidence of grammatical knowledge of the phenomenon. For example, Marinis, Roberts, Felser, and Clahsen (2005) report a self-paced reading study in which the integration of the fronted object *the nurse* with the embedded verb *angered* in (13a) was facilitated for native English speakers by the availability of a purported intermediate syntactic gap at the clause boundary (e_i'), compared to object-extraction sentences of the same length that did not contain an intermediate gap (13b) (see also Gibson & Warren, 2004), since reading times were faster following *angered* in (13a) than in (13b).

(13) a. The nurse [who$_i$ the doctor argued [e_i' that the rude patient had angered e_i]] is refusing to work late.

b. The nurse [who$_i$ the doctor's argument about the rude patient had angered e_i] is refusing to work late.

The native speakers appeared to activate the fronted constituent at the grammatically determined position, and this re-activated it in memory and made it more easily available for integration with the verb (*angered*) in (13a) in comparison to (13b).[4]

Even though the bilinguals were able to comprehend the sentences, no difference was observed in the processing cost of the two conditions for any of the bilingual groups that they tested – even those in whose L1 relative clause constructions are formed in the same way (Greek, German versus Japanese, Chinese). That is, a dependency was formed on-line between the fronted constituent (*the nurse*) and the subcategorising verb (*had angered*) – as evidenced by processing difficulty relative to additional non-extraction conditions that were tested – but no use was made of any structurally determined intermediate position. Similarly, in a cross-modal priming study, Felser and Roberts (2007) examined whether the fronted indirect object (*peacock*) in object relative clauses like (14) would be re-activated at the structurally appropriate gap site (#1) for advanced Greek L2 learners of English.

(14)   John saw the peacock to which the small penguin gave the #2 nice birthday present #1 in the garden.

The participants listened to sentences presented auditorily and then made an alive/not-alive discrimination decision to an identical (*peacock*) or unrelated picture (*carrot*) that was presented either at the gap site (#1) or at a position earlier in the sentence (#2). Like native participants in an earlier study (Roberts, Marinis, Felser, & Clahsen, 2007), the learners responded faster to the identical target (*peacock*) than to the unrelated target, but critically, for the bilinguals this was the case at both positions (#1) and (#2), suggesting that the argument was maintained in memory throughout the processing of the sentence. In contrast, the natives showed facilitation for the fronted object only at the grammatically appropriate position (#1) (see also Love, Mass, & Swinney, 2003).

Arguing against qualitative differences between bilingual and native speaker processing, some researchers claim that parallel effects to those of native speakers could be observed with sentences like (14) if the bilinguals had been given enough time (e.g., Dekydtspotter, Schwartz, & Sprouse, 2006), particularly given the findings in the bilingual processing literature that there are often speed and/or efficiency differences in general (e.g., Fender, 2001; Hoover & Dwivedi, 1998; Hopp, 2006; 2010; Jiang, 2004, 2007). Indeed, the L2 learners in the Felser et al. study were not tested at later points in the sentence. However, the finding in Felser and Roberts (2007) that the learners re-activated the fronted element at the earlier, control position, argues against the idea that re-activation effects would have become visible later.

Clahsen and Felser (2006a) argue that these and other results showing non-native-like syntactic processing irrespective of L1 background (e.g., Williams et al., 2001) or limited processing resources (Juffs, 2005), together with the relative clause attachment data that indicate learners are less able to apply structural processing principles on-line (Felser et al., 2003; Papadopoulou & Clahsen, 2003) support the SSH.

Debate on this topic also centres on the extent to which bilinguals are sensitive to grammatical constraints like those purported to govern the interpretation of *wh*-constructions. Evidence against (a strong version of) the SSH comes from studies in which it is demonstrated that, like native speakers (e.g., Traxler & Pickering, 1996), bilinguals do not attempt to link a *wh*-filler inside a relative clause island (15a), as shown in the total reading times in an eye-tracking study with German and Chinese L2 learners of English by Cunnings, Batterham, Felser, and Clahsen (2010). Both the native speakers and bilinguals attempted to integrate the filler (*book/city*) with the first available subcategoriser (*wrote*) only in the non-island sentences (15b), with longer fixation durations when this resulted in an implausible dependency (*wrote the city* versus *wrote the book*), but, critically, there was no effect of the plausibility of the filler, for either group.

(15) a. Everyone liked the book (city) that the author who **wrote continuously** and with exceptionally great skill **saw whilst** waiting for a contract.
(island condition)

b. Everyone liked the book (city) that the author **wrote continuously** and with exceptionally great skill **about whilst** waiting for a contract.
(non-island condition)

The L2 learners, therefore – and irrespective of the typological closeness of their first language (German/Chinese) – respected relative clause islands, prohibiting the establishment of filler-gap dependencies within them (see also, Omaki & Schulz, 2011; Juffs, 2005, Juffs & Harrington, 1995). Similarly to the results of the studies on filler-gap processing in multiple clauses reported above (e.g., Jackson & Bobb, 2009), only the native speakers showed evidence of on-line recovery, with higher reading times where the dependency was ultimately resolved (*saw whilst/about whilst*) for items which had initially led to a plausible interpretation (*wrote the book*). For the bilinguals, there was no effect of plausibility at this position, with overall reading times higher for the island versus the non-island conditions.

These results go against predictions of the SSH, but only if one assumes that island constraints are grammatical in nature (cf., the Subjacency Condition, Chomsky, 1973). However, there is debate in both the syntax and the processing literature as to whether island effects are best accounted for in terms of grammatical constraints applied on hierarchical representations which restrict the parser's search domain for a gap (e.g., Phillips, 2006; Traxler & Pickering, 1996; Stowe, 1989; Wagers & Phillips, 2009), or whether they reflect processing difficulties encountered at the clause boundary of the second relative clause (*who wrote*) as the parser attempts to link a filler NP (e.g., *the author*) with the relative pronoun while keeping the filler (*the book*) active in memory (e.g., Kleunder, 1998, 2004). This problem with definition highlights one difficulty in the attempt to falsify the SSH: many of the proposed structural phenomena and/or parsing procedures examined could be argued to reflect processing rather than grammatical constraints.

Referential processing

The fact that bilinguals may have difficulty in general with grammatical processing is also in evidence in the results of studies looking at how bilinguals establish dependencies on-line between pronominals and their potential antecedents, which suggest that integrating syntactic knowledge with knowledge from other sources (e.g., discourse-pragmatic) may cause processing disruption in comparison to native speakers. For example, Felser and Cunnings (2012) investigated whether Japanese and German L2 learners of English – who had been shown via a judgment task to have acquired the locality requirement of English reflexive pronouns – would establish the dependency between a reflexive pronoun and its antecedent (16) like native English speakers. That is, immediately linking a reflexive anaphor with only a grammatically appropriate or *binding-accessible* NP (*Richard*) and not an inappropriate NP (*John/Jane*) in the earlier discourse (Sturt, this volume; Nicol & Swinney, 1989), but at a later stage possibly considering inappropriate but discourse-prominent antecedents (Sturt, 2003; Badecker & Straub, 2002).

(16) John (Jane) and Richard were very worried in the kitchen of the expensive restaurant. *John (Jane)* noticed that Richard had cut *himself* with a very sharp knife.

The native speakers' first-pass fixation times showed an immediate effect of such locality constraints. In contrast, the bilinguals were slower in conditions where the matrix subject – the non-local but discourse-prominent antecedent (John) – matched in gender, even though their final interpretation of the reflexive anaphors was native-like (as also demonstrated in grammaticality judgment tasks). The authors argue that the results support the SSH because both groups of learners' initial analyses are constrained by discourse-level constraints rather than grammatically determined locality conditions, even though German patterns like English (and unlike Japanese) with no long-distance binding permitted.

The fact that bilinguals' on-line interpretation of a referring expression can be disrupted by having a matching competitor antecedent in the discourse, irrespective of the language background of the learners was also observed in an eye-tracking study with Turkish and German learners of Dutch (Roberts, Gullberg, & Indefrey, 2008). In ambiguous contexts ([17a] *Peter/Hans*), the German learners' off-line interpretation for the pronoun patterned like the native Dutch, with an overwhelming preference to resolve to the local antecedent (*Peter*). In contrast, the Turkish participants often resolved the pronoun towards the non-local referent (*Hans*), under the influence of their L1, a null subject language in which an overt pronoun would indicate disjoint, rather than local co-reference.

(17) a. *Peter$_i$ en Hans zitten in het kantoor. Terwijl Peter$_i$ aan het werk is, eet hij$_i$ een boterham.*
'*Peter$_i$ and Hans are in the office. While Peter$_i$ is working, he$_i$ is eating a sandwich.*'

b. *De Werknemers zitten in het kantoor. Terwijl Peter$_i$ aan het werk is, eet hij$_i$ een boterham.*
'The workers are in the office. While *Peter$_i$* is working, *he$_i$* is eating a sandwich.'

Unlike the off-line findings in the Felser and colleagues' studies, there was an L1 influence effect in the learners' ultimate interpretations for the pronouns; however, this L1 effect was not observed in the on-line data. Both the German and Turkish bilinguals took longer to read the subject pronoun (*hij* 'he') in the ambiguous contexts (17a) than when there was only one grammatically available referent for the pronoun (*Peter* [17b]). This was in contrast to the native Dutch, whose reading times were shorter in (17a), arguably because the discourse context (re-introducing a referent) plus the concordant grammatical information in the verb and pronoun facilitated resolution.

Since the learners' L1 can account for the off-line but not for the on-line data, the authors argue that it is the integration of information from multiple sources (e.g., grammatical, discourse-pragmatic) during real-time comprehension that is more problematic for L2 learners than native speakers, and so causes processing slow-downs, even when the L1 and the L2 are typologically closely related (German, Dutch), and irrespective of a comprehender's final interpretation for the pronoun (see also Ellert, Järvikivi, & Roberts, forthcoming).

Accounting for differences between bilingual and native speaker sentence processing

Taken together, the results reported in the above overview show that, like native speakers, bilinguals most often do not wait to integrate each constituent of the input into the emerging parse. Their on-line analyses of the L2 are constrained by subcategorization (e.g., Juffs & Harrington, 1995, 1996) and verb bias information (e.g., Dussias & Cramer Scaltz, 2008), and are affected by plausibility (e.g., Roberts & Felser, 2011) and other semantic factors such as noun animacy (e.g., Jackson & Roberts, 2010). It is when processing across clause boundaries, with more structurally complex sentences in general, and when information from multiple sources must be integrated, that bilinguals' parsing appears to diverge from that of native speakers, even when the specific grammatical knowledge has been independently established.

There is a marked lack of L1 influence on bilinguals' grammatical processing, and so one cannot always attribute L1–L2 processing differences to this factor. That is, the data on syntactic processing show that learners most often pattern together and differently from native speakers – even with a maximally comparable L1 and L2 (e.g., Havik et al., 2009; Jackson & Dussias, 2009; Marinis et al., 2005; Roberts et al., 2008; cf. Juffs, 1998a, b, 2005). Given the findings indicating that lexical information from both languages is active during the processing of either (e.g., Jared & Kroll, 2001) this striking contrast to the subtle L1 transfer effects observed in the domain of lexical-semantics (e.g., Frenck-Mestre & Pynte, 1997; Roberts, 2008) is perhaps unexpected.

As regards the effects of processing capacity limitation, there are mixed results. Overall, there is evidence that bilinguals of lower proficiency and/or working memory capacity have more trouble with grammatical processing, particularly with revision and handling non-local dependencies (e.g., Jackson & Bobb, 2009; Jackson & van Hell, 2011). Processing in one's less dominant language puts a strain on cognitive resources, and so reduced memory span has been observed in L1 versus L2 (Dornič, 1980). Furthermore, the more L2 proficiency/experience increases, the less memory capacity is consumed (Service, Simola, Metsanheimo, & Maury, 2002) and reliable correlations have been found between reading span and phonological memory span scores in the L1 and L2, and with L2 proficiency (Berquist, 1997; Ellis, 1996; Havik et al., 2009; Harrington & Sawyer, 1992; Miyake & Friedman, 1998; Osaka & Osaka, 1992). However, working memory has often been treated as a variable to be controlled for (e.g., Felser & Roberts, 2007; Jackson & Roberts, 2010) rather than one for explicit investigation to explain differences in bilinguals' real-time parsing, which may explain the mixed findings (see Juffs & Harrington, 2011), as too might the fact that the role of working memory in monolingual sentence comprehension is controversial (Baddeley, 2003; Traxler, Williams, Blozis, & Morris, 2005; Waters & Caplan, 1996).

Bilingual parsing may also be affected by processing speed; i.e., differences in the time taken for lexical access, the accessing of syntactic rules, applying semantic interpretation, and so on, to the language input. Processing speed, like working memory capacity, also tends to correlate with proficiency. Bilinguals are often almost twice as slow at reading (e.g., Fender, 2001; Kilborn, 1992), and even more so if having to read in a different script (Juffs, 2005; Marinis et al., 2005). However, despite sometimes showing delayed and/or prolonged effects (e.g., Frenck-Mestre, 2002, 2005; Hopp, 2006; Jackson, 2008), being slower does not appear to qualitatively affect bilinguals' processing procedures. In fact, it may be that because bilinguals are slower than native speakers, some effects that are not visible during monolingual processing show up with bilinguals (e.g., for 'easy' English GP sentences: Roberts & Felser, 2011; on the auxiliary preceding the thematic verb in L2 Dutch, Jackson & Roberts, 2010).

Differences between children's and adult native speakers' sentence processing (over-use of bottom-up grammatical information at the expense of discourse-pragmatics, e.g., Traxler, 2002) has been attributed to children's lack of processing resources, thus to differences in cognitive capacity between adults and children. Therefore, the lack of cognitive capacity effects obverved in bilingual sentence processing has been taken as evidence by proponents of the SSH that L2 learners' processing is fundamentally different from that of native speakers.

However, as reported above, with bilinguals, working memory is tightly correlated with other factors and it is not clear how these affect processing individually, nor in combination with each other. One SSH prediction is that native speakers of lower processing capacity should also shallow process. It is possible that such speakers are less able to predict upcoming material, furthermore it is possible that it is *both* incremental processing *and* creating expectations of the input on the basis of current analyses that is the problem, and this would also be interesting to test with a bilingual population.

The fact that at least under some circumstances bilinguals apply parsing procedures similarly to natives argues against a qualitative difference account (cf., the SSH) for bilingual processing (Indefrey, 2006a). For instance, performing metalinguistic tasks as well as comprehending a sentence can enable bilinguals to attend to the details of the input, and, under these conditions, they often show parallel parsing performance to native speakers (Havik et al., 2009; Hopp, 2006; Jackson & Bobb, 2009; Juffs & Harrington, 1995, 1996; Juffs, 2005; Williams et al., 2001).

The SSH as a fundamental difference hypothesis is also weakened by the findings that native speakers may shallow parse under certain circumstances (cf., 'chunking', Abney, 1991), and may perform 'Good Enough' analyses: as evidenced by the findings that even when confronted with contradictory syntactic evidence, native speakers may sometimes be unable to revise a strongly plausible initial misanalysis (e.g., Christianson, Hollingworth, Halliwell, & Ferreira, 2001; Ferreira, Bailey, & Ferraro, 2002). Furthermore, Townsend and Bever (2001) suggest that comprehenders apply simple heuristics to the input as well as performing full parsing using the grammar. Given the findings reviewed above, it appears that such shallow parsing is relied on more in bilingual processing, specifically in the absence of an accompanying metalinguistic task, rather than it being the only parsing option available, as assumed by the SSH (see e.g., Gillen Dowens & Carreiras, 2006; and supporting hemodynamic data, Indefrey, 2006b).

Conclusion

Although bilingual sentence processing has only recently become a topic of interest, researchers are beginning to build a picture of how bilinguals comprehend the L2 input in real time in comparison to native speakers. However fundamental these differences may be, it is clear that it is grammatical processing that differs between bilingual and native speaker parsing. The above overview indicates that different processing modes may be in operation, and that if bilinguals are motivated to pay attention to the morpho-syntactic details of the input and given high enough proficiency and/or cognitive capacity, they can perform deep on-line analyses. Otherwise, their processing is shallower than that of native speakers.

One of the many questions that remain concerns the role of parsing in the learning process. Some work has looked at how sensitive lower-proficiency learners are to morpho-syntactic information (e.g., Keating, 2009; Schimke, 2009; Tokowicz & MacWhinney, 2005), but there is very little work on how parsing the input helps to develop linguistic knowledge in either L1 or L2 (see Dekydtspotter, Kim, et al., 2008 and Fodor, 1998, for discussion; also Osterhout & colleagues, e.g., McLaughlin, Tanner, Pitkänen, Frenck-Mestre, Inoue, K., Valentine, & Osterhout, 2010, on EEG findings of the grammaticalisation process in L2 acquisition), yet this is an important topic, given that learners at some point must parse the input with limited grammatical knowledge. It is hoped that such future work – with that on the effects individual difference factors such as cognitive capacity and proficiency/exposure – will shed light on the human sentence-processing mechanism in general, and thus will be of great interest to researchers in the fields of both language acquisition and sentence processing.

Notes

1. Most of the studies reported in this overview focus on 'late' L2 learners, that is, those acquiring the L2 after puberty, rather than 'simultaneous' bilinguals who acquire two languages from birth. The terms 'bilingual' and 'second language learner' are used interchangeably throughout, and where the participants differ from this post-childhood learner group, it is noted in the text.
2. These results argue against both a syntax-first account of the parsing of relative clauses, e.g., the Active Filler Strategy (e.g., Frazier, 1987), which predicts that a subject-relative is built independently of semantic information and memory-load accounts, which would predict that object relative clauses are more computationally costly (e.g., Gibson, 1998). The results (as well as those of Mak et al., 2006) are more in line with a constraint-based (e.g., Gibson, Desmet, Grodner, Watson, & Ko, 2005; Kaan, 2001) or statistical frequency-based account (e.g., Desmet, De Baecke, Drieghe, Brysbaert, & Vonk, 2006).
3. See van Hell and Tokowicz (2010) for a recent overview of EEG findings in bilingual sentence processing.
4. The authors assume a trace-based account, for other theoretical accounts of this phenomenon see Gibson and Warren (2004).

References

Abney, S. (1991). Parsing by chunks. In R. Berwick, S. Abney, & C. Tenny (Eds.), *Principle-based parsing* (pp. 257–278). Dordrecht, The Netherlands: Kluwer.

Baddeley, A. (2003). Working memory and language: An overview. *Journal of Communication Disorders*, 36, 189–208.

Bader, M., & Meng, M. (1999). Subject–object ambiguities in German embedded clauses: An across-the-board comparison. *Journal of Psycholinguistic Research*, 28, 121–143.

Badecker, W., & Straub, K. (2002). The processing role of structural constraints on the interpretation of pronouns and anaphors. *Journal of Experimental Psychology: Learning, Memory, and Cognition*, 28, 748–769.

Berquist, B. (1997). Individual differences in working memory span and L2 proficiency: Capacity or processing efficiency? In A. Sorace, C. Heycock, & R. Shillcock (Eds.), *Proceedings of the GALA '97 conference on Language Acquisition* (pp. 468–473). Edinburgh: Human Communication Research Centre, University of Edinburgh.

Boland, J. E., Tanenhaus, M. K., Garnsey, S., & Carlson, G. N. (1995). Verb argument structure in parsing and interpretation: Evidence from *wh*-questions. *Journal of Memory and Language*, 34, 774–806.

Carlson, G., & Tanenhaus, M. (1988). Thematic roles and language comprehension. In W. Wilkins (Ed.), *Syntax and Semantics. Thematic Relations*, Vol. 21 (pp. 263–89). New York: Academic Press.

Chomsky, N. (1973). Conditions on transformations. In S. R. Anderson and P. Kiparsky (Eds.), *A Festschrift for Morris Halle* (pp. 232–286). New York: Holt, Rinehart & Winston.

Christianson, K., Hollingworth, A., Halliwell, J., & Ferreira, F. (2001). Thematic roles assigned along the garden path linger. *Cognitive Psychology*, 42, 368–407.

Clahsen, H., & Felser, C. (2006a). Grammatical processing in language learners. *Applied Psycholinguistics*, 27, 3–42.

Clahsen, H., & Felser, C. (2006b). How native-like is non-native language processing? *Trends in Cognitive Sciences*, 10, 564–570.

Clifton, C. Jr. (1993). Thematic roles in sentence parsing. *Canadian Journal of Experimental Psychology*, *47*, 222–246.
Cunnings, I., Batterham, C., Felser, C., & Clahsen, H. (2010). Constraints on L2 learners' processing of *wh*-dependencies: Evidence from eye-movements. In B. VanPatten & J. Jegerski (Eds.), *Research in second language processing and parsing* (pp. 87–110). Amsterdam: John Benjamins.
Dekydtspotter, L., Donaldson, B., Edmonds, A. C., Liljestrand Fultz, A. L., & Petrush, R. A. (2008). Syntactic and prosodic computations in the resolution of relative clause attachment ambiguity by English-French learners. *Studies in Second Language Acquisition*, *30*, 453–480.
Dekydtspotter, L., Kim, B., Kim, H. J., Wang, Y.-T., Kim, H.-K., & Lee, J. K. (2008). Intermediate traces and anaphora resolution in the processing of English as a second language. In H. Chan, E. Jacob, & E. Kapia (Eds.), *Proceedings of BUCLD 32* (Vol. 1, 84–95). Somerville, MA: Cascadilla Press.
Dekydtspotter, L., Schwartz. B., & Sprouse, R. A. (2006). The comparative fallacy in L2 processing research. In M. G. O'Brien, C. Shea, & J. Archibald (Eds.), *Proceedings from the 8th Generative Approaches to Second Language Acquisition Conference (GASLA 2006)* (pp. 33–40). Somerville, MA: Cascadilla Proceedings Project.
Desmet, T., De Baecke, C., Drieghe, D., Brysbaert, M., & Vonk, W. (2006). Relative clause attachment in Dutch: On-line comprehension corresponds to corpus frequencies when lexical variables are taken into account. *Language and Cognitive Processes*, *21*, 453–485.
De Vincenzi, M. (1991). *Syntactic parsing strategies in Italian*. Dordrecht: Kluwer Academic Publishers.
Dornič, S. (1980). Language dominance, spare capacity and perceived effort in bilinguals. *Ergonomics*, *23*, 369–377.
Dussias, P. E. (2003). Syntactic ambiguity resolution in L2 learners. *Studies in Second Language Acquisition*, *25*, 529–557.
Dussias, P. E. (2004). Parsing a first language like a second: The erosion of L1 parsing strategies in Spanish-English bilinguals. *International Journal of Bilingualism*, *8*, 355–371.
Dussias, P. E., & Cramer Scaltz, T. R. (2008). Spanish-English L2 speakers' use of subcategorization bias information in the resolution of temporary ambiguity during second language reading. *Acta Psychologica*, *128*, 501–513.
Dussias, P. E., & Piñar, P. (2010). Effects of reading span and plausibility in the reanalysis of *wh*-gaps by Chinese-English L2 speakers. *Second Language Research*, *26*, 443–472.
Dussias, P. E., & Sagarra, N. (2007). The effect of exposure on syntactic parsing in Spanish-English bilinguals. *Bilingualism: Language and Cognition*, *10*, 101–116.
Ellert, M., Järvikivi, J., & Roberts, L. (forthcoming). Resolving ambiguous pronouns in a second language: A visual-world eye-tracking study in L2 German and Dutch. *International Review of Applied Linguistics*.
Ellis, N. C. (1996). Phonological memory, chunking and points of order. *Studies in Second Language Acquisition*, *18*, 91–126.
Felser, C., Clahsen, H., & Münte, T. F. (2003). Storage and integration in the processing of filler-gap dependencies: An ERP study of topicalization and *wh*-movement in German. *Brain and Language*, *87*, 345–354.
Felser, C., & Cunnings, I. (2012). Processing reflexives in a second language: The timing of structural and discourse-level information. *Applied Psycholinguistics*, *33*, 571–603.

Felser, C., & Roberts, L. (2007). Processing *wh*-dependencies in a second language: A cross-modal priming study. *Second Language Research, 23,* 9–36.

Felser, C., Roberts, R., Marinis, T., & Gross, R. (2003). The processing of ambiguous sentences by first and second language learners of English. *Applied Psycholinguistics, 24,* 453–489.

Fender, M. (2001). A review of L1 and L2/ESL word integration skills and the nature of L2/ESL word integration development involved in lower-level text processing. *Language Learning, 51,* 319–396.

Fernández, E. M. (1999). Processing strategies in second language acquisition: Some preliminary results. In E. Klein & G. Martohardjano (Eds.), *The development of second language grammars: A generative approach* (pp. 217–240). Amsterdam: John Benjamins.

Ferreira, F., Bailey, K., & Ferraro, V. (2002). Good enough representations in language comprehension. *Current Directions in Psychological Science, 11,* 11–15.

Fiebach, C., Schlesewsky, M., & Friederici, A. (2002). Separating syntactic memory costs and syntactic integration costs during parsing: The processing of German *wh*-questions. *Journal of Memory and Language, 47,* 250–272.

Fodor, J. D. (1998). Learning to parse? *Journal of Psycholinguistic Research, 27,* 285–319.

Frazier, L. (1978). *On comprehending sentences: Syntactic parsing strategies.* Doctoral Dissertation, University of Connecticut.

Frazier, L. (1987). Sentence processing: A tutorial review. In M. Coltheart (Ed.). *Attention and performance XII: The psychology of reading.* Hillsdale, NJ: Erlbaum.

Frazier, L., & Clifton, C. (1996). *Construal.* Cambridge, MA: MIT Press.

Frazier, L., & Flores d'Arcais, G. B. (1989). Filler-driven parsing: A study of gap filling in Dutch. *Journal of Memory and Language, 28,* 331–344.

Frenck-Mestre, C. (2002). An on-line look at sentence processing in the second language. In R. Heredia & J. Altaribba (Eds.), *Bilingual sentence processing* (pp. 217–236). Amsterdam: Elsevier.

Frenck-Mestre, C. (2005). Ambiguities and anomalies: What can eye-movements and event-related potentials reveal about second language processing? In J. F. Kroll & A. M. B. de Groot (Eds.), *Handbook of bilingualism* (pp. 268–284). Oxford: Oxford University Press.

Frenck-Mestre, C., & Pynte, J. (1997). Syntactic ambiguity resolution while reading in second and native languages. *Quarterly Journal of Experimental Psychology, Section A: Human Experimental Psychology, 50A,* 119–148.

Friederici, A. D., & Frisch, S. (2000). Verb-argument structure processing: The role of verb-specific and argument-specific information. *Journal of Memory and Language, 43,* 476–507.

Gibson, E. (1998). Linguistic complexity: Locality of syntactic dependencies. *Cognition, 68,* 1–76.

Gibson, E., Desmet, T., Grodner, D., Watson, D., & Ko, K. (2005). Reading relative clauses in English. *Cognitive Linguistics, 16,* 313–353.

Gibson, E., Pearlmutter, N., Canseco-Gonzalez, E., & Hickok, G. (1996). Recency preference in the human sentence processing mechanism. *Cognition, 59,* 21–39.

Gibson, E., & Warren, T. (2004). Reading-time evidence for intermediate linguistic structure in long-distance dependencies. *Syntax, 7,* 55–78.

Gillen Dowens, G., & Carreiras, M. (2006). The shallow structure hypothesis of second language sentence processing: What is restricted and why? *Applied Psycholinguistics, 27,* 49–52.

Gorrell, P. (1995). *Syntax and parsing.* Cambridge: Cambridge University Press.
Hahne, A., & Friederici, A. (2001). Processing a second language: Late learners' comprehension mechanisms as revealed by event-related brain potentials. *Bilingualism: Language and Cognition, 4*, 123–141.
Harrington, M., & Sawyer, M. (1992). L2 working memory and L2 reading skill. *Studies in Second Language Acquisition, 14*, 25–38.
Havik, E., Roberts, L., van Hout, R., Schreuder, R., & Haverkort, M. (2009). Processing subject-object ambiguities in the L2: A self-paced reading study with German L2 learners of Dutch. *Language Learning, 59*, 73–112.
Hernandez, A. E., Bates, E. A., & Avila, L. X. (1994). On-line sentence interpretation in Spanish-English bilinguals: What does it mean to be 'in between'? *Applied Psycholinguistics, 15*, 417–446.
Hoover, M. L., & Dwivedi, V. D. (1998). Syntactic processing in skilled bilinguals. *Language Learning, 48*, 1–29.
Hopp, H. (2006). Syntactic features and reanalysis in near-native processing. *Second Language Research, 22*, 369–397.
Hopp, H. (2010). Ultimate attainment in L2 inflectional morphology: Performance similarities between non-native and native speakers. *Lingua, 120*, 901–931.
Indefrey, P. (2006a). It is time to work toward explicit processing models for native and second language speakers. *Applied Psycholinguistics, 27*, 66–69.
Indefrey, P. (2006b). A meta-analysis of hemodynamic studies on first and second language processing: Which suggested differences can we trust and what do they mean? *Language Learning, 56(1)*, 279–304.
Isel, F. (2007). Syntactic and referential processes in second-language learners: Event-related brain potential evidence. *Neuroreport, 18*, 1885–1889.
Jackson, C. N. (2008). Proficiency level and the interaction of lexical and morphosyntactic information during L2 sentence processing. *Language Learning, 58*, 875–909.
Jackson, C. N., & Bobb, S. C. (2009). The processing and comprehension of *wh*-questions among second language speakers of German. *Applied Psycholinguistics, 30*, 603–636.
Jackson, C. N., & Dussias, P. E. (2009). Cross-linguistic differences and their impact on L2 sentence processing. *Bilingualism: Language and Cognition, 12*, 65–82.
Jackson, C. N., & van Hell, J. G. (2011). The effects of L2 proficiency level on the processing of *wh*-questions among Dutch second language speakers of English. *International Review of Applied Linguistics, 49*, 195–219.
Jackson, C., & Roberts, L. (2010). Animacy affects the processing of subject-object ambiguities in L2 processing: Evidence from self-paced reading with German L2 learners of Dutch. *Applied Psycholinguistics, 31*, 671–691.
Jared, D., & Kroll, J. F. (2001). Do bilinguals activate phonological representations in one or both of their languages when naming words? *Journal of Memory and Language, 44*, 2–31.
Jiang, N. (2004). Morphological insensitivity in second language processing. *Applied Psycholinguistics, 25*, 603–634.
Jiang, N. (2007). Selective integration of linguistic knowledge in adult second language learning. *Language Learning, 57*, 1–33.
Juffs, A. (1998a). Main verb versus reduced relative clause ambiguity resolution in L2 sentence processing. *Language Learning, 48*, 107–147.
Juffs, A. (1998b). Some effects of first language argument structure and syntax on second language processing. *Second Language Research, 14*, 406–424.

Juffs, A. (2004). Representation, processing, and working memory in a second language. *Transactions of the Philological Society, 102*, 199–225.

Juffs, A. (2005). The influence of first language on the processing of *wh*-movement in English as a second language. *Second Language Research, 21*, 121–151.

Juffs, A. (2006). Processing reduced relative versus main verb ambiguity in English as a second language: A replication study with working memory. In R. Slabakova, S. Montrul, & P. Prevost (Eds.), *Inquiries in Linguistic Development in Honor of Lydia White* (pp. 213–232). Amsterdam: John Benjamins.

Juffs, A., & Harrington, M. (1995). Parsing effects in second language sentence processing: Subject and object asymmetries in *wh*-extraction. *Studies in Second Language Acquisition, 17*, 483–516.

Juffs, A., & Harrington, M. (1996). Garden path sentences and error data in second language processing research. *Language Learning, 46*, 286–324.

Juffs, A., & Harrington, M. (2011). Aspects of working memory in L2 Learning. *Language Teaching: Reviews and Studies, 42*, 2, 137–166.

Kaan, E. (2001). Effects of NP type on the resolution of word-order ambiguities. *Journal of Psycholinguistic Research, 30*, 529–547.

Keating, G. D. (2009). Sensitivity to violations in gender agreement in native and nonnative Spanish: An eye-movement investigation. *Language Learning, 59*, 503–535.

Kilborn, K. (1992). On-line integration of grammatical information in a second language. In R. Harris (Ed.), *Cognitive processing in bilinguals* (pp. 337–350). Elsevier: Amsterdam.

Kluender, R. (1998). On the distinction between strong and weak islands: A processing perspective. In P. Culicover & L. McNally (Eds.), *Syntax and Semantics 29: The limits of syntax* (pp. 241–279). San Diego, CA: Academic Press.

Kluender, R. (2004). Are subject islands subject to a processing account? In V. Chand, A. Kelleher, A. J. Rodríguez, & B. Schmeiser (Eds.), *Proceedings of the 23rd WCCFL*. Somerville, MA: Cascadilla Press.

Konieczny, L., Hemforth, B., Scheepers, C., & Strube, G. (1997). The role of lexical heads in parsing: Evidence from German. *Language and Cognitive Processes, 12*, 307–348.

Lenneberg, E. (1967). *Biological foundations of language*. New York: John Wiley and Sons.

Love, T., Maas, E., & Swinney, D. (2003). The influence of language exposure on lexical and syntactic language processing. *Experimental Psychology, 50*, 204–216.

Mak, W. M., Vonk, W., & Schriefers, H. (2006). Animacy in processing relative clauses: The hikers that rocks crush. *Journal of Memory and Language, 54*, 466–490.

Marinis, T., Roberts, L., Felser, C., & Clahsen, H. (2005). Gaps in second language processing. *Studies in Second Language Acquisition, 27*, 53–78.

McLaughlin, J., Tanner, D., Pitkänen, I., Frenck-Mestre, C., Inoue, K., Valentine, G., & Osterhout, L. (2010). Brain potentials reveal discrete stages of L2 grammatical learning. *Language Learning, 60(2)*, 123–150.

Miyake, A., & Friedman, N. (1998). Individual differences in second language proficiency: Working memory as language aptitude. In A. Healy & L. Bourne (Eds.), *Foreign language learning* (pp. 339–364). Mahwah, NJ: Lawrence Erlbaum.

Miyao, M., & Omaki, A. (2006). No ambiguity about it: Korean learners of Japanese have a clear attachment preference. In D. Bamman, T. Magnitskaia, & C. Zaller (Eds.), *Proceedings of the 30th annual Boston University conference on language development supplement*, 4–6 November, 2005.

Mitchell, D., & Cuetos, F. (1991). The origins of parsing strategies. In C. Smith (Ed.), *Current issues in natural language processing* (pp. 1–12). Center of Cognitive Science, University of Austin, Texas.

Nicol, J., & Swinney, D. (1989). The role of structure in co-reference assignment during sentence comprehension. *Journal of Psycholinguistic Research, 18*, 5–20.

Omaki, A., & Schulz, B. (2011). Filler-gap dependencies and island constraints in second language sentence processing. *Studies in Second Language Acquisition, 33*, 563–588.

Osaka, M., & Osaka, N. (1992). Language-independent working memory as measured by Japanese and English reading span tests. *Bulletin of the Psychonomic Society, 30*, 287–289.

Papadopoulou, D. (2006). *Cross-linguistic variation in sentence processing: Evidence from RC attachment preferences in Greek*. Dordrecht, The Netherlands: Springer.

Papadopoulou, D., & Clahsen, H. (2003). Parsing strategies in L1 and L2 sentence processing: A study of relative clause attachment in Greek. *Studies in Second Language Acquisition, 25*, 501–528.

Phillips, C. (2006). The real-time status of island phenomena. *Language, 82*, 795–823.

Pickering, M., Clifton, C. Jr, & Crocker, M. (2000). Architectures and mechanism in sentence comprehension. In M. Crocker, M. Pickering, & C. Clifton Jr. (Eds.), *Architectures and Mechanisms for Language Processing* (pp. 1–28). Cambridge: Cambridge University Press.

Pickering, M. J., & Traxler, M. J. (1998). Plausibility and recovery from garden-paths: An eye-tracking study. *Journal of Experimental Psychology: Learning, Memory, and Cognition, 24*, 940–961.

Pritchett, B. (1992). *Grammatical competence and parsing performance*. Chicago, IL: University of Chicago Press.

Roberts, L. (2003). Syntactic processing in second language learners. Unpublished Ph.D. Dissertation. University of Essex.

Roberts, L. (2008). Processing temporal constraints and some implications for the investigation of second language sentence processing and acquisition. *Language Learning, 58(1)*, 57–61.

Roberts, L., & Felser, C. (2011). Plausibility and recovery from garden-paths in second language sentence processing. *Applied Psycholinguistics, 32*, 299–331.

Roberts, L., Gullberg, M., & Indefrey, P. (2008). On-line pronoun resolution in L2 discourse: L1 influence and general learner effects. *Studies in Second Language Acquisition, 30*, 333–357.

Roberts, L., Marinis, T., Felser, C., & Clahsen, H. (2007). Antecedent priming at gap positions in children's sentence processing. *Journal of Psycholinguistic Research, 36*, 175–188.

Schimke, S. (2009). The acquisition of finiteness in Turkish learners of German and Turkish learners of French. Unpublished Ph.D. Thesis, Max Planck Institute for Psycholinguistics, The Netherlands.

Schlesewsky, M., Fanselow, G., Kliegl, R., & Krems, J. (2000). The subject preference in the processing of locally ambiguous *wh*-questions in German. In B. Hemforth & L. Konieszny (Eds.), *German sentence processing* (pp. 65–93). Dordrecht: Kluwer.

Schriefers, H., Friederici, A. D., & Kühn, K. (1995). The processing of locally ambiguous relative clauses in German. *Journal of Memory and Language, 34*, 499–520.

Service, E., Simola, M., Metsanheimo, O., & Maury, S. (2002). Bilingual working memory span is affected by language skill. *European Journal of Cognitive Psychology, 14*, 383–408.

Slabakova, R. (2009). The Fundamental Difference Hypothesis twenty years later. *Studies in Second Language Acquisition*, 2. Cambridge: Cambridge University Press.

Stowe, L. (1989). Thematic structures and sentence comprehension. In G. Carlson & M. Tanenhaus (Eds.), *Linguistic structure in language processing*. Dordrecht: Kluwer.

Sturt, P. (2003). The time-course of the application of binding constraints in reference resolution. *Journal of Memory and Language*, *48*, 542–562.

Sturt, P., & Crocker, M. (1996). Monotonic syntactic processing: A cross-linguistic study of attachment and reanalysis. *Language and Cognitive Processes*, *11*, 449–494.

Tokowicz, N., & MacWhinney, B. (2005). Implicit and explicit measures of sensitivity to violations in second language grammar. *Studies in Second Language Acquisition*, *27*, 173–204.

Townsend, D. J., & Bever, T. G. (2001). *Sentence comprehension. The integration of habits and rules*. Cambridge, MA: MIT Press.

Traxler, M. J. (2002). Plausibility and subcategorization preference in children's processing of temporarily ambiguous sentences: Evidence from self-paced reading, *The Quarterly Journal of Experimental Psychology*, *55A*, 75–96.

Traxler, M. J., & Pickering, M. (1996). Plausibility and the processing of unbounded dependencies: An eye-tracking study. *Journal of Memory and Language*, *35*, 454–475.

Traxler, M. J., Williams, R. S., Blozis, S. A., & Morris, R. K. (2005). Working memory, animacy, and verb class in the processing of relative clauses. *Journal of Memory & Language*, *53*, 204–224.

Van Hell, J. G., & Tokowicz, N. (2010). Event-related brain potentials and second language learning: Syntactic processing in late L2 learners at different L2 proficiency levels. *Second Language Research*, *26*, 43–74.

Wagers, M., & Phillips, C. (2009). Multiple dependencies and the role of the grammar in real-time comprehension. *Journal of Linguistics*, *45*, 395–433.

Waters, G. S., & Caplan, D. (1996). The measurement of verbal working memory capacity and its relation to reading comprehension. *Quarterly Journal of Experimental Psychology: Human Experimental Psychology*, *49*, 51–79.

Weinberg, A. (1999). A minimalist theory of human sentence processing. In S. Epstein & N. Hornstein (Eds.), *Working minimalism* (pp. 283–315). Cambridge, MA: MIT Press.

Williams, J. N. (2006). Incremental interpretation in second language sentence processing. *Bilingualism: Language and Cognition*, *9*, 71–81.

Williams, J. N., Möbius, P., & Kim, C. (2001). Native and non-native processing of English *wh*-questions: Parsing strategies and plausibility constraints. *Applied Psycholinguistics*, *22*, 509–540.

10 Syntactically based sentence comprehension in aging and individuals with neurological disease

David Caplan

Introduction

The study of the effects of aging and neurological disease on the ability to use language is of interest for many reasons. From a practical point of view, understanding these changes may help older individuals and those with neurological disease, and the people who interact with them, adapt to changes in their abilities to communicate (and, likely, to formulate certain concepts internally) brought on by changes in their language abilities; it also provides information that can help professionals combat age- and disease-related reductions in language functions. From a theoretical point of view, language abilities may differ in aging and neurological disease from those of young, healthy individuals, whose study has provided most of the data upon which models of language processing have been based, and these differences may provide data that confirm, extend, contradict, or amplify these models.

This review focuses on the comprehension of sentences in which syntactic and interpretive processing are required for understanding. I will briefly outline the questions that have been raised in this research before beginning the review.

In the area of aging, the two major questions that have been raised are whether there is an age-related decline in the ability to structure sentences syntactically and use that structure to determine meaning and, if there is, whether that decline is due to age-related declines in other cognitive functions, in particular verbal working memory (WM). The second question—the relation of any age-related decline in syntactically based comprehension to age-related declines in WM—bears on the issue of whether the verbal WM system tested in laboratory tasks such as complex span, n-back, and others is utilized in the process of syntactic comprehension. Work on patients with Alzheimer's Disease also largely focuses on these questions. In contrast, the main question that has been raised about vascular aphasic patients is what the nature of their disorders in the area of syntactically based comprehension is. Answers to this question have been provided in linguistic and processing terms. A second question that has been raised about these disorders is whether particular disorders arise after damage to particular brain areas. I shall not deal with this second question in this chapter.

The major change that has occurred in how sentence processing is studied is the increasing emphasis on on-line methods in the past 10 years. This change has mostly affected work on aphasia. Until recently, with some notable exceptions, the main evidence regarding aphasic patients' assignment of syntactic structure consisted of end-of-sentence responses in tasks such as sentence–picture matching, grammaticality judgment, and enactment (object manipulation). Inferences were drawn from these end-of-sentence performances about the nature of deficits in on-line parsing and interpretation in these patients. The models based on these data have been called into question by direct on-line observations that I will review below. The literature on parsing and interpretation in aging developed later than that on these processes in patients and relied on on-line measures to a greater extent from its onset. The emphasis on on-line measures leads to two new questions that I shall discuss in the review below.

The first is that, in both the literature on aging and that on disease, on-line measures have been interpreted as indications of on-line parsing and interpretation. The literature on "typical" populations, however, shows that comprehension is incrementally "situated"; that on-line observations reflect the interaction of context with comprehension (Altmann & Kamide, 2007; Farmer, Anderson, & Spivey, 2007; Spivey & Grant, 2005; Tanenhaus, Spivey-Knowlton, Eberhard, & Sedivy, 1995). The incremental use of context makes it necessary to distinguish between the effects of context and those of parsing and interpretation in on-line measures.

One type of context, that has not been studied in young healthy subjects to my knowledge but that recent work suggests is relevant to on-line performance measures in aging and vascular aphasia, is the intentional context set up by task demands. It is clear that task demands affect the operations that a listener/reader must perform: encoding meaning into a short duration memory is needed in verification and not plausibility judgment; mapping meaning onto visual-scene analysis is needed in picture matching and not verification. These operations very likely occur incrementally, raising the possibility that age- and disease-related changes in on-line measures reflect both age- and disease-related changes in parsing and interpretation and changes in the incremental performance of task-related operations. A related question is whether age- and disease-related changes in on-line processing reflect effects of age- and disease-related changes in cognitive functions such as WM capacity on parsing and interpretation or on the performance of task-related operations. These questions have begun to be approached by examining the effect of these factors on performances in different tasks.

A second question is how on-line and end-of-sentence performances are related, and how aging and disease affect their relation. Both the literature on "typical" and "atypical" populations generally assumes that longer on-line processing times are reflections of less efficient processing, but they could also be the result of persistence in performing normally efficient operations or applying operations that are not usually engaged at a given on-line point.

Caplan, DeDe, Waters, Michaud, and Tripodis (2011) suggested an approach to this question based on the relation of on-line processing times to task performance accuracy. This approach is far from perfect—the relation between on-line processing and end-of-sentence performance may be obscured by the many factors that intervene between points of processing during the presentation of a sentence and a response made at the end of the sentence. However, the application of this approach has yielded some suggestive results.

The study of syntactic comprehension in aging, aphasia, and Alzheimer's Disease has thus changed significantly in the past 10 years, and, as the reader must have anticipated, there are many gaps and loose ends in what we know about the issues that have been raised. Although the review that follows points to results that raise more than settle issues, I present it as an indication of where I think studies of these topics are heading. I will begin with age, then turn to disease. In both areas, the review is selective and heavily reliant upon work in my own lab.

Sentence processing and comprehension in aging

The literature provides clear evidence that accuracy on sentence comprehension tasks declines in aging. There are mixed results regarding the effects of age on on-line processing. These can be illustrated in studies using self-paced presentation. Three effects of age on on-line processing times have been reported—increases of on-line processing times at points of demand in aging; decreases in processing times at those points; no effect of age at those points. Illustrative studies are the following.

Stine-Morrow, Ryan, & Leonard (2000) studied sentences with subject and object relative clauses ((1) and (2)).

(1) Subject relative: The pilot that admired the nurse dominated the conversation

(2) Object relative: The pilot that the nurse admired dominated the conversation

They found that older subjects showed less of an increase in self-paced reading at the verb of an object relative clause (*admired* in (2)) than younger subjects. Kemper and Kemtes (1999) found that among elderly, but not young, adults, those with lower WM capacities had longer reading times for ambiguous sections of questions such as *to paint* in "Who did John ask to paint?" than those with higher WM capacities. In several studies using the auditory moving windows paradigm with end-of-sentence plausibility judgment, we have failed to find age effects on on-line processing times at these points (Waters & Caplan, 2001, 2005; see Waters & Caplan, 1999, for review).

Caveats need to be entered about these specific studies and others in the literature. For instance, in the Kemper and Kemtes (1999) study, WM affected reading times for both young and old subjects in the unambiguous portions of the sentences, making the implications of the effect of WM on ambiguity resolution in aging less clear. However, such issues aside, the major problem is how to interpret the different patterns of on-line data. Based on the fact that other, expected, effects were present in the data, we suggested that the null results in our studies were not due to lack of power but true indications of an absence of an effect of age on on-line parsing efficiency. Both Stine Morrow and her colleagues and Kemper and Kemtes argued that their results indicated that parsing efficiency declined with age. Stine-Morrow et al. (2000) argued that older participants stopped attempting to assign the structure and meaning of the more complex sentences at the point of increased computational load, resulting in shorter processing times. Kemper and Kemtes (1999) argued that the longer processing times in low-WM older participants resulted from parsing inefficiency in that group.

The attribution of both longer and shorter on-line processing times at points of demand to parsing inefficiency in aging (or a subset of the older population) led us to look for constraints on the interpretation of on-line measures. As noted above, we suggested that the relation of on-line processing times to accuracy provides clues as to the processes that determine longer on-line processing times (Caplan et al., 2011). Longer on-line processing times could be due to less efficient processing (which we called "compensatory" processing) or to applying operations that are not usually engaged at a given on-line point (which I shall call "augmentative" processing). "Compensatory" increases in on-line times would bring performance up the level achieved by a more efficient processor (if the compensation were fully effective) and would lead to negative correlations between on-line processing time and end-of-sentence performance if the compensation were less than fully effective; "augmentative" prolongations of on-line processing should improve compensation, leading to positive correlations of on-line processing time and end-of-sentence comprehension.

Caplan et al. (2011) applied this approach to the interpretation of the effects of age, WM, and speed of processing on on-line processing, with some suggestive results. Caplan et al. (2011) studied two hundred healthy individuals equally divided into four age groups (18–29, 30–49, 50–69, 70–90 years), and measured WM and speed of processing. Subjects participated in two self-paced reading studies, a plausibility judgment study using cleft structures and relative clauses ((3)–(6)) and a verification study using sentential complement (7) and doubly center embedded relative clauses ((8); Grodner, Gibson, & Tunstall, 2002) (plausible sentences only shown):

(3) Subject cleft: It was the movie that terrified the child because it showed a monster

(4) Object cleft: It was the child that the movie terrified because it showed a monster

(5) Subject relative: The picture that included the advertisement depicted the product

(6) Object relative: The picture that the advertisement included depicted the product

(7) Sentential complement: The dealer indicated that the jewelry that was identified by the victim implicated one of his friends

(8) Doubly embedded relative: The dealer who the jewelry that was identified by the victim implicated was arrested by the police

Age was associated with longer self-paced reading times (after regression for length) at verbs of all but cleft subject and subject relative sentences (a floor effect), and these correlations remained significant after speed of processing and WM were partialled out. Multilevel models showed that aging led to longer reading times for embedded verbs in cleft object and object relative sentences compared to those in matched cleft subject and subject relative sentences. Age was negatively correlated with accuracy on cleft object, subject–object, and doubly embedded relative clauses (the lack of a correlation with the other sentences is due to ceiling effects in accuracy). Correlations of residual self-paced reading times for embedded verbs in each of the sentence types with accuracy were not significant (with one exception to be discussed below), consistent with a compensatory view of increased on-line processing time. These findings suggest that age reduces the efficiency of on-line syntactic processing independent of any age-related change in either speed of processing or WM.

Greater WM and faster speed of processing were associated with greater accuracy, and with faster reading times for verbs in the verification task used to test sentences (7) and (8), again with one exception. The fact that the on-line effects of WM and speed of processing were only seen in the verification and not the plausibility task suggests that faster speed of processing and greater WM capacity are associated with more efficient encoding of thematic roles into memory for later verification.

As noted, there was one point at which some of the results differed—the second verb of doubly center embedded relatives (*implicated* in (8)). At this point, the correlation between residual reading time and accuracy was significantly positive, consistent with "augmentative" processing at that point, and there was no relation between WM and residual reading time. Caplan et al. (2011) suggested that the absence of a correlation between WM and residual reading times at this point occurred because individuals with lower WM spent more time there to compensate for their inefficiency at encoding thematic roles into memory, and individuals with higher WM spent more time engaging in ancillary cognitive operations that lead to better comprehension.

Overall, the results of this study suggest that age, speed of processing, and WM affect different types of on-line operations: age affects parsing and interpretation; speed of processing and WM affect encoding of thematic roles into memory; WM also affects use of ancillary cognitive operations to determine structure and meaning. Aside from moving towards a better understanding of the effects of age, WM, and speed of processing on on-line syntactic processing and its relation to the ability to perform tasks based upon the comprehension of a sentence, these results have several possible implications for models of on-line sentence processing.

One is that they provide evidence that operations related to task demands affect on-line processing. The fact that WM and speed of processing affected reading times in the verification and not the plausibility judgment task suggests that task-related operations (encoding thematic roles into memory) occur incrementally, and are affected by general cognitive abilities.

Second, the effect of age on the ability to assign meaning to sentences on the basis of syntactic structure (parsing and interpretation of sentences) bears on the role of experience in the development of processing efficiency. Some authors have argued that experience with syntactic structures leads to more efficient processing (Reali & Christiansen, 2007; Wells, Christiansen, Race, Acheson, & MacDonald, 2009; Misyak & Christiansen, 2011). While this may be true in short-term learning studies in young individuals, this does not seem to be the case with respect to the experience that accrues with age. Age appears to be associated with a decrease in sentence-processing efficiency that is not entirely due to age-related decreases in speed of processing or WM; any age-related increase in efficiency due to age-related experience with sentence processing (if any exists) appears to be more than offset by age-related declines in sentence-processing efficiency. We note that our previous studies with auditory moving windows presentation (DeDe, Caplan, Kemtes, & Waters, 2004; Waters & Caplan, 2005), found no effect of age on on-line syntactic processing in a subset of the sentences used in Caplan et al. (2011). One might speculate that the additional age-related experience associated with the auditory modality more fully compensates for an age-related decline in sentence-processing efficiency; however, no study has shown an increase in sentence-processing efficiency in aging.

To summarize, consideration of the relation between on-line measures and end-of-sentence performance has suggested that it might be possible to distinguish between individual differences in the efficiency of incrementally successful comprehension processes and the use of augmentative processes in sentence comprehension. Expansion of studies of the effects of age, WM, and other general cognitive factors on on-line sentence comprehension to include examination of task effects has suggested that these factors may affect different aspects of on-line processing. These early results will require replication, extension to other structures, comparison with results of other techniques, and extension to other cognitive functions (e.g., inhibitory function; decision-making processes) to be confirmed and to yield a full picture of the processes that occur during on-line comprehension and the changes that occur in them in aging.

Sentence processing and comprehension in neurological disease

The nature of the deficits

As opposed to the focus on whether there are age-related changes in sentence comprehension and the relation of any such changes to changes in age-related domain-general cognitive capacities, the major focus of work on sentence processing and comprehension in individuals with neurological disease, in particular stroke, has been the nature of the deficit(s) in sentence processing seen in these individuals. The most important fact that has been discovered about sentence comprehension in patients with vascular aphasia is that these patients can have disorders of sentence comprehension that are both severe and selective. The literature has focused on whether patients with certain types of aphasia have comprehension deficits that can be characterized in linguistic terms, and on the nature of their deficits in processing syntactic structure.

The critical observations were first made by Caramazza and Zurif (1976). These authors described patients who could match sentences to pictures when the thematic roles in the sentence could be inferred from lexical meaning and real-world knowledge, as in (9), but not when the thematic roles could not be inferred on the basis of word meaning and knowledge of the world and the sentences were syntactically complicated, as in (10). These patients also systematically misunderstood sentences such as (11), assigning thematic roles according to real world likelihood rather than syntactically determined meaning:

(9)   The apple the boy is eating is red

(10) The girl the boy is chasing is tall

(11) The boy the apple is eating is tall

The pattern they described—a deficit in which understanding semantically reversible syntactically complex sentences falls to chance or below and the ability to understand semantically irreversible sentences with the same syntactic structures is retained—does not occur in aging, to the best of my knowledge. A major focus of aphasiology that is not applicable to aging is thus the characterization of disorders affecting syntactically based comprehension to this extent.

I have reviewed descriptions of aphasic disorders of syntactically based comprehension in many places (see, Caplan, 2003, 2006, 2011 and Caplan & Waters, 2006, for overviews; and Caplan, Baker, & Dehaut, 1985; Caplan, DeDe, & Michaud, 2006; Caplan, Hildebrandt, & Makris, 1996; Caplan, Waters, DeDe, Michaud, & Reddy, 2007a; and Caplan, Waters, & Hildebrandt, 1997, for studies and reviews) and will only summarize (my reading of) this literature briefly here. Collapsing over what I take to be variants on a theme, there are two basic types of theories (models) of aphasic disorders of syntactically based comprehension: specific deficit models and resource reduction models. The first see these disorders as ones selectively affecting particular linguistic representations or parsing/interpretive operations; the second see them as reductions in the ability to apply a "resource" (such as WM) to parsing/interpretation. The prototypical model of the first type is Grodzinsky's (1986, 2000) "trace deletion hypothesis"; Caplan and Hildebrandt (1988) provide analyses suggesting a more extensive range of specific deficits. Examples of resource reduction models are the "slowed processing" models of Haarman and Kolk (1991), Haarman, Just, and Carpenter (1997), Frazier and Friederici (1991), Love, Swinney, and Zurif (2001), and Love, Swinney, Walenski, and Zurif (2008); the resource reduction model of Miyake, Carpenter, and Just (1994); and an account in which the resource reduction occurs in the interaction of a specialized parser/interpreter and processes that perform tasks (Caplan et al., 2006, 2007a).

Advocates of specific deficit models claim that individual patients, or groups of patients with certain types of aphasia (e.g, Broca's, or agrammatic, aphasics), or patients with lesions of certain types (usually stroke) in certain areas of the brain (most often, Broca's area), show abnormal comprehension of semantically reversible sentences with particular linguistic features. For instance, Grodzinsky (2000) has argued that patients with Broca's aphasia (or agrammatic aphasics, or patients with both either Broca's or agrammatic aphasia and a lesion in Broca's area) perform at chance on sentences with elements known as "traces" in Chomsky's (1986, 1995) theory of syntax. Caplan and Hildebrandt (1988) presented a series of case studies in which they argued that individual patients had selective deficits affecting each of the different types of co-indexation operations involving noun phrases in English postulated in Chomsky's model of syntactic structure (traces, PRO, anaphors (*himself, herself*), and pronominals (*him, her*)). All these studies suffer from significant limitations.

In many, critical control sentence types have not been tested. For instance, Caplan and Hildebrandt (1988) and Caplan et al. (1996, 2007a) are the only studies in which sentences with reflexives and pronouns have been presented to the same patients as were tested on passives and object relatives. Without data on the ability to find antecedents of overt referentially dependent items such as reflexives and pronouns, one cannot conclude that poor performance on sentences with what are considered to be phonologically empty referentially dependent items, such as the "traces" found in passives and object relatives, reflect selective failures of co-indexation of one type of empty referentially dependent noun phrase.

Second, patients have very rarely been tested on more than one task requiring comprehension. When this has been done, they often do not perform the same way on both tasks (Cupples & Inglis, 1993; Caplan et al., 1997, 2006, 2007a). Gutman, DeDe, Liu, Michaud, and Caplan (2011a) and Gutman, DeDe, Caplan, and Liu (2011b) found that Rasch models are better fits to aphasic performance when they contain a task factor.[1] Dissociation in processing one structure in two comprehension tasks (e.g., object manipulation and sentence–picture matching) may result from failure to integrate on-line task-related operations with accruing propositional or discourse-related aspects of sentence meaning derived from parsing and interpretation (see Caplan et al., 2006, 2007a, for discussion), or from failure to use the products of comprehension of certain sentence types in one task. Regardless of its origin, task-specificity undermines models that see aphasic deficits as specific impairments of linguistic representations or parsing or interpretive operations, because the putatively affected sentences are shown to be understood normally when comprehension is measured in one task.

Resource reduction accounts find support from several results. Unrotated factor analyses of patient accuracy and of both patient and control RT data in studies in which many sentence types were presented to groups of people with aphasia (Caplan et al., 1985, 1996, 2007a; DeDe & Caplan, 2006) have shown first factors that are positively weighted roughly equally for all sentences types that accounted for the great majority of the variance in performance (usually 66 percent or more). In only a few cases was even a second factor retained in the analysis. Confirmatory factor analyses showed that one-factor solutions were preferred to two-factor solutions for these analyses, and that imposing a factor structure that reflected the groupings of sentence types corresponding to the different structures in the experiments did not account for more variance than the structure that emerged from the unconstrained analysis (DeDe & Caplan, 2006). Rotated factor analyses have never shown factors on which sentences with particular linguistic features or that required particular psycholinguistic operations loaded (Caplan et al., 1985, 1996, 2007a; DeDe & Caplan, 2006). These results suggest that aphasic performance results from variability in a single latent capacity, and not from disorders affecting different types of theoretically specifiable syntactic elements or operations to any significant degree. Caplan et al. (2007a) found superadditive interactions between overall severity of patients' syntactic comprehension performance and the syntactic complexity of sentences; these would result from more frequent failures to understand more complex sentences as the resources needed to understand sentences declined. Finally, Caplan and Hildebrandt (1988) reported that individual patients often were able to show comprehension of a sentence that required either of two types of syntactic operation, but failed when both operations were needed. These results all provide evidence that the inability to perform multiple syntactic operations determines much of aphasic patients' performance on these tasks. They do not, of course, show that specific deficits do not exist, and they do not provide answers to basic questions such as what the nature of the resources are, what tasks and functions are supported by a given resource system, and whether disturbances in functions such as lexical access, phonological or semantic short-term memory, or general WM or slowing of cognitive processing might underlie the resource reduction that leads to these comprehension deficits.

The evidence that supports or disconfirms these models is almost exclusively derived from end-of-sentence comprehension performance. As noted, the major advance in the past decade of study of aphasic deficits in syntactically based comprehension is the increased application of on-line observational methods to the question of what underlies these abnormal performances. The evidence is still sparse, but a common thread runs through it—on-line processing of syntactic structure appears to be much more intact in aphasic patients than was thought on the basis of end-of-sentence task performance.

Tyler (1985) reported that an agrammatic aphasic, DE, whose end-of sentence, anomaly judgments were much less accurate than those of controls, showed several features in a word monitoring task that suggest intact on-line parsing: longer latencies for word targets in syntactically correct, semantically anomalous sentences than in normal sentences; faster reaction times in the second and last thirds of normal sentences but not in word salad; and normal effects of semantic and syntactic anomalies on monitoring times for the words following an anomalous word. DE did not show faster reaction times in the second and last thirds of anomalous sentences, which led Tyler to suggest that his on-line syntactic processing was restricted to local constituents and did not extend to global sentence-wide structures. Shankweiler, Crain, Gorrell, and Tuller (1989) reported that six agrammatic aphasics showed some normal aspects of performance in an on-line wellformedness judgment task with auditorily presented sentences: judgments were faster as each sentence progressed; RTs were faster when the distance between the anomalous and licensing segments was smaller; and patients were better able to detect syntactic anomalies that involved between-grammatical-class substitutions than semantic anomalies that involved within-class substitutions. These studies raise doubts about inferences regarding on-line processing abnormalities that are based solely on end-of-sentence performance.

Swinney, Zurif, Prather, and Love (1996) and Swinney and Zurif (1995) reported a series of lexical priming studies in which they found semantic priming in healthy control subjects for written words immediately after the presentation of the head noun of a relative clause and again at a later point at which the word would have been re-accessed (the verb in the relative clause) but not at an intermediate point during the auditory presentation of a sentence and interpreted this pattern as evidence for on-line activation of the antecedent of the trace at that point (see McKoon, Ratcliff, & Ward, 1994; McKoon & Ratcliff, 1994; and Nicol, Fodor, & Swinney, 1994, for discussion of cross modal priming). They reported that eight patients with anomic aphasia who performed poorly on end-of-sentence comprehension measures showed the normal pattern of cross-modal priming. Blumstein, Byma, Kurowski, Hourihan, Brown, and Hutchinson (1998) also reported that the normal pattern was retained in four Broca's aphasics. These results provide evidence for the integrity of some syntactic and interpretive operations in both the major clinical groups of aphasic patients.

An important advance has been the separation of on-line observations made in trials on which end-of-sentence responses are correct and erroneous. Chance performance on forced-choice end-of-sentence tasks has been interpreted as a result of failure of assignment of syntactic structure and the application of a guessing strategy to the response selection process. In some models (e.g., Grodzinsky, 2000), this guessing strategy applies after the comprehension of a sentence is complete. This would entail that on-line syntactic and interpretive processing would not differ in trials on which end-of-sentence responses are correct and erroneous when performance is at chance. However, several studies have reported different on-line performance in correctly and incorrectly interpreted sentences when performance is at chance.

Caplan et al. (2007a) found that, when patients made correct responses, their listening times (corrected for spoken word duration and word frequency) in moving auditory windows presentations with sentence-picture and grammaticality judgment tasks showed normal effects of syntactic structure, but that self-paced listening times were abnormal at points of high demand in complex sentences when patients made errors. In a study of 28 aphasic patients using auditory moving windows and plausibility judgment, Caplan and Waters (2003) found that, for cleft structures, poor comprehending patients (based on essentially a median split in a separate test of syntactic comprehension) had longer residual listening times for the embedded verb in cleft object sentences than for the embedded verb or noun phrase in cleft subject sentences to which they responded correctly, comparably to normal performance, and disproportionately long residual listening times for the embedded verb in cleft object sentences to which they responded erroneously (compared to the embedded verb in cleft object sentences to which they responded correctly). These residual listening times in cleft object sentences suggest these low comprehending patients attempted to assign the structure and meaning of these sentences on-line. When they succeeded, their residual listening times showed the normal pattern; failures were associated with longer listening times at the most demanding phrase of the sentence, suggesting continuing and unsuccessful efforts to parse and interpret the sentences.

Dickey and Thompson (2005) reported 12 Broca's aphasics eye fixations on pictures of words designated in *wh* questions (*Which boy did the girl push . . .*) as the sentences were spoken. Patients made many more errors than controls in a comprehension test. However, at the embedded verb (*push*), they fixated on the picture of the object (boy) as frequently as controls did; their errors were associated with an increased frequency of late looks to the subject noun phrase. Thompson and Choy (2009) reported similar findings in eight agrammatic patients at points of presentation of pronouns and reflexives. The authors suggested that their patients initially processed the sentences normally, to the point of initially understanding the thematic roles in object extracted structures and co-indexing overt referentially dependent noun phrases in the same way as controls. In their view, errors were due to patients' initial understanding being overridden at a later point in processing by an alternative interpretation of the sentences. The difference between aphasics and controls, in this view, is not that aphasics' initial comprehension processes are disturbed, but that aphasics are less capable than controls of determining that a syntactically derived meaning, as opposed to a meaning derived in some other fashion, is correct. This deficit would be a failure of some sort of control, or perhaps of a labeling process, not of assigning syntactic structure or using it to determine sentence meaning *per se*. Hanne, Sekerina, Vasishth, Burchert, and De Bleser (2011) reported similar results in 11 German patients using case marked sentences with non-canonical object–verb–subject order in a sentence–picture matching task. In their study, there was a difference between eye fixations of controls and aphasics only in incorrect trials, although patients' fixations were slowed relative to controls on correct trials. In incorrect trials, aphasics first fixated on the incorrect picture, then on the correct one, and then returned to the incorrect picture—a pattern not seen in controls. Hanne et al. suggested this pattern indicated "an unsuccessful attempt to reanalyse the structure" (p. 237) and "fail[ure] to compute reanalysis even when one is detected" (p. 221).

A well-known set of results are the reports by Swinney and his colleagues (Swinney & Zurif, 1995; Swinney et al., 1996; Zurif, Swinney, Prather, Solomon, & Bushell, 1993) that Broca's aphasics did not show the lexical-semantic priming pattern described above for normal adults and anomic patients, which they interpreted as evidence for on-line re-activation of the head noun of a relative clause; the absence of priming at the embedded verb was interpreted as indicating an on-line impairment activating the antecedent of a trace, consistent with the trace deletion hypothesis. It has become clear, however, that those studies cannot be unequivocally interpreted in this fashion, for two reasons. First, the authors did not separate correct and erroneous trials. Second, the Broca's aphasics tested in the Swinney/Zurif studies showed no priming effects at any position, not just at the verb of the relative clause, and were not tested for word-to-word priming effects in isolation; the absence of any priming effects may thus have been due to a failure of these patients to show lexical priming, as has been documented for Broca's aphasics by Milberg and Blumstein (1981; Blumstein, Milberg, & Shrier, 1982). Follow-up studies in other Broca's aphasics (Love et al., 2001, 2008) showed delayed priming after both the initial presentation of the head noun and the relative clause verb, leading Love et al. to conclude that the patients experienced a delay in activation of lexical semantic or conceptual representations that interfered with parsing and interpretation. This conclusion was supported by the finding that the patients' comprehension improved significantly when the object relative sentences were presented at a slower speed (see also Friederici & Kilborn, 1989, and Kilborn & Friederici, 1994, for models that involve slowing of lexical activation or syntactic processing, and Waters & Caplan, 2003, for discussion).

Summarizing these on-line studies, there is considerable evidence that aphasic patients whose end-of-sentence performances in tasks that require syntactically based comprehension are abnormal retain considerable on-line parsing and interpretive abilities. This is not to say that their on-line processing is completely normal. In some studies, on-line processing was found to be abnormal for some sentences in all trials. For example, Caplan and Waters (2003) found that their poor performing patients did not show the normal increase in residual listening times at the verbs of object extracted relative clauses (as opposed to clefts; see above). In other studies, on-line processing was found to be abnormal in erroneous trials. The literature suggests that there are a variety of abnormalities that can affect on-line processing: failure to accomplish parsing and interpretive processing (Caplan & Waters, 2003: relative clauses); failure to do so when errors are made (Caplan & Waters, 2003: clefts; Caplan et al., 2007a); failure to choose syntactically licensed propositional meanings over those derived by other processes (Dickey & Thompson, 2005; Thompson & Choy, 2009); failure to reanalyze simple sentences with non-canonical word order (Hanne et al., 2011). There is every reason to believe that this list will grow as more studies are done.

All the studies reviewed above have interpreted on-line measures as reflections of on-line syntactic processing and comprehension; as discussed above, they may also reflect other processes that occur simultaneously with parsing and interpretation. There is some evidence that this is the case. Caplan et al. (2007a) reported that patients' self-paced listening times were longer for the same sentences in a sentence picture matching than in a grammaticality judgment task, suggesting that these responses partly reflect the time it takes to begin to accomplish the task while patients are self-pacing themselves through a sentence word-by-word. The issue of whether on-line measures measure parsing and interpretation or other processes is particularly important in aphasia because of the evidence from end-of-sentence tasks that many deficits affect certain structures in only one task (Linebarger, Schwartz, & Saffran, 1983; Linebarger, 1995; Cupples & Inglis, 1993; Caplan et al., 2006, 2007a). A related question that requires study is the relation of on-line and end-of-sentence performance. While the studies reviewed above that separate on-line processing of trials with correct and erroneous responses provide evidence about some aspects of this relation, many questions remained unanswered. The range of relations between time spent in different aspects of on-line processing and end-of-sentence performance has not been thoroughly studied.

Disorders of syntactic comprehension and WM in neurological disease

The review of studies of parsing and interpretation in aging indicated that an important topic in that literature is the relation of age-related changes in these functions to age-related changes in domain general capacities such as speed of processing and WM. The question of the relation of syntactically based comprehension deficits to WM has also arisen about patients with neurological disease.

Baddeley's model of WM (Baddeley, 1986; Baddeley & Hitch, 1974), and extensions of that model, provides the most commonly used framework for relating WM to sentence processing in aphasia. On that account, verbal, visual, and episodic buffers are used to maintain information in an active state as computations are being performed. The capacity of the individual buffers is limited, and they are directed by a central executive, which has its own storage and computational functions. Martin and her colleagues have suggested that another component of the WM system maintains lexical semantic representations (Martin, 2003).

The application of this model of WM to sentence processing has led researchers to consider two related questions. The first is what component of WM is involved in sentence comprehension. Baddeley's model provides two mechanisms whereby verbal information can be stored—the verbal slave system (the Phonological Buffer and the Articulatory Loop), in which information is maintained in a phonological and articulatory form, and the Central Executive, in which information is maintained in more abstract form (not fully specified in Baddeley's model), either of which might support maintenance of information in sentence comprehension. The second question is whether the WM capacity underlying sentence processing is shared with other cognitive tasks (the *shared resources* hypothesis), or whether sentence processing has its own distinct WM system (the *dedicated resource hypothesis*). Baddeley's model includes separate verbal and spatial slave systems, and subsequent research (e.g., Miyake, Friedman, Rettinger, Shah, & Hegarty, 2001) has provided evidence for similar verbal and spatial specializations within the Central Executive component of his model; advocates of the dedicated resources hypothesis carry this fractionation one step further to separate the memory system utilized in language processing from that used in other verbally mediated tasks.

Initial data suggesting that phonological representations were maintained in memory during sentence processing came from studies of patients with deficits in the Phonological Store and Articulatory Loop ("short term memory" patients), whose comprehension of various types of sentences was shown to be abnormal (e.g., Martin & Caramazza, 1982). However, in a review of all published cases at the time, Caplan and Waters (1990) argued that these data were inconclusive. Evidence that a short duration semantic memory system plays a role in sentence processing comes from patients who have shown no sensitivity to semantic variables in short-term memory tests and who have a characteristic problem in sentence comprehension consisting of difficulty understanding sentences in which multiple pieces of information must be maintained in memory before they are integrated into a concept (e.g., *The boy liked the large, black, expensive, handmade briefcase* versus *The boy liked the briefcase that was large, black, expensive, and handmade*; Martin & He, 2004). However, the abnormalities in sentence comprehension seen in the semantic short-term memory patients are not those predicted by the WM model of sentence comprehension (deficits affecting sentences with more complex syntactic structures); see also Caplan, Waters, and Howard (2012) for review of the construct of semantic short-term memory). If the verbal memory slave systems are not used in memory during sentence comprehension, and lesions of the semantic short-term memory system do not lead to predicted working-memory-related comprehension deficits, then if WM supports sentence comprehension, some other component of the system must do so. The only possible remaining component is the Central Executive, and many researchers have concluded that the Central Executive is the WM component that is critical for syntactically based comprehension (Just & Carpenter, 1992).

The second question researchers have addressed is whether the Central Executive is fractionated into a component that supports aspects of sentence processing and one that supports other verbally mediated functions (the dedicated resource theory) or not (the shared resource model; Just & Carpenter, 1992; King & Just, 1991). There have been two approaches to this question —the study of individual differences, and the study of dual task effects. The logic is as follows: If individuals differ in their WM capacity, and if those WM differences affect both linguistic and non-linguistic verbal processing, then individual differences in WM capacity should correlate with individual differences in the magnitude of the effects of variables that affect WM demands in sentences. Similarly, if a single WM system underlies both linguistic and non-linguistic verbal processing, increasing the WM demands of each should lead to superadditive interactions in dual task performance when linguistic and non-linguistic verbal tasks are performed together (Waters & Caplan, 1996). Both these approaches have been applied in patients with neurological disease.

The individual differences approach has been used to contrast performance of controls and patient groups, including patients with Alzheimer's and Parkinson's Diseases (associated with low WM) and those with aphasia following stroke. Reports differ somewhat but, as reviewed in Caplan and Waters (1999), patients with Alzheimer's Disease have often not shown end-of-sentence performances that are worse than those of matched controls on syntactically complex semantically reversible sentences. We have also found that effects of on-line load (e.g., the load found at verbs of object extracted relative clauses and clefts) were increased relative to baseline positions in subject extracted clauses in patients with Alzheimer's Disease to the same extent as in controls in self-paced listening tasks (Waters & Caplan, 1997). Patients with Alzheimer's Disease performed worse than controls on end-of-sentence tasks for sentences with two propositions, suggesting a disturbance in encoding propositional content (Rochon, Waters, & Caplan, 1994). Applying the dual task approach, we (Caplan, Waters, & DeDe 2007b) found that a concurrent digit load did not disproportionately affect self-paced listening time at points of load (verbs of object relatives) in Alzheimer's Disease compared to controls.

Almor, MacDonald, Kempler, Andersen, and Tyler (2001) reported that patients with Alzheimer's Disease and controls showed the same sensitivity to violations in subject–verb number agreement in a short sentence condition and similar degradation of this sensitivity in a long sentence condition. Performance in neither condition was related to WM. However, patients with Alzheimer's Disease were less sensitive than controls to pronoun–antecedent number agreement violations across sentences, and this performance was correlated with measures of WM. Almor, Kempler, MacDonald, Andersen, & Tyler (1999) also found that patients with Alzheimer's Disease had longer reading times for inappropriate pronouns in the third sentence of a text and the magnitude of the effect was correlated with a measure of WM. This suggests that the memory impairment seen in Alzheimer's Disease does not interfere with on-line grammatical processing within sentences, but affects on-line processing across sentences.

As reviewed above, as a group, aphasic patients with stroke show the effects of syntactic complexity predicted by resource reduction models, and often have very reduced spans; the questions in this population are whether the reductions in span are due to limitations of the Central Executive or a slave system, and whether the two performances (memory and comprehension) are related. To my knowledge, the signatures of integrity of the slave systems (phonological similarity and word-length effects in span; primacy effects in free recall) have not been explored in aphasic patients with stroke whose comprehension meets criteria for a resource reduction account, so the answer to the first question does not receive an empirical answer. However, two studies suggest that, whatever the answer to the first question, the answer to the second is negative. Miyake et al. (1994) simulated aphasic performance in enactment and actor identification tasks by reducing resources in Just and Carpenter's (1992) CC-READER model of sentence comprehension. A reanalysis of their results by Caplan and Waters (1995) showed that the simulation results matched the aphasic data for sentences with two propositions but not for sentences with object relatives, consistent with the results in Alzheimer's Disease, which suggest that reductions in general WM underlie the effect of increasing the number of propositions only. Caplan and Waters (1996) approached the issue empirically in a dual task study, in which they found that the effect of sentence type on ten aphasic patients' enactment performance did not change under a concurrent digit load.

It would be inappropriate to end this discussion without mentioning that theoretical developments outside the areas of cognitive aging and aphasiology put this work on WM and syntactic comprehension in these populations in a new light. Modern work on short-term memory has essentially eliminated the concept of the Central Executive as an entity that has both storage and computational functions, replacing it with a Central Store with very limited storage (Cowan, 2000, 2010; Verhaeghen et al., 2007) and relegating domain-specific computations to specialized processors (Engle, 2010; Engle, Kane, & Tuholski, 1999a; Engle, Tuholski, Laughlin, & Conway, 1999b). Retrieval based parsing models have related retrieval mechanisms that apply in the Central Store to retrieval in syntactic processing (Gordon, Hendrick, Johnson, & Lee 2006; Gordon, Hendrick, & Levine, 2002; McElree, 2006; Van Dyke & Lewis, 2003; Van Dyke & McElree, 2006; Lewis, Vasishth, & Van Dyke, 2006). In this view, measures of retrieval mechanisms from the Central Store would be more appropriate measures of WM than performance on complex span and similar tasks. The fact that capacity, as measured on complex span tasks, is low in aging and neuropathology does not entail that retrieval mechanisms would differ in these populations as well. A large set of studies will be needed to determine if this is the case.

Summary

Research on the effects of age and neurological disease on sentence comprehension has increasingly used methods employed in the study of young healthy individuals and focused on issues raised in that literature. Results are beginning to document the nature of on-line processing changes that occur in these groups and the relation of these on-line changes to end-of-sentence comprehension performance. These results have some possible implications for models of on-line sentence processing.

Acknowledgments

This research was supported by a grant from NIDCD (DC 00942).

Note

1. In the simple Rasch model, the probability of a correct response is modeled as a logistic function of the difference between the person's ability and the item's difficulty. The Gutman et al. results show that the simplest model is not optimal and that tasks affect item difficulty in aphasic comprehension.

References

Altmann, G. T. M., & Kamide, Y. (2007). The real-time mediation of visual attention by language and world knowledge: Linking anticipatory (and other) eye-movements to linguistic processing. *Journal of Memory and Language, 57(4)*, 502–518.

Almor, A., Kempler, D., MacDonald, M. C., Andersen, E. S., & Tyler, L. K. (1999). Why do Alzheimer's patients have difficulty with pronouns? Working memory, semantics, and reference in comprehension and production in Alzheimer's disease. *Brain & Language, 67*, 202–228.

Almor, A., MacDonald, M.C., Kempler, D., Andersen, E. S., & Tyler, L. K. (2001). Comprehension of long distance number agreement in probable Alzheimer's disease. *Language and Cognitive Processes, 16*, 35–63.

Baddeley, A. (1986). *Working memory*. Oxford: Oxford University Press.

Baddeley, A. D., & Hitch, G. J. L. (1974). Working memory. In G. A. Bower (Ed.), *The Psychology of Learning and Motivation: Advances in Research and Theory, 8*, 47–89.

Blumstein S. E., Milberg W., & Shrier R. (1982). Semantic processing in aphasia: Evidence from an auditory lexical decision task. *Brain and Language, 17*, 301–315.

Blumstein, S. E., Byma, G,. Kurowski, K., Hourihan, J., Brown, T., & Hutchinson, A. (1998). On-line processing of filler-gap constructions in aphasia. *Brain and Language, 61(2)*, 149–169.

Caplan, D. (2003). Syntactic aspects of language disorders. In K. Heilman and E. Valenstein (Eds.), *Clinical neuropsychology*, Fourth Edition (pp. 61–91). London: Oxford University Press.

Caplan, D. (2006). Aphasic disorders of syntactic comprehension, *Cortex, 42*, 797–804.

Caplan, D. (2011). Syntactic aspects of language disorders, in K. Heilman and E. Valenstein (Eds.), *Clinical neuropsychology*, Fifth Edition (pp. 61–91). London: Oxford University Press.

Caplan, D., Baker, C., & Dehaut, F. (1985). Syntactic determinants of sentence comprehension in aphasia. *Cognition, 21*, 117–175.

Caplan, D., DeDe, G., & Michaud, J. (2006). Task-independent and task-specific syntactic deficits in aphasic comprehension. *Aphasiology, 20*, 893–920.

Caplan, D., DeDe, G., Waters, G. S., Michaud, J., & Tripodis, Y. (2011). Effects of age, speed of processing and working memory on comprehension of sentences with relative clauses, *Psychology and Aging, 26*, 439–450.

Caplan, D., Hildebrandt, N., & Makris, N. (1996). Location of lesions in stroke patients with deficits in syntactic processing in sentence comprehension. *Brain, 119*, 933–949.

Caplan, D., & Hildebrandt, N. (1988). *Disorders of syntactic comprehension*. Cambridge, MA: MIT Press (Bradford Books).

Caplan, D., & Waters, G. S. (1990). Short-term memory and language comprehension: A critical review of the neuropsychological literature. In T. Shallice and G. Vallar (Eds.), *The neuropsychology of short-term memory* (pp. 337–389). Cambridge: Cambridge University Press.

Caplan, D., & Waters, G. S. (1995). Aphasic disturbances of syntactic comprehension and working memory capacity. *Cognitive Neuropsychology, 12*, 637–649.

Caplan, D., & Waters. G. S. (1996). Syntactic processing in sentence comprehension under dual-task conditions in aphasic patients. *Language and Cognitive Processes, 11* (5), 525–551.

Caplan, D., & Waters, G. S. (1999). Verbal working memory capacity and language comprehension. *Behavioral and Brain Science, 22*, 114–126.

Caplan, D., & Waters, G. S. (2003). On-line syntactic processing in aphasia: Studies with auditory moving windows presentation. *Brain and Language, 84*(2), 222–249.

Caplan, D., & Waters, G. S. (2006). Comprehension disorders in aphasia: The case of sentences that require syntactic analysis. In M. Traxler and M. Gernsbacher (Eds.), *Handbook of psycholinguistics*, Second Edition (pp. 939–968). San Diego, CA: Academic Press.

Caplan, D., Waters, G. S., DeDe, G. (2007b). Specialized verbal working memory for language comprehension. In A. Conway, C. Jarrold, M. Kane, A. Miyake, and J. Towse (Eds.), *Variation in working memory* (pp. 272–302). Oxford: Oxford University Press.

Caplan, D., Waters, G. S., DeDe, G., Michaud, J., & Reddy, A. (2007a). A study of syntactic processing in Aphasia I: Behavioral (psycholinguistic) aspects, *Brain and Language, 101*, 103–150.

Caplan, D., Waters, G., & Hildebrandt, N. (1997). Syntactic determinants of sentence comprehension in aphasic patients in sentence–picture matching and enactment tasks. *Journal of Speech and Hearing Research, 40*, 542–555

Caplan, D., Waters, G., & Howard, D. (2012). Slave systems in verbal short term memory, *Aphasiology, 26*, 279–316.

Caramazza, A., & Zurif, E. B. (1976). Dissociation of algorithmic and heuristic processes in language comprehension: Evidence from aphasia. *Brain & Language, 3*, 572–582.

Chomsky, N. (1986). *Knowledge of language*. New York: Praeger.
Chomsky, N. (1995). *The minimalist program*. Cambridge, MA: MIT Press.
Cowan, N. (2000). The magical number 4 in short-term memory: A reconsideration of mental storage capacity. *Behavioral and Brain Sciences, 24*, 87–185.
Cowan, N. (2010). The magical mystery four: How is working memory capacity limited, and why? *Current Directions in Psychological Science, 19*, 51–57.
Cupples, L., & Inglis, A. L. (1993). When task demands induce "asyntactic" comprehension: A study of sentence interpretation in aphasia. *Cognitive Neuropsychology, 10*, 201–234.
DeDe, G., & Caplan, D. (2006). Factor analysis of syntactic deficits in aphasic comprehension, *Aphasiology, 20*, 123–135.
DeDe, G., Caplan, D., Kemtes, K., Waters, G. (2004) The relationship between age, verbal working memory, and language comprehension. *Psychology and Aging, 19*, 601–616.
Dickey, M., & Thompson, C. (2005). Real-time comprehension of *wh-* movement in aphasia: Evidence from eyetracking while listening. *Brain and Language, 100*, 2.
Engle, R. W. (2010). Role of working memory capacity in cognitive control. *Current Anthropology, 51*, S17–26.
Engle, R. W., Kane, M., & Tuholski, S. (1999a). Individual differences in working memory capacity and what they tell us about controlled attention, general fluid intelligence, and functions of the prefrontal cortex. In A. Miyake & P. Shah (Eds.), *Models of working memory: Mechanisms of active maintenance and executive control* (pp. 102–134). Cambridge: Cambridge University Press.
Engle, R. W., Tuholski, S., Laughlin, J., & Conway, A. R. A. (1999b). Working memory, short-term memory, and general fluid intelligence: A latent variable approach. *Journal of Experimental Psychology: General, 128*, 309–331.
Farmer, T. A., Anderson, S. E., & Spivey, M. J. (2007). Gradiency and visual context in syntactic garden-paths. *Journal of Memory and Language, 57(4)*, 570–595.
Frazier , L., & Friederici, A. (1991). On deriving the properties of agrammatic comprehension *Brain and Language, 40*, 51–66.
Friederici, A., & K. Kilborn (1989). Temporal constraints on language processing: Syntactic priming in Broca's aphasia. *Journal of Cognitive Neuroscience, 1*, 262–272.
Gordon, P. C., Hendrick, R., & Levine, W. H. (2002). Memory-load interference in syntactic processing. *Psychological Science, 13*, 425–430.
Gordon, P. C., Hendrick, R., Johnson, M., & Lee, Y. (2006). Similarity-based interference during language comprehension: Evidence from eye tracking during reading. *Journal of Experimental Psychology: Learning, Memory, and Cognition, 32*, 1304–1321.
Grodner, D., Gibson, E., & Tunstall, S. (2002). Syntactic complexity in ambiguity resolution. *Journal of Memory and Language, 46*, 267–295.
Grodzinsky, Y. (1986). Language deficits and the theory of syntax. *Brain and Language, 27*, 135–159.
Grodzinsky, Y. (2000). The neurology of syntax: Language use without Broca's area. *Behavioral and Brain Sciences, 23*, 47–117.
Gutman, R., DeDe, G., Liu J. H., Michaud, J., & Caplan, D. (2011a). Rasch models of aphasic performance on syntactic comprehension tests. *Cognitive Neuropsychology, 27(3)*, 230–244.
Gutman, R., DeDe, G., Caplan, D., & Liu, J. H. (2011b). Rasch model and its extensions for analysis of aphasic deficits in syntactic comprehension, *Journal of the American Statistical Association, 106*, 1304–1316.

Haarmann, H. J., & Kolk, H. H. (1991). Syntactic priming in Broca's aphasics: Evidence for slow activation. *Aphasiology*, *5*, 247–263.

Haarmann, H. J., Just, M. A., & Carpenter, P. A. (1997). Aphasic sentence comprehension as a resource deficit: A computational approach. *Brain and Language*, *59*, 76–120.

Hanne, S., Sekerina, I., Vasishth, S., Burchert, F., & De Bleser, R. (2011). *Aphasiology*, *25*, 221–244.

Just, M. A., & Carpenter, P. A. (1992). A capacity theory of comprehension: Individual differences in working memory. *Psychological Review*, *99*, 122–149.

Kemper, S., & Kemtes, K. (1999). Limitations on syntactic processing. In S. Kemper & R. Kliegl (Eds.), *Constraints on language: Aging, grammar, and memory* (pp. 79–105). Boston/Dordrecht/London: Kluwer Academic Publications.

Kilborn, K., & Friederici, A. (1994). Cognitive penetrability of syntactic priming in Broca's aphasia. *Neuropsychology*, *8*, 81–90.

King, J. W., & Just, M. A. (1991). Individual difference in syntactic processing: The role of working memory. *Journal of Memory and Language*, *30*, 580–602.

Lewis, R. L., Vasishth, S., & Van Dyke, J. A. (2006). Computational principles of working memory in sentence comprehension. *Trends in Cognitive Sciences*, *10*, 44–54.

Linebarger, M. C. (1995). Agrammatism as evidence about grammar. *Brain and Language*, *50*, 52–91.

Linebarger, M. C., Schwartz, M. F., & Saffran, E. M. (1983). Sensitivity to grammatical structure in so-called agrammatic aphasics. *Cognition*, *13*, 361–392.

Love, T., Swinney, D., & Zurif, E. (2001). Aphasia and the time-course of processing long distance dependencies. *Brain and Language*, *79*, 169–170.

Love, T., Swinney, D., Walenski, M., & Zurif, E. (2008). How left inferior frontal cortex participates in syntactic processing: Evidence from aphasia. *Brain and Language*, *107*, 203–219.

McElree, B. (2006). Accessing recent events. In B. H. Ross (Ed.), *The psychology of learning and motivation*, Vol. 46. San Diego, CA: Academic Press.

McKoon, G., & Ratcliff, R. (1994). Sentential context and on-line lexical decision. *Journal of Experimental Psychology: Learning, Memory, and Cognition*, *20*, 1239–1243.

McKoon, G., Ratcliff, R., & Ward, G. (1994). Testing theories of language processing: An empirical investigation of the on-line lexical decision task. *Journal of Experimental Psychology: Learning, Memory, and Cognition*, *20*, 1219–1228.

Martin, R. C. (2003). Language processing: Functional organization and neuroanatomical basis. *Annual Review of Psychology*, *54*, 55–89.

Martin, R. C., & Caramazza, A. (1982). Short-term memory performance in the absence of phonological coding. *Brain and Language*, *1*, 50–70.

Martin, R. C., & He, T. (2004). Semantic short-term memory deficit and language processing: A replication. *Brain and Language*, *89*, 76–82.

Milberg, W., & Blumstein, S. E. (1981). Lexical decision and aphasia: Evidence for semantic processing. *Brain and Language*, *14*, 371–385.

Misyak, J. B., & Christiansen, M. H. (2011). Statistical learning and language: An individual differences study. *Language Learning*, *62(1)*, 302–331.

Miyake, A., Carpenter, P., & Just, M. (1994). A capacity approach to syntactic comprehension disorders: Making normal adults perform like aphasic patients. *Cognitive Neuropsychology*, *11*, 671–717.

Miyake, A., Friedman, N. P., Rettinger, D. A., Shah, P., & Hegarty, M. (2001). How are visuospatial working memory, executive functioning, and spatial abilities related? A latent-variable analysis. *Journal of Experimental Psychology: General, 130*, 621–640.

Nicol, J., Fodor, J. D., & Swinney, D. (1994). Using cross-modal lexical decision tasks to investigate sentence processing. *Journal of Experimental Psychology: Learning, Memory, and Cognition, 20(5),* 1229–1238.

Reali, F., & Christiansen, M. H. (2007). Processing of relative clauses is made easier by frequency of occurrence. *Journal of Memory and Language, 57*, 1–23.

Rochon, E., Waters, G. S., & Caplan, D. (1994). Sentence comprehension in patients with Alzheimer's Disease, *Brain and Language, 46*, 329–349.

Shankweiler, D., Crain, S., Gorrell , P., and Tuller, B. (1989). Reception of language in Broca's aphasia. *Language and Cognitive Processes, 4*, 1–33.

Spivey, M. J., & Grant, E. R. (2005). Eye-movements and spoken language comprehension: Effects of visual context on syntactic ambiguity resolution. *Cognitive Psychology, 45*, 447–481.

Stine-Morrow, E. A. L., Ryan, S., & Leonard, J. S. (2000). Age differences in on-line syntactic processing. *Experimental Aging Research, 26*, 315–322.

Swinney, D., & Zurif, E. (1995). Syntactic processing in aphasia. *Brain and Language, 50*, 225–239.

Swinney, D., Zurif, E., Prather, P., & Love, T. (1996). Neurological distribution of processing resources underlying language comprehension. *Journal of Cognitive Neuroscience, 8*, 174–184.

Tanenhaus, M. K., Spivey-Knowlton, M. J., Eberhard, K. M., & Sedivy, J. C. (1995). Integration of visual and linguistic information in spoken language comprehension. *Science, 268*, 1632–1634.

Tanenhaus, M., Maghuson, J. S., Dahan, D., & Chambers, C. (2000). Eye-movements and lexical access in spoken-language comphrension: Evaluating a linking hypothesis between fixations and linguistic processing. *Journal Psycholinguistic Research, 29*, 557–580.

Thompson, C. K., & Choy, J. (2009). Pronominal resolution and gap filling in agrammatic aphasia: Evidence from eye-movements. *Journal of Psycholinguistic Research, 38*, 255–283.

Tyler , L. (1985). Real-time comprehension processes in agrammatism: A case study. *Brain and Language, 26*, 259–275.

Van Dyke, J. A., & Lewis, R. L. (2003). Distinguishing effects of structure and decay on attachment and repair: A cue-based parsing account of recovery from misanalyzed ambiguities. *Journal of Memory and Language, 49*, 285–316.

Van Dyke, J. A., & McElree, B. (2006). Retrieval interference in sentence comprehension. *Journal of Memory and Language, 55*, 157–166.

Verhaeghen, P., Cerella, J., Basak, C., Bopp, K. L., Zhang, Y., & Hoyer, W. J. (2007). The ins and outs of working memory: Dynamic processes associated with focus switching and search. In N. Osaka, R. Logie, and M. D'Esposito (Eds.), *Working memory: Behavioural & neural correlates* (pp. 81–98). Oxford: Oxford University Press.

Waters, G. S., & Caplan, D. (1996). The capacity theory of sentence comprehension: A reply to Just and Carpenter (1992). *Psychological Review, 103*, 761–772.

Waters, G. S., & Caplan, D. (1997). Working memory and on-line sentence comprehension: Evidence from patients with Alzheimer's disease. *Journal of Psycholinguistic Research, 26* (4), 377–400.

Waters, G. S., & Caplan, D. (1999). Verbal working memory capacity and on-line sentence processing efficiency in the elderly. In S. Kemper & R. Kliegel (Eds.), *Constraints on language: Aging, grammar and memory* (pp. 107–136). Boston: Kluwer.

Waters, G. S., & Caplan, D. (2001). Age, working memory and on-line syntactic processing in sentence comprehension. *Psychology and Aging, 16*, 128–144.

Waters, G. S., & Caplan, D. (2003). The reliability and stability of operation span measures. *Behavioral Research Methods, Instruments & Computers, 35* (4), 550–564.

Waters, G. S., & Caplan, D. (2005). The relationship between age, processing speed, working memory capacity, and language comprehension. *Memory, 13*, 403–413.

Wells, J., Christiansen, M. H., Race, D. S., Acheson, D., & MacDonald, M. C. (2009). Experience and sentence processing: Statistical learning and relative clause comprehension. *Cognitive Psychology, 58*, 250–271.

Zurif, E., Swinney, D., Prather, P., Solomon, J., & Bushell, C. (1993). An on-line analysis of syntactic processing in Broca's and Wernicke's Aphasia. *Brain and Language, 45*, 448–464.

Index

action-compatibility effects (ACE) 179–80
active filler strategy 26, 225
adjuncts 33, 165–6
aging 247–53, 263
agreement 32, 85–6, 261
Alzheimer's disease 14, 261
animacy 232
anticipatory eye movements *see* predictive processing
anticipatory processing *see* predictive processing
aphasia 14, 248, 254–8
aphasics *see* aphasia
argument structure 57, 118–19, 126–7, 165, 167, 205
arguments 165–6
aspectual coercion 169
atypical development 191
augmentative processing 250–1
autism 191
automaticity 21–2

backwards anaphora 151–3
Bayes's rule 91
bilingual sentence processing 12–14, 221–39
binding as an initial filter account 138–41, 146, 149, 154
binding constraints *see* Principles A, B and C
bottom-up processing 201, 204
broad-coverage evaluations 103–4

capacity-based theories 191
cardinal quantifiers 173–4

career of metaphor hypothesis 178
case marking 29, 32, 37
c-command 138, 152, 157
central executive 260–2
central store 262
centre embedding 80, 82–4
children's sentence processing 12, 189–213
coercion 166–70
cohort effects 207
compensatory processing 250–1
competition 8–9, 31, 63–4, 66, 117
competition-integration model 61–7
complement coercion 167–9
computational models 61–71, 88
computer mouse tracking 129–30
connectionist models 58
constraint-based theories 8–9, 51–71, 117–19, 130
content-addressable memory 83
context effects 6, 38–9, 57, 116–31, 193, 198–200, 203–4
coordinated interplay account network (CIANet) 69–70
corpus analyses 59–60, 90
cross-linguistic differences 5, 34–40, 230–1
cross-modal priming 139, 142
cue-based recall *see* similarity-based interference

dative alternation 206
dedicated resources hypothesis 260–1
defeasible filter account 145–7
deficits in language comprehension 248, 253–63

dependency locality theory (DLT) 9, 82–3, 99–100, 103
diagnosis model 28–9
dual reference hypothesis 178
dual task paradigm 195

early left-anterior negativity 209, 210–11
embodied sentence interpretation 179–80
enriched composition 167–70
entropy 97
ERPs *see* event related potentials
event related potentials (ERPs) 2, 12, 125, 197, 208
executive function 212
expectation-based comprehension *see* anticipatory processing
eye movements *see* eye tracking
eye tracking 2, 129, 144–45 *see also* visual-world method

filler-gap dependencies *see* long-distance dependencies
first language influence 236–7
first-mention bias 203–4
fMRI *see* functional magnetic resonance imaging
frequency *see* structural frequency
functional magnetic resonance imaging (fMRI) 196
fundamental differences account 222, 233, 239

garden-path theory 3–5, 9, 25–7, 53, 116–17
gender (linguistic) 204
good enough processing 28
grammaticality judgement 1, 3

head direction 35
head-final constructions 35, 101, 226–30

incremental interactive theory 57
incrementality 1, 13, 64, 89, 91, 160–6, 174–6, 192, 194, 212, 222–30, 232
information structure 38–9
integration cost 9, 82–3
interactive constraint view 143
interactivity 8, 61–2, 117, 192, 200, 212

interference *see* similarity-based interference
intersective adjectives 161–2
island constraints 234–5

language acquisition 191, 210
late closure 4, 26, 231
lexical bias *see* structural frequency
lexical priming 155–6
lexicalist models 55
literal meaning 176–9
local coherence effects 24, 87
logophor 148–9
long-distance dependencies *see* syntactic dependencies

memory constraints *see* working memory
memory limitations 80–4, 101–4, 221 *see also* working memory
memory span 225, 228, 238, 262–3
methods for studying sentence comprehension 1–2, 142–5, 193–7, 256
metonomy 177
minimal attachment 3, 26
minimal chain principle 37, 225
mirror neurons 180
modularity 6, 8, 25, 53, 191, 198, 210
movement *see* syntactic dependencies

N400 2, 124–5, 209, 232
neurological disease *see* deficits in language comprehension
non-literal language 176–9
normalised recurrence algorithm 62–3
novel verb generation 205
null subject 36–7

offline production norming tasks 58–9
on-line processing 145, 222, 226, 229, 232–3, 248–50, 252, 256, 258–9
optimal perceptual discrimination 97
optimal preparation 99

P600 2, 124, 209, 232
parallelism 30–1, 54
Parkinson's disease 261
picture noun phrase 147–50

plausibility 13, 170–2 201, 224 *see also* semantic information
predicate proximity 231
predictive processing 71, 88, 94, 101–2, 105, 128–9, 166
Principle A 137–8, 144, 146–50, 154
Principle B 136, 138–141, 143, 148–150, 154, 202–3
Principle C 138, 152–3
probabilistic context-free grammar 90–6, 104
probabilistic selection theories *see* unrestricted race model
processing speed 233, 238, 251–2
proficiency in the second language 221, 226–7, 231–3, 237–9
pronouns 11, 36–7, 136–43, 147–55, 202–4, 236
prosody 30, 41–43, 163, 193, 199

quantifier scope ambiguity 175
quantifiers 173–5

random walk 97–8
rational agent 97, 99
rational cognitive models 96
re-activation 234, 258
reading span *see* memory span
reanalysis 8–9, 27–31, 33, 116, 118, 123, 131, 222–6
reanalysis failure 28, 198, 223–4, 258
recency 231
reciprocals 137
recurrent network 67–9, 104
referential context *see* context effects
referential processing 11, 136–57, 202–4, 235–7
referential theory 6, 30, 120–1
reflexives 11, 136–9, 143–5, 147–50, 154, 156, 202–3, 235–6
relative clause attachment 5, 34, 230–2
reranking cost 97
resource reduction models 254–5, 262
R-expression 138

scrambling 38–9
selective binding 170
self-paced reading 2
semantic anomaly 2, 171, 208

semantic compositionality 166
semantic information 7, 52, 64, 118–19, 172, 201, 223–4
semantic interpretation 11
sense ambiguity 168
sentential wrap up 162–3
shallow structure hypothesis 13, 221, 233–6, 238–9
shared resources hypothesis 260–1
short-term memory 255, 260
similarity-based interference 10, 83–4, 87
single quantifier expressions 174
standard pragmatic view 176
storage cost 9, 83
structural complexity 9, 80–2, 224, 253, 255, 261–2
structural constraints 3–5, 11
structural frequency 7, 55–6, 68, 193, 199, 223
structural priming 23, 205–8
subcategorisation information 55–6, 94–5, 164–5, 222–3, 232
subject-verb-object (SVO) bias 55
subsective adjectives 161–2
surprisal theory 10, 89–106
syntactic complexity *see* structural complexity
syntactic dependencies 13, 26, 31, 39–40, 82, 101–2, 224–30, 234–5
syntactic priming *see* structural priming
syntactic representations 12, 23, 205, 211–12
syntax 13–14, 21–4, 115–16
syntax-first models 116, 130 *see also* garden-path theory

thematic fit 55, 64
thematic roles 11, 27–8, 57, 69–70, 128–9, 163–6, 251–3
theta attachment principle 27
top-down processing 201, 204, 211–12

underspecification 27, 33
unrestricted race model 8–9, 31, 66, 117

verb bias *see* structural frequency
verb final constructions *see* head final constructions
verb island hypothesis 205, 210

verb subcategorization preferences *see* structural frequency
visitation set gravitation model 67–9
visual context *see* visual world method

visual-world method 2–3, 6, 12, 57, 69–70, 126–9, 195–6

working memory (WM) 14, 191, 221, 225–6, 228–9, 237–8, 247–55, 259–62